MW00834861

McFarland Classics

HOLLYWOOD CAULDRON

Thirteen Horror Films from the Genre's Golden Age

by Gregory William Mank

McFarland Classics

McFarland & Company, Inc., Publishers
Jefferson, North Carolina, and London

Gregory W. Mank is also the author of
Karloff and Lugosi (McFarland, 1990); and the two-volume set
Women in Horror Films, 1930s and
Women in Horror Films, 1940s (both McFarland, 1999)

The present work is a reprint of the library bound edition of
Hollywood Cauldron: Thirteen Horror Films from the Genre's
Golden Age, *first published in 1994.* **McFarland Classics** *is an
imprint of McFarland & Company, Inc., Publishers, Jefferson,
North Carolina, who also published the original edition.*

Library of Congress Cataloguing-in-Publication Data

Mank, Gregory W.
    Hollywood cauldron : thirteen horror films from the genre's golden
age / by Gregory William Mank.
        p.   cm.
    Contents: Dr. Jekyll and Mr. Hyde — The old dark house — The
mask of Fu Manchu — Mark of the vampire — Mad love — The black
room — The walking dead — Cat people — The lodger — Bluebeard —
The picture of Dorian Gray — Hangover Square — Bedlam.
    Includes index.
    ISBN 0-7864-1112-0 (softcover : 50# alkaline paper) ∞
    1. Horror films — United States — History and criticism.   I. Title.
PN1995.9.H6M315   2001   791.43'616 — dc20   92-56663

British Library cataloguing data are available

On the cover: Frances Drake in the 1935 film *Mad Love*

Manufactured in the United States of America

McFarland & Company, Inc., Publishers
  Box 611, Jefferson, North Carolina 28640
  www.mcfarlandpub.com

For my beautiful Barbara
as before, and for always
my greatest blessing

TABLE OF CONTENTS

INTRODUCTION AND ACKNOWLEDGMENTS

The horror genre spawned much of Hollywood's richest creativity and folklore—especially during its Golden Age of the 1930s and 1940s. These films' imaginative flair sparks a special fascination, but today their history commands an equal interest: the backstage intrigues of their stars, directors, writers, studios, and the whole wild process of their creation.

Along with a fascination come questions: What were some of the most far-reaching influences of the horror genre? How did some of literature's most beloved horror tales translate to the screen? How could one compare an MGM deluxe horror show with a Poverty Row shocker? What artists were the most overrated—and underrated? Were contemporary critics able to assess the horror films fairly or incisively? What part did censorship play? Who really prospered in the genre? And who was destroyed by it?

Hence the present work, which examines a baker's dozen of the most offbeat but still widely influential terror films of Hollywood's grandest era, noting how they popped and sometimes fizzled in Hollywood's fantasy cauldron and offering a glimpse behind the soundstage door as these pictures were produced.

I have authored two previous books on the horror film: *It's Alive! The Classic Cinema Saga of Frankenstein* and *Karloff and Lugosi*. These books (for better or worse) read rather like novels (or so many reviewers have said). The first covered the awesome intrigues of Universal Studios from *Frankenstein* in 1931 through *Abbott and Costello Meet Frankenstein* in 1948, while the latter book covered the real-life melodrama on horror movies, of the Boris and Bela professional and private relationship. This third book, *Hollywood Cauldron*, is intended as a historical and critical examination of thirteen Hollywood horror films that have had a particularly meaningful impact on the genre:

I. *Dr. Jekyll and Mr. Hyde:* A review of the three most famous performances of Stevenson's dual role, those of Barrymore, March, and Tracy. Each man brought a wildly different style (and personal insight) to the horrific Hyde.

II. *The Old Dark House* (1932), Universal's "lost" horror classic. The first reunion of star Karloff and director James Whale after *Frankenstein* and a stylish, bizarre lampoon, predating Monty Python comedies by forty years.

III. *The Mask of Fu Manchu* (1932). Karloff's lisping Fu Manchu, Myrna Loy's nymphomaniacal Fah Lo See, and MGM's art deco style produced Hollywood's greatest comic book of a horror movie, today widely considered racist.

IV. *Mark of the Vampire* (1935). The glorious Metro-Goldwyn-Mayer lot gave the famous Tod Browning an opportunity to create the greatest vampire movie ever made, even presenting him with Bela Lugosi from the director's *Dracula;* what the studio got was something else altogether. Did MGM ruin the film by cutting it or was Browning to blame?

V. *Mad Love* (1935). Mixing the French Grand Guignol theatre with surgical dismemberment, MGM unleashes the most horrible horrors of all. The movie that introduced Peter Lorre as a Hollywood star and cast Colin Clive (Universal's *Frankenstein*) as victim rather than mad scientist. This final directorial credit of horror great Karl Freund was a box office failure almost as colossal as Metro's notorious *Freaks*.

VI. *The Black Room* (1935). Columbia creates one of the most charming horror movies ever made, complete with Karloff's tour de force performance as good and evil twins, a fairy tale ambience, and masterful strokes by horror's (perhaps) most underrated director—Roy William Neill.

VII. *The Walking Dead* (1936). Warner Bros. gets Karloff, packages for him a horror movie mixed with gangster melodrama, and somehow ends up with one of the most religiously profound and moving shockers of the era.

VIII. *Cat People* (1942). RKO's erudite producer Val Lewton threatens to revolutionize horror with a chiller based on . . . frigidity? lesbianism? One of the most influential "B" movies ever produced and the terror debut of one of horror's most meteoric, brilliant personalities.

IX. *The Lodger* (1944). 20th Century–Fox produced Hollywood's most famous treatment of Jack the Ripper. A full-blown, outlandish "A" film starring young, doomed, brilliant character actor Laird Cregar as the Ripper, directed by gifted, underrated John Brahm, and offering proof of what Hollywood could do to create a top melodrama.

X. *Bluebeard* (1944). PRC, the most lowly of the Poverty Row lots, produces one of the most classy, sublime, "psychological" horror shows of the Golden Age. A major credit for "cult" director Edgar G. Ulmer and the finest horror showcase for its star, John Carradine.

XI. *The Picture of Dorian Gray* (1945). MGM meets Oscar Wilde. The most sophisticated horror movie ever made—or the most overblown? The film filled with hints of perversions never dreamed of by Louis B. Mayer, is famous for the Technicolor Albright painting of the horrid Dorian and the enigmatic title performance by Hurd Hatfield.

XII. *Hangover Square* (1945). Fox's Victorian sex melodrama was in many ways more frightening than *The Lodger,* with the same producer, director, writer, and star. The most disturbing thing about the film is its revelation of an anguished, dying Laird Cregar, who never lived to see the film's release.

XIII. *Bedlam* (1946). RKO, Val Lewton, and Boris Karloff ring down a wonderful final curtain on the Golden Age of Horror with a movie that advances the complexity of villainy, the power of a heroine, and the potential of the horror picture.

A major intent of this book is to cover the style of the various studios—MGM, Paramount, Columbia, Warner Bros., RKO, 20th Century–Fox, PRC and (of course) Universal. The films were selected as "flagships" of that particular lot's output. If MGM dominates in number with four films, it is because the style of Metro, both in product and production, varied so widely. *Mark of the Vampire* and *Mad Love* are two entirely different horror films—one too cold, one too hot—yet both were produced on the same lot in the same year. Also, while a period of only twelve years separates the filming of *The Mask of Fu Manchu* and *The Picture of Dorian Gray,* these movies were light years apart in terms of their sophistication and MGM's manner of producing them.

Writing any book is an adventure. This was no exception. Being a film historian in the 1990s is no longer the dusty, armchair pundit position it used to be. A researcher of Hollywood's Golden Age works more like Lee Tracy in *Doctor X* or Glenda Farrell in *Mystery of the Wax Museum*—an ambulance-chasing, fancy-footwork, fast-talking journalist on the prowl for interviews, confidential studio sources, and elusive illustrations. Having played Prof. Harold Hill in several stage productions of *The Music Man,* I found myself playing him again in this "racket," although all I wanted was memories. My experiences in researching *Hollywood Cauldron* ranged widely, wildly, and unforgettably.

Fortunately, the kindnesses of so many people (and the fanaticism they share for Hollywood's past) made writing a book like this not an arid affair but often an exciting drama.

Thanks go first of all to the professionals who gave interviews: Gil Perkins, a double in the 1931 *Dr. Jekyll and Mr. Hyde* and Tracy's double as Hyde in the 1941 version; Gloria Stuart, the beautifully blonde Margaret Waverton of *The Old Dark House;* Carroll Borland, the immortal "Luna" of *Mark of the Vampire;* Frances Drake, the glorious Yvonne Orlac of *Mad Love;* Marian Marsh, the breathtaking Thea of *The Black Room;* Ruth

Lewton, widow of Val Lewton, and their son Val Lewton, Jr.; the late Alan Napier, player in *Cat People* and *Hangover Square* and devoted friend of Val Lewton; Jane Randolph, the strikingly sophisticated heroine of *Cat People* and its sequel *Curse of the Cat People;* Elizabeth Russell, the "cat woman" herself of *Cat People* and beautiful familiar of the Lewton films; Shirley Ulmer, loving widow of Edgar G. Ulmer and his script supervisor on *Bluebeard;* Hurd Hatfield, star of *The Picture of Dorian Gray;* Anna Lee, the crusading leading lady of *Bedlam;* Glen Vernon, *Bedlam's* "gilded boy"; and Robert Clarke, *Bedlam's* "Dan the Dog."

Special thanks go to the late DeWitt Bodeen, writer of *Cat People* and, until his death in 1988, a leading film historian—not only for his input on that chapter but for so much kindness and encouragement to me that, sadly, I was never able to repay.

I am very grateful to Ned Comstock of the University of Southern California's Performing Arts Library. Ned was friendly and resourceful as he searched through the awesome files of USC to put into my hands such materials as MGM's hysterical story ideas for *The Mask of Fu Manchu,* drafts of *Mark of the Vampire* and *Mad Love,* test stills from *The Lodger,* various script drafts for *Hangover Square,* and even Karloff's annotated script from *Bedlam.* Many writers on movie history have found Ned Comstock a tower of strength, as I did.

Sincere gratitude is expressed, too, to the Lincoln Center Library of Performing Arts and the Margaret Herrick Library of the Academy of Motion Picture Arts and Sciences.

Many thanks go to Buddy Barnett of Hollywood's Cinema Collectors memorabilia shop (1507 Wilcox Avenue) and his colleague, Karl Thiede. Buddy generously provided many of the pictures in this book, as well as leads and encouragement, while Mr. Thiede made available many facts and figures from studio archives that made it possible to assess accurately the resources and box office performance of several of the films covered here.

I would like to thank also the many writers, researchers and historians whose work helped build this book. Whenever possible, I've cited author and source within the text of each chapter, be it a book or magazine feature, to give proper credit. I am especially grateful to such influential gentlemen as William K. Everson *(The Bad Guys* and *Classics of the Horror Film),* Joel E. Siegel *(The Reality of Terror),* Paul Jensen *(Boris Karloff and His Films),* Richard Bojarski *(The Films of Boris Karloff* and *The Films of Bela Lugosi),* Thomas Schatz *(The Genius of the System),* David J. Skal *(Hollywood Gothic),* and John Brunas, Michael Brunas and Tom Weaver *(Universal Horrors).*

Many thanks go to Forrest J Ackerman, Ed Bansak, Edward Bernds, Ron Borst, Eddie Brandt's Saturday Matinee, Frederick S. Clarke *(Cine-*

fantastique), Robert Clarke, Hazel Court, David Del Valle, Vince Di Leonardi, Eve Golden, Dan Gunderman, the late Steve Jochsberger, Maria Jochsberger, Tom Johnson, Don Leifert, the late David Lewis, Jessie Lilley *(Scarlet Street* magazine), Bill Littman, Donna Lucas, Tim Lucas *(Video Watchdog)*, Mark Martucci, Julie May, Richard May, Bill Neal, Mark D. Neel, Scott Allen Nollen, John Norris, John E. Parnum *(Cinemacabre)*, Garydon Rhodes, Philip J. Riley, Richard Schmidt, Curt Siodmak, Don G. Smith, Sally Stark, Michael Stein, George Stover *(Cinemacabre)*, Gary J. Svehla *(Midnight Marquee* magazine), Sue Svehla, Jim Trocki, George Turner, Richard Valley *(Scarlet Street)*, Sharon Lind Williams *(Filmfax)*, Scott Wilson, and Stella Zucco.

Finishing a project like this bequeaths one happy memories of the generosity of friends also caught up in this crazy business—colleagues like Doug Norwine, who, when this project was near its final stages, surprised me with the inspiring gift of a Colin Clive autograph and, a little later, a Laird Cregar signature. Also, as ever, I acknowledge a very special debt to Tom Weaver, whose contributions to film history are sure to be well known to many readers of this book; he reviewed drafts of the book as they developed, gave me leads for interviews, and extended to me the freedom to crash at his house in North Tarrytown (not far from the Headless Horseman bridge) whenever I ventured to New York for research.

Finally, my deepest thanks go to my wife Barbara, my beloved partner in these adventures, and my children Jessica and Christopher, who so lovingly tolerate having a writer for a father. Sharing this work with them (along with everything else) remains my deepest joy.

Gregory William Mank
Delta, Pennsylvania
April 1993

HOLLYWOOD HORROR CHRONOLOGY, 1929–1948

April 28, 1929   Carl Laemmle, founder of Universal Studios, gives his son, Carl Jr., the post of general manager of Universal. "Junior" soon wins 1930 Best Picture Oscar for *All Quiet on the Western Front.*

July 16, 1929   Tod Browning completes *The Thirteenth Chair* at MGM. Bela Lugosi, "Dracula" of the Broadway stage and national tour, plays Inspector Delzante at $1000 per week. Studio's first "talkie" melodrama makes a profit of $148,000.

August 26, 1930   Lon Chaney, "The Man of a Thousand Faces," dies at St. Vincent's Hospital, Los Angeles, of throat cancer less than two months after his "talkie" debut, MGM's *The Unholy Three.*

September 29, 1930   Tod Browning begins shooting Junior Laemmle's new production, *Dracula,* on the back lot of Universal City. Bela Lugosi, star of the Broadway play and national company, reprises his role of the count; desperate for part, he takes $500 per week. Edward Van Sloan, his stage colleague from New York and tour, again plays Prof. Van Helsing. Final cost: $341,191.20. Film opens at Roxy Theatre, New York City, February 12, 1931, to excellent box office.

May 1, 1931   Warner Bros.' *Svengali,* starring John Barrymore, with Marian Marsh as Trilby, premieres in New York City.

August 24, 1931   James Whale begins shooting *Frankenstein* at Universal, starring Colin Clive in the title role and Boris Karloff as the monster. Makeup by Jack P. Pierce. Final cost: $291,129.13. Premieres at the Mayfair Theatre, New York City, December 4, 1931, and proves a sensation.

February 10, 1932   Universal's *Murders in the Rue Morgue,* directed by Robert Florey, starring Bela Lugosi, opens in New York City.

February 20, 1932   MGM releases *Freaks,* directed by Tod Browning, starring Olga Baclanova and real circus freaks. Film is one of MGM's great disasters.

July 28, 1932 *White Zombie,* starring Bela Lugosi, released by United Artists, opens in New York City.

August 2, 1932 MGM's *Kongo,* a remake of Tod Browning's *West of Zanzibar* that had starred Lon Chaney, begins shooting. Walter Huston re-creates his stage role as "Dead Legs." Film is MGM's cheapest sound horror film ($160,000) until the 1937 remake of *The Thirteenth Chair* ($145,000).

August 3, 1932 Warner Bros.' *Doctor X,* shot in two-strip Technicolor, premieres in New York City. Stars Lionel Atwill and Fay Wray will team again for Majestic's *The Vampire Bat* and Warner's two-strip Technicolor *Mystery of the Wax Museum,* both 1933 releases.

August 6, 1932 MGM begins shooting *The Mask of Fu Manchu.* Metro borrows Boris Karloff from Universal to star as Fu; Myrna Loy wins role of nymphomaniacal daughter, Fah Lo See. Film released December 1932.

October 27, 1932 Universal's *The Old Dark House,* starring Boris Karloff, directed by James Whale, opens in New York City.

October 28, 1932 A Los Angeles newspaper reports that Bela Lugosi has declared bankruptcy.

November 18, 1932 In the Fiesta Room of the Ambassador Hotel, Los Angeles, Fredric March wins the Academy Award as Best Actor for Paramount's *Dr. Jekyll and Mr. Hyde,* directed by Rouben Mamoulian. Later in the evening, it is noted that Wallace Beery of MGM's *The Champ* lost to March by only one vote, so Beery gets an Oscar too.

January 6, 1933 Universal's *The Mummy* lures huge crowds at New York City's Mayfair Theatre. Giant Broadway display advertises "Karloff the Uncanny." In Jack P. Pierce makeup(s), Karloff scores a new triumph. Leading lady, Zita Johann; director, Karl Freund. Production cost: $196,000.

January 11, 1933 Paramount's *Island of Lost Souls,* based on H. G. Wells's *Island of Dr. Moreau,* opens in New York City. Charles Laughton stars as whip-cracking Moreau, Bela Lugosi is hairy "sayer of the law," Kathleen Burke the highly touted "panther woman." Film banned in England.

March 2, 1933 Boris Karloff and wife Dorothy take an American Airways plane this night for New York, where they will sail to England for Karloff to star in *The Ghoul.* It is Karloff's first trip home since he left England for Canada in 1909.

March 24, 1933 RKO's *King Kong* premieres at Grauman's Chinese Theatre in Hollywood. Merian C. Cooper/Ernest Schoedsack film becomes an instant classic. RKO contractee Julie Haydon later claims to have dubbed Fay Wray's screams.

November 17, 1933   Universal's *The Invisible Man,* directed by James Whale, opens at the Roxy in New York City. Film soon requires two theatres to accommodate the Manhattan crowds. Claude Rains, as "the invisible one," becomes a star. John P. Fulton's special effects still amaze.

May 3, 1934   *The Black Cat,* first of Universal's Karloff and Bela Lugosi shows, premieres at the Hollywood Pantages Theatre. Edgar G. Ulmer directs the film, also designing costumes and sets and collaborating on adapting Poe's tale. Final cost (including three days of retakes): $95,745.31. Boris, Bela, and leading lady Jacqueline Wells all make personal appearances at the opening.

January 2, 1935   Universal begins shooting *The Return of Frankenstein,* fated to be released that spring as *Bride of Frankenstein.* Karloff and Colin Clive reprise monster and monster maker; James Whale directs. Cast boasts Ernest Thesiger, Dwight Frye, Valerie Hobson, and—as Mary Shelley and the bride—Elsa Lanchester. Whale finishes film in 46 days (10 days over schedule) at a cost of $397,023.79 (more than $100,000 over budget). Film considered the climax of 1930s Hollywood horror.

January 12, 1935   Tod Browning begins shooting *Vampires Over Prague,* a remake of his 1927 *London After Midnight* that had starred Lon Chaney. New production has Lionel Barrymore, Bela Lugosi, and as "Luna," the bat woman, Carroll Borland. Film premieres at two different Broadway theatres simultaneously in May 1935 titled *Mark of the Vampire.*

February 23, 1935   Universal completes *Werewolf of London.* Henry Hull plays the title role, replacing originally announced Karloff. Warner Oland plays tragic Dr. Yogami, a part once envisioned for Lugosi. Stuart Walker directs. Valerie Hobson co-stars. Final cost: $195,393.01.

April 5, 1935   Universal "wraps" *The Raven,* new Karloff and Lugosi vehicle. Louis Friedlander (aka Lew Landers) shoots film on a 15-day schedule; final cost: $115,209.91. Film opens 4th of July in New York City. Lugosi, en route to England for *The Mystery of the Marie Celeste,* makes personal appearance there to, in his words, "take some bows."

May 6, 1935   *Mad Love* starts shooting at MGM, starring Peter Lorre, Frances Drake, and Colin Clive, directed by Karl Freund. *The Black Room* starts filming at Columbia, starring Karloff, directed by Roy William Neill.

October 25, 1935   Universal completes *The Invisible Ray,* third Karloff and Bela Lugosi vehicle. Leading lady, Frances Drake. Director, Lambert Hillyer. Film runs 12 days over schedule and, at final cost of $234,875.74, ends up $68,000 over budget. Opens in January 1936.

February 20, 1936   Karloff and wife Dorothy set sail for England. Star will top-bill two 1936 British films: *The Man Who Lived Again* and *Juggernaut.*

February 29, 1936   Warner Bros.' *The Walking Dead,* starring Karloff, opens in New York City.

March 10, 1936   Universal completes *Dracula's Daughter,* directed by Lambert Hillyer, starring Gloria Holden and Edward Van Sloan, who reprised his Van Helsing from 1931 *Dracula.* Final cost: $278,380.96. Lugosi, eliminated from the final script, collects $4000 for the time he has forfeited expecting to be in the film.

March 14, 1936   The Laemmles lose Universal City to new, antihorror movie management.

April 29, 1936   Tod Browning completes *The Devil-Doll* for MGM, starring Lionel Barrymore. Cost: $391,000. Film proves Browning's most popular horror film of the '30s, with a profit of $68,000.

September 14, 1936   Irving G. Thalberg, MGM "boy wonder," dies of pneumonia at his Santa Monica beach house. *Freaks* remembered as one of his few disasters.

January 1, 1937   Great Britain issues the "H" certificate, limiting audience for horror films.

June 25, 1937   Colin Clive dies at Cedars of Lebanon Hospital, Hollywood, from consumption and alcohol.

January 13 (a Friday), **1939**   Universal's *Son of Frankenstein,* starring Basil Rathbone in the title role, Boris Karloff as the legendary monster, Bela Lugosi as broken-necked Old Ygor, and Lionel Atwill as one-armed Inspector Krogh, premieres at Hollywood's Pantages Theatre. The $420,000 production (over budget by $120,000 and over schedule by 19 days), produced and directed by Rowland V. Lee, is a smash hit. Horror films—dead for over two years after the Laemmles' loss of Universal and the British "H" certificate censoring terror films—are back with a Gothic vengeance.

May 20, 1939   Tod Browning begins shooting *Miracles for Sale* at MGM, starring Robert Young, Florence Rice, and Henry Hull; he completes the film June 20, 1939, at a cost of $297,000. The movie flops, losing $39,000. Browning retires to Malibu.

May 26, 1939   20th Century–Fox jumps on the Hollywood horror bandwagon (sort of) as *The Gorilla* opens on Broadway. The film stars the Ritz brothers, Bela Lugosi, and Lionel Atwill.

September 20, 1939   *The Man They Could Not Hang,* first of Columbia's "Mad Doctor" series for Karloff, premieres in New York City.

November 22, 1939   Warner Bros. opens *The Return of Doctor X* in New York. Playing the blood-seeking zombie: Humphrey Bogart.

December 2, 1939   Universal's M. F. Murphy files a report on John P.

Fulton's painstaking trick shots on *The Invisible Man Returns:* "Some of the trick shots we have already seen are highly successful—others have not worked out so well on the first attempts—but we believe the final results will be more than satisfying." The film, starring Vincent Price, premieres in January of 1940 and wins Fulton an Academy nomination for Best Special Effects. Other "Invisible" sagas to follow at Universal: *The Invisible Woman* (1941), *Invisible Agent* (1942), and *The Invisible Man's Revenge* (1944).

December 15, 1939   Universal's *Tower of London,* starring Basil Rathbone as Richard III and Karloff as bald, club-footed, axe-swinging Mord, premieres at the Warfield Theatre in San Francisco. The Rowland V. Lee production also features 28-year-old Vincent Price as Clarence, who is drowned in a wine vat by Basil and Boris. On hand for the San Francisco festivities: co-stars Karloff, Nan Grey, and John Sutton. Also dispatched by Universal to join the fun: Bela Lugosi.

January 18, 1940   *Black Friday,* Lugosi's final Universal film with Karloff (they don't share a single scene) finishes shooting. Bela plays his death scene in the film supposedly under hypnosis. Karloff claims Bela really was hypnotized and jokes that he had never seen him keep his back to the camera for so long.

April 10, 1940   Paramount premieres *Dr. Cyclops* in New York—the first full-Technicolor horror movie. Albert Dekker stars. Ernest (*King Kong*) Schoedsack directs.

September 20, 1940   Universal releases *The Mummy's Hand*—all $84,000 worth of it. Tom Tyler plays "Kharis," the mummy, with George Zucco as the evil Egyptian high priest. Three sequels will follow: *The Mummy's Tomb* (1942), *The Mummy's Ghost* (1944), and *The Mummy's Curse* (1945), all with Lon Chaney as the mummy.

December 14, 1940   Lon Chaney completes work on Universal's *Man Made Monster,* co-starring with Anne Nagel. His performance as "Dynamo Dan the Electrical Man" wins him a Universal contact.

January 8, 1941   Evelyn Ankers signs a contract with Universal City, following work in British theatre and films and the Broadway play *Ladies in Retirement.*

January 10, 1941   The play *Arsenic and Old Lace* opens on Broadway. Boris Karloff, as the evil Jonathan, says he killed a man because "He said I looked like Boris Karloff!" and brings down the house. The play becomes one of the biggest hits in New York theatre history.

May 7, 1941   Lugosi's *Invisible Ghost*—his first film for Sam Katzman's Banner Productions at Monogram—braves New York City.

November 25, 1941   Associate producer/director George Waggner wraps *The Wolf Man* at Universal. Released in December, the film wins major celebrity for Lon Chaney, Jr., coronates Evelyn Ankers as "Queen of Horrors," and proves a monster hit. Scriptwriter Curt Siodmak's "Even a man who is pure in heart" ditty becomes Universal folklore.

March 13, 1942 Universal releases *The Ghost of Frankenstein*. Lon Chaney replaces Karloff as the monster. Lugosi returns as Ygor.

March 16, 1942 Val Lewton joins RKO–Radio Studios to produce low-budget horror films and is appalled by his first audience-tested title: *Cat People*.

October 15, 1942 Lionel Atwill is convicted of perjury. He has confessed to lying under oath that he did not own stag films, which he allegedly showed at an "orgy" at his Pacific Palisades house during Yuletide, 1940. Sentence: five years probation. Atwill has just begun *Frankenstein Meets the Wolf Man*, in which he plays the mayor; Universal keeps him in the picture. (Atwill's lawyer succeeds in having the decision reversed via a legal technicality in April 1943.)

November 5, 1942 Bela Lugosi collapses on the set of *Frankenstein Meets the Wolf Man*, in which he plays the Frankenstein monster. A doctor blames it on the strain of his makeup and costume and sends him home. The same day, Maria Ouspenskaya and Lon Chaney are hurt in a carriage accident, and Madame Ouspenskaya goes to the hospital.

December 7, 1942 Val Lewton's *Cat People* opens at the Rialto Theatre, New York City, and makes box office history. Hot on its paws: Lewton's *I Walked with a Zombie*, *The Leopard Man*, *The Seventh Victim*, *The Ghost Ship*, and *The Curse of the Cat People*.

January 21, 1943 Universal begins shooting *Phantom of the Opera*, starring Nelson Eddy, Susanna Foster, and—as the phantom—Claude Rains. The Technicolor spectacular will cost $1,750,000 and prove one of the biggest hits in Universal's history.

June 4, 1943 Universal releases *Captive Wild Woman*, starring Acquanetta as the studio's latest monster—Paula the Ape Woman. Inspires two hairy sequels: the 1944 *Jungle Woman* (with Acquanetta again), and the 1945 *Jungle Captive* (with Vicky Lane inheriting the role of Paula).

August 21, 1943 Columbia begins *The Return of the Vampire*, starring Bela Lugosi. Due to Universal's copyright on *Dracula*, Bela's vampire is called "Armand Tesla." Lugosi receives the same fee he had received for the 1931 *Dracula:* $3500.

October 16, 1943 Monogram begins *Voodoo Man*, Sam Katzman's latest. Lugosi stars in the title role; Carradine plays a bongo-playing moron named Toby; George Zucco, in warpaint and feathers, acts as high priest of Ramboona. Eight days later, Carradine opens as Hamlet with his Shakespearean stage company in San Francisco.

November 7, 1943   Dwight Frye suffers a fatal heart attack on a Hollywood bus, while returning with his family from a movie. He is only 44 years old and had been working nights at the Douglas aircraft plant. Frye had been set to play Secretary of War Baker in 20th Century–Fox's *Wilson;* Reginald Sheffield replaces him.

January 19, 1944   20th Century–Fox's *The Lodger* premieres at the Roxy on Broadway. Laird Cregar, a sensation as Jack the Ripper, makes personal appearances at the Roxy throughout the run.

February 1, 1944   Universal begins shooting *The Climax,* starring Susanna Foster, Turhan Bey, and—in his first Technicolor film—Boris Karloff, who has returned to Hollywood after starring in *Arsenic and Old Lace* on Broadway and national tour.

March 2, 1944   Susanna Foster sings "The Star-Spangled Banner" at the Academy Awards ceremony at Grauman's Chinese Theatre. Her *Phantom of the Opera* wins two Oscars: Best Color Cinematography and Best Color Interior Decoration.

April 4, 1944   Boris Karloff begins work on Universal's *The Devil's Brood,* destined to be released as *House of Frankenstein.* Also in the cast: Lon Chaney (as the wolf man), John Carradine (as Dracula), Glenn Strange (as Frankenstein's monster), J. Carrol Naish (as a hunchback), Elena Verdugo (as the Gypsy girl), plus Anne Gwynne, Lionel Atwill, and George Zucco.

May 18, 1944   Boris Karloff signs a two-picture contract with RKO-Radio to star in Val Lewton pictures.

May 31, 1944   Edgar G. Ulmer begins shooting *Bluebeard,* starring John Carradine, at PRC Studios. Film reportedly shot in six days.

August 5, 1944   Director Albert Lewin completes *The Picture of Dorian Gray,* starring Hurd Hatfield, George Sanders, and Angela Lansbury, at MGM after 127 days of shooting. Cost is near $2,000,000.

August 21, 1944   John Brahm begins *Hangover Square* for 20th Century–Fox. Laird Cregar, who originally rejected the project, stars as a mad pianist, with Linda Darnell and George Sanders.

December 9, 1944   Laird Cregar, having lost 102 pounds, suffers two heart attacks following a hernia operation and dies at Good Samaritan Hospital at age 31. *Hangover Square* is presented at a trade show in January 1945.

May 10, 1945   *The Body Snatcher* opens at Hollywood's Hawaii Theatre. It stars Boris Karloff, Henry Daniell, and Bela Lugosi and is directed by Robert Wise. Val Lewton's version of the Robert Louis Stevenson tale is the producer's biggest hit since *Cat People* and breaks records at the Hawaii.

July 18, 1945   Val Lewton's *Bedlam* begins shooting for RKO, starring Karloff and Anna Lee. Mark Robson directs.

December 21, 1945   Universal's second "monster rally," *House of Dracula,* becomes the Christmas attraction at New York City's Rialto. Film features Dracula (John Carradine), Frankenstein's monster (Glenn Strange), and the wolf man (Lon Chaney)—the last getting a cure for his hirsute affliction. Film also boasts a mad doctor (Onslow Stevens), a hunchbacked nurse (Jane Adams), a police inspector (Lionel Atwill), and a blonde (Martha O'Driscoll).

February 4, 1946   Lionel Atwill, fatally ill with bronchial cancer, completes his death scene (he is exploded to atoms in an airplane) in Universal's serial *Lost City of the Jungle.* He is too ill to finish his other scenes, and the studio engages a double (George Sorel) to complete his character's part.

April 19, 1946   *Bedlam* premieres at New York's Rialto Theatre to excellent reviews.

April 22, 1946   Lionel Atwill dies at his Pacific Palisades home, leaving a 29-year-old widow, a 6-month-old baby, and a $250,000 estate.

October 1, 1946   Universal merges with William Goetz's International Pictures; Universal-International pledges prestige pictures.

June 25, 1948   Universal-International previews *Abbott and Costello Meet Frankenstein.*

Double, double, toil and trouble,
Fire burn and cauldron bubble.
   —The Three Witches
   in Shakespeare's *Macbeth,*
   Act IV, sc. i

Dr. Jekyll and Mr. Hyde

JOHN BARRYMORE VERSION

Studio: Paramount-Artcraft Pictures; Producer: Jesse Lasky; Director: John Stuart Robertson; Screenplay: Clara S. Beranger (from the story, "The Strange Case of Dr. Jekyll and Mr. Hyde," by Robert Louis Stevenson, and the play created for Richard Mansfield); Cinematographer: Roy Overbaugh; Running Time: seven reels.

Filmed at the Famous Players Studio, New York City, January–February 1920. Opened at the Rivoli Theatre, New York City, March 28, 1920.

The Players: Dr. Henry Jekyll/Mr. Edward Hyde (John Barrymore); Millicent Carew (Martha Mansfield); Miss Gina (Nita Naldi); Sir George Carew (Brandon Hurst); Dr. Richard Lanyon (Charles Lane); Edward Enfield (Cecil Clovelly); Poole (George Stevens); John Utterson (J. Malcolm Dunn); Music Hall Proprietor (Louis Wolheim).

FREDRIC MARCH VERSION

Studio: Paramount; Producer/Director: Rouben Mamoulian; Screenplay: Samuel Hoffenstein and Percy Heath (based on the story by Robert Louis Stevenson); Cinematographer: Karl Struss; Makeup: Wally Westmore; Art Director: Hans Drier; Costumes: Travis Banton; Editor: William Shea; Assistant Director: Bob Lee; Running Time: 98 minutes.

Filmed at Paramount Studios, Fall, 1931. Opened at the Rivoli Theatre, New York City, December 31, 1931.

The Players: Dr. Henry Jekyll/Mr. Edward Hyde (Fredric March); Ivy Pierson (Miriam Hopkins); Muriel Carew (Rose Hobart); Dr. Lanyon (Holmes Herbert); Brigadier-General Carew (Halliwell Hobbes); Poole (Edgar Norton); Mrs. Hawkins (Tempe Pigott); Briggs (Eric Wilton); Utterson (Arnold Lucy); Hobson (Colonel MacDonnell); Student (Douglas Walton); Doctor (Murdock MacQuarrie); Waiter (John Rogers); Dance Extra (Major Sam Harris); Stuntmen (Chick Collins, Gil Perkins).

1

SPENCER TRACY VERSION

Studio: MGM; Producer/Director: Victor Fleming; Screenplay: John Lee Mahin (based on the Robert Louis Stevenson story); Cinematographer: Joseph Ruttenberg; Musical Score: Franz Waxman; Dance Director: Ernst Matray; Recording Director: Douglas Shearer; Art Director: Cedric Gibbons (Daniel B. Cathcart, Associate); Set Decorations: Edwin B. Willis; Special Effects: Warren Newcombe; Montage Effects: Peter Ballbusch; Gowns: Adrian; Men's Wardrobe: Gile Steele; Editor: Harold F. Kress; Makeup: Jack Dawn; First Assistant Director: Tom Andre. Running Time: 114 minutes.

Filmed at Metro-Goldwyn-Mayer studios, February 4–April 8, 1941. Trade show, Ambassador Hotel, Los Angeles, July 21, 1941.

The Players: Dr. Henry Jekyll/Mr. Edward Hyde (Spencer Tracy); Ivy Peterson (Ingrid Bergman); Beatrix Emery (Lana Turner); Sir Charles Emery (Donald Crisp); Dr. John Lanyon (Ian Hunter); Sam Higgins (Barton MacLane); The Bishop (C. Aubrey Smith); Poole (Peter Godfrey); Mrs. Higgins (Sara Allgood); Dr. Heath (Fredric Worlock); Intern Fenwick (William Tannen); Marcia (Frances Robinson); Freddie (Dennis Green); Mr. Weller (Billy Bevan); Old Prouty (Forrester Harvey); Colonel Weymouth (Lumsden Hare); Mrs. Weymouth (Winifred Harris); Dr. Courtland (Lawrence Grant); Constable (John Barclay); Mrs. Marley (Doris Lloyd); Mr. Marley (Lionel Pape); Mrs. French (Gwen Gaze); Mrs. Arnold (Hillary Brooke); Wife (Mary Field); Husband (Eric Lonsdale); Hobson (Olaf Hytten); Briggs (Brandon Hurst); Landlady (Martha Wentworth); Interne Fenwick (William Tannen); Lady Copewell (Lydia Bilbrook); Mrs. Courtland (Gwendolyn Logan); Uncle Geoffrey (Claude King); Inspector (Aubrey Mather); Cart Driver (Bobby Hale); Blind Man (Harold Howard); Hanger-On (Jimmy Aubrey); Waiter (Alec Craig); Chairman (Yorke Sherwood); Thug (C. M. "Slats" Wyrick); Choir Master (Milton Parsons); Dowager in Church (Susanne Leach); Old Woman (Clara Read); Spinster (Vangie Beilby); French Attendant (Jacques Vanaire); Young Man (Jimmy Spencer); Young Girl (Frances McInerney); Hostler (Herbert Clifton); Messenger (Edldon Gorst); Footman (David Dunbar); Cockney (Douglas Gordon); Man (Stuart Hall); Woman (Pat Walker); Drunks (Pat Moriarty, Cyril McLaglen, Frank Hagney); Constables (John Power, Al Ferguson, Colin Kenny, Jack Stewart); Townspeople (Patrick J. Kelly, Rita Carlyle, Mel Forrester); Stunt Double for Tracy (Gil Perkins).

●

He put the glass to his lips, and drank at one gulp. A cry followed; he reeled, staggered, clutched at the table and held on, staring with injected eyes, gasping with open mouth; and as I looked, there came, I thought, a change...

"O God!" I screamed, and "O God!" again and again; for there before my eyes—pale and shaken, and half-fainting, and groping before him with his hands, like a man restored to death—there stood Henry Jekyll!

—from "Dr. Lanyon's Narrative" in Robert Louis Stevenson's story, "The Strange Case of Dr. Jekyll and Mr. Hyde" (1886)

One night at "Skerryvore," his house in Scotland, Robert Louis Stevenson lay tossing in his sleep. His wife Fanny, hoping to end her husband's nightmare, awakened Stevenson—and received a reprimand for terminating the "fine bogy tale" haunting his rest. Stevenson quickly penned the first draft of his nightmare story, at which time Fanny redeemed herself. Why, she critiqued, simply write a Gothic thriller? Why not expand the dream into a supernatural tragedy, with a theme fascinating to the Victorian world—the dissection of good and evil in every man's soul?

The result, "The Strange Case of Dr. Jekyll and Mr. Hyde," was a sensation when first published in January 1886. The international success established Stevenson as a major author and spawned a great lineage of theatrical versions.

In Boston on May 9, 1887, Richard Mansfield (1854–1907) first played the dual role on the stage, reaping screams from the gallery ladies as the 32-year-old matinee idol turned into Hyde before their eyes. Mansfield premiered his *Dr. Jekyll and Mr. Hyde* in New York at the Madison Square Theatre on September 12, 1887. He would star in two New York revivals (New Amsterdam Theatre, March 15, 1904, and the Garrick Theatre, March 20, 1905), and spend much of the last 20 years of his life touring the melodrama in repertory with his other great stage roles.

Mansfield did face one disaster in his triumph. In a classic case of bad timing, Mansfield's Hyde lunged across the stage of London's Lyceum Theatre in the summer of 1888—just in time for Jack the Ripper's reign of terror. Mansfield had to close the show after the headlines of the Whitechapel mutilations spoiled the Londoners' taste for horrors!

Dr. Jekyll and Mr. Hyde first flickered onto a movie screen in 1908 when film pioneer Col. William Selig of Chicago's Polyscope Company filmed a stage play version (complete with the curtain). The star was the great, barnstorming Thomas E. Shea, who had produced and starred in the 1897 road company of *Dr. Jekyll and Mr. Hyde;* his repertory company joined O'Shea (who died in Cambridge, Massachusetts, on April 23, 1940, at the age of 79) in what is documented as the first U.S.-filmed horror movie.* *Dr. Jekyll and Mr. Hyde,* with its powerful themes and showcase for great actors, has made it one of the most revived properties of all time;

There were numerous pre–Barrymore versions. Denmark's Den Skæbnevs Abgre Opfindelse, *released by Nordisk Films in 1909, had Alwin Neuss playing the dual role (and discovering it all to be a dream). In 1910, Wrench Films in England released* The Duality of Man; *in 1912, Thanhouser released* Dr. Jekyll and Mr. Hyde, *starring James Cruze in the roles. (Or so audiences believed; in 1963, a forgotten octogenarian named Harry Benham claimed he had played Hyde in that film of half-a-century before.) There were two 1913 versions: one from Universal, starring King Baggott in the title roles, the other from Urban's Kineto-Kinemacolor Co., with Murdock J. Mac-Quarrie as Jekyll and Hyde, and an early color gimmick so complicated that it discouraged exhibitors from booking the film.*

Jack Palance, Kirk Douglas and Michael Caine are just three of the contemporary stars to indulge themselves in the dream role(s).

For most film disciples, however, there are only three genuine Jekyll/ Hydes: John Barrymore, Fredric March, and Spencer Tracy. If March, perhaps, fairly well claims the role (Hollywood's only Oscar-winning horror performance until Anthony Hopkins in *The Silence of the Lambs,* 60 years later), each star created his own unique interpretation of Stevenson's timeless nightmare.

●

> I, that am curtailed of this fair proportion, Cheated
> of feature by dissembling nature,
> Deformed, unfinished, sent before my time into
> this breathing world scarce half made up,
> and that so lamely and unfashionable
> That dogs bark at me as I halt by them. . . .
> —from Richard's first soliloquy in
> Shakespeare's *Richard III,* Act I, sc. 1

On March 6, 1920, John Barrymore (1882–1942) made theatre history at New York's Plymouth Theatre as Shakespeare's "foul lump of deformity," Richard III. For 4½ hours, Barrymore, with crookback and long, raven-black wig, cackled the great soliloquies, finally performing an acrobatic death scene in his black copper armor which became so hot under the lights that costumers had to spray it with a hose before Barrymore could remove it.

Then, on March 28, 1920, just a few blocks from the Plymouth at Broadway's Rivoli Theatre, Barrymore made cinema history in the title roles of *Dr. Jekyll and Mr. Hyde.*

Although the 38-year-old Barrymore had played in a dozen silent films (notably *Raffles, the Amateur Cracksman* in 1917) by 1920, Lionel and Ethel's younger brother had little respect for movies or his work in them:

> In the Silent days, I found myself continually making frantic and futile faces to try to express unexpressable ideas—like a man behind a closed window on a train that is moving out of a station who is trying, in pantomime, to tell his wife, on the platform outside, that he forgot to pack his blue pajamas and that he wants her to send them to him care of Detweiler, 1032 West 189th Street, New York City!

Yet when Jesse Lasky offered Barrymore the star spot in the Famous Players' *Dr. Jekyll and Mr. Hyde,* the actor found the temptation irresistible. Barrymore's true dream had been to illustrate definitively the works of Poe; he despised the "lover" roles his "exquisite paper-knife" profile had sentenced him to play (dismissing his stage role of Peter Ibbettson as "a marshmallow in a blond wig"). For John Barrymore, the role of horrific Edward Hyde was a dream come true.

Production of *Dr. Jekyll and Mr. Hyde* began at Lasky's Famous Players Studio on West 56th Street in New York; Barrymore then was co-starring with brother Lionel on Broadway in *The Jest,* and large pieces of that play's "palazzo" served as scenery for the movie. John Stuart Robertson directed (he directed Mary Pickford silents, and later, MGM's 1928 Garbo show *The Single Standard),* while Clara Beranger's screenplay developed the now-traditional concept of the two women—the pure fiancée (Martha Mansfield) and the sensual showgirl (Nita Naldi)—to cater respectively to Jekyll and Hyde. Director and writer created some memorable moments: in one vignette, as Jekyll lies sleeping, a monstrous phantom spider crawls over his bedcovers and melts into his body. Jekyll awakens—as Hyde!

The real show, naturally, was Barrymore. The star vowed to transform from Jekyll to Hyde à la Richard Mansfield—before the camera, and with very little makeup. After quaffing the evil drug, the actor suffers maniacally (indeed, acrobatically)—then swings his face toward the camera to reveal his horribly twisted, leering visage. Then the camera cuts to a close-up and we see a conical warped skull and a wild scraggly wig have assisted the grotesque Hyde transformation. Barrymore relished the Hyde makeup, especially the skeletal fingers (his own fingers were short and stubby, and he hated them). The transformation is unforgettable.

"Perhaps the most wonderful moment in the film," writes David J. Skal on Barrymore's *Dr. Jekyll and Mr. Hyde* in *The Horror Show,* "is Hyde's removing his pointed hat, revealing that it conforms all too neatly to the shape of the head beneath."

Barrymore's Jekyll is fascinating: he has the poise of a Beau Brummel in a Victorian painting, a tinge of Dorian Gray in his fascination with the soul of man. His masterpiece, of course, is Hyde. A red, eight-legged tarantula with a gray bald spot had inspired Barrymore to play Richard III; while the actor was simultaneously preparing for the play and shooting *Dr. Jekyll and Mr. Hyde,* the tarantula affected his interpretation of Hyde. In his old black hat, flowing black rags, and bestial face, Barrymore's Hyde conjures the image of a great, poisonous spider as he scuttles about the shadows of the Soho sets.

Richard III was so wonderful a success that *Dr. Jekyll and Mr. Hyde* had a phenomenal appeal when it opened at the Rivoli on Sunday, March 28, 1920. So eager was the opening day throng to see the film that hysteria broke out in the lines outside the theatre, and the crowd shattered two windows and broke a door of the Rivoli. At the film's finale, applause of the volume rarely heard in a movie theatre filled the Rivoli. The *New York Times* reported:

> It is what Mr. Barrymore himself does that makes the dual character of Jekyll and Hyde tremendous. His performance is one of pure motion picture pantomime on as high a level as has ever been attained by anyone.

Richard III closed only a few days after *Dr. Jekyll and Mr. Hyde* opened. Barrymore, exhausted not only by his roles as Richard, Jekyll and Hyde, but also by his relationship with authoress Michael Strange (his lover, who become his second wife), suffered a total physical and nervous collapse. As he recovered in a White Plains sanatorium, *Dr. Jekyll and Mr. Hyde* became one of the greatest hits of the Silent Era. It totally squashed a rival *Dr. Jekyll and Mr. Hyde*, a "featurette" slapped together by not yet prestigious producer Louis B. Mayer and released by Pioneer Film Corp. This rival production starred Sheldon Lewis and featured a classically camp line voiced by the good doctor's butler: "Dr. Jekyll is not himself!" (It also contained a cop-out, all-a-dream ending.) There was glory for Barrymore, Famous Players/Lasky, and the emerging film industry.*

For all the laurels Barrymore won as Jekyll and Hyde, the actor, in his later years, professed little admiration for his triumph:

> The critics said my portrayal of the horrible Hyde was something magnificent. All I did was put on a harrowing makeup, twist my face, claw at my throat, and roll on the floor. That, the critics said, was acting. And, may my worthy ancestors forgive me, I began to agree with them!

Truthfully, Barrymore had great affection for his *Dr. Jekyll and Mr. Hyde*. In the famous memoir of Barrymore, *Good Night Sweet Prince*, Gene Fowler wrote of the time that Barrymore slyly reprised Mr. Hyde in a plot to buy his magnificent estate high above Beverly Hills, which he christened "Bella Vista." Henry Hotchener, Barrymore's business manager, drove to the site with Barrymore hiding on the car floor. As Hotchener and the real estate agent began exploring the grounds, the agent (not aware of the client's true identity) looked at the car and saw Hyde, in black hat and

---

A German screen version also appeared in 1920: Der Januskopf: Eine Tragödie am Rande der Wirklichkeit (The Head of Janus: A Tragedy on the Border of Reality). The director was the legendary F. W. Murnau, the star was the great Conrad Veidt, and the role of Jekyll's butler was played by Bela Lugosi. Making it even more curious is the fact that this filming of Stevenson's tale was unauthorized—hence Dr. Jekyll and Mr. Hyde became Dr. Warren and Mr. O'Connor.

scraggly wig, peeking over the car window, cackling maniacally, and kissing his pet monkey, Clementine.

"Have to humor him with pets," said Hotchener nonchalantly.

Doubting if the maniac and his keeper were men of means, the agent fell prey to Barrymore's trick and slashed the price of the estate from $60,000 to $50,000.

Each actor who plays Dr. Jekyll and Mr. Hyde brings his own nature to the roles; in Barrymore's case, this nature was profound. Barrymore was tragically fated to play those very roles before the gaping eyes of the public. Jekyll was the young Barrymore, the classically handsome man with the beauty of a Raphael angel, making his Broadway bow as Richard III and Hamlet, captivating movie audiences as Ahab in *The Sea Beast* and in the title role in *Don Juan,* and loving the sea, his yacht, his animals. Hyde was the elderly Barrymore, the sordid alcoholic, reading his lines in "B" movies from blackboards, urinating in restaurant lobbies, a jowly, flabby man struggling into a girdle (sold after his 1942 death for $4.50 at an auction of the insolvent actor's personal effects) as he played his final act as a hammy buffoon.

It seems poetic that Barrymore's genius of physically becoming Hyde never left him. In her 1964 memoir, *All My Sins Remembered,* Elaine Barrie Barrymore, John's fourth and final wife (who had played Ariel to his Caliban in the raucous headlines), remembered an evening late in his life, before their divorce, when she promised her husband a beer if he would "do Jekyll and Hyde for me." Barrymore posed as Jekyll at the fireplace, pantomimed drinking the concoction from an empty glass, clutched wildly at his throat and heart, and turned toward her:

> My blood ran cold. There wasn't a feature that was recognizable. His face was contorted by the presence of sheer evil. No! It wasn't even evil. This was no cliche of cruelty or bestiality.... This was utter amorality. The smile made you crawl with its obscenity. The secrets of hell were unlocked.... I sat frozen in terror as he slowly hobbled toward me like a giant crab. One wasn't frightened of death at this monster's hands but of the unknown. The look of lechery did not spell rape or violence but something unheard of, so loathsome that man had still to articulate it. I almost fell into a faint.

Instead, her dog, Timmy, bared his teeth and barked hysterically until Mrs. Barrymore feared the dog was going mad. "For God's sake, stop!" she screamed at Barrymore, who immediately turned off Hyde and began petting the relieved Timmy.

"Best audience I ever played to," said Barrymore, hugging the dog.

"What an actor this man was!" wrote Elaine Barrymore. "What an artist! And he had forgotten the beer!"

●

He was ugly, but boy, he had a heart in him.
> —Rouben Mamoulian, director of
> the 1931 *Dr. Jekyll and Mr. Hyde,*
> describing Fredric March's Hyde

Of all the movie versions of *Dr. Jekyll and Mr. Hyde,* it was Paramount's first "talkie" version, premiering New Year's Eve, 1931, which is the most celebrated and controversial. It boasts Fredric March's Academy Award–winning performance, Rouben Mamoulian's wildly theatrical direction, and even a long history of suppression and censorship that officially ended when MGM Video released a restored version of the milestone shocker in 1989.

In 1931, John Barrymore, who had triumphed as Svengali at Warner Bros. that year, rejected a reported $25,000 per week Paramount offer to remake *Dr. Jekyll and Mr. Hyde;* he preferred to join MGM and go glamorous in such hits as *Grand Hotel* (1932). Nevertheless, the story had not been filmed since the 1920s, and the studio was hell-bent on producing a remake of the Barrymore hit.

So was director Rouben Mamoulian (1897–1987). He had won celebrity as a great cinema stylist via only two films—*Applause* in 1929 and *City Streets* in 1931. Both had been made at Paramount, which prized Mamoulian enough to allow him to experiment within the factory atmosphere of the lot. Mamoulian had his own concept of *Dr. Jekyll and Mr. Hyde* and explained it to John A. Gallagher in a *Cinemacabre* interview:

> The thing that interested me in the story was that I changed the basic nature of it. The original was about good and evil. Jekyll wanted to assume the different existence in order to commit acts of evil. I thought that was a very specific horror thing that the audience would hardly get involved with. I thought that if I changed that and made it a conflict not between good and evil but between the spiritual and the animal in man, that would be a part of every one of us.
>
> We have base instincts and high instincts. We have the flesh and the spirit.... That would be much more interesting, because every person could identify with the dilemma of Jekyll and Hyde....
>
> I think that's what makes the movie very topical even today ... it's right in with the direction of the youth today, looking for an expansion of consciousness, for love, for the good things. And they end up taking dope, trying this, trying that, and many times they fall victim to it. That's exactly what happened to Dr. Jekyll. But his original purpose was very lofty and quite heroic.

Mamoulian entrusted his concept to poet Samuel Hoffenstein (who would work on the screenplay of Universal's 1943 *Phantom of the Opera*)

Rouben Mamoulian and Fredric March exchange pleasantries on the set for the 1931 *Dr. Jekyll and Mr. Hyde*.

and Percy Heath. As for casting, Mamoulian related his troubles to Al Taylor:

> When Paramount asked me to direct *Dr. Jekyll and Mr. Hyde*, they had the star already picked out. They wanted to use Irving Pichel, a fine middle-aged character actor who later became a director. I thought the idea was atrocious, and said I wouldn't be interested in doing the film with him.

They said he would make such a wonderful Hyde. "I'm not worried about Hyde," I said. "I'm worried about Jekyll. I want Jekyll to be young and handsome, and Mr. Pichel can't play that." I wanted to use Freddy March, who was at that time a light comedian. He had just done a film called *Laughter.* They said, "You're crazy. How can March play this part?" I told them if I couldn't use Freddy March, I wouldn't do the film.

March (1897–1975), a Paramount contractee, had begun his Broadway career as Lionel Atwill's understudy in *Deburau* (1920), progressing to matinee idol glory in such plays as Broadway's *The Devil in the Cheese* (1926, co-starring with Bela Lugosi and Dwight Frye) and the Los Angeles production of *The Royal Family.* The latter was a lampoon of the Barrymore's, and March's take-off on John delighted everyone, including Barrymore himself, who saw March in the play. March triumphed in the role again in Paramount's 1930 film version, so his position as heir apparent to the Barrymore role shouldn't have shocked the studio as much as Mamoulian reported.

Mamoulian wooed Miriam Hopkins (1902–1972), Paramount's Georgia-born, super-temperamental blonde to play Ivy, Hyde's doomed concubine, while Rose Hobart, recently released by Universal after battles with Junior Laemmle, took the part of Jekyll's tightly laced fiancée Muriel. Added to the cast was a "lucky charm": Edgar Norton, who reprised the role of the butler, Poole, a part he had previously played on stage with Richard Mansfield. Norton would also play the butler in 1939's *Son of Frankenstein.*

The restored *Dr. Jekyll and Mr. Hyde* opens with about 2½ minutes of long-cut footage featuring Mamoulian's "seeing eye" approach to Dr. Henry M. Jekyll. As March plays his organ, we only hear him; via the director's stylistics and the camera wizardry of Karl Struss, *we* are Jekyll. As Mamoulian explained on January 21, 1971, when he appeared at the American Film Institute in Washington, D.C., in conjunction with a revival of the movie (as reported by Bill Thomas in *Cinefantastique,* Summer 1971):

> The "first" in *Dr. Jekyll and Mr. Hyde* is the use of the camera in a subjective manner. . . . The camera begins by being Jekyll and Hyde. In other words, *you* are Jekyll, the audience is Jekyll, being the camera . . .
>
> Now I did that because I wanted to use that device in the transformation of Jekyll into Mr. Hyde. In other words, I wanted to put the audience into Jekyll's shoes and make them feel a little sharper this vertigo that Jekyll goes through.

Finally, 34-year-old, classically handsome Fredric March appears before his mirror, cocks his top hat, and sets off to lecture the medical students. And as he leaves the house, the camera again becomes subjective as he bounds into his carriage and later tosses his cape and hat to the

Birdseye view of the set for the 1931 *Dr. Jekyll and Mr. Hyde*.

doorman at the lecture hall. It is an impressive piece of movie legerdemain, but perhaps a bit too avant-garde: most of the segment was pruned for reissues.

"If these two selves could be separated from each other—how much freer the good in us would be!" barnstorms Jekyll to his rapt medical students. "What heights it might scale! And the so-called evil, once liberated, would fulfill itself, and trouble us no more."

The students are dazed, but the older doctors, such as Henry's stuffy crony, Dr. Lanyon, are appalled. Holmes Herbert, of Tod Browning's *The Thirteenth Chair* (both 1929 and 1937 versions) and *Mark of the Vampire*, and a later fixture in Universal's Sherlock Holmes sagas, is a fine foil for March, with his potato dumpling face and fluffy toupee. Both are expected that night at a dinner party hosted by Brigadier-General Carew (Halliwell Hobbes), father of Jekyll's brunette fiancée, Muriel (Rose Hobart). Before arriving, the liberal Jekyll inspires a little blonde waif to walk without her crutches (another long-lost minute restored for video) and operates on an old charity crone.

Rose Hobart, destined to play in such fare as Universal's *Tower of London* (1939) and *The Mad Ghoul* (1943) as well as Columbia's *Soul of a Monster* (1944), was also doomed to be a victim of the Hollywood witch-hunt. The outspoken, gutsy lady, now living at the Motion Picture Country House, recalled *Dr. Jekyll and Mr. Hyde* for a *Filmfax* interview with Michael Brunas and Tom Weaver:

> [Mamoulian] really was a fine, fine director. The only thing that really bothered me about the way he directed was that I thought he really dotted his i's and crossed his t's because when he finished a scene he would always have something symbolic of the scene to finish up with. That was really overdoing it! ... I got along fine with Fredric March, a great actor, and his wife, Florence Eldridge, was an equally great actress.

"You've opened a gate for me into another world," says Jekyll to Muriel at the Carew mansion; Mamoulian festoons the love scene with a camera pan of statuary in the Carew garden and by the fountain. The passionate couple pleads with General Carew to allow the wedding to take place soon, but the Victorian stoic ("I waited five years for your mother," he tells Muriel) refuses, insisting on a "decent observance" before the nuptials.

As Jekyll walks home with Lanyon (himself taken by Muriel's charms), they pass through a slummy section of Soho, where a blonde saloon girl named Ivy Pierson is fighting with one of her "callers." Jekyll intervenes and carries the girl from the streets to her bedroom.

"You mustn't wear so tight a garter," Jekyll teases the girl. "Bad for you. It impedes the circulation."

What follows is one of the classic erotic vignettes of the early '30s: sly Ivy, attracted to Jekyll, takes off her garter and seductively tosses it to Jekyll. She also strips off her clothes ... and when Lanyon, waiting outside, impatiently opens the door, he sees Jekyll passionately kissing Ivy.

Lanyon leaves in disgust and Jekyll follows. As he stands at the door, Ivy, a garter back on her bare thigh, teasingly rocks her leg back and forth over the edge of the bed.

Miriam Hopkins as Ivy, displaying her notorious garter in *Dr. Jekyll and Mr. Hyde* (1931).

"Come back," Ivy sighs. "Come back soon, won't you?"

Out in the streets, Jekyll confesses his desires to the aghast Lanyon. "I want to be clean," he says, "not only in my conduct but in my innermost thoughts and desires. There is only one way to do it. . . . Separate the two natures in us."

"Oh, you are mad," snaps Lanyon.

"Mad, eh, Lanyon?" asks Jekyll. "Oh, we'll see."

In his Gothic laboratory, Jekyll looks at a steaming vial and then drinks it. The laboratory starts swimming about him, as he sees images of General Carew sneering "Positively indecent," Lanyon insisting "You're mad," and Ivy of the gartered thigh crying, "Come back."

Once again, Mamoulian staged this transformation as a cinema tour de force. As he told Charles Higham and Joel Greenberg in their book, *The Celluloid Muse:*

> We had a problem with the sequence in which Jekyll takes a drink and is physically transformed: how do you make the audience believe it? I decided to make them feel what Jekyll is feeling. Showing subjectively his demented whirlings round his laboratory. I had the camera revolve around upon its axis, and all four walls of the set were lit completely; this had never been done on the screen. The cameraman had to be tied to the top of the camera: he had to lean down and control the focus from up there. He was as small as a jockey, luckily.

The director needed a sound to accompany the visual; after experimenting with various effects—a gong sound run backwards, a snare drum, Hawaiian drums, Indian tom-toms—Mamoulian finally ran up and down stairs, recording his own heartbeat for accompaniment. "When I say my heart was in Jekyll and Hyde," he laughed, "I meant that literally!"

And, as for Hyde himself, Mamoulian always was outspoken about the makeup for March's Hyde. He told Al Taylor:

> As a prototype for Hyde, I didn't take a monster, but our common ancestor, the Neanderthal man. Mr. Hyde is not a monster but a primeval man—closest to the earth, the soil. When the first transformation takes place, Jekyll turns into Hyde, who is not the evil but the animal in him. . . . The first Hyde is this young animal released from the stifling manners and conventions of the Victorian period.

March's Hyde, indeed, looks like a sinister chimp, an escapee from hell's monkeyhouse. As Fredric March remembered the makeup agony:

> For six weeks, I had to arrive at the studios each morning at 6:00 A.M., so that Wally Westmore could spend four hours building pieces on my nose and cheeks, sticking fangs in my mouth, and pushing cotton wool up my nostrils.

It is a fantastic makeup—indeed, it's too much for some audiences, just as it was too much for Karl Struss, Mamoulian's cinematographer. Decades later, in the book *Karl Struss: Man with a Camera* (edited by John and Susan Harvith), Struss griped:

> I never agreed with the business of making a monkey out of Hyde. . . .
> He had two sets of false teeth, which I spoke to Mamoulian about because
> I thought that one was plenty. It could have been a gorilla or Wally Beery,
> it was no longer Fredric March to me. I said to Mamoulian, "Listen,
> you're going to have the audiences rolling in the aisles." He just shrugged
> his shoulders and he did it. He wanted it. He was the captain of the ship,
> I was only the first lieutenant.

March's first appearance as hairy Hyde, as he creeps around a corner
of the laboratory, was in fact so hilarious to some audiences that Paramount soon cut it. The approximately 25 seconds of stretching, dancing
and mugging was long sentenced to a trim can and only recently restored
to the video copy. As it is, March's first appearance in the cut version—
grinning in his mirror and exulting, "Free. . . . If you could see me now,
what would you think!" was enough to elicit a blast of derisive laughter
from a grimy audience at Los Angeles's Vagabond Theatre when the film
was revived there in 1976.

But to appreciate fully *Dr. Jekyll and Mr. Hyde*, it is essential to
understand that Mamoulian wanted Hyde to be funny, at least in the early
part of the show. "He is like a kitten, a pup, full of vim and energy," said
the director. Historian/writer/professor Paul Jensen once attended a showing of *Dr. Jekyll and Mr. Hyde* with Mamoulian present and remembers
that the director openly laughed loud and long at Hyde in his early scenes.
He is supposed to be funny, grotesquely so—a fascinating insight, too
often lost on new viewers of the film, who find the Westmore makeup
"camp."

The restored tape now presents over six minutes of previously cut
footage: Poole arriving at the lab, knocking on the door, and having a
returned-to-normal Jekyll answer it; Jekyll and Muriel debating whether
or not to wed without the old general's consent; a rainy day in the lab, with
Jekyll boiling over just as Mamoulian cuts to a chemical boiler, which explodes and boils over; and the next transformation of Jekyll to Hyde. It is
a remarkable special effect, and Struss explained:

> It was done by using a red filter on a strong red makeup, so that when
> you photographed red with a red filter the object was white. In front of
> the lens you put a two-inch square red "A" filter that had the same speed
> as a green "B" filter so that when you went from one exposure to the
> other, the density remained the same. . . . When the transition started it
> would slowly change and with the green filter you could see the image,
> the face, become quite dark, with lines and so forth, depending on how
> much makeup we had put on in the first place. I controlled the makeup
> with the makeup man.

Hyde, in cape and top hat, runs out into the night and the rain; in an
unforgettable scene, he bares his face to the rain, exulting in it, virtually

baptizing his new self. He seeks Ivy, calling at her house. When the house-keeper comes out on the porch above, Hyde playfully sticks his cane up her dress—a rather risqué (and funny) touch in the pre–Production Code days. Hyde finds Ivy at the Variety Music Hall, where the blonde is singing her song:

> Champagne Ivy is my name,
> Champagne Ivy is my name,
> Good for any game at night, my boys,
> Come and join me in a spree.

Hyde lures Ivy to his table with a bottle of champagne. When Ivy's previous admirer of the evening tries to interfere, Hyde threatens him with a broken bottle. And when Ivy tries to leave, Hyde brutally shoves her back into the chair.

"Forgive me, my dear," hisses Hyde to the terrified doxy. "You see, I hurt you because I love you. I want you. What I want, I get. I'll grant you I'm no beauty. But under this exterior, you'll find a very flower of a man."

"She was always upstaging everyone, all the time," said Rose Hobart of Miriam Hopkins. Indeed, the powerhouse actress appears out to steal *Dr. Jekyll and Mr. Hyde*. As Hobart remembers, Mamoulian became so exasperated with Hopkins's attempts to upstage March and hog the camera that he lied to her during the pub scene about where the camera was. Only after the scene was shot did the director reveal the true camera, concealed behind a curtain, much to the actress's wrath.

Hyde is soon keeping Ivy in her flat on Diaden Court, Soho. There Hyde visits; in a wonderfully comic touch, he trips over a bearskin rug, growls, and kicks the bear in the mouth. It is there in the flat that Hyde reads in the paper that the general and Muriel are back in London from a vacation. Realizing he must transform back into Jekyll to reclaim his fiancée, Hyde hugs Ivy up against the bedpost and tells her he must go away "for a few days." She breaks into a smile. When he looks up and catches her expression, she instantly reverts to being poker-faced—another great comic touch that is played by both stars with the timing of vaudeville comics.

"Remember you belong to me, do you hear?" snarls Hyde. "You belong to me. If you do one thing that I don't approve of while I'm gone—the least little thing, mind you—I'll show you what horror means!" Sadistically, Hyde demands that the horrified girl sing "Champagne Ivy," and as she does so, crying, she becomes hysterical and throws herself on the bed. Hyde, roaring with joy, follows.

"Look, my darling, how tight your garter is!" mocks Hyde. "You mustn't wear it so tight. It'll bruise your pretty tender foot!" Hyde grabs

Ivy in his arms, and he kisses her passionately as this scene fades out.

After the transformation, Jekyll is remorseful. He orders Poole to take £50 to Ivy. He calls on Muriel and persuades the general to agree to an early wedding. Jekyll is joyous, celebrating at home, playing his great organ, as Poole announces a caller, Miss Pierson. Ivy, shy in Jekyll's presence, timidly gives him back the £50. He asks why she won't take it.

"Here's why!" cries Ivy, baring her back to Jekyll. "Pretty, ain't it? It's a whip, that's what it is, *a whip!*"

Hysterical, Ivy pours out her dread of Hyde to Jekyll. She has tried to drown herself and failed. "And if you don't help me," she weeps, "you who has the kindest heart in the world, sir, then give me poison so I can kill myself."

Jekyll comforts the girl, who looks up at him in adoration and with longing. "You're an angel, sir. I'll do anything you like. I ain't as bad as you think. And I ain't a bad looker, either. I'll work for you. I'll slave for you. I'll love you."

"I give you my word," vows a repentant Jekyll, "that you will never be troubled with Hyde again."

On the night of the engagement party at Carew's, Jekyll strolls across the park, sits on a bench, and beholds a singing bird. In probably the most famous restored scene of the 1931 *Dr. Jekyll and Mr. Hyde,* March's Jekyll recites:

> Thou was not born for Death, immortal bird!
> No hungry generations tread thee down.
> Thou was not born for Death.

Then Jekyll sees a cat sneaking up the tree to attack the bird and devour it. The approximately 40 seconds of ode, bird, and cat all spent decades cut from the film although they acted as a prelude to Jekyll's new transformation into an even more horrible Hyde.

"But it *is* Death!" Hyde snarls into the camera.

Mamoulian's favored split screen technique shows Muriel, sadly waiting at the party, amidst her whispering guests, while Ivy toasts herself with champagne. "Here's hoping that Hyde rots wherever he is—and burns where he oughta be!" says Ivy. "And here's hoping that Dr. Jekyll will think of Ivy once in a while. He's an angel, he is. Here's to you, my angel."

Her door opens. It is Hyde.

"You took the word of that snivelling hypocrite Jekyll against mine!" rants Hyde. "You went down on your knees to the man I hate more than anybody in the world! ... You wanted him to love you, didn't you? Well, I'll give you a lover now. His name is *death!*"

Ivy runs, but Hyde traps her on the couch, where he finds the money that Jekyll made her keep.

"Listen my dear . . . I'm going to let you into a secret. A secret so great that those who share it with me cannot live. I *am Jekyll!* I am the angel whom you wanted to slave for and love. I'm going to take you in my arms and hold you close. Close, my little lamb . . . my dove . . . my bird . . . Isn't Hyde a lover after your own heart?"

Ivy's screams sound below, but help comes too late. Hyde escapes as Ivy's corpse lies on the bed.

Hyde cannot take sanctuary in Jekyll's laboratory because Jekyll has destroyed the key in his vow never to transform back into Hyde. So late that night, after Lanyon has returned from the Carew's sad party, he receives a note of despair, begging him to go to Jekyll's laboratory and take the vials marked A.H.S.T.R.M. from the E cabinet. Lanyon returns to his own house with the phials, and Hyde pays him a call.

Hyde grabs the vials and whirls to leave, but Lanyon pulls a gun. "Take me to Dr. Jekyll or you'll not leave this room!"

Mixing the potion, Hyde holds up the smoking flask and gives Lanyon one last warning. "Do you want to be left as you are, or do you want your eyes and your soul to be blasted by a sight that would stagger the devil himself?"

Lanyon cannot be dissuaded.

"What you are about to see," promises Hyde, "is a secret you are sworn not to reveal. And now, you who have sneered at the miracles of science, you who have denied the power of man to look into his own soul, you who have derided your superiors—look. *Look!*"

Hyde gulps down the potion. Before Lanyon's gaping eyes and Struss's camera, the beast becomes Henry Jekyll.

A melting candle shows the night wearing on. "There is no help for you, Jekyll," judges Lanyon. "You've committed the supreme blasphemy. I've warned you! . . . There is no help for you here. Nor mercy beyond. You're a rebel, and see what it has done for you. You are in the power of this monster that you've created!"

"I'll never take that drug again!" swears Jekyll.

"Yes, but you told me you became that monster tonight, not of your own accord. It will happen again."

Jekyll pleas for Lanyon's help, however. Lanyon finally agrees, making Jekyll vow never to mix the drug again and to give up Muriel.

When Jekyll calls at the Carew house, Muriel overrides her father's command that he not be admitted. The big scene between Jekyll and Muriel is one of the best in the film, the restored version providing over two long-lost minutes of the showdown. It is a wonderfully theatrical scene, the kind of lyceum drama that would have won bravos and an early bow for each player at its finish. When Jekyll falls to the floor in his misery, Muriel strokes him and comforts him.

"I give you up because I love you so," March climactically proclaims. "This is my proof, this is my penance. Do you hear, O God? *This is my penance!*"

The star marches out; Hobart's heartbroken Muriel falls at the piano, crashing out a chord—a dramatic touch that was also later cut but is now restored. Hearing her weeping, the heartbroken Jekyll approaches the French doors from the garden to take a final look at his beloved. And as he stands there, he feels a change.

"Oh God!" prays Jekyll. "Oh God don't let me! Don't let me! Save me!"

Muriel feels warm breath on her neck. She turns and sees Hyde. As the beast attacks, the general and his butler run to the rescue and Hyde crashes through the French doors. The men follow, and Hyde insanely bashes in the general's skull, leaving his broken cane as he flees.

The police, led by Lanyon, break down the door of Jekyll's laboratory seconds after the doctor has reverted from Hyde. Jekyll claims Hyde ran through the laboratory and out the back door. But Lanyon stops the police.

"Your man has not escaped," says Lanyon, pointing at Jekyll. "There! There he is! There's your man!"

Before the shocked eyes of the police and Poole and Lanyon, Jekyll slowly reverts to the horrible Hyde—more grotesque than ever. All through the film, the Westmore makeup has become more ghastly each time, and now it is truly nightmarish, the skin under the eyes stretched under the sockets. Wildly, he attacks the police, and like a demonic ape, leaps atop Jekyll's shelves, where a policeman shoots him.

The body falls, crashing amidst the vials and chemicals of Jekyll's great table. The corpse of the bestial, Neanderthal Hyde returns to that of the handsome, brilliant, and doomed Dr. Henry M. Jekyll.

And as Lanyon and the police behold the body, as Poole weeps and prays, Mamoulian's camera retreats, back through Jekyll's fireplace and over the blazing cauldron, bubbling madly, satanically. Is it symbolic of the damnation Henry Jekyll now faces for eternity? Or the everlasting hell he perhaps escaped in his penance of surrendering Muriel before Hyde overtook him?

While that is left to the audience to decide, the last scene of *Dr. Jekyll and Mr. Hyde* presents, truly, Hollywood's own cauldron—the melting pot of man's battle with his soul that is the true trademark of the Golden Age's greatest horror movies.

Paramount completed *Dr. Jekyll and Mr. Hyde* in about seven weeks;

the cost was probably about $500,000. The final "Hyde" almost destroyed Fredric March for real, as Rose Hobart remembered:

> Of course, the worst thing to happen to Freddie on that picture was when the makeup man, who should have known better, was trying to make the masks, because Hyde got progressively worse. All of them were just too mask-like and Freddie couldn't move. So they made a mask and put it on Freddie with liquid rubber. He was in the hospital for three weeks! It took his whole face off! It was lucky he wasn't ruined for life! That's the kind of thing they used to do in those days and that's why I hated pictures! They didn't give a shit about people!

The big night was New Year's Eve, 1931—the year in which *Dracula* and *Frankenstein* had proved sensations with the Depression public. And the theatre was New York's Rivoli, where Barrymore's *Dr. Jekyll and Mr. Hyde* had premiered 11 years before.

The *New York Times* reported:

> With the audibility of the screen and the masterful photography, the new pictorial transcription of Stevenson's spine-chilling work *Dr. Jekyll and Mr. Hyde* emerges as a far more tense and shuddering affair than it was as John Barrymore's silent picture. . . . Rouben Mamoulian . . . has gone about his task with considerable enthusiasm, and the way in which Jekyll changes into Hyde is pictured with an expert cunning. . . . Mr. March's portrayal is something to arouse admiration, even taking into consideration the camera wizardry. As Dr. Jekyll he is a charming man, and as the fiend he is alert and sensual. . . . Miriam Hopkins does splendidly as the unfortunate Ivy.

Variety, too, was impressed. As always, "the show business Bible" has its eye on box office, reporting ideally through the eyes of the midwestern theatre owner trying to capture a no-nonsense, middle-class audience. Given this perspective, the magazine was sometimes almost hilariously obtuse in recognizing the artistry of some films of the era, especially the horror films. *Variety* praised Mamoulian's avant-garde *Dr. Jekyll and Mr. Hyde*, however:

> The picture is a fine work of the studio art. As a literal transcription, the picture is the last word in artistic interpretation, done by understanding adaptors and an extremely skillful director. . . . March does an outstanding bit of theatrical acting. His Hyde is a triumph of realized nightmare.

Variety did have one major reservation:

> The element that detracts from its highest box office possibilities is that
> it runs overtime on footage. Labored adornment of the original simplicity
> weakens the production for mob appeal. High pitch of emotional horror
> is difficult to maintain beyond some certain degree of elapsed time, and
> the 98 minutes this picture runs carries it past that human limit.

Perhaps *Variety*'s lament was instrumental in the many cuts the film
soon suffered. Nevertheless, *Dr. Jekyll and Mr. Hyde* was a terrific hit in
its first release. It was one of the top money-making films of 1932, placed
on the "Ten Best" list of both the *New York Times* (#5) and *Film Daily*
(#6), and played at the original 1932 Venice Film Festival, where audiences voted it "Most Original Film" and voted March "Favorite Actor."
However, while *Dracula* and *Frankenstein* had saved Universal, Paramount's horror hit couldn't save its studio from an awesome financial
disaster: in 1932, Paramount lost $16 million and toppled into bankruptcy.

Paramount took some consolation at the fifth Academy Awards
ceremony banquet, held November 18, 1932, at the Fiesta Room of the
Ambassador Hotel in Los Angeles. The nominees for Best Actor of 1931/
1932: Wallace Beery for MGM's *The Champ,* Alfred Lunt for MGM's *The
Guardsman,* and Fredric March for Paramount's *Dr. Jekyll and Mr. Hyde.*
Both Beery and March were present. Norma Shearer announced the winner: Fredric March.

"I must thank Wally Westmore, who made my task an easy one," said
the victor. "Wally, who I consider a great artist, is responsible for the
greater measure of my success."

A little later in the evening, after Lionel Barrymore had named Helen
Hayes Best Actress for *The Sin of Madelon Claudet* and William Le Baron
had named *Grand Hotel* Best Picture, Conrad Nagel announced *another*
Best Actor winner: Wallace Beery. A vote checker had discovered that
Beery had lost to March by only one vote, and by Academy rules, this con-
stituted a "tie." Another Oscar was found, and Beery took home an
Academy Award, too. March laughed over the whole spectacle.

"It seems a little odd," joked March, noting that he and Beery had just
adopted children, "that Wally and I were given awards for best male performance of the year!"

It was the first of Fredric March's two Academy Awards; he later won
again for Goldwyn's 1946 *The Best Years of Our Lives.* March would reprise
Dr. Jekyll and Mr. Hyde on radio's "Theatre Guild," November 19, 1950,
with Barbara Bel Geddes and Hugh Williams.

Oddly, Mamoulian received no Best Director nomination (he never
won an Oscar in his career), although *Dr. Jekyll and Mr. Hyde* copped
nominations for Best Writing for Percy Heath and Samuel Hoffenstein
(Edwin Burke won for Fox's *Bad Girl*) and Best Cinematography for Karl
Struss (his Paramount colleague Lee Garmes won for *Shanghai Express*).

Hailed for its sleek exotica in the early '30s cinema, Paramount did little in the horror genre following *Dr. Jekyll and Mr. Hyde*. The studio's *Island of Lost Souls* (1932), based on H. G. Wells's novel and starring Charles Laughton as mad Dr. Moreau, Bela Lugosi as the hairy Sayer of the Law, and Kathleen Burke as "The Panther Woman," was banned in Britain and caused a stir that led the studio largely to forsake the genre. Nevertheless, its infrequent forays were interesting—including *Murders in the Zoo* (1933), in which a wild-eyed, insanely jealous Lionel Atwill tosses his young spouse (Kathleen Burke) into an alligator pool. Paramount's '40s output was curious, as well—such as *Dr. Cyclops,* horror's first full-Technicolor feature, and the nasty *The Monster and the Girl,* both 1940 films.

Dr. Jekyll and Mr. Hyde would soon face suppression and a long limbo in the vaults of rival MGM before being resurrected in its new, restored, videocassette release. Mamoulian, who later displayed his strikingly theatrical stylistics in such films as Paramount's *Song of Songs* (with Dietrich, 1933) and 20th Century–Fox's *Blood and Sand* (with Tyrone Power, Linda Darnell, and Rita Hayworth, 1941), spoke of the film's lasting power in *Cinemacabre:*

> You know, we have to realize that art is a magic wand that touches stone and turns it into gold, metaphorically speaking. It turns everything into gold. Today, we touch everything and it turns to lead. It's ugly. We portray man wallowing in a gutter, full of foibles and sickness, falling short. They say life is like that, but it isn't true. . . . We still have great people, spiritual people. We have great aspirations and ideals. You take Shakespeare. He always had balls, he knew there was such a thing as conscience, such a thing as good. You've got to have both sides. I don't care how debased or how sordid your subject is, like *Dr. Jekyll and Mr. Hyde,* you must portray the whole truth of life, not partial truth, because partial truth is worse than a lie.

●

> Sex was more psychological in MGM's two-hour super version, with the transformation designed as a special montage by Peter Ballbusch; giraffes' necks were never so phallic. Ingrid Bergman and Lana Turner were the women in Spencer Tracy's double life, which he played in little makeup. The most superior monster movie ever made.
> —Denis Gifford, *Movie Monsters*
> (Great Britain, 1969)

The 1941 *Dr. Jekyll and Mr. Hyde* does have its admirers, such as the aforementioned Mr. Gifford; it is also this author's favorite cinema treatment of the Stevenson tale. I confess that "critical aberration" while admitting at the same time that the film needs a strong defense, both in its MGM gloss and its production machinations.

After Robert Donat won the 1939 Best Actor Oscar for MGM's *Goodbye Mr. Chips*, Metro announced a new *Dr. Jekyll and Mr. Hyde* as a vehicle for the peculiar, asthmatic star. He rejected it, whereupon MGM bestowed the property on its celebrated Spencer Tracy (1900–1967), winner of Oscars for *Captains Courageous* (1937) and *Boy's Town* (1938) and, in 1940, the nation's number two box office star, right between MGM's Mickey Rooney (#1) and Clark Gable (#3).

Tracy also pushed for his own vision for the new *Dr. Jekyll and Mr. Hyde*. According to Bill Davidson's book *Spencer Tracy: Tragic Idol* (Dutton, 1987), Tracy, tormented by his own alcohol problems and "perhaps thinking of his own dual personae . . . proposed to MGM executive Eddie Mannix that the story be done as a lesson in how alcohol and drugs can bring out the evil side of a man." In her 1991 best-seller, *Me: Stories of My Life*, Katharine Hepburn remembered Tracy telling her about his original concept not long after making *Dr. Jekyll and Mr. Hyde*. Tracy told Hepburn:

> Believe it or not, when they first mentioned *Jekyll and Hyde*, I was thrilled. I had always been fascinated by the story and saw it as a story of the two sides of a man. I felt that Jekyll was a very respectable doctor— a fine member of society. He had proposed to a lovely girl and was about to marry her. But there was another side to the man. Every once in a while, Jekyll would go on a trip. Disappear. And either because of drink or dope or who knows what, he would become—or should I say turn into?—Mr. Hyde. Then in a town or neighborhood where he was totally unknown, he would perform incredible acts of cruelty and vulgarity. The emotional side of Jekyll was obviously extremely disturbed. The girl, as his fiancee, is a proper lady. But as his fantasy whore, the girl matched his Mr. Hyde. She would be capable of the lowest behavior.
>
> The two girls would be played by the same actress; the two men would be me.

As Hepburn added, "Oddly enough, when he had this notion, I was the girl he had in mind. At this time we had never met. It still seems the most fascinating idea to me...."

Of course, this avant-garde approach wasn't to be. Davidson quoted Eddie Mannix as saying:

> It was an interesting idea to me, but Mr. Mayer wouldn't go for it. . . . Mr. Mayer thought that if Spence flipped out when he drank booze and took dope, it would be too close to home for a lot of people, and besides, it would make a "message picture," which L. B. hated.

A good woman—
A bad woman—
He needed the
love of both!
SPENCER TRACY
INGRID BERGMAN · LANA TURNER
IN
VICTOR FLEMING'S production of
Dr. Jekyll and Mr. Hyde
with
DONALD CRISP · IAN HUNTER
BARTON MacLANE · C. AUBREY SMITH
Screen Play by JOHN LEE MAHIN
BASED ON THE NOVEL BY ROBERT LOUIS STEVENSON
Directed by VICTOR FLEMING
A Metro-Goldwyn-Mayer PICTURE

MGM knew all too well of Tracy's alcohol binges, which were the stuff of ugly Hollywood legend. Possibly the idea of parading that side of the beloved star before the public gave a true feeling of horror to the front office. They opted to go the traditional route by buying Paramount's old script and securing all copies of the 1931 version.

A traditional *Dr. Jekyll and Mr. Hyde* frightened Tracy. The movies' most "natural" actor was terrified of the makeup and the theatrics; he also hated the idea of following rival Fredric March in the role that had won March an Academy Award. According to Jackson J. Benson's excellent 1984 biography, *The True Adventures of John Steinbeck, Writer,* Tracy finally agreed to *Dr. Jekyll and Mr. Hyde* with the proviso that MGM would allow him to narrate *The Forgotten Village,* an independent film his friend Steinbeck had made in Mexico.

The production shaped up most impressively. Victor Fleming (1883–1949), who had directed Tracy in *Captains Courageous* and *Test Pilot,* was the producer and director of *Dr. Jekyll and Mr. Hyde.* It was his first film since his Oscar-winning work on Selznick's 1939 *Gone with the Wind.* MGM engaged Ingrid Bergman (1915–1982) for Jekyll's fiancée (now named "Beatrix") and Lana Turner for Ivy. They switched assignments because Lana was afraid of the heavy dramatics of the Ivy role and Ingrid desired to do something provocative after her wholesome U.S. performances.

John Lee Mahin provided the script, following the structure of the 1931 film. Indeed, the Screen Achievement Records Bulletin for the 1941 *Dr. Jekyll and Mr. Hyde,* noting Mahin as screenplay author, added beside "Other Substantial Contributors" the name Samuel Hoffenstein, with the words, "Received credit on old produced picture." Jack Dawn designed the makeup.

The shooting of *Dr. Jekyll and Mr. Hyde* began February 4, 1941. And as production began, MGM rescinded permission for Tracy to narrate Steinbeck's *The Forgotten Village*—"knowing," Steinbeck theorized, "he wouldn't stop a picture already in production." Tracy was angry, but it was only the beginning of his troubles on *Dr. Jekyll and Mr. Hyde.*

There are some surprises in the Metro product: it opens, to the strains of Franx Waxman's celestial music, in a glorious church, where a bishop (C. Aubrey Smith) delivers his sermon. Suddenly, a deranged man (Barton MacLane) jumps up, cackles lewdly, and starts to tell the congregation what "a real man" thinks about. Jekyll, at worship with Beatrix and her father (Donald Crisp), turns around for a dramatic first close-up, helps the man's distraught mother (Sara Allgood, later memorable in *The Lodger*), and examines the man—diagnosing that his evil, sordid side has been unleashed by an accident.

Opposite: **Poster for the Spencer Tracy *Dr. Jekyll and Mr. Hyde* (1941).**

Indeed, the tone of the 1941 version is not so much the macabre, as it is a sexual sadism—quite strikingly delivered for the era. Perhaps the most notorious demonstration is Jekyll's de Sade–ish nightmare after quaffing the drug. In the Peter Ballbusch–designed montage, we see those phallic giraffe necks and such little spectacles as Bergman, with a sexy smile, being shoved by a giant corkscrew into a bottle, which, as any Freudian might expect, explodes. The dream also features the famous flagellation scene in which Jekyll imagines himself madly driving a chariot pulled by his steeds Lana and Ingrid as he merrily whips them both. As Lana Turner recalls in her biography:

> Creating the scene was hellishly uncomfortable. We had to sit astride mechanical horses, which bucked worse than live ones, while machines drove gale-force winds through our long hair. That sequence is often cut out when the picture is replayed on television—I suppose because it is too suggestive.

There were personal problems. Ingrid Bergman fell in love with Victor Fleming; Tracy was reportedly also infatuated with Ingrid, and she with him. Fleming, still nursing his wounds after the battles with Vivien Leigh on *Gone with the Wind*, had no patience with either leading lady; he got Lana to cry for a scene by twisting her arm behind her back, and he produced tears from Ingrid by smacking her face.

The real surprise of MGM's *Dr. Jekyll and Mr. Hyde*, however, is Tracy. His Hyde, all bedecked in Victorian top hat and cape, is magnificent—a toothy, eye-flashing sadist who virtually reeks of sexual perversion, reveling in his own cruelty. Tracy delivers the richly sinister dialogue with relish, as when he kills Bergman's screaming Ivy:

> Yes, dance—dance and dream. Dream that you're Mrs. Henry Jekyll . . . dancing with your own butler and six footmen! Dream that they've all turned into white mice and crawled into an eternal pumpkin!

While he seems to be enjoying his Hyde in the film, the wildly insecure Tracy was in fact terrified by the challenge and so self-conscious in the subtle Jack Dawn makeup that he rode to and from the set in a limousine with curtains over the windows. To add to his discomfiture, a story quickly circulated through Hollywood that Somerset Maugham had visited the *Jekyll and Hyde* set to watch Tracy in action. "Which one is he playing now?" Maugham supposedly inquired.

Tracy never got over this quip, the makeup, having to follow the Oscar-winning Fredric March, or MGM's betrayal regarding Steinbeck's *The Forgotten Village*. He threw himself into the roles with everything he had, however. Gil Perkins, veteran Australian stuntman who had acted with Tracy at MGM on such films as *Captains Courageous* (and had played in the fight scene outside the Carew home in the 1931 *Dr. Jekyll and Mr. Hyde*), was his double on *Dr. Jekyll and Mr. Hyde:*

> To double Tracy as Mr. Hyde, I had to get into the MGM makeup department at 5:30 in the morning, and it would take them a couple of hours to put the rubber mask all over my head. Then they would make up the mask, and put a wig on top of it, and fill in down around the neck. ... At lunchtime, I used to have to drink my lunch through a straw, because I couldn't eat anything—I could only get this straw in my rubber mouth. Jack Dawn and Bill Tuttle were the two guys responsible for all that.
>
> All I know is that Tracy did everything very professionally—he always was the ultimate professional. And Victor Fleming was one of the best directors in the business. ... Spence had a great respect for Vic, and they got along very well.

No expense was spared. MGM completed *Dr. Jekyll and Mr. Hyde* April 8, 1941 (retakes began April 16); the final negative cost was $1,140,000. On July 21, 1941, MGM proudly hosted a trade show at the Ambassador Hotel in Los Angeles. "To see it is to indulge in an emotional binge," hailed *The Hollywood Reporter:*

> Victor Fleming's production of *Dr. Jekyll and Mr. Hyde* is a master screen work and a first calibre dramatic hit. Magnificent are the performances of Spencer Tracy and Ingrid Bergman, the thoughtful direction of Fleming, and the artful screenplay writing of John Lee Mahin. ... Tracy wisely chooses to play Hyde with the smallest application of makeup. ... His Jekyll and Hyde is the top portrayal of a top actor's career. ... It will be impossible hereafter to draft any list of the screen's great actresses without including the name of Ingrid Bergman. ... Excelling in every technical department, the film is one in which MGM can take justifiable pride.

Dr. Jekyll and Mr. Hyde opened in New York City on August 12, 1941. The luxuriant trade reviews were not repeated; *Time* nailed Tracy, claiming "He is not so much the fiend incarnate as the ham rampant." Tracy himself agreed. The late Ralph Bellamy, one of Tracy's best friends, remembered the actor coming to his house one night, very drunk, begging Bellamy to hide him as he had just ruined his career; Tracy had just seen *Dr. Jekyll and Mr. Hyde.*

While some current historians claim the 1941 film bombed, such was hardly the case. *Dr. Jekyll and Mr. Hyde* earned a domestic gross of $1,279,000 with a foreign gross of $1,072,000—all for a worldwide gross of $2,351,000. The movie's profit was $350,000. The picture rated

Academy nominations for Joseph Ruttenberg's black-and-white cinematography, Franz Waxman's magnificent musical score, and Harold F. Kress's film editing; it won no Oscars.

Tracy's horror at his own performance may not have been based on his acting. His Hyde is horribly convincing; perhaps, in this Gothic portrayal, Tracy revealed a glimpse of the alcoholic, tormented man who used to go to a New York hotel and drink himself senseless in a bathtub, who once wrecked a sound stage during his pre–MGM days on a binge at Fox, the actor whom Katharine Hepburn nursed through so many violent depressions. For critics used to hailing Tracy's "naturalistic" underplaying, this was a daring stretch.

"That notion," wrote Katharine Hepburn of Tracy's original conception of *Dr. Jekyll and Mr. Hyde,* "I couldn't get it out of my mind. Was there some very personal connotation?" Even in the "traditional" *Dr. Jekyll and Mr. Hyde,* perhaps Spencer Tracy had seen a "personal connotation" that had scared him. As Hepburn wrote:

> Who was he? I never really knew. He had locked the door to the inside room. I have no idea even whether he himself had the key. I only suspected that inside that room was a powerful engine which ran twenty-four hours a day at full speed. It turned out some remarkable people— yes—all those different people.

One of the most powerful attributes of the 1941 *Dr. Jekyll and Mr. Hyde* is its finale. After Tracy's dead Hyde turns back into Jekyll, Franz Waxman's music swells beautifully, with a religious fervor, as a chorus sings the words from the 23rd Psalm, "He restoreth my soul." The implication is that the Almighty has forgiven Henry Jekyll for his blasphemy, and it is a welcome and moving interpretation.

When MGM produced the 1941 *Dr. Jekyll and Mr. Hyde,* it condemned the 1931 prints to deep in the vaults to avoid any comparison between that version and the remake. It was not until the late 1960s that Raymond Rohauer discovered the Mamoulian version, long-lost in the Metro catacombs, and presented the cut film in an October 1967 Mamoulian retrospective. The film made a slow comeback in revival theatres and television as the Metro production played constantly. But it was MGM/UA Video that officially repented, eventually restoring the long-cut Mamoulian version and releasing it in 1989, just as the company had released the Tracy version.

Over the years, there have been many Jekyll and Hyde remakes, spin-offs, homages and spoofs. There was Columbia's *The Son of Dr. Jekyll* (1951), starring Louis Hayward and directed by Seymour Friedman; Allied Artists provided *Daughter of Dr. Jekyll* (1957), directed by Edgar G. Ulmer, with Gloria Talbott in the title role and Arthur Shields as the lecherous monster. Britain's Hammer Films got into the act with *The Two Faces of Dr. Jekyll* (1960), directed by the prolific Terence Fisher and starring Paul Massie as Jekyll and Hyde. In 1972, Hammer outdid itself with *Dr. Jekyll and Sister Hyde*, in which the alter ego of the doctor (Ralph Bates) is a lethal lady (Martine Beswick); Bates, director Roy Ward Baker, and (especially) Beswick all made it work. British Lion-Amicus Pictures provided the Christopher Lee/Peter Cushing *I, Monster* (1972), with Lee as "Dr. Charles Marlowe" and "Edward Blake" and Cushing as Mr. Utterson, his "personal attorney and close friend." The accent was on Freud; Cushing called it "not the best film I've ever worked on." *Edge of Sanity* (1989) found Anthony Perkins doing the Jekyll/Hyde bit, and turning into Jack the Ripper.

Naturally, there have been many comic spin-offs: Universal-International's *Abbott and Costello Meet Dr. Jekyll and Mr. Hyde* (1953) (starring Boris Karloff as Jekyll and Hyde, with Eddie Parker performing the strenuous "Hyde" action); Paramount's *The Nutty Professor* (1963), with Jerry Lewis directing himself as Professor Julius F. Kelp and his hyper-cool alter-ego, "Buddy Love" (who some believe is Lewis's lampoon of Dean Martin). There's been Oliver Reed as *Dr. Heckyl and Mr. Hype* (1980) and Mark Blankfield in *Jekyll and Hyde . . . Together Again* (1982).

As for television, CBS's "Suspense!" telecast "Dr. Jekyll and Mr. Hyde" September 20, 1949, with Ralph Bell in the title roles. Faced with the challenge of the transformation before the early television cameras, director Robert Stevens (in a twist of the Mamoulian approach) made the camera Hyde, only showing Hyde's hands as Bell (and the audience) "became" Hyde. On March 6, 1951, "Suspense!" offered a new version—this time starring Basil Rathbone as Jekyll and Hyde. CBS's "Climax" offered Michael Rennie as "Dr. Jekyll and Mr. Hyde" on July 28, 1955, in an adaptation by Gore Vidal. On March 8, 1957, NBC's "Matinee Theatre" presented the melodrama with Douglass Montgomery in the dual roles. On January 7, 1968, there was a 2½ hour ABC color special of *The Strange Case of Dr. Jekyll and Mr. Hyde*, starring Jack Palance and produced by Dan Curtis, with makeup by Dick Smith. (In one scene as Hyde, running along a garden wall to his laboratory, Palance became so excited that he scorned a stunt man, performed the action himself, fell through a flimsy part of the set, crashed to the studio floor 15 feet below and fractured his arm. He was hospitalized for three days.) NBC followed March 7, 1973, with a 90-minute musical version starring Kirk Douglas. Most recently, it was Michael Caine who tackled the venerable role in a 1990 made-for-television movie.

It is curious to compare the three most famous *Dr. Jekyll and Mr. Hyde* star performances: Barrymore's scuttling, leering conehead, which he could instantly reprise at the promise of a beer; March's smirking, steadily degenerating Neanderthal man, whose impact (according to the modest Oscar-winner) was largely due to the makeup man; Tracy's grinning sexual sadist that horrified the actor himself.

Each great actor, in his own way, illuminated the eternal fascination of Stevenson's old nightmare. And each man managed to conjure Stevenson's most profound theme: that the worst horror, after all, is what might lurk deep within our own souls and consciousness.

The Old Dark House

Studio: Universal; Producer: Carl Laemmle, Jr.; Director: James Whale; Associate Producer: E. M. Asher; Screenplay: Benn W. Levy (from J. B. Priestley's 1928 novel *Benighted*); Dialogue: R. C. Sherriff; Cinematography: Arthur Edeson; Editor: Clarence Kolster; Art Director: Charles D. Hall; Makeup: Jack P. Pierce (assistant, Otto Lederer); Special Effects: John P. Fulton; Set Decorations: R. A. Gausman; Music: David Broekman and Heinz Roemheld; Recording Supervisor: C. Roy Hunter (Western Electric Recording); Sound Technician: William Hedgcock; Assistant Director: Joseph McDonough; Camera Operator: King Gray; Assistant Cameraman: Jack Eagen; Stills: Roman Freulich; Running Time: 71 minutes.

Filmed at Universal City, California, April–May 1932; opened at the Rialto Theatre, October 27, 1932.

The Players: Morgan (Boris Karloff); Roger Penderel (Melvyn Douglas); Sir William Porterhouse (Charles Laughton); Gladys DuCane (Lilian Bond); Horace Femm (Ernest Thesiger); Rebecca Femm (Eva Moore); Philip Waverton (Raymond Massey); Margaret Waverton (Gloria Stuart); Sir Roderick Femm (John [Elspeth] Dudgeon); Saul Femm (Brember Wills).

> They were all godless here. They used to bring their women here—brazen, lolling creatures in silks and satins. They filled the house with laughter and sin, laughter and sin. And if I ever went down among them, my own father and brothers—they would tell me to go away and pray ... and I prayed—and left them with their lustful red and white women.
>
> —Eva Moore, in *The Old Dark House*

A cataclysmic storm crashes in the night outside a foreboding old house high in the mountains of Wales. Inside, within a candlelit, decaying Victorian bedroom, a lovely blonde of porcelain beauty stands in a silk slip, changing her rain-soaked clothes while a leering old hag, mad with religion, watches.

31

"That's fine stuff," says the hag, feeling the dress into which the blonde has wriggled—"but it'll rot." And then, eyeing the young lady's bosom: "*That's* finer stuff still—but it'll rot too, in time!"

The heroine explores the Gothic hall—and a monstrous, drunken, literally Karloffian butler suddenly looms over her. He attacks, chasing the screaming beauty about the hall, overturning a giant dining table in crashing pursuit.

Add to the show such macabre accoutrements as a skeletal, prissy avowed atheist, actually terrified of God; a boorish knight and his chorus line girlfriend; a "wicked, blasphemous old man" of 102 (actually played by a squeaky-voiced old woman in a beard); a giggling pyromaniac who fondles a carving knife; two wild climaxes; a grand cast; dazzling cinematography; and the bravura style of James Whale; and the concoction is Universal's long-lost horror classic of 1932—*The Old Dark House*.

For many years, *The Old Dark House* languished in film limbo, condemned by legal entanglements resulting from William Castle's dismal 1963 remake. While Whale's *Frankenstein, The Invisible Man,* and *Bride of Frankenstein* all became beloved cinema folklore, *The Old Dark House* was considered lost. Now, via archival showings and "bootlegged" video prints, this elegant black comedy has been making a slow, almost underground comeback.

One wishes the comeback could be more official. For *The Old Dark House* is one of Universal's most striking horror tales, one of Hollywood's most delightfully visual melodramas, and one of James Whale's most personal and fascinating works.

> The man who played the Monster in *Frankenstein* now transforms himself into the mad butler, in *The Old Dark House* ... Another whale of a picture directed by James Whale, who also directed *Frankenstein.*
> —Universal publicity for *The Old Dark House*

> I owe it all to Dr. Frankenstein's jolly old monster!
> —Boris Karloff

> I am getting quite to like Hollywood. It makes me so brown and beautiful.
> —James Whale

Once upon a time, in the summer of 1931, a little band of fascinating misfits gathered under the giant, purple mountains of Universal City, California, to make a movie based on Mary Shelley's *Frankenstein*.

A Woolworth Christmas window display, promoting *The Old Dark House*.

The portrayer of Frankenstein was Colin Clive, a fraught, anguished, chainsmoking Englishman. In real life, Clive played the role(s) of Dr. Jekyll and Mr. Hyde; he was the kindly Jekyll only when he was sober.

The director was "Jimmy" Whale, tall, foxy, cheroot-smoking "ace" of Universal, an English "aristocrat," with Byronic poses, red hair with silver streaks, and a sardonic flair. Hailed as "the genius who made

Journey's End," Whale was actually not an aristocrat at all, but a bitter homosexual who based his life-style on the "gentleman lovers" he had known in the London theatre. The movie colony later referred to him slyly as "the Queen of Hollywood."

And there was Boris Karloff, "the monster," gaunt, haunting, doe-eyed—an English black sheep. Karloff would soon be beloved in Hollywood as "dear Boris," a gentle, poetry-loving man who between scenes of *Frankenstein* took refuge high in the Universal hills, smoking a cigarette and laughing and playing with the lambs who grazed on the hillside.

Jack P. Pierce, the genius makeup wizard, came to makeup each morning in a surgeon's smock, like a doctor performing an operation. Dwight Frye, portrayer of the dwarf Fritz, once a versatile Broadway leading man, was now horrified to find himself Hollywood's fly-eater of *Dracula* and hunchback of *Frankenstein*. The producer, Carl Laemmle, Jr., Universal's 23-year-old "crown prince," was an Academy Award winner for *All Quiet on the Western Front*. A weaselly hypochondriac barely 5' tall, Laemmle had been given Universal City by his founding father, "Uncle Carl" Laemmle, as a 21st birthday present. Junior was so fearful of catching cold that he wore Kotex in his trousers.

If there was a blasphemy in Universal releasing Mary Shelley's saga of the man-made monster during Yuletide, 1931, nobody seemed to mind; *Frankenstein* was a sensation. There was glory for all, but "Uncle Carl" and "Junior" were exalting two offbeat Englishmen—Karloff and Whale—the saviors of Universal City.

Boris Karloff, born William Henry Pratt in Dulwich, England, November 23, 1887, was the youngest (and possibly illegitimate) son of a family of British diplomats. Educated at King's College, black sheep Karloff was exiled at age 21 to Canada due to his scandalous love of the theatre. Laboring first as a farmer and a lumberjack, Karloff was soon barnstorming all over western America, playing everything from Shakespeare to *The Virginian* to one of the ugly sisters in *Cinderella*. He acted many a melodrama night in top hat and black cape, leering at heroines and clutching at mortgages. Making his Hollywood debut in Fairbanks's 1919 *His Majesty the American,* Karloff went on to play nearly 80 bits and parts in the movies. These included the sinister jailbird Galloway in *The Criminal Code,* in the Los Angeles stage and the Columbia 1931 screen version, as well as follow-ups like dope-peddler "Cokey Joe" in RKO's *Young Donovan's Kid* and pervert Isopod of Warner's *Five Star Final*. In the meantime, Karloff contracted at least four marriages.

James Whale, born in Dudley, England, on July 22, 1889 (he claimed 1896), was educated at public schools (he claimed private tutors). An art student with a dream, Whale received his baptism in drama as a POW in

Gloria Stuart and Eva Moore in *The Old Dark House*.

World War I, directing and acting in shows at a Holzminden, Germany, prison camp. After training in Shakespeare at Stratford-upon-Avon, Whale triumphed as Charles Laughton's mad son in the 1928 play *The Man with Red Hair.* He then directed the great London hit *Journey's End* with heart-rending power and duplicated his success in the New York and Chicago companies. His next stop was Hollywood, where he ghost directed Howard Hughes's *Hell's Angels* and the 1930 Tiffany screen version of *Journey's End.* Whale began a Universal contract with *Waterloo Bridge,* starring Mae Clarke as the doomed streetwalker Myra.

It had been amidst the make-believe cowboys, gangsters, and glamour girls of Universal's commissary that Whale spied Karloff's face and invited him to test for "a damned awful monster!" By almost miraculous luck, Whale had found the actor who could portray all the quirky sensitivity he had hoped for in Frankenstein's monster. "A very fine director, indeed" was Karloff's salute to Whale late in his life.

Whale spoke very little of Karloff during his career. In 1983, I asked the late David Lewis, the gifted producer *(Dark Victory, Kings Row)* who had lived with Whale from 1929 to the early 1950s (when Whale surprisingly returned from Paris with a new lover), about the Whale and Karloff relationship. Lewis responded:

> As far as I know, Whale had high respect for Karloff and for his work. Whale never gave interviews about his feelings for actors, not even about Colin Clive, for whom he had the highest admiration. I don't know why people expect others to verbalize about their feelings. I had great respect for Bette Davis and great admiration for Errol Flynn, but it never crossed my mind to say so to the press. It seemed sufficient that I kept working happily with them. . . . Karloff was a gifted actor and there was more than a little sadness about him, but I never heard him complain. He was an intelligent man and intelligence often breeds sadness.

There was also a bizarre, sad aspect to the Karloff and Whale relationship.

In October 1957, five months after Whale's suicide, "This Is Your Life" honored Karloff. Jack P. Pierce, creator of Universal's *Frankenstein* makeup (who had been dropped by the studio a decade previous), was a guest. Karloff laughed with joy when he heard Pierce's voice, and the makeup wizard remembered the lake location shoot of the "flower game" scene with Little Maria.

"And after that," beamed the ebullient Pierce, "we left the location, and came back to the studio—"

"And worked all that night!" said Karloff.

"All that night," crowed Pierce, "with Colin Clive on your back—the bloodhounds chasing you!"

"I remember it!" smiled Karloff.

Left out of this story, by both gentlemen, was the frightening ego-tripping of Whale during this adventure. The director already resented the attention Karloff's monster was reaping. Marilyn Harris, the seven year old who had played Little Maria and loved Karloff, never knew that "the monster" had led a quiet rebellion at the lake, protesting the death of the child. Indeed, Karloff argued, why must she die at all? The company emotionally sided with Karloff, against Whale.

"You see, it's all part of the ritual," decreed Whale at last.

So, in a vengeance that might have titillated Marilyn's sadistic stage mother, Whale took Karloff back to Universal and ordered the exhausted actor to run up the hill to the windmill, away from the bloodhounds and the torch-bearing villagers, with Colin Clive on his back, all through the night, over and over and over again. It was the monster's penance for challenging the Almighty.

"What a stamina!" said Pierce of Boris Karloff.

"What a sadist!" Karloff might have said of James Whale, but he kept the story private. He remembered it vividly, though, when he became one

James Whale, center, hand on hip, relaxes with cast and crew of *The Old Dark House*.

of the founders of the Screen Actors Guild in 1933 and when he suffered from back trouble in later life.

Karloff and Whale: they had made *Frankenstein* a legend, and they belonged to Universal. As *Frankenstein* made its fortune, Karloff played in two Universal releases. In *The Cohens and Kellys in Hollywood,* he guest-starred as himself at the Coconut Grove and hobnobbed with such Universal stars as Tom Mix, Genevieve Tobin, and Sidney Fox. In *Night World,* he played a nightclub proprietor Happy MacDonald ("Hello, Big Shot!" he lisps in his British accent), who is gunned down in the finale. Whale, meanwhile, had directed Mae Clarke in *The Impatient Maiden,* with a climax that centered around an appendicitis attack. A new horror show, reuniting the Universal saviors, was in order.

●

The dreadful drama of *Dracula* ... Plus the stark terror of *Frankenstein* and the vivid portrayals of *Dr. Jekyll & Mr. Hyde!*
　—Universal publicity for *The Old Dark House.*

Junior Laemmle wanted a shocker for overnight star Karloff; Whale preferred a showcase to luxuriate his own quirky sense of humor. The chosen vehicle, J. B. Priestley's 1928 novel of madness—*Benighted*—did both. The tale of travelers who spend a horrific night in a gloomy house high in the Welsh mountains presented Karloff with the role of the mute, scarred, drunken, and bearded butler Morgan, while the eccentrics populating the abode (along with the visual potential) delighted Whale.

Benn Levy fashioned Priestley's novel into a screenplay; Whale surrounded himself with familiar and stimulating co-workers. R. C. Sherriff, who had written *Journey's End*, Whale's passport to glory on the London, Broadway, and Chicago stage (and the 1930 Tiffany movie version) penned the dialogue; cinematographer Arthur Edeson (1891–1970), who had filmed Whale's *Waterloo Bridge, Frankenstein,* and *The Impatient Maiden* (and would be cameraman of *The Invisible Man*) would be behind the camera.

It was a powerhouse cast, each personally selected by the director:

• Karloff, of course, would play Morgan, the drunken, homicidal butler, and reported to Jack Pierce to create a new horrific face.

• Melvyn Douglas (1901–1981) won the part of Roger Penderel, the cynical, war veteran hero (replacing Russell Hopton, who had gone so far as to get into costume and pose for candids with Karloff). Douglas would find his greatest thespic satisfaction late in life, winning a Broadway Tony for *The Best Man* (1963) and Oscars for Best Supporting Actor in *Hud* (1963) and *Being There* (1979); he was deeply unhappy playing conventional leading-men roles in fare ranging from Garbo's *As You Desire Me* (MGM, 1933) to *The Vampire Bat* (Majestic, 1933).

• Charles Laughton (1899–1962) made his Hollywood debut as Sir William Porterhouse, the knighted, boisterous bore. Laughton was on contract to Paramount, where he scored later in 1932 as whip-cracking Dr. Moreau in *Island of Lost Souls;* he would win the 1933 Best Actor Oscar for *The Private Life of Henry VIII.* On their first night in Hollywood, Laughton and his wife, Elsa Lanchester, dined with Whale—who not only had played Laughton's crazy son in *A Man with Red Hair,* but had been stage manager of a 1926 revue, *Riverside Nights,* in which Elsa sang in black top hat and tutu.

"You'll like it here, Charles," Elsa remembered Whale telling her spouse. "I'm pouring the money through my hair!"

• Lilian Bond (1910–1991) played Gladys DuCane, Sir William's chorus line girlfriend. The London-born actress soon returned to Broadway, co-starring with Brian Donlevy in the French farce *Three and One* (1933); she would show up in later years in bit roles in such films as *The Picture of Dorian Gray* (1945) and *Man in the Attic* (1953).

• Ernest Thesiger (1879–1961) was Whale's choice for Horace Femm, morbid master of the Old Dark House. The prissy Thesiger was a great character of the London stage, famous for his roles of Captain Hook in *Peter Pan* (1921), the Dauphin in Shaw's *Saint Joan* (1924), and Mephistopheles in *Doctor Faustus* (1925). (Thesiger enjoyed remembering the review that claimed he played the devil "like a maiden lady from Balham.") His favorite role would be Polonius in Hamlet, but his fame rested in his female impersonations. Thesiger had just made his Broadway debut in 1932 in *The Devil Passes,* with Basil Rathbone and Diana Wynyard; Whale found Thesiger simply fascinating. He admired Thesiger not only for his idiosyncrasies, but also for his supposed royal lineage; Thesiger was fated to play his most famous role, Dr. Septimus Pretorius, in Whale's *Bride of Frankenstein.*

• Eva Moore (1870–1955), mother of actress Jill Esmond (and mother-in-law of Laurence Olivier) played Rebecca Femm, Horace's nearly deaf, religious-fanatic sister.

• Raymond Massey (1896–1983), destined for greatness in roles like Lincoln and John Brown, here played stranded married sophisticate Philip Waverton. Referring to *The Old Dark House* many years later in his 1979 memoir, *A Hundred Different Lives,* Massey dismissed his role as a "juvenile," reported he had never seen the movie, and launched into a story about a Santa Monica party where one of the Countess di Frasso's dogs bit off the tip of his finger.

• Gloria Stuart, Universal's beautiful blonde contractee, played Margaret Waverton. Stuart had scored at the Pasadena Playhouse in Chekhov's *The Sea Gull,* and Paramount and Universal had so vied for her favor that the studios had to settle on a coin toss.

"Unfortunately," says Stuart today, more with humor than anger, "Universal won! I mean, Paramount had great stars, great directors, and Universal had nobody—except Boris Karloff and James Whale."

• Finally, for the role of Saul, the locked-away pyromaniac, Whale especially imported a British actor named Brember Wills, on whom information is scarce indeed (he died in 1948). (One wonders why Whale didn't send for Dwight Frye, who had played mad Renfield in *Dracula* and hunchbacked Fritz in *Frankenstein;* the diminutive actor would have been ideal for the role—and a lot closer to Universal.)

In the spring of 1932, all these talents gathered at Universal City for *The Old Dark House,* the elegant Whale in command.

> *The Old Dark House* was very interesting for a southern California girl like myself. My first impression of James was that he was very austere, very cold, very English—very removed from the scene. He was not at all "cozy" or anything....
> With James, every single line, every single movement, your

whole approach to the character was very meticulously discussed. He was the most prepared director I ever worked for.

Today, Gloria Stuart, painter, author, actress is still a striking lady.
She continues her acting career, recently playing in the acclaimed PBS
special *There Were Times, Dear,* dealing with Alzheimer's disease, which
had stricken her late husband, writer Arthur Sheekman. Living in Brent-
wood in West Los Angeles, Stuart vividly remembers *The Old Dark House*
and James Whale, who would direct her in three films:

> All the actors in *The Old Dark House* were very sophisticated, knowl-
> edgeable, and experienced, and Whale ran a very tight ship. Karloff was
> very quiet—after all, he had been under all the heavy makeup beginning
> at 4 in the morning—but he was beautifully educated, very soft-spoken,
> and charming. Laughton was there, with his "Method"; he had to huff
> and puff in a scene, so he ran up and down the stage to huff and puff,
> which was an eye-opener for me—I can huff and puff without moving a
> muscle! Eva Moore, who was the mother of the actress Jill Esmond, had
> been a great Victorian belle, and the "lady friend" of Edward, Victoria's
> son. It was very hard looking at her then to realize that—but now, looking
> at myself some days, I can understand it!
>
> All the actors—Raymond Massey, Melvyn Douglas, all of them—they
> were all stage-trained, very fine, accomplished actors, they all rehearsed
> a great deal until James had everything exactly the way he wanted it.

The opening episode of *The Old Dark House* is set in the stormy Welsh
mountains; it is night and Philip and Margaret Waverton (Massey and
Stuart) and fellow traveler Roger Penderel (Douglas) are caught in their
car, beleaguered by the apocalyptic storm. When Massey sarcastically laments how much he loves water running down his back, Whale and Edeson focused on a little cascade running off the brim of his hat; when the car
rides through a lake of water in the road, Douglas merrily warbles "Singin'
in the Rain." Stuart shivers as she remembers filming the scene:

> Ugh! We did it all night, from 6 P.M. to 5 o'clock in the morning, with
> rain machines and wind machines on the back lot. . . . Oh, it was awful!
> Fortunately, I was very young, and at the time, I thought it was great. But
> I must say, Melvyn and Raymond complained a lot.

The storm sends them to a dark old house, where Karloff's bearded
Morgan opens the door. In Whale fashion, we at first see only part of the
Jack P. Pierce makeup through the semiopened door; one eye, a sliver of
broken nose, a gash of cruel mouth. When Massey pleads for shelter,
Karloff's mad, mute butler replies the only way he can—with a bestial
muttering.

"Even Welsh ought not to sound like that," says Douglas.

The Morgan makeup is superb. "Jack Pierce was very fussy, a martinet," says Gloria Stuart, "but enormously talented, and he was wonderful with Karloff."

Inside, Whale and Edeson survey the cold, Gothic interior; the Charles D. Hall set is a masterpiece, destined to be rented by other studios. Melvyn Douglas found himself on the same set when he joined Lionel Atwill, Fay Wray, and Dwight Frye in Majestic's *The Vampire Bat* (1933). Ernest Thesiger, with the screen's most memorable nostrils, also enjoys a Whale theatrical entrance as sissified, atheistic Horace Femm. He walks down the stairs like a jovial skeleton, announcing to Edeson's low-angled camera, "My name is Femm! Horace Femm!" Thesiger merrily tosses off some of the film's best lines: "My sister was on the point of arranging these flowers"—just as he tosses them into the fireplace. He toasts Douglas with: "I give you—illusion!" And there's his masterfully delivered, "We make our own electric light here—and we're not very good at it." Eva Moore, as religious fanatic Rebecca Femm, is equally memorable, underscoring the offbeat sexual tones of Whale's work as she caws, "No beds! They can't have beds!"

At times the dialogue sounds very much like popular British comedy of today; such a scene occurs when Stuart tries to get through to the deaf Rebecca:

> STUART: It's a dreadful night.
> MOORE: What?
> STUART: I say, it's a dreadful night.
> MOORE: Yes, it's a very old house. Very old.
> STUART: It's very kind of you to let us stay.
> MOORE: What?
> STUART: I say, you're very kind!
> MOORE: Yes, it is a dreadful night.

This leads to one of the movie's best scenes: in a Victorian bedroom, Stuart, strikingly lovely in her slip and silk stockings, changes her clothes by candlelight, as Moore watches in evil fascination. The storm is terrible, and the hag shows Margaret the bed where her sister Rachel died:

> She was a wicked one. Handsome and wild as a hawk. All the young men used to follow her about, with her red lips and her big eyes and her white neck. But that didn't save her! She fell off her horse, hunting. Hurt her spine. On this bed, she lay—month after month. Many a time I used to sit here, listening to her screaming. ... She used to cry out to me to kill her, but I'd tell her to turn to the Lord. She didn't. She was Godless to the last!

Karloff as Morgan the butler in *The Old Dark House.*

Then Moore's Rebecca, her witch's face nightmarishly distorted in a mirror, tells of the house, of its sinful evenings of yore with the "lustful red and white women" favored by her brothers and her father—"a wicked, blasphemous old man" of 102, still alive upstairs.* Then she turns on Margaret:

*Eva Moore's soliloquy on the "lustful red and white women" would turn up in Haunted Honeymoon *(1986), where it was delivered by Dom DeLuise in drag.*

You're wicked too! Young and handsome. Silly and wicked! You think of nothing but your long straight legs, and your white body, and how to please your man! You *revel* in the joys of fleshly love, don't you?

The sermon on sin and vanity over, Rebecca exits, pausing to check her hair in the mirror. Rebecca's image haunts the heroine (who unwittingly opens a window and allows the storm to blast inside). In a virtuoso piece of direction and cinematography, Stuart gazes in the mirror at her own distorted face, imagines the warped reflection of Rebecca leering, "Lustful red and white women!" and then sees the spying face of Morgan, before she runs hysterically into the halls, the curtains blowing madly in the storm's wind.

The vignette is beautiful—superbly festooned by Whale with shadowy hues, candlelight, that perverse mirror and, finally, Stuart's dress, described by the *New Times Times* reviewer as "a stunning creation." Whale personally masterminded this gown, and Stuart recalls:

> James put me in what we used to call a Jean Harlow dress—a pale, pink, bias-cut, satin velvet evening dress, with spaghetti straps; I had crystal earrings, pearls. I said, "James! We just arrived an hour ago, sopping wet, in the wind and the mud, everything—everybody else is in rain-drenched clothes, and here I am, changing, in the spaghetti straps. Why me? Why do I get dressed?"
>
> And James said, "Because, Gloria, Boris is going to chase you, up and down the corridors, and I want you to appear like a white flame!"
>
> So I said, "OK—I'm a white flame!"

It was also, as Stuart discovered, strikingly visual, the sort of episode that Whale, former cartoonist for the London *Bystander,* loved creating.

The film rolls on: Sir William Porterhouse (Charles Laughton, broad and boisterous in his Hollywood bow) and his girlfriend Gladys DuCane (Lilian Bond) arrive. "I tell you, it's coming down in bucketfuls!" roars Laughton in his Lancashire accent. "I wouldn't be surprised if we caught our death!" Whale makes the most of the duo's entrance. Penderel gives Gladys his shoes for her wet feet; the delighted chorus girl jumps up and dances about in them, singing "Ach der Lieber Augustin," while old Rebecca sneers all the while.

There is a funereal dinner: "Have a potato," drolls Thesiger repeatedly. Douglas and Bond fall quickly in love and woo each other in the stable, a potentially stuffy scene that Whale initiates and ends with an insomniac rooster crowing irreverently. Back in the house, there is a charming touch: Stuart, before a wall, passes a few moments casting animal shadows with her hands. Suddenly, Moore's own frumpy shadow invades the scene, destroys Stuart's "animal," and stalks off.

The most horrific episode follows: Karloff's Morgan, drunk and violent, creeps up behind Miss Stuart and attacks.

As the blonde screams, darting about in that dress with the spaghetti straps, Karloff, his eyes rolled up into his head, rapaciously pursues. Whale aims Edeson's camera for a wicked series of Halloween closeups: a profile shot of the panting butler; a full shot of his leering, bearded scarface; frightening perusals of the mad eyes, the broken nose, and the twitching mouth. Morgan overturns the giant dinner table in his mania, smashing the dishes; finally, Massey knocks him out by hitting him with a lamp and sending him crashing down the steps, where he lies temporarily unconscious.

Stuart and Massey, recovering from the mad near-rape and wild fight, share a wonderfully understated dialogue:

> MARGARET: Philip, this is an awful house!
> PHILIP: It isn't very nice, is it?

Meanwhile, during such morbid adventures, Whale kept the company charmingly entertained; every day there was teatime. Gloria Stuart recalls: "The English contingent had tea at 11 and 4, and neither Melvyn nor I were ever asked! The real 'host' at tea was Ernest Thesiger. He was a brilliant character actor. As for his offscreen personality—the word 'rigid' doesn't begin to describe him!" It was a caste touch that hurt the young actress. As *The Old Dark House* progressed, however, the relationship between the arch (and homosexual) Whale and Gloria Stuart changed:

> It was interesting ... I was separated from my first husband at the time, and James took me to the theatre many times—Jane Cowl, Katharine Cornell, all the greats that came to Los Angeles—and he was a wonderful companion. Off the set, he had a very sharp sense of humor, and he could be very cutting, too—he could really cut you off at the pass. Away from the set, he was charming and relaxed, but back on the set the next morning, it was "Ach-tung" time.

Perhaps Karloff was lucky to be invited to tea, even though he was an Englishman. For according to the late Elsa Lanchester, Whale was cruelly derisive of Karloff, contemptuously referring to him as a "truck driver"— one of the survival jobs Karloff had worked between movies in the 1920s. It was a sad irony. Karloff, in fact, was from the lofty British background that Whale so idolized and had never known himself. It was an ego hangover from *Frankenstein*.

High in the house, Stuart and Massey discover Sir Roderick Femm, age 102, sprawled in his long-suffering death bed. Sir Roderick cackles how two of his children died young; how "madness came"; how his eldest son, Saul, hopelessly insane, is locked behind a door high in the house to keep him from setting fire to it; how Morgan serves as mad Saul's keeper. Perhaps Whale's sly approach to *The Old Dark House* is most clearly evidenced by the fact that Whale cast a woman named Elspeth Dudgeon in the part. Although she was only 60 when she played in *The Old Dark House*, Miss Dudgeon was the oldest-looking human being Whale knew, so he had Jack Pierce paste a beard on her, allowed her to deliver her lines in her own falsetto tones, and coyly billed good sport Elspeth as "John Dudgeon." (She later worked for Whale, under her own name and gender, as a pipe-smoking Gypsy in *Bride of Frankenstein* [1935], a mother superior in *Showboat* [1936], and the "Old Witch" in *The Great Garrick* [1937]. Elspeth Dudgeon was still acting as late as MGM's 1949 *The Great Sinner*, and died December 11, 1955—one week after her 84th birthday.)

"None of us knew that 'he' was a 'she,'" says Gloria Stuart. "In fact, we didn't know about 'him/her' until almost the cast party! It was James's secret, and he enjoyed it—and it was fun!"

Now, however, Whale mischievously shifts *The Old Dark House* into truly frightening melodrama for the last part of the film. First Morgan attacks again; a wild, violent struggle in which the men crash against a grandfather clock and through the hall, Edeson's camera breathlessly following as Morgan struggles and gurgles. The butler is hardly subdued before a second climax follows: a ghostly hand is clutching the banister. Saul Femm (Brember Wills), a raving, Bible-obsessed pyromaniac, has been let loose by the drunkenly vindictive Morgan. The waiflike madman informs Douglas that the family keeps him locked up because he knows they killed injured Rachel. Was the family guilty of a mercy killing? Is it the raving of a lunatic? The truth stays lost in the house's ominous shadows; Saul hopes to incinerate the house as a fiery offering to God.

"Flames are really knives," says Saul. "Sharp and cold.... They burn like ice!"

Telling the Bible story of Saul and David, the maniac sickly taunts Douglas with a carving knife:

> And it came to pass on the morrow that evil spirits came upon Saul ... and David played upon the harp with his hand, and there was a javelin in Saul's hand, and Saul *cast* the javelin!

Saul finally throws the knife at Penderel's head and misses; then the insanely cackling Saul runs wild, setting the balcony afire as the hero chases him. The men fight; in a chilling touch, Whale has Saul rabidly bite Penderel on his neck. Finally, the two crash through the balcony railing and fall.

"He's alive!" exults Bond, hysterically (and familiarly) over Douglas; Saul is dead.

And it is here that Whale presents his most wicked vignette.

Karloff's Morgan, crashing through the mayhem, finds Saul's corpse. Hugging the cadaver, the mad butler breaks down and weeps pitifully. Then Morgan picks up Saul and miserably minces up the steps, rocking him, his hips swaying effeminately, as if he were some nightmarish mother cradling a dead, horrific infant.

"The cold light of day," signaled by that irreverent rooster, provides the denouement. The Wavertons leave, (Massey mercifully unaware that years later he would be made up by Warner Bros. to look like Boris Karloff in the film version of Karloff's stage hit *Arsenic and Old Lace*). Thesiger's Horace waves goodbye like a foppish Roman emperor. Eva Moore's Rebecca emits a farewell croak like a dyspeptic raven. Laughton's Porterhouse, having lost his girlfriend to the romantic lead, snores good naturedly. And Douglas, his head bandaged, proposes to Miss Bond for a romantic fadeout, punctured and punctuated by Laughton's snores.

The final result, completed in May 1932 was a highly peculiar and individual work, purely stylized by James Whale. He was a director in every sense of the word; he had even orchestrated a full cacophony of stormy sound effects that underscored the movie. Gloria Stuart, who would star for Whale in his *The Kiss Before the Mirror* and *The Invisible Man*, says:

> Whale loved making films. Every morning—oh, he was so enthusiastic. He'd come in and he had every single set-up on the left hand side of the page opposite the dialogue. He had a wonderful cameraman, Arthur Edeson, and they just worked hand-in-glove. But Whale was the one who said what the set-ups were. Most directors would say to the cameraman, "What do you think?" but James just said, "I want it there"—and that's where it was.
>
> Working with James, I thought all movies were going to be like that. Well, forget it! When I made *Roman Scandals,* the director, Frank Tuttle, used to say, "OK, kids, believe it." Another of my favorite nondirectors used to say, "OK, kids, let's go laughing and scratching!" But James Whale...

J. B. Priestley's
THE OLD
DARK HOUSE
A Universal Picture with
Karloff
The Monster of *Frankenstein*
supported by a superb cast...

Directed by James Whale, Director of *Frankenstein*

Brember Wills and Boris Karloff in a scene from Universal's *The Old Dark House*.

> Ten souls storm-bound in a house
> accursed! Murderous maniac—drink—
> mad monster—harpy—coward—fire fiend.
>
> Two beautiful women to be protected
> —three decent men not enough!
> > —Premiere eve publicity for *The Old
> > Dark House, New York Times,* Oc-
> > tober 26, 1932

The Old Dark House became Universal's Halloween "Boo" of 1932. "A remarkable picture with a remarkable cast," promised one poster; another heralded, "The best-selling novel by J. B. Priestley comes to life and chizzles your backbone!" Karloff's Morgan, heralded the PR, was "A characterization that will make the world talk!" while Gloria Stuart "steals your heart and soul!" Finally, Universal, with the eggs primarily in Karloff's basket, added a foreword following the credits that was underscored by David Broekman's whimsically scary music:

> Producer's Note: Karloff, the mad butler in this production, is the same Karloff who created the part of the mechanical monster in *Frankenstein.*

We explain this to settle all disputes in advance, even though such disputes are a tribute to his great versatility.

The Old Dark House opened at New York's Rialto Theatre at 9:30 A.M., October 27, 1932. The *New York Times* praised the film:

> There is a wealth of talent in this production. . . . This current thriller, like *Frankenstein,* has the advantage of being directed by James Whale, who again proves his ability. . . . Mr. Laughton . . . gives a splendid portrayal . . . Gloria Stuart is both clever and charming . . . Mr. Thesiger is very capable . . . Eva Moore is distinctly fearsome . . . Mr. Karloff . . . leaves no stone unturned to make this character thoroughly disturbing.

The Old Dark House, however, was certainly not for everyone. "Abel" of *Variety* basically respected the film but found much of Whale's elegant Gothic comedy way over his head and was stunned by Gloria Stuart's Whale-designed gown:

> A somewhat inane picture, its eeriness and general spooky character, further fortified by Boris "Frankenstein" Karloff's presence in the cast, should make *The Old Dark House* worthwhile at the box offices of the lesser strands. . . . There are sundry inanities throughout. . . . Gloria Stuart as Mrs. Waverton gives excellent account of herself, although that extreme decolletage was rather uncalled for, considering the locale. Still, if there wasn't the s.a. angle, mebbe Morgan wouldn't get all hot and bothered as he did. And maybe there'd been no picture as a result, and mebbe that was a good idea, too.

The Old Dark House played three weeks at the Rialto, performed solid business, and enjoyed rereleases right into the early 1950s. The film was destined, however, for a strange, ignominious fate mercifully spared all other Universal classics.

The Old Dark House was not a part of Universal's *Shock!* package, sold via Screen Gems to television, that premiered in the fall of 1957—just months after the mysterious death of James Whale. It was rumored lost; a seeming death blow came via William Castle's 1963 *The Old Dark House,* for Columbia. The remake (with nice title backgrounds by Charles Addams) starred Tom Poston as Penderel, Robert Morley as Roderick Femm, and replaced the other eccentrics with new ones, jettisoning Morgan entirely. It was a horrible film, properly roasted critically, and guilty of entangling the rights so cruelly that all hopes of revival of the 1932 version seemed dashed.

Enter Curtis Harrington. The director of AIP's *Planet of Blood* (1966, starring Basil Rathbone) had joined Universal, directing the stylish *Games*

(1967, with Simone Signoret). Harrington had met Whale in the late 1940s and later crossed paths with him in Paris and London, where, at the British Film Institute, Harrington arranged a showing of *The Old Dark House,* with Whale as guest of honor. In Danny Peary's anthology *Close-Ups* (Workman Publishing, 1978), Harrington wrote how he pestered Universal to make a real search for *The Old Dark House.*

It was a new Universal by 1966; the "Black Tower" had arisen, housing the executives of MCA—most of whom had no knowledge of or interest in a 1932 film. Yet Harrington persisted. Finally word arrived from the Universal office in New York: both the original negative and the "lavender" protection print had been discovered. However, part of the negative had shriveled and shrunk with age. Financing would be necessary for restoration.

Who to turn to? Universal apparently would have none of it; after all, Columbia owned the rights. Harrington knew better than to appeal to Carl Laemmle, Jr.; the little "crown prince" was a vegetable, crippled and forgotten; after the Laemmles lost Universal in 1936, Junior had never produced another movie. (Junior died in his Beverly Hills home on September 24, 1979—the 40th anniversary of the death of Laemmle, Sr.) It was James Card of Eastman House, salvation of many a damaged vintage film, who came to the rescue, financing the restoration of *The Old Dark House.*

Happily, at this time Boris Karloff was paying one last visit to Universal, guesting on "The Name of the Game"—the final televised appearance of his lifetime (November 29, 1968). Harrington found "Morgan," over 36 years after he had chased Gloria Stuart around the Gothic dining hall, now a venerable octogenarian, sitting serenely on the set sidelines in a wheelchair. Triumphantly, Harrington told Karloff of the restoration of *The Old Dark House.*

"Yes," smiled Karloff, "haven't seen it in years, but that *was* a good film. How nice. How good of you to tell me."

As the fifth (possibly sixth) very caring Mrs. Karloff wheeled her husband off the set, Harrington could hear his idol saying, "That young man told me they've saved *The Old Dark House.*" A few months later, February 2, 1969, Boris Karloff died in his beloved England. He was 81.

At long last, in January of 1970, *The Old Dark House* played at the Bing Auditorium of the Los Angeles County Museum as part of a series of rare vintage films, "Here Comes the Parade." Kevin Thomas, in the *Los Angeles Times,* reported:

> Film buffs and children should be delighted. . . . With its great looming sets *The Old Dark House* is one of those unabashedly extravagant melodramas. . . . The dialog is gloriously highfalutin, and the cast was

allowed a field day under the direction of Whale.... The one subtle, timeless performance is given by Karloff.

The movie tentatively made a very limited comeback in archival showings in sad 16mm versions. Presently, 35mm prints have become available (although they are limited). The legal rights remain in a mess; while Universal/MCA has released beautiful prerecorded videos of Whale's "big three" horror epics, video collectors can only secure bootlegged copies of *The Old Dark House*, of wildly varying quality.

Thus, forlornly, erratically, and (perhaps) illegally does *The Old Dark House* presently survive.

> Karloff expanded his range in *The Old Dark House*, stealing the show from an all-star cast.... Directed by James Whale, melding the haunted-house formula and comedy of manners à la Ernest Lubitsch.... Audiences were pleased with the results, which indicated the range of Whale's and Karloff's talents and the flexibility of the horror genre—how easily the surreal logic and visual stylization of the form could be pushed into parody and self-conscious humor.
> —Thomas Schatz, *The Genius of the System* (Pantheon, 1988)

Today, one might whimsically imagine that the ghost of James Whale is haunting Hollywood. On the morning of May 29, 1957, Whale had thrown himself into his Pacific Palisades pool, leaving a sad, rambling suicide note, which said in part:

> To ALL I LOVE,
>   Do not grieve for me—My nerves are all shot and for the last year I have been in agony day and night—except when I sleep with sleeping pills.... I have had a wonderful life but it is over and my nerves get worse and I am afraid they will have to take me away—so please forgive me—all those I love and may God forgive me too....
>   —Jimmy

There was a sad postscript requesting he be cremated ("so nobody will grieve over my grave") and hoping that his fortune ($600,000) "will help my loved ones to forget a little." Strangely, Whale's note was a pitiful paraphrase of the monster's classic curtain line in *Bride of Frankenstein:* "We belong dead."

Indeed, Whale had seemingly enjoyed playing a Hollywood monster himself in his later years. Exiled from the studios since 1941, Whale hosted notorious homosexual parties at his Graeco/Roman poolhouse in his final years—soirees his old friend Alan Napier casually described as "orgies."

The Hollywood "villagers" seemed to take a revenge upon his demise; many of his best films were "lost" or legally locked away. Even his sad, heartbreaking suicide note was packed away in a closet, not made public until James Curtis's biography *James Whale* (Scarecrow Press, 1982). This suppression of the note left Kenneth Anger free to report in *Hollywood Babylon* that Whale's head had been bashed in and his body tossed into the pool by a beachboy whose nude portrait Whale was painting.

Now, over 30 years later, "Jimmy" Whale's ghost is amok and strange things are happening. One could almost hear the ghost laughing sardonically in 1986 when Universal/MCA "restored" *Frankenstein,* including the shot of the monster tossing Little Maria into the lake—the scene that had caused Karloff to rebel, the episode that had been cut after the outcry of a shocked preview audience. The ghost was delighted when the 1936 *Show Boat,* which Whale once hailed his "pride and joy," chugged down the Mississippi again after decades of repression (following MGM's 1951 version)—first on public television and now in a beautiful video transfer from MGM/UA/Turner. Even *Hell's Angels,* which Whale "ghost-directed" for Howard Hughes in 1929 and which has long-circulated in poor, cut-down prints, has played in restored glory on cable TV's *American Movie Classics*—complete with the original Technicolor sequences showing the platinum blonde of Harlow's mane and the oranges and purples of the exploding German dirgible. It too is now available on MCA/Universal video cassette.

In late 1990, a new surprise delighted the ghost: *Classic Film Collector* ran an advertisement offering *Journey's End.* As late as 1976, only two prints of Whale's classic (one of them edited) were rumored to exist, presumably in the hands of manic zealots who guarded them fanatically. British television ran the 1930 film; an enterprising video dealer, Burk Communications of Indiana, transferred the British cassette to the American VCR system; and now, audiences can finally see Colin Clive's magnificently ravaged Stanhope and the wonderfully sensitive, poetic direction that launched Whale's fame.

So, at long last, almost all of James Whale's films are available, filled with visual beauty; his elegant filmic style, spiked with grand theatricality; a sly, bizarre humor; and, finally, Whale's own sense of isolation, alienation, and bitterness. All these touches were part of a unique man—one who created his own Byronic public self out of a poor boy from Dudley, England, only to destroy that self in his Palisades pool in 1957.

There is a special delight in the slow-but-steady comeback of *The Old Dark House.* It is unique amidst Whale's famous, oft-seen horror shows: it survives, almost bitterly, almost defiantly, as the director's most unusual work, a terror tale showcasing his own style, with the least incense-burning to public taste. Stocked with horror flourishes, it is primarily a high exercise in macabre comedy, peopled with ensemble eccentrics, playing on a mad level above the head of many audiences, perhaps delighting the vision of the director more than any audience member who paid $.35 till 1:00 P.M. at the Rialto to see the new Karloff show in 1932. Karloff's Morgan is legendary, full of the "queer, penetrating personality" that Whale cited as his reason for casting Karloff in *Frankenstein;* surely, much of the impetus behind *The Old Dark House*'s rise from oblivion is the chance to see a classic, long-lost Karloff performance. While Thesiger and Moore have the juiciest lines and are wonderful grotesques, there is no doubt that Karloff's Morgan claimed the lion's share of attention in 1932, just as he does today. Still, the role is small. And, with no historic special effects, the star of *The Old Dark House* really and truly is the director.

The ingenious, egomaniacal James Whale saw the public acclaim inspired by *Frankenstein, The Invisible Man,* and *Bride of Frankenstein* serenade others; he himself (for all of Universal's hype) was largely sentenced to the low public profile that shadowed most directors of the 1930s. With *The Old Dark House,* however, it is the eerily sophisticated vision of an eccentric, superb director that truly shines—joyously communicated by wonderful talents who respectfully never upstage it.

One might fancifully imagine that the long limbo of *The Old Dark House* was posterity's revenge for so offbeat a work. One might also guess that its long-in-coming reinstatement to public accessibility is hampered by its bizarre, highly personal style.

Nevertheless, *The Old Dark House,* with Karloff's drunken leers, Gloria Stuart's delicacy and spaghetti straps, Ernest Thesiger's "Have a potato," Eva Moore's distorted reflection, Brember Wills's cackle, and Arthur Edeson's enchanted camera, seems destined to continue its rise from oblivion to fascinate more and more audiences.

And—again fancifully—one might imagine that if one looks closely enough into the foreboding shadows of *The Old Dark House,* one might see the sardonic ghost of James Whale, enjoying himself hugely and winking slyly.

The Mask
of Fu Manchu

Studio: Metro-Goldwyn-Mayer/Cosmopolitan Productions; Production Supervisor: Hunt Stromberg; Director: Charles Brabin (Charles Vidor, uncredited); Screenplay: Irene Kuhn, Edgar Allan Woolf, and John Willard (based on Sax Rohmer's 1932 novel *The Mask of Fu Manchu*); Cinematographer: Tony Gaudio; Editor: Ben Lewis; Art Director: Cedric Gibbons; Costumes: Adrian; Make-Up: Cecil Holland; Special Electrical Properties: Kenneth Strickfaden; Recording Director: Douglas Shearer; Running Time: 68 minutes.

Filmed at MGM Studio, Culver City, California, August 6–October 21, 1932; New York City premiere, Capitol Theatre, December 2, 1932.

The Players: Dr. Fu Manchu (Boris Karloff); Sir Dennis Nayland Smith (Lewis Stone); Sheila Barton (Karen Morley); Fah Lo See (Myrna Loy); Terry Granville (Charles Starrett); Professor Von Berg (Jean Hersholt); Sir Lionel Barton (Lawrence Grant); McLeod (David Torrence); Goy Lo Sung (E. Alyn Warren); British Museum Officials (Ferdinand Gottschalk, C. Montague Shaw); Chinese Steward on Ship (Willie Fung); Double for Karloff (in electricity long shots) (Kenneth Strickfaden).*

●

More Stars than the Heavens.
—Credo of Metro-Goldwyn-Mayer
Studios, 1930s

In their book Making a Monster (Crown, 1980), authors Al Taylor and Sue Roy reported that Strickfaden, the famous electricity wizard of Universal's Frankenstein series, doubled as Karloff in the long-shot scene where Fu Manchu places his fingernails into the electrical lightning rays. It was a dangerous stunt, and the authors noted, "Strickfaden had grounded one of his legs with a piece of wire, but when he moved his ungrounded leg near a metal floor conduit, he went flying."

The *newest* Sax Rohmer sensation! The Frankenstein of the
Orient—and his devilish daughter's love drug!
—MGM 1932 publicity for *The Mask
of Fu Manchu*

Fu Manchu is an ugly, evil homosexual with five-inch finger-
nails while his daughter is a sadistic sex fiend.
—Letter from the Japanese-American
Citizens League to MGM, requesting
the removal of *The Mask of Fu
Manchu* from Metro's catalogue, 1972

It was a shambles, it really was—it was simply ridiculous.
—Boris Karloff, remembering *The
Mask of Fu Manchu*

"Ars Gratia Artis." MGM, Metro-Goldwyn-Mayer, Hollywood's
grandest, gaudiest, most glorious studio. The holy sacristy of Garbo, the
glamorous jungle of Leo the Lion.

Best Picture Academy Award winner of 1931/1932: MGM's *Grand
Hotel.* Best Actress Academy Award winner: Helen Hayes for MGM's *The
Sin of Madelon Claudet.* Best Actor Academy Award winner (sharing the
honor with Fredric March of Paramount's *Dr. Jekyll and Mr. Hyde*):
Wallace Beery for MGM's *The Champ.*

MGM had five of the ten best pictures of 1932 in *Film Daily's* nationwide poll: *Grand Hotel* (#1), *The Champ* (#2), *The Guardsman* (#4),
Smilin' Through (#5), and *Emma* (#7). MGM's 1932 fiscal record (in
a year that Universal lost $3.8 million, Warner Bros. $14 million, Paramount $16 million, and Fox $17 million): a dizzy $8 million Depression
profit.

Squat, bespectacled mogul Louis B. Mayer, former Brooklyn junk
dealer, and frail, aesthetic "boy wonder" Irving Thalberg, former office
boy to Universal's "Uncle Carl" Laemmle: together these "make-believe saints" (as late MGM story-editor Samuel Marx called them) presented 1932 audiences with some of their most sensational movie memories.

They included *Grand Hotel,* with Garbo sighing to John Barrymore's
left profile, "But I want to be alone"; *Red Dust,* with platinum blonde Jean
Harlow flirting with Gable while bobbing naked in a rain barrel; *Tarzan
the Ape Man,* with Johnny Weissmuller fighting a gorilla monster in a pit;
Rasputin and the Empress, boasting all three Barrymores, climaxed by John
maniacally assassinating Lionel and screaming, "Get back in hell!" as the
mad monk rises bloody and chanting from the floor; Norma Shearer (aka
Mrs. Thalberg), shot to death in her wedding gown by spurned lover
Fredric March in *Smilin' Through.*

It all came true at MGM, 10202 Washington Boulevard, Culver City, California, pantheon of attractions from Marion Davies to Marie Dressler to Laurel and Hardy.

And during 1932, its Circus Maximus year, MGM released two classic horror pictures.

Tod Browning's infamous *Freaks* lost money, shocked audiences, was the shame of the studio, and was sold off to an independent exhibitor—like a deformed baby abandoned on a doorstep.

Metro's second horror show of 1932, *The Mask of Fu Manchu,* was a box office success, starring Boris Karloff as a marvelous black mamba of a Fu, featuring Myrna Loy as his evil daughter Fah Lo See, and parading a bevy of resplendent torture devices with all of MGM's Barnum and Bailey showmanship.

Come the video age, nearly 60 years later, MGM reconciled with its own long forsaken *Freaks* and released it to cable TV, even treating it to a tub-thumped video release and going into the vaults to restore a finale not seen for decades. A few years later, MGM released on video a cut version of *The Mask of Fu Manchu.*

Why was the film cut? Was it because of Karloff's gay, lisping dragon of a Fu Manchu, looking like Carmen Miranda from hell in his fruit basket hat and five-inch fingernails? Was it because of the wriggle of Myrna Loy as Fah, the nympho daughter of Fu? Was it because of the spectacle of Lewis "Judge Hardy" Stone on a torturous seesaw, which lowers his venerable gray head into the jaws of grinning crocodiles? Was it because of the sight of Jean "Kindly Dr. Christian" Hersholt, gasping and sweating between spiked walls that slowly come together to perforate him? No. It was because of certain aspects of the film that had come to be seen as racist.

●

> Lon Chaney's gonna get you, if you don't watch out!
> He's liable to pounce upon you, with a shout!
> You'll find him in the teapot, you'll find him in the zoo,
> He may be only half a man—and then he may be two.
> —Song from MGM's *Hollywood
> Revue of 1929*

Gus Edwards warbled this tune in a gala production number of Metro's lavish *Hollywood Revue of 1929,* serenading the glory of MGM's own "man of a thousand faces." Two dancers, one adorned in a skeleton suit and the other garbed as Fu Manchu, led a parade of Halloween-costumed characters onto the stage. They swooped the chorus girls from their beds, they all kicked a wild Charleston, and the girls cavorted in a circle under the soundstage-ceiling camera à la the June Taylor dancers.

For a grand finale, the whole group descended through a trap door with a climactic scream and a cloud of brimstone.

Horror, via Lon Chaney, was a cornerstone of the power and the glory of Metro-Goldwyn-Mayer. Although his cinema immortality rests on Universal's hallowed ground for his roles in *The Hunchback of Notre Dame* (1923) and *The Phantom of the Opera* (1925), Chaney was an MGM star. In fact, the studio's first official release was *He Who Gets Slapped* (1924), starring Chaney (as the hapless clown "He"), Norma Shearer, and John Gilbert. Chaney would be the last MGM great to start making sound pictures; six months after Garbo's *Anna Christie*, Chaney's *The Unholy Three* opened on Broadway as a 4th of July 1930 premiere.

"The Man of a Thousand Voices!" shouted the publicity. At 12:55 A.M., August 26, 1930, however, at St. Vincent's Hospital in Los Angeles, Lon Chaney—all thousand voices destroyed by throat cancer—died. Metro sent Chaney off to his anonymous crypt at Forest Lawn with all the studio's usual florid ballyhoo: at the Hollywood funeral, the theme from Chaney's *Laugh Clown Laugh* (MGM, 1928) pealed away on the organ, and the honorary pallbearers included Mayer, Thalberg, MGM president Nicholas Schenck, studio director Fred Niblo, and MGM stars Lionel Barrymore, Harry Carey, Ramon Novarro, William Haines, Lawrence Tibbett, Wallace Beery, and Jack Benny. All solemnly marched with the casket.

And so did the man who directed Lon Chaney in ten films, including eight MGM silent hits: *The Unholy Three* (1925), *The Blackbird* (1926), *The Road to Mandalay* (1926), *The Unknown* (1927), *London After Midnight* (1927), *The Big City* (1928), *West of Zanzibar* (1929), and *Where East Is East* (1929). He was a Kentucky boy who had run away from home at age 16 to join a contortionist act, had later become a blackface carnival performer and circus ringmaster, and finally had entered films as an assistant to D. W. Griffith.

His name was Tod Browning.

●

The Edgar Allan Poe of the Screen.
—Publicity for Tod Browning

Perhaps some day a film historian will truly produce an honest, fair, revealing biography of Tod Browning. Did Browning really work in carnivals as a geek under the name "Bosco the Snake Eater?" Did he really almost fade in Hollywood in the early '20s after his wife Alice temporarily left him and he vowed "to drink up all the bad liquor in the world"? Did he really attack an assistant manager at San Francisco's St. Francis Hotel (who sought to control Browning's behavior one wild New Year's Eve) by yanking out his own upper and lower false teeth, throwing them at the man and shouting, "Go bite yourself"?

One certainty: the Chaney and Browning collaboration at MGM was legendary—the most incredible catalogue of vengeance, cruelty, deformity, and sexual aberration in horror history. Take the Browning/Chaney 1925 *The Unholy Three:* Chaney capers through much of it in drag as an old lady; a midget (Harry Earles) kicks in a child's teeth; and when the "Strong Man" (Victor McLaglen) falls in love with the "heroine" (Laurel and Hardy's old nemesis, Mae Busch), the midget, out of sexual jealousy, unleashes a mad gorilla upon him. Or take *The Unknown* (1927): Chaney's "Alonzo the Armless" so loves a frigid circus girl (Joan Crawford), whose early molestations made her despise men's arms, that he has his own arms amputated and then stands by in insane jealousy as she falls in love with (and into the arms of) the Strong Man. Castration, sexual humiliation, mad obsessions—Browning and Chaney hinted at (or outright displayed) them all, and one can only imagine the cathartic release director and star experienced from their bizarre teamings.

Certainty #2: this "sick" collaboration was incredibly profitable, solidly supporting such giant MGM hits as *The Big Parade* (1925), *Ben-Hur* (1926), and *The Flesh and the Devil* (1927). In his book *The Genius of the System* (Pantheon, 1988), Thomas Schatz reports on the "Lon Chaneys":

> Frequently, Lon Chaneys were written and directed by Tod Browning. They were nominally supervised by Thalberg but required little of his input, given Browning and Chaney's excellent track record at MGM. A Chaney cost anywhere from $200,000 to $250,000, just below the studio's average cost for A-class features. The relatively low cost was due primarily to two factors: Chaney's films rarely required a major studio player to co-star—indeed Chaney occasionally played more than one role himself—and Browning generally contributed the story and scenario as well as the direction.

Another certainty: these "Lon Chaneys" have become one of Hollywood's saddest myths, revealed, as each of the "lost" Browning/Chaney works rises for rediscovery, to be colossal disappointments, the fascinating kinky content emasculated by Browning's stagy, dull direction. "Not only borderline horror," writes *Fangoria*'s film historian Tom Weaver of the Browning/Chaney canon, "but borderline entertainment," and one can't blame Chaney—who was almost embarrassingly dour in assessing Browning:

> I like his work. I think Victor Seastrom and Benjamin Christensen are great directors. Their values are finer. But I don't really worry over who they hand me.

Although Browning's first "talkie" for Metro, *The Thirteenth Chair* (a 1929 film sparked by Bela Lugosi as Inspector Delzante), earned the studio a profit of over $100,000, Thalberg dropped Browning after this film — due (unofficially) to his alcohol bouts. But now, the MGM "family" took note of Browning at Chaney's funeral. It took greater note when Browning directed Universal's *Dracula,* which made movie history when it was released in February 1931. That *Dracula* was, is, and always will be a classic is due entirely to the macabre magic of Bela Lugosi, and the film succeeds in spite of Browning's woefully unimaginative direction rather than because of it. Yet the glory rubbed off on Browning, and after he directed Jean Harlow in Universal's *Iron Man* (1931), MGM wooed Browning back to the Culver City fold. In light of the tradition of Lon Chaney, the profits of Universal's *Dracula,* and the news of Universal's plan to score again with *Frankenstein,* MGM wanted to make horror movies, and Tod Browning seemed to be the man to make them.

"Give me something more horrifying than *Frankenstein!*" commanded Thalberg.

Browning's response: *Freaks,* the carnival shocker that the former (and presumably pseudo) snake eater had long envisioned. The source was the short story "Spurs" (*Munsey's* magazine, February 1923), written by Tod Robbins (author of *The Unholy Three*). Cedric Gibbons, MGM's famed, multi–Oscar-winning (and Oscar-designing) art director (and a childhood friend of Robbins, who had supposedly typed some of his manuscripts), persuaded his studio to pay $8000 for the story.* Browning saw *Freaks* as his potential masterwork and sent word across the country that he was casting the MGM horror show with real "freaks."

From carnivals and circuses all over the country, they came. Schlitze, the Pin-Head, whose true gender was a mystery (a dress was the usual attire), had collected a fortune in jewelry and real estate from obsessed admirers. Prince Randian, the Hindu Human Torso, sported an earring and could roll his cigarettes sans arms or legs. Johnny Eck was the Half-Boy, whose body ended at the waist (Eck died in 1991 in Baltimore, where he had achieved recognition as a painter). Violet and Daisy Hilton, the famous Siamese twins, had led their own jazz band.

Browning began shooting November 9, 1931, with a $290,468.82

Perhaps Gibbons had personal reasons for being attracted to such a "sado/maso" property. In his memoir Bring on the Empty Horses *(1975), the late David Niven remembered the Santa Monica house of the "good-looking, military-moustached" Gibbons and his actress wife, Dolores del Rio: "Dolores had a large sunny room on the first floor containing a huge and inviting bed. Gibbons lived in comparative squalor in a small room immediately below. The only connection between these two rooms was by way of a stepladder which could be lowered only when a trapdoor in the floor of Dolores' room had been raised." The couple divorced in 1941. Gibbons later wed MGM showgirl Hazel Brooks; he died in 1960.*

budget, a 24-day schedule, and supervision via MGM studio manager Eddie Mannix. The true star of *Freaks* was Olga Baclanova (1899–1974), the evil blonde amazon transformed by the vengeful freaks from "The Peacock of the Air" into the squawking "Chicken Woman" of the climax. Three decades later, Baclanova (in her thick Russian tongue) remembered MGM's *Freaks* in John Kobal's book, *People Will Talk:*

> Tod Browning. I loved him. He say, "I want to make a picture with you, Olga Baclanova. . . . Now I show you with whom you are going to play. But don't faint." . . . I wanted to faint. I wanted to cry when I saw them. . . . Now, after we start the picture, I like them all so much.

Not everyone shared Miss Baclanova's compassion. "People run out of the commissary and throw up!" wailed Harry Rapf, a Metro production supervisor (whose background had been in carnivals). It all proved too much for the tummy of F. Scott Fitzgerald, then paying Zelda's sanatorium bills as a $1200-per week Metro writer. One noon he glimpsed the Siamese twins smiling over the commissary menu, bolted outside, and threw up.

Browning completed *Freaks* December 16, 1931; on December 23, he began retakes. These came just in time for a major MGM event, as described in Charles Higham's new book *Merchant of Dreams: Louis B. Mayer, MGM, and The Secret Hollywood* (Fine, 1993):

> On Christmas Eve, the studio was the scene of an astonishing orgy, which soon became an annual event. While Mayer drove home to the beach house and Irving Thalberg took off to dinner with Norma Shearer, Eddie Mannix and Benny Thau spread it around that any man and woman could have as much booze as they wanted, and that they could choose a partner who appealed to them and make love against desks, on the floor, against the walls, anywhere they wanted.
>
> A stranger wandering about in those sacred corridors of the executive building would have been able to see naked or partly dressed couples of all ages frenziedly copulating—even on Irving Thalberg's desk (Mayer kept his office locked). Some vigorous clerks serviced two or three women in succession. If this incident had leaked, it would have been the end of MGM.

Following a disastrous *Freaks* preview, Thalberg made cautious cuts. (One of the unkindest cuts, reputedly, was the freaks' castration of Cleopatra's Strong Man lover, Hercules, played by Henry Victor, glimpsed in the original finale in the same freak show as Chicken Woman Cleopatra; he was now fat and singing in falsetto.)*

Nevertheless, *Freaks* went on to infamy. Final cost: $310,607.37. Shooting Days: 36. Release date: February 20, 1932. Overall critical reaction: horror, outrage, and a 30-year ban in England. Financial loss: $164,000.

Mayer apoplectically cut the MGM logo of his beloved lion Leo from the prints of *Freaks*. On August 7, 1932, only 30 days after *Freaks* had finally braved New York's Rialto Theatre, MGM took a fast $50,000 from Dwain Esper, an independent exhibitor, who got *Freaks* on a 25-year distribution deal and milked the scandalous picture (under such titles as *Nature's Mistakes*) for all of its sensationalism.

In 1962, the Cannes Festival Repertory exhumed *Freaks,* and it made a round of the revival houses. Vincent Canby of the *New York Times* hailed it as "one of the perhaps half-dozen great horror films of all time." By 1990 it was playing on the TNT Cable Network and had received (with considerable fanfare) release on MGM/UA Home Video. While film critics rapturously praise its "compassion," it is hard to find any compassion in the climax. The sight of the Pinhead, the Human Torso, the Half-Boy, and those other poor souls wriggling and crawling through the stormy climax with knives and guns, hellbent on transforming Cleopatra into the Chicken Woman, makes them truly monstrous as Browning crumbles under the temptation to present his freaks as a nightmarish herd of goblins.

Freaks had been one of the great failures and embarrassments in the history of MGM. And in its desire to be supreme in every genre, Metro vowed to make a new horror picture, this one attacking a new defenseless minority group: the Chinese race.

●

Little by little that night, and on many more nights, I built up Dr. Fu Manchu until I could both hear him and see him. . . . I seemed to hear a sibilant voice saying, "It is your belief that you have made me. It is mine that I shall live when you are smoke."

—Sax Rohmer, on his literary
creation, Fu Manchu

MGM proclaimed that by 1932, 100,000,000 readers had thrilled to the nefarious exploits of Fu Manchu—"The Yellow Peril" brainchild of

---

MGM later filmed a revised ending in which Wallace Ford and Leila Hyams, as Phroso and Venus, witness Harry Earles's Hans reconciling with Daisy Earles's Frieda. This was the ending restored by the studio for the video release.

Sax Rohmer (aka Arthur Henry Sarsfield Ward, 1883–1959). One night, in an alley in London's Chinatown, Fleet Street journalist Rohmer had spied on a mysterious Chinese man, whom he believed was the kingpin of a dope-smuggling coven. The memory inspired the author's two short stories and thirteen novels about the diabolic, torture-loving, gloriously mad Fu Manchu. As Rohmer described his arch-villain in the first novel, *The Insidious Dr. Fu Manchu* (1913):

> Imagine a person, tall, lean and feline, high-shouldered, with a brow like Shakespeare and a face like Satan, a close-shaven skull, and long, magnetic eyes of true cat-green. Invest him with all the cruel cunning of an entire Eastern race, accumulated in one giant intellect. . . . Imagine that awful being, and you have a mental picture of Dr. Fu Manchu, the yellow peril incarnate in one man.

Fu's stiff-upper-lip adversaries were Sir Dennis Nayland Smith of Scotland Yard and Smith's trusty familiar, Dr. Petrie, who narrated the tales. A real-life adversary was the Chinese government, who pleaded with Rohmer to kill off Fu Manchu in the interest of the Chinese international image. Rohmer did so, but the author (who loved posing in Oriental robes and smoking a pipe à la Sherlock Holmes) couldn't resist bringing Fu back from two different demises to vow again the destruction of the white race. The author would write Fu Manchu thrillers for over 40 years; the last novel, *Emperor Fu Manchu,* was published in 1959.

Fu Manchu was an actor's dream. Harry Agar Lyons played Fu in the 15-chapter British serial *The Mystery of Dr. Fu Manchu* (Stoll, 1923); A. E. Coleby produced and directed, and the cast included Fred Paul as Nayland Smith and H. Humberstone Wright as Dr. Petrie. The same company got together for the 15-chapter *The Further Mysteries of Dr. Fu Manchu* (1924), with Paul not only reprising Nayland Smith, but adapting and directing the cliffhanger. Fu Manchu also took to the U.S. radio airwaves, as Arthur Hughes played Fu Manchu in a series of 12-chapter serials on radio's "The Collier Hour" in 1927.

It was Warner Oland (1880–1938) who first scored in Hollywood as Fu Manchu in Paramount's "all-talking" *The Mysterious Dr. Fu Manchu* (1929). The film is a fun curiosity today, with its talent force of director Rowland V. Lee (destined to direct *Son of Frankenstein* [1939]), Jean Arthur (as Lia, Fu's evil Caucasian ward), O. P. Heggie (here as Nayland Smith, later the blind hermit of *Bride of Frankenstein* [1935]), and Neil Hamilton (as John, whose love redeems Lia; he later played Commissioner Gordon of TV's "Batman"). The film was a hit. As played by the Swedish, slant-eyebrowed Oland, Fu Manchu was a deadly (but rather bovine) menace, a lethal relative to Charlie Chan (whom Oland would play so

Karloff in all his kinky glory in *The Mask of Fu Manchu*.

winningly for Fox) and rather sympathetic. Paramount, as if perceiving racial troubles decades away, was careful to give Fu a motivation for his mania: his wife and son had been slain during the Boxer Rebellion. Hence Fu's hatred of the white race, Oland's hangdog performance in *The Mysterious Dr. Fu Manchu*, and the two Paramount sequels that followed.*

*Paramount's 1930 The Return of Dr. Fu Manchu *(aka* The New Adventures of Fu Manchu*) reunited director Lee, Oland, Arthur, Heggie, Hamilton, and William Austin, who provided fey*

MGM, lusting for the mad, almighty Fu Manchu of the Sax Rohmer novels, would change all that. "A *new* Fu Manchu . . . not to be confused with the Fu Manchu of other pictures!" Metro's copy would proclaim as the studio nailed down the rights to Rohmer's latest opus, *The Mask of Fu Manchu.* Colliers magazine was serializing the melodrama from May 7 to July 23, 1932 (with Rohmer reaping a reported $30,000 for the serialization). MGM plotted a fall movie release, just as Rohmer's 330-page novel would hit the bookstores (via Doubleday and Doran). Unlike the disastrous *Freaks,* MGM was now marketing a bogey man with proven appeal in novels, radio, and movies; it was all showmanship with a vengeance.

On July 19, 1932, MGM publicity chief Howard Strickling, with the blessing of Louis B. Mayer, promised the world that Metro-Goldwyn-Mayer would now "go all out for sex" — and indeed, it would be a major spice of *The Mask of Fu Manchu.* To guarantee the sensation, MGM announced that only one Hollywood star was worthy of the role of Fu Manchu: Metro would borrow Boris Karloff, "Frankenstein's monster" himself, from Universal City.

Deep in the MGM archives, an August 4, 1932, contract reveals Metro's engagement (via Universal Pictures) of Karloff. The star was fresh from the triumph of *Frankenstein,* had completed *The Old Dark House* (set for October release), and was looking forward to Universal's *The Mummy;* he received a Metro $3500 guarantee. It was a pivotal role for Boris. In *Frankenstein,* the actor had growled, howled, and screamed; in *The Old Dark House,* he had madly gurgled; in *The Mask of Fu Manchu,* he would use his lisping voice for the first time to scare the crowds.

MGM called her Garbo; Universal called him Karloff. Now, the only two members of the Hollywood "surname only" club were working on the same lot.

Hunt Stromberg, whose most famous Metro show would be Best Picture Oscar-winning *The Great Ziegfeld* (1936), produced *The Mask of Fu Manchu.* MGM's "good guys" for the movie included three real-life heroes: an ex-officer from the Spanish American War (MGM's own Lewis Stone, who played Sir Nayland Smith); a former Dartmouth football star

---

comic relief as Sylvester Wadsworth. Fu Manchu "perished" in the climax, falling into the river with a bomb. Yet Oland's Fu Manchu returned once more in Paramount's 1931 Daughter of the Dragon, directed by Lloyd Corrigan (who worked on the scripts of all three Paramount Fu Manchus). In this film, Fu Manchu has merely a cameo, being killed virtually at the outset; the real star of the show is Anna May Wong (as Fu's daughter, Princess Ling Moy). Also in the cast: Sessue Hayakawa (as Fu's new adversary, Detective Ah Kee), Bramwell Fletcher (Little Billee of Svengali and mad Norton of The Mummy, here as romantic lead Ronald Petrie), Frances Dade (Lugosi's doomed Lucy of Dracula, here as ingenue Joan Marshall), and Holmes Herbert (Lanyon of March's Dr. Jekyll and Mr. Hyde, here playing Sir John Petrie, a mature version of the part Neil Hamilton had played in the first two Paramount films).

(Charles Starrett, who played hero Terry Granville); and a future founder of the Motion Picture Relief Fund (Metro's Jean Hersholt, who took the part of archaeologist/professor Von Berg). Two Metro "featured ladies" filled out the leading roles: Karen Morley, who already in 1932 had acted at MGM with the Barrymore brothers in *Arsene Lupin* and with Garbo in *Mata Hari,* played heroine Sheila Barton, while Myrna Loy (who, reportedly, had been considered for the Baclanova role in *Freaks*) would be Fu's "devilish daughter," Fah Lo See. (Rohmer had introduced this temptress in *The Mask of Fu Manchu,* with the name Fah Lo Suee; MGM, possibly fearing the response of pig farmers in the audience, made the adjustment.)

As director, Metro chose 32-year-old, Budapest-born Charles Vidor, formerly of the Austro-Hungarian army. Vidor would direct everything from Rita Hayworth stripteasing to "Don't Put the Blame on Mame" in *Gilda* (Columbia, 1946) to Danny Kaye singing "Wonderful, Wonderful Copenhagen" in *Hans Christian Andersen* (Goldwyn, 1952). *The Mask of Fu Manchu* would be his directorial debut.

Behind the camera, capturing the exotic look of *The Mask of Fu Manchu,* was Tony Gaudio (1885–1951), later star cinematographer for Warner Bros., where he would win the Academy Award for his work on *Anthony Adverse* (1936).

The atmosphere at MGM was becoming delirious. On August 2, 1932, as *Fu Manchu* neared its starting date, Metro began shooting the jungle melodrama *Kongo,* a remake of the Lon Chaney/Tod Browning 1927 silent *West of Zanzibar.* Walter Huston starred as "Dead-Legs," who hopes to avenge himself on the man who crippled him (C. Henry Gordon) by transforming the man's daughter (Virginia Bruce) from a convent virgin to a brandy-addicted whore; of course, she turns out to Dead-Leg's own daughter. William Cowan directed. The $160,000 production featured such sideshows as Huston preparing to yank out Lupe Velez's tongue with a wire, and Conrad Nagel purging his own dope addiction in a swamp of thirsty leeches.

Meanwhile, as Karloff reported to MGM, there was a big problem: *The Mask of Fu Manchu* had no finished script. If Universal's Karloff expected fastidious production at the great MGM Studios, he got a big surprise:

> I shall never forget, about a week before we started, I kept asking for a script—and I was met with roars of laughter at the idea that there would *be* a script!

On August 1, 1932, producer Stromberg had began dictating the storyline, scattershooting plots, tortures, and melodrama that Irene Kuhn,

John Willard, and Edgar Allan Woolf would all tackle over the next two-and-a-half months of production. The MGM collection at the University of Southern California features at least 20 of these off-the-cuff inspirations from Stromberg, who set the tone of the show:

> Fah Lo See's Boudoir
> Sees Fah Lo See leering.
> Sheila draws back in horror. She could have almost stood anything but this—death for Terry would have been better—but this idea of sex creeping in—the fact that he has slept with this Chinese girl—that would serve to arouse any woman who has loved a man.
> ...flays Fu ... says: "You monster—fiend—etc." It is then that he rather enjoys this—get light and shade in this scene. A new interest comes into his eyes. He picks her up, struggling, and starts out of the room.

On Saturday, August 6, 1932, *The Mask of Fu Manchu* began shooting.

●

> Say, this is obscene!
> —Myrna Loy, upon studying her role
> of Fah Lo See in *The Mask of Fu
> Manchu*

Leo growls. *The Mask of Fu Manchu* unspools its credits, with creepy (and uncredited) Oriental music with a crashing gong. The credits proclaim it an MGM/Cosmopolitan Production—Cosmopolitan being the unit camped at MGM by William Randolph Hearst, primarily to showcase his famous paramour, Marion Davies.

The scene is night in London in the quarters of Scotland Yard's Sir Nayland Smith. He has sent for Sir Lionel Barton.

"I want to ask you a very funny question," says Smith, instantly setting up the jingoistic tone. "Do you love your country?"

Gray-fringed, poker-faced Lewis Stone (1879–1953) is Sir Nayland; after Lionel Barrymore, he was Mayer's most adored actor. The ever-venerable Stone (who had gone gray at age 20) co-starred in ten MGM 1932 releases, sharing the screen with Harlow in *Red-Headed Woman,* with Garbo in *Mata Hari,* with Crawford in *Letty Lynton,* and with Garbo *and* Crawford in *Grand Hotel* (one of his best roles, as scarfaced Dr. Otternschlag). Of course, the somber Stone ("I'm not a motion picture actor, I'm just an actor trying to act in motion pictures") was fated to be hearth-and-home icon Judge James Hardy in the Mickey Rooney *Andy Hardy* films (Mayer's favorite product). Stone's casting as Nayland Smith is thus, retrospectively, all the more enjoyable (and campy) here.

Stone was at MGM the rest of his days; on Saturday night, September 12, 1953, Stone heard a gang of punks creating a disturbance at his pool, ran out of the house to chase them, and dropped dead. A sad fate for a true gentleman (who would have been shocked at the two-page spread of his body that appeared in Kenneth Anger's *Hollywood Babylon*). Stone's dialogue as Nayland Smith is so "veddy" patriotic:

> SMITH: Sir Lionel, the British government is asking you to risk your life again.
> BARTON (Cheerfully): Oh! Very well!

Lawrence Grant (1870–1952, who played in Paramount's 1931 Fu Manchu thriller *Daughter of the Dragon* and later was the Burgomaster in Universal's 1939 *Son of Frankenstein* and 1942 *The Ghost of Frankenstein*) makes a keen old rover boy of Sir Lionel, who has a mission: to lead archaeologists to the Gobi Desert tomb of Genghis Khan in order to claim the tyrant's golden mask and scimitar before it falls into the clutches of Fu Manchu. Stone's Sir Nayland warms to the mission:

> Should Fu Manchu put that mask across his wicked eyes and take that scimitar into his boney, cruel hands, all Asia rises. He'll declare himself Genghis Khan come to life again — and he'll lead hundreds of millions of men to sweep the world.

At the British Museum, Sir Lionel meets his archaeologists, including McLeod (David Torrence) and bespectacled Professor Von Berg (Jean Hersholt, 1886–1956). Hersholt was a Copenhagen-born character actor, who played everything from the heavy of von Stroheim's *Greed* (1924) to Shirley Temple's grandfather in *Heidi* (Fox, 1937) to "kindly Dr. Christian" of the RKO series. Then under Metro contract (and another alumnus of *Grand Hotel*, as Senf the porter), Hersholt was a great humanitarian, who won special Oscars for his real-life role as a major founder of the Motion Picture Relief Fund. The Academy established the "Jean Hersholt Humanitarian Award" after his demise. That Fu Manchu is also after the treasures of Genghis Khan's tomb hardly intimidates Hersholt's Von Berg.

"A Chinaman beat me? He couldn't do it!"

However, out in the museum, in the caskets, mummies stir, and they jump out and kidnap Sir Lionel.

Sir Nayland breaks the news to Barton's daughter Sheila (Karen Morley) and her beau, Terry Granville (Charles Starrett). The blonde Morley, memorable as Paul Muni's flashy moll, "Poppy," in *Scarface* (1932), was a fine, all-purpose leading lady at MGM. Making her first appearance in a mournful dark suit and hat, she plays the heroine on a shrill note of soignee hysteria. Starrett (best-remembered as Columbia's "The Durango Kid") stands stolidly by (in a role one MGM reader suggested was ideal for Clark Gable).

"You know what they say about him in the East!" barnstorms Morley of Fu, as if she believed there might be an Academy Award in the role of Sheila. "His cruelty, his unspeakable tortures!"

Sir Nayland is worried—"They have ways in the East of shattering the strongest courage!"—and is more concerned as Terry and blonde, white woman Sheila insist on going along on the expedition.

The opulent MGM set for the Gobi Desert lair of Fu Manchu was masterminded by Cedric Gibbons. It is a mixture of fairy tale castle, Frankenstein laboratory, and Oriental whorehouse. And here we meet Dr. Fu Manchu—Karloff. The introductory close-up is marvelous; Karloff's Fu, his face monstrously reflected into a mandarin-mustached gargoyle on a great hanging mirror, grins satanically and quaffs an unholy, smoking vial.

Boris had to leave his Toluca Lake bungalow very early in the morning to arrive at MGM for the 2½ hour makeup job applied by the late, great Cecil Holland:

> In *Fu Manchu* I had to speak lines. This meant I could not use any of the many types of false teeth which were such potent parts of disguise in silent days. Lon Chaney once told me speech had made impossible about fifty of his best makeup devices. In *Fu Manchu* we used some thin shell teeth that covered the front of the natural teeth only. Slanting eyebrows, which usually can be simulated by a strip of thin membrane that is cemented to the skin and then painted, bind the muscles of the face and make speech impossible. So we used two tiny celluloid clips instead.

One of the most notorious features of the makeup, along with the pointed ears and false eyelashes, was the long fingernails, and MGM publicity regaled the prurient by saying that Boris couldn't "scratch himself" while wearing these fabulous fakes. The mind boggles at the other prosaic necessities that must have been impossible when Karloff was in full Fu Manchu regalia.

Karloff remembered his *The Mask of Fu Manchu* adventure:

> On the morning that we started shooting, I went into the makeup shop and worked there for about a couple of hours getting this extremely bad makeup on, as a matter of fact, for Fu Manchu. It was ridiculous! And, as I was in the makeup chair, a gentleman came in and handed me about four sheets of paper which was one enormous, long speech. That was to be the opening shot in the film and I was seeing it for the first time, then and there. It was written in the most impeccable English. Then, I said, "This is absolute nonsense. I can't learn this in time to do it," and he said,

"well, it will be all right. Don't worry." So I got my makeup on and, on my way to the stage from the makeup shop, I was intercepted by some-body else who took those pages away from me and gave me some others that were written in pidgin English! They had about five writers on it and this was happening all through the film. Some scenes were written in beautiful Oxford English, others were written in—God knows what!

A crash of musical gong chimes, and minions drag in Sir Lionel, who has been drugged for days. "You're Fu Manchu, aren't you?" sneers the Britisher. Karloff lisps one of his many joyously memorable lines of *The Mask of Fu Manchu:*

> I'm a doctor of philosophy from Edinborough. I'm a doctor of Law from Christ's College. I'm a doctor of medicine from Harvard. My friends, out of courtesy, call me Doctor!

One wonders how many 1932 audiences, noticing Karloff's famous lisp for the first time, felt he was affecting the "hiss" as Fu Manchu.

Sir Lionel refuses an offer of one million pounds to divulge the loca-tion of Khan's tomb, so Fu offers his daughter Fah Lo See (Myrna Loy). "Explain to this gentleman the rewards that might be his. Point out to him the delights of our lovely country—the promise of our beautiful women."

"Even my daughter," Karloff pimps passionately. "Even *that* for you!"

Fah Lo See is played by 27-year-old Myrna Loy. The Montana-born, pert-nosed, redhead was then one of Hollywood's most lethal screen vamps; MGM had just loaned her to RKO to play the Javanese/Indian half-caste who slays all her patronizing white schoolmates (save Irene Dunne) in *Thirteen Women*. In her memoir *Myrna Loy: Being and Becom-ing* (written with James Kotsilibas-Davis, Knopf, 1987), the actress, who five years after *Fu Manchu* was voted "Queen of Hollywood," wrote:

> Metro then tossed me into *The Mask of Fu Manchu* as Fah Lo See, the nefarious daughter of the title character, played by Boris Karloff. That script was really the last straw. ... I'd been reading Freud, and appar-ently the writers hadn't. "I can't do this," I told our producer, Hunt Stromberg. "I've done a lot of terrible things in films, but this girl's a sadistic nymphomanic."
>
> "What's that?" he said.
>
> "Well, you better find out, because that's what she is and I won't play her that way." I did play her, of course; there was nothing I could do about it. But Hunt Stromberg was no fool; he simply hadn't been reading Freud. He did some research, and in the end the character's worst ex-cesses were toned down. She wasn't Rebecca of Sunnybrook Farm.

Sir Lionel wants nothing to do with a sadistic nymphomaniac (at least not a Chinese one), so he soon finds himself tied to a slab under *Fu Manchu* torture #1: the great bell. Karloff leers, smiling like Ann-Margret in *Kitten with a Whip*, and says:

> The torture of the bell. . . . Just a bell ringing—but the percussion and the repercussion of sound against your eardrums will soften and destroy them, until the sound is magnified a thousand times. You can't move . . . you can't sleep . . . you will be frantic with thirst . . . you will be unspeakably foul! But here you will lie, day after day—until you tell!

The bell begins to peal. And Karloff's Fu Manchu lopes away in sadistic bliss.

Karloff, with his Ann-Margret smile, false eyelashes, Adrian-designed gowns, dragon-lady fingernails, and lisping, come-hither delivery, has created a wild, kinky, archfiend of a Fu; part Yellow Peril, part Frederick's of Hollywood. Yet saving the performance (and assuring its taste) is a wonderful, crazy, bravura humor in Karloff's acting. As Myrna Loy wrote:

> Boris and I brought some feeling and humor to those comic book characters. Boris was a fine actor, a professional who never condescended to his often unworthy material.

The film keeps returning to that bell; we see Fu Manchu merrily running a bouquet of grapes over Sir Lionel's delirious face. Later, Fu returns to give a drink to his "guest"—which Sir Lionel spews out.

"Oh, I forgot to tell you," laughs Karloff, grinning from pointed ear to pointed ear, stroking Grant's hair. "It was *salt!*"

MGM loved that bell. In 1972, when MGM rereleased *The Mask of Fu Manchu* on a triple feature with *Mark of the Vampire* and Paramount's *Dr. Jekyll and Mr. Hyde,* the studio publicity department was still sending out releases about the notorious giant bell:

> One of the authentic details re-created by the MGM art department of the time was a gigantic bell copied from a Chinese original in the British Museum. . . . After the bell was reconstructed, it was found to have a thunderous low-frequency vibration. The sound equipment of the time could not record its frequency. So, bit by bit, a machinist shaved away paper-thin slices of metal until a recordable tone was reached.

MGM's *The Mask of Fu Manchu* pressbook hailed "the great feast of the Mongols" as one of the film's "dramatic thrills," and it does survive as one of the movie's best hoots. In a banquet hall, two warriors fight with swords as reclining Mongols stuff their faces and Karloff, in pagoda-style hat, grins appreciatively at the warriors' half-naked bodies. Then the host has an announcement.

> I have brought you here for great tidings! I am the most unfortunate of men. I have no son to follow me. Therefore, in shame, I ask you to receive a message from my ugly and insignificant daughter!

Like the intro to a crazy Busby Berkeley number, an army marches in, does a brisk left face to the camera, separates, and there is Miss Loy's breathtaking Fah Lo See. (When Myrna Loy received an honorary Oscar in 1991, the Academy Awards telecast featured this closeup in its homage to the actress.) After the camera dutifully surveys the leers of the Mongols, Fah Lo See delivers:

> I have seen a vision. The prophecy is about to be fulfilled. Genghis Khan . . . comes back to us! I see the vision of countless hordes swarming to recapture the world. I see them victorious. I've heard the shouts of the dead and the dying drowned by the victorious cries of our people. Genghis Khan comes back. *Genghis Khan leads the East against the world!*

Meanwhile the archaeologists' band has arrived in the Gobi Desert and has discovered the tomb. Even these scenes of "the good guys" move with color and pace. Terry removes the golden mask from the skeleton of Genghis Khan, and a tarantula wriggles in the eye socket of the decayed tyrant's skull. There is the murder of McLeod, staged with acrobatics worthy of the Big Top, as a Fu minion swings one-handed along a high wire by night, from tree to mosque, to throw a knife in McLeod's back. The explorer dies, but lives long enough to shoot his assassin, who falls screaming to the ground. And in an especially grisly shot, as Terry stands under a tree, a dismembered hand (Sir Lionel's, naturally) falls from the branches, nearly beaning the hero on the head. Meanwhile, Stone's Sir Nayland, who has joined the group, spews white supremist lines and paranoia:

> Will we ever understand these Eastern races? . . . Do you suppose for a moment Fu Manchu doesn't know we have a beautiful white girl here with us? . . . He knows everything, he knows every move we make, his spies are all around us, I can't even trust our own coolies.

To soothe Sheila's Old Vic outbursts, Terry decides to bargain with Fu Manchu. Before Sir Lionel loses any more body parts, he will give Fu Manchu the Genghis Khan sword in exchange for his returning to Sheila her beloved (and mostly intact) father. Little does Terry know that Smith has buried the real sword with McLeod, leaving a facsimile. Equipped with

Sir Lionel Barton (Lawrence Grant) undergoes the dreaded bell torture as Dr. Fu Manchu (Boris Karloff) tries to extricate the location of the tomb of Genghis Khan.

the pseudo-sword, Terry visits the palace of Fu Manchu. The result, whether the cast, director, and writers were aware of it or not, is one of the most outrageous phallic vignettes in movie history.

"What can one so poor as Dr. Fu Manchu do for you?" flirts Karloff, reading the line for all its ridiculous rhythm. As Fu Manchu and Fah Lo See watch eagerly, stalwart Starrett slowly pulls out his giant sword, and the camera cuts to Loy, cooing and waving her hands in delight at the sword's size. Not to be outdone, Karloff grabs the sword, clutching it passionately—"Genghis Khan!" he ejaculates soulfully. Then he thrusts the sword, striking macho poses with it.

The sword must undergo a test—an electrical ray designed for the movie by Kenneth Strickfaden, who masterminded Karloff's "creation" in the spectacular laboratory effects of *Frankenstein*. Smiling satanically, Karloff's Fu Manchu subjects the sword to the lightning ray, and it sparks, and melts, and shrivels.

"You accursed son of a white dog!" shrieks Karloff.

Minions drag off poor Terry. They hang him from a ceiling, strip him half-naked, and whip him. Fah Lo See, of course, watches.

"Ahi!" squeals Fah. "Faster! Faster! *Faster!"* as Karloff's Fu plays voyeur, grinning at the sadism from a window above.

Naturally, poor, whipped, unconscious Terry ends up in the oh-if-walls-could-talk boudoir of Fah Lo See, where his muscular body lies sprawled on her bed. As daughter paws over him, father pays a visit:

> FAH: He is not entirely unhandsome, is he, my father?
> FU: For a white man, no!

●

> Metro-Goldwyn-Mayer is having trouble with two of its current films, the all–Barrymore *Rasputin* and *The Mask of Fu Manchu.*
> —*New York Times,* August 28, 1932

Now if at this point in the chapter, any reader finds *The Mask of Fu Manchu* awful, or revolting, or simply silly, ponder this: the version discussed is Metro's second version of the same project—with the same cast.

In mid–August of 1932, MGM brass began looking at the rushes of *The Mask of Fu Manchu* and were appalled. Fearful of another *Freaks,* the front office shut down production #640. "The Chinese picture has been halted," reported the *New York Times,* "while the story is being rewritten, several of the writers having been formed into a shock-troop to get something filmable out in a hurry."

And to make a clean break, MGM fired director Charles Vidor, canning him from what was to have been his Hollywood directorial debut. Reportedly, most (if not all) of what Vidor had shot was scrapped; the shooting would begin all over again. Vidor's career fell into limbo, languishing for over a year until he landed his next directing job, *Sensation Hunters* (1934), for Monogram.

Meanwhile, there was trouble on the set of *Rasputin and the Empress.* Lionel, as black-bearded Rasputin, was growling that brother John was stealing their scenes. John, so tightly corseted into his uniforms as Prince Paul that he couldn't sit down, was drinking heavily and trying to seduce young Jean Parker, who was playing one of the princesses. Ethel was Ethel. Bored by movie-making, worried she might not finish the film in time to return East for a stage engagement, she one day went to the stage phone, called Louis B. Mayer, and announced so all on the soundstage could hear: "See here, Mayer, let's get rid of this Brahbin or Braybin or what's-his-name."

His name was Charles Brabin (1883–1957), and as Richard Boleslawski took over *Rasputin and the Empress,* Brabin took over *The Mask of*

Director Charles Brabin (right of camera) gives instructions to actors Jean Hersholt and Charles Starret.

Fu Manchu. Liverpool-born Brabin's directorial career dated back to the 1914 Edison serial *The Man Who Disappeared;* he had recently directed Jean Harlow's debut as an MGM star in the 1932 gangster saga, *The Beast of the City.* Brabin himself was no doubt disgusted by this kind of studio politics: he had been fired from MGM's 1926 spectacular *Ben-Hur* and replaced by Fred Niblo; losing *Rasputin and the Empress* was his second great career humiliation. Brabin would retire (at age 51) after Metro's 1934 *A Wicked Woman,* happily married to great screen vamp Theda Bara (whom he had directed in silents), living quietly until his death in Santa Monica in November 1957.

The "shock troop" of writers working on the *Fu* script included Edgar Allan Woolf (a Metro contract writer who contributed to such Metro films as *Freaks* and *The Wizard of Oz*), John Willard (author of the venerable melodrama play *The Cat and the Canary*), and Irene Kuhn, who, based on available data, never worked on another picture.

Then, just as *The Mask of Fu Manchu* was beginning anew, a real-life horror/sex melodrama erupted right in the midst of the MGM Studios.

It is amazing that the censors didn't burn Jean Harlow at the stake, red wig, black garter belt, fishnet stockings, and all, after MGM released *Red-Headed Woman* on June 25, 1932. Metro's "scandalous" comedy made Production Code history: "Adultery, sometimes necessary plot material, must not be explicitly treated, or justified, or presented attractively." And in the wake of *Red-Headed Woman,* Thalberg's brilliant producer Paul Bern, supervisor of *Grand Hotel* and co-supervisor of *Red-Headed Woman,* died of a gunshot to the head after midnight of Labor Day, 1932.

His death occurred only 65 days after his July 2, 1932, marriage to Jean Harlow.

MGM was a circus. Mayer, Thalberg, MGM PR chief Howard Strickling (but *not* Harlow) were all at the newlyweds' Bavarian hideaway, 9820 Easton Drive, high in Benedict Canyon, early the next morning, beholding the naked body of the 42-year-old Bern, sprawled in the bedroom, drenched in Harlow's Mitsouko perfume, with this infamous note nearby:

> Dearest Dear/
>
> Unfortunately this is the only way to make good the frightful wrong I have done you and to wipe out my abject humiliation/I love you
>
> —Paul
>
> You realize that last night was only a comedy

Harlow probably had spent the night at her mother's. Mayer took control. Legend would claim Bern blew his brains out, humiliated over his impotence, and that his alluded "comedy" was a pathetic attempt to make love to MGM's platinum blonde while sporting a dildo.

However, in *Deadly Illusion: Jean Harlow and the Murder of Paul Bern* (Random House, 1990), Thalberg's now-late story editor Samuel Marx and Joyce Vanderveen argue that MGM fabricated the impotence saga to protect Harlow. They assert that Bern was actually murdered by Dorothy Millette, his common-law wife, who, after years in a Connecticut sanatorium and a San Francisco hotel, had now come to Hollywood. According to the authors, Millette was a raving religious lunatic who vengefully confronted Bern with his bigamy and maniacally demanded he star her in a religious epic. The authors argue that while Jean was away, Dorothy was at the house that night, shrieking on the Japanese lantern-lit patio, gobbling devil's food cake that had been saved for Jean, taking a dip in the pool with Paul, shooting him in the head in the bedroom, unleashing an "unearthly scream" heard by his housekeeper, and escaping in the limousine Bern had called MGM for at 1:04 A.M. that night to drive

Myrna Loy as Fah Lo See.

a woman to San Francisco. Two nights later, Dorothy Millette jumped off the *Delta King* steamboat and drowned in the Sacramento River.

"This is the most terrible moment in the history of our company!" howled Mayer to his producers, fearing the scandal could bring on the downfall of of MGM.* And Harlow was in the midst of filming a new picture, *Red Dust*, with Gable and Mary Astor. *Red Dust*'s supervisor was

---

In the most recent book to take a crack at this scandal, Charles Higham's 1993 Merchant of Dreams, the author accepts the impotence/suicide theory, stating that Paul Bern was "underdeveloped sexually"; he also notes that Bern's probate file contains a bill from a Culver City bookshop for four books, all bought in the summer of 1932, concerning male genitalia, female sexual needs, and hormone disorders. For the most authoritative word on Jean Harlow, see the excellent new Harlow biography, Platinum Girl, by Eve Golden, published by Abbeville Press.

Hunt Stromberg, the same man simultaneously producing *The Mask of Fu Manchu.*

Following Bern's cremation, where MGM staff mysteriously and fanatically guarded the body, Harlow (affectionately known at MGM as "The Baby") bravely returned to *Red Dust*—only to collapse.

Hunt Stromberg certainly had his hands full. On September 9, he was back to dictating ideas for *The Mask of Fu Manchu*. The studio that announced its plan to "go all out for sex" was having it blow up in its face, professionally and personally. And as Stromberg coped with the Metro hysteria, the day-to-day condition of Harlow, and the melodrama on the *Red Dust* set, his other film went on shooting.

●

Fu minions deliver Sir Lionel's body, a dragon tattooed on his head, giving Miss Morley a new chance for hysterics. Stone's Sir Nayland, who has the real sword of Genghis Khan, takes off for the House of 10,000 Joys, which he thinks leads to Fu Manchu. At "the House," we get a tour of an opium den, a musical comedy number from a Chinese floozie, and a fire, courtesy of Sir Nayland, as he penetrates the lair of Fu Manchu. The Yellow Peril aims a gun at Sir Nayland's back in a cave of vipers as a snake slithers at Sir Nayland's feet.

"Is this a friend of your family's?" deadpans Sir Nayland.

Fu Manchu leads his enemy to see the half-naked hero at the mercy of Fah Lo See. Fu explains his plan to inject a serum into Terry to control his will—"so much better than hypnotism."

"I see—another of your Oriental tricks," sneers Stone's Sir Nayland. "In the name of the British government, I demand the release of this boy!"

"British government! I'll wipe them and the whole accursed white race off the face of the earth when I get the sword and mask!"

Fu promises to show Sir Nayland the sword himself—"Just before I dispatch you to your cold, saintly, Christian paradise!" And as Nayland is dragged off, Fu leers over Terry's naked torso, stroking his super fingernails over it.

The operation begins. Fu, in surgical mask and gown, dominates his stark laboratory, where lizards and reptiles wriggle out of their crystal test tubes and the hero lies strapped to a table. Fu's loinclothed minions stand by, strangely glistening, for all the world like Oscar statues (which perhaps isn't all that surprising; Cedric Gibbons, the movie's scenic designer, also designed the Oscar statue for the Academy). The doctor extracts poison from a tarantula. Then a giant snake is pulled up from a trapdoor; two slaves aim its fangs like a knife and shove them into a hapless sacrifice. The poison is then extracted from the snake's dying victim.

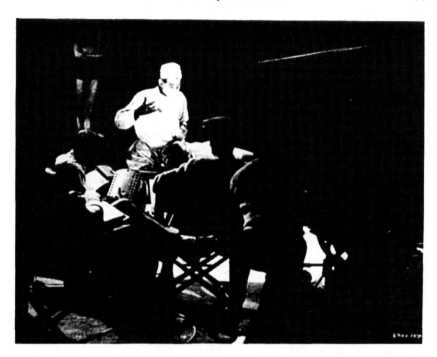

Not as scary as it looks: the scene that caused Karloff and "victim" Charles Starrett to go home laughing from *The Mask of Fu Manchu*.

Fu offers this running commentary:

> This serum, distilled from dragon's blood, my own blood, the organs of different reptiles, and mixed with a magic brew of the Sacred Seven Herbs, will temporarily change you into the living instrument of my will. You will do as I command! I am only going to give you the very smallest amount . . . because I want you to be your very self when I hand you over to my gentle daughter!

And Fu Manchu jabs the needle of serum into Terry's neck.

It is an incredibly sadistic scene, one which, in actuality, caused the cast to have hysterics of a different type. In Cynthia Lindsay's book *Dear Boris* (Knopf, 1975), Charles Starrett remembered:

> Boris was a subtle, good-humored man—an actor's actor. . . . Never blew a line—except once—in *Mask*. I, the hero, was lying strapped to a table; he as Fu Manchu was about to inject a hypodermic needle into the back of my neck—we couldn't get it right—it never looked like the real thing—so the director, I think it was Charles Brabin, suddenly yelled, "I've got it!" He sent to the commissary for four especially-baked

potatoes—he tucked one of them into the collar of my shirt and said to Boris, "Go ahead—jab it in—it can't hurt him—it will only go into the potato." We started the scene. Boris plunged the needle into (allegedly) my neck—the potato exploded with a great pop, got all over Boris and all over me. The two us couldn't stop laughing—we went through three more takes, using up the rest of the potatoes with the same results until we were hysterical. Finally the director said—"you two just go home—you're no use—we'll shoot it in the morning."

"This just isn't Terry!" wails Sheila as a doped and dopey-looking Terry returns to headquarters, but Hersholt's Von Berg and company agree to Terry's summons to meet Sir Nayland. They depart in a wild storm that night, Terry leering so moronically at Sheila in the carriage that she gasps. In a very effective scene, the drugged hero laughs wildly in the storm as his friends are trapped by Fu's forces. Fu Manchu now has the real sword and mask of Genghis Khan. The sword passes the electricity test.

"It will be your honor to be the first white martyrs to perish at the hands of the new Genghis Khan. I congratulate you!" The film is nearing its climax, and so are the xenophobic one-liners.

"You hideous yellow monster!" shrieks Morley's Sheila. "...Do you want to destroy us all?"

"Yes!" rants Karloff's Fu. "This is only the beginning! I will wipe out your whole accursed white race!"

By force of love, Sheila manages to snap Terry out of his trance and out of his love for Fah Lo See.* "Listen, Sheila...," wails Terry, "I love you!" as the heathens drag him away. While Stromberg had envisioned Karloff's Fu so turned on by Sheila's nasty zingers that he scooped her up and ran off to have his way with her, she (presumably) retains her honor in the release print.

It is now, however, that MGM proudly presents The Mask of Fu Manchu's top tantalizers—the torture scenes.

The torture devices are indeed a rich, wild experience, realized with all of Metro-Goldwyn-Mayer's glistening production value—each a hoot

*MGM toyed with various ideas about the fate of Fah Lo See. At one point, Stromberg envisioned Smith and Terry freeing Sheila and substituting Fah in the sacrificial white robes; Fu Manchu, forced to go through with it, would sacrifice his own daughter and, "heartbroken," kill himself. Another idea transformed Miss Loy's Fah Lo See into the heroine of the show. MGM's pressbook for The Mask of Fu Manchu synopsized that Fu "has a huge robot, controlled by a mysterious ray, which he plans to use in his uprising. The Oriental's daughter becomes infatuated with Terry ... and through this friendship Fu Manchu is defeated." It is possible such a climax was filmed, since stills survive showing Terry and Fah romantically cuddling. Obviously, MGM had second thoughts about having a "sadistic sex fiend" save the day, and Miss Loy's Fah Lo See simply disappears in the release print.

"Conquer and breed": Karloff's Yellow Peril versus Karen Morley's blonde in *The Mask of Fu Manchu*.

and each conceived by designer Cedric Gibbons, perhaps as he fantasized under Dolores del Rio's trap door.

• There are the "slim, silver fingers"—walls of wicked spikes that slowly come together, aimed to impale the plump, wild-eyed, sweating Jean Hersholt.

• There is the crocodile pit, a seesaw weighted by sand. Stone lies strapped to this sadistic teeter-totter as he is slowly dipped into the mire of the crocodiles, each growling and grunting and flashing Jimmy Durante smiles for the camera.

Starrett's Terry is off to become the drugged, pitiful plaything for Fah Lo See, while Morley is all gussied up in white maiden's robes in the Room of the Golden Peacock to be a fetishist sacrifice, to be sliced into pieces at a dawn ceremony by Fu and his Sword of Genghis Khan.

At dawn the scene is like opening day at Yankee Stadium. The Mongols, with torches, march to the ceremony, the extras filling a Metro soundstage. Karloff's Fu, wearing the Genghis Khan mask, sporting a fruit basket hat that looks like a cast-off from Carmen Miranda or, perhaps, Flub-a-Dub, takes center stage on a huge altar before a giant statue of Genghis Khan that holds the sword. A trumpet blares, and Karloff barnstorms to the shrieking, howling crowd: "Genghis Khan ... may he rain down on the white race—and *burn* them!"

The crowd screams. In march minions carrying on a sacrificial bed Morley, who swoons as the slavering mob roars and reaches for her, trying to touch the blonde.

"The sacrifice to our God!" rants Fu. "Would you all have maidens like this for your wives?"

A *big* cheer.

"Then," climaxes Karloff, *"Conquer and breed! Kill the white man, and take his women!"*

A *very* big cheer. Even the monstrous statue seems excited as it comes to life and presents the sword of Genghis Khan to Fu Manchu.

"Ahi!" banshees Karloff.

He raises the sword to slice Miss Morley as the Mongols scream.

"In the blood of Shiva's bride, I baptise this sword!"

But Sir Nayland has chewed off his bonds to escape the crocodiles, Terry has beaten up those live Academy Award statues who wanted to drug him for Fah Lo See, and the men have rescued Von Berg from the slim, silver fingers. In a room above the altar, the heroes find an electric ray gun. They aim it through the trap door, and it zaps the Genghis Khan sword right out of Fu's hands.

Starrett's Terry runs onto the altar, grabs the sword, and hacks Karloff's Fu, an act that in 1932 must have caused the cheers of the movie audiences to mix with the roars of the screen Mongols. White man picks up white woman and runs for it. The Mongols take this very badly and charge him, screaming in bloodlust, but Sir Nayland aims the ray gun lightning down at them, zapping them all, mowing them down like insects. He leaves the ray gun on as the heroes escape, and the ray cuts down any Mongols who happen to slink into its path.

The next scene is set at night on a ship back to London. Our little band of heroes—Von Berg, Terry, Sheila, and Sir Nayland—are on deck. Nayland is going to drop the Genghis Khan sword into the sea, so it can never fall into the dragon-nailed hands of another like Dr. Fu Manchu.

"By golly," laughs Von Berg, "after all that's happened, I wouldn't be surprised to see the hand of that fella Fu Manchu come out of the ocean and grab it!"

Sir Nayland goes to drop the sword, and a gong is heard. But it's not Fu Manchu.

It's little Willie Fung, comic Chinese actor, then playing Gable's silly servant ("Me come again, beep! beep!") in *Red Dust*. Plump, jolly, missing front teeth, Willie plays a steward who has come to announce dinner by hitting a gong; he giggles as Stone questions him.

"You aren't by any chance a doctor of philosophy? law? medicine?"

"I no think so, sir!" yuk-yuks Willie, showing his toothless gap. This is a Chinaman Hollywood can live with. "I congratulate you," says Sir Nayland.

"Well, as I was saying," says Stone, for the curtain line, "wherever you are, Genghis Khan, I give you back your sword!"

And *The Mask of Fu Manchu* ends, with a splash.

●

"God forgive us for shooting what we have," dictated Hunt Stromberg on September 19, 1932. *The Mask of Fu Manchu* began "retakes and added scenes," carrying on for another month of shooting. One grisly retake bears reporting: on October 18, 1932, Stromberg ordered the scene in which a Fu Manchu minion tosses Sir Lionel's dismembered hand into the headquarters yard reshot: "Retake the shot where the hand drops in — getting a real hand from the morgue and avoiding any bounce."

The Mask of Fu Manchu finally "wrapped" at MGM on Friday, October 21, 1932, after a bloody two-and-a-half months of shooting. Final cost: $327,627.26.* Karloff escaped the hothouse Metro climate and returned to Universal, where he was shooting *The Mummy* as Metro slowly pieced together *The Mask of Fu Manchu.*

As the film reached completion and premiere, there were a couple of curious developments. First of all, MGM's new melodrama got a "hypo" at the box office as CBS premiered a new radio show, "Fu Manchu," on September 26, 1932. John C. Daly was Fu (not the John Charles Daly of TV's "What's My Line!"), Charles Warburton was Nayland Smith, and Sundra Love was Karamenheh, "slave to the evil scientist's powers." Campana Balm sponsored the half-hour show, produced in Chicago, and Sax Rohmer himself was on hand for the premiere episode. (Harold Huber and Charlotte Manson later replaced Daly and Love; the show ran through April 24, 1933.)

On a more personal level, although Charles Vidor had lost *The Mask of Fu Manchu,* the fired director had a last laugh at Metro's expense; he secretly wed the movie's leading lady Karen Morley in November 1932. To the wrath of MGM, Morley didn't announce the wedding for over a month. The Vidors had a child, Michael, in 1933. By the time they divorced in 1943, Miss Morley's career was all but over, while Mr. Vidor's directorial skills were in top demand. He married actress Evelyn Keyes and (later) Doris Warner Le Roy (daughter of Warner Bros. president Harry Warner), and ultimately returned to Metro to direct such stars as Eliza-

*Many thanks to Cinema Collector's Buddy Barnett and MGM/UA's Karl Thiede for unearthing these studio figures.

beth Taylor in *Rhapsody* (1954), James Cagney in *Love Me or Leave Me* (1955), and Grace Kelly in *The Swan* (1956). Vidor would be replaced one other time in his career; he died June 5, 1959, while directing Columbia's *Song Without End* (based on the life of Franz Liszt), and George Cukor completed the picture.

●

> In an astounding makeup, Boris Karloff goes through amaz-
> ing adventures in *The Mask of Fu Manchu*.... Weird intrigues,
> sensations, mysteries, thrills, torture chambers, the fantastic
> laboratory of the "death ray," the lost tomb of Genghis Khan
> in the Gobi Desert.
> —From MGM's pressbook for *The
> Mask of Fu Manchu*

On Friday, December 2, 1932, MGM's *The Mask of Fu Manchu* had a gala New York City premiere at the Capitol Theatre, Metro's flagship Broadway movie house. "Boris 'Frankenstein' Karloff" top-lined the posters; "Mad, Oriental tortures! Crazed, heartless desires!" teased the promotional copy, along with the blurb: "This Oriental monster almost wrecked civilization with his love-drug."

The big stage show at Major Edward Bowes's 5486-seat Capitol offered a show business history curiosity: the headliner was Bing Crosby and the M. C. was Bob Hope. This was eight years before they teamed for Paramount's *The Road to Singapore*. Also on the bill were Cass, Mack, and Owen; Betty Jane Cooper and Lathrop Bros.; Abe Lyman and his Famous Californians; and NBC's "Radio Rubes," who, amazingly, according to the *New York Times,* won "the heartiest applause."

As for *The Mask of Fu Manchu,* the New York *American* saluted the movie as "a chilling, thrilling hour of hair-raising entertainment"; Britain's *Film Weekly* hailed it as "A blood-and-thunder thriller of nightmare dimensions." Most critics, however, were aghast. The movie's merry sado/masochism appalled many of the fourth estate, and Karloff's glee-fully mad Fu caused a number of nervous critics to yearn for Warner Oland's kinder, gentler Yellow Peril. *Variety* righteously hissed the picture, as myopic as ever to the show's most juicy offerings:

> This time they should have let the doctor rest in peace.... The
> diabolical stuff is piled on so thick at the finish, audiences are liable to
> laugh where they oughtn't. The audience at the Capitol did.... It's
> strange how bad such troupers as Stone and Hersholt can look when up
> against such an assignment as this. Miss Morley, miscast, is never her
> sophisticated self in this picture, and disappointing.... Boris Karloff,

borrowed from Universal, makes the doctor a monster instead of the cunning, shrewd fellow that he usually is. That Karloff is still doing the Frankenstein Monster is hardly concealed by a mandarin's robe. Myrna Loy, as the wicked daughter, is playing stock.

Of course, Karloff's wildly wicked Fu Manchu was thespic light years away from his beautiful, bewildered monster. Over the decades, he became the screen's definitive, most famous Fu Manchu, while Miss Loy's "stock" Fah Lo See won praise as one of the most exquisite villainesses of '30s melodrama. With Karloff's crazy bravado, Miss Loy's evil exotica, and MGM's big parade of torture devices, *The Mask of Fu Manchu* became the greatest horror comic book of Hollywood's Golden Age. Domestic gross, $377,000; foreign gross, $248,000; net profit: $62,000.

How might *The Mask of Fu Manchu* have haunted the liberal consciences of its stars? Karloff became one of the founders of the very controversial Screen Actors Guild in 1933. Myrna Loy reminds readers throughout her memoir of the various liberal causes she campaigned for throughout her life. Karen Morley followed *The Mask of Fu Manchu* with such "social conscience" films as UA's *Our Daily Bread* (1934) and Warners' *Black Fury* (1935), actively campaigned for the Progressive Party Platform in 1948, and in 1951, became one of the tragedies of the Hollywood witch-hunt, as at least three actors named her as a Communist in the House Un-American Activities Committee hearings (where Morley had taken the Fifth Amendment). She soon dropped out of sight in the entertainment world; she lives today in Los Angeles, widowed, alone, and rejecting requests for interviews and autographs.

●

When I played Fu Manchu in the Republic serial, *Drums of Fu Manchu* [1940], I'd go to a theatre nearby here in Hollywood, where they showed it, and sit among the kids (they never recognized me)—and I *loved* their reactions. Within two or three episodes, they were on *my* side! It was because I was brighter than the others, and the kids went for intelligence, whether it was bad or good.

But the PTAs—they didn't like it at all, because the kids would wet their beds after seeing it. And the Chinese government raised *plenty* of hell! And that's childish, because I consider Fu Manchu a fairy tale character—it's not to be taken seriously, for God's sake!

—Henry Brandon, 1986, interview
with the author

Fu Manchu returned over the decades in various incarnations. He leered in the mid–'30s in WOW comics and Detective comics; 1939 saw a syndicated "Shadow of Fu Manchu" 15-minute serial radio show. In 1940, Republic released the serial *Drums of Fu Manchu*, which starred the late Henry Brandon (evil "Barnaby" of Laurel and Hardy's 1934 *Babes in Toyland*) as a bald-pated Fu and was directed by William Witney and John English. Fu's mania included trying to feed the hero to an octopus, and the serial proved so popular that Republic planned a follow-up cliffhanger, *Fu Manchu Strikes Again*. The studio had to drop the concept in 1942, however, after the Chinese government appealed to the State Department. As a consolation prize to itself, Republic released an edited feature version of the 1940 serial in 1943.

The Yellow Peril was diplomatically still during the remainder of the war years, although there was a 1945 Spanish feature, *El Otro Fu Manchu*, directed by Ramon Barreiro, with Manuel Requena in the title spot. Then, in 1950, NBC produced a pilot for a "Fu Manchu" teleseries that starred John Carradine as Fu and Sir Cedric Hardwicke as Sir Nayland and was directed by William Cameron Menzies.* Retrospectively mouth-watering, the series reportedly failed to sell due to sponsor dissatisfaction with scripts. In 1955, Republic paid Sax Rohmer a reported $4 million for the Fu Manchu film/TV/radio rights. This transaction resulted in the 1956 syndicated TV series "The Adventures of Fu Manchu," with Glen Gordon as Dr. Fu Manchu. In this series, Fu headed Subtly, a terrorist organization. During these Eisenhower years, the producers borrowed Paramount's old excuse for Fu Manchu's mania: British officer Jack Petrie (Clark Howat) had inadvertently killed Fu's wife and son during the Boxer Rebellion. Republic proudly announced 78 half-hour episodes, but "The Adventures of Fu Manchu" fizzled after only 13 installments.

In 1965, Christopher Lee, who had played Frankenstein's monster, Count Dracula, the Mummy, and Rasputin, added Dr. Fu Manchu to his repertoire in *The Face of Fu Manchu*, a British production written and co-produced by Harry Alan Towers, directed by Don Sharp, filmed in Ireland, and released by 7 Arts. The brisk production had a charming 1920s atmosphere, and the publicists had great fun inviting Sax Rohmer's widow to the set and even launching a campaign to elect Fu Manchu mayor of New York. *The Face of Fu Manchu* (called *The Mask of Fu Manchu* in preproduction) proved a hit, despite Lee's very stiff performance, a problem he blamed on

---

The great director/art director Menzies had directed Fox's Chandu the Magician, *"hokum" à la Fu Manchu, starring Edmund Lowe in the title role and Bela Lugosi as the villainous Roxor. It was released in September 1932 almost three months before* The Mask of Fu Manchu. *It is curious that both Karloff and Lugosi were playing comic book villains at virtually the same time.*

the plastic eyelids I had to wear. I couldn't look up, I couldn't look down. I could only play, so to speak, from side to side. I had to rely entirely on the inflection of the voice and the "lack" of movement to put over the character.

Nevertheless, a series of Lee Fu Manchus followed. *The Brides of Fu Manchu* (1966) featured Don Sharp's direction, 12 beautifully lethal "brides," a death ray, and this critical advice from the *New York World-Journal Tribune:* "Fu-get it." *The Vengeance of Fu Manchu* (1968), directed by Jeremy Summers, was saluted by the *New York Times* as "a dignified, hilariously restrained continuation of the Fu of yore." However, with box office returns sagging, 7 Arts withdrew financing. Lee carried on (along with Tsai Chin, who played Fu's evil daughter in all five films of the series) in *Blood of Fu Manchu* (1969) and *Castle of Fu Manchu* (1972), both directed by Jess Franco and shot on the cheap in Spain. In fact, *Blood of Fu Manchu* was released in some markets as *Kiss and Kill* and *Against All Odds*, and *Castle of Fu Manchu* was marketed under the title *Assignment Istanbul*, which shows just how sadly the once mighty name of Fu Manchu had faded in the public consciousness. When Fu Manchu stirred once more cinematically, it was pure farce: *The Fiendish Plot of Dr. Fu Manchu* (1980), directed by Piers Haggard, and starring Peter Sellers in the dual roles of Fu Manchu *and* Nayland Smith. It wasn't nearly as much fun as the 1932 movie, and, sadly, it was Sellers's final film.

●

> Boris Karloff as the evil Fu Manchu—his passion for power twisting his brilliant mind—as he revels in the horrors of human sacrifice!
> —Trailer for the 1972 rerelease of *The Mask of Fu Manchu*

In 1972 MGM conceived the delightful idea of theatrically releasing a horror classic triple bill: *The Mask of Fu Manchu,* Tod Browning's 1935 *Mark of the Vampire,* and the Rouben Mamoulian 1931 *Dr. Jekyll and Mr. Hyde* (made, of course, by Paramount, but long imprisoned in the Metro vaults since the MGM Spencer Tracy version of 1941).

It was a different world now, one of greater social consciousness—and *The Mask of Fu Manchu* got nailed. On May 7, 1972, *Variety* reported that the Japanese-American Citizens League had fired off a letter to MGM requesting that *The Mask of Fu Manchu* "be removed from its catalogue immediately" and protesting that the 40-year-old movie was "offensive and demeaning to Asian-Americans." The League lamented that the vintage melodrama falsely depicts Asians as a mindless horde blindly worshipping the bloody activities of Genghis Khan and Fu Manchu. When United States Foreign Policy is reaching out for understanding of Asian people, this rehash of Yellow Peril cannot be tolerated by any patriotic American.

The League also complained that white actors had all the speaking roles, while the Asian actors were only extras, and insisted that "This insulting pattern of discrimination in motion picture casting does not need reenforcement."

The fire was lit, and *The Mask of Fu Manchu* attracted more and more flak, some of it from historians themselves. "In an age when man is rising above the old-age prejudices," editorialized Frank Dello Stritto in his article "Karloff Vs. Lugosi" in the defunct *Photon* magazine, "there is little wonder why a film whose hero is devoted to keeping the yellow man in his place and whose villain intends to destroy all white males to mate with their females should be kept in hiding."

Throughout the brouhaha, MGM declined to comment.

> Charles J. Brabin's film (based on the famous pulp novel by Sax Rohmer) is one of the most enduring splendors of the 1930s fantastic cinema, a spectacle of stylized performance and art direction that takes full and potent advantage of its pre-code status. Boris Karloff stars as Rohmer's criminal mastermind. . . . Myrna Loy, in another of her early exotic femme fatale roles . . . is memorably cast as Fu's cool-of-veneer and hot-of-blood daughter, Fah Lo See. If the heroic performances of Lewis Stone (as Nayland Smith) and Charles Starrett are less memorable, it is because the tortures designed for them by the insidious Dr. Fu Manchu are so upstagingly clever.
>
> — *Video Watchdog*, March/April 1993

Ever since video cassettes changed show business history in the early 1980s, many film buffs have believed that Karloff's magnificent leer, Myrna Loy's evil oomph, the Genghis Khan mask and sword, the smiling crocodiles, the great title, and the "wild and woolly" reputation would make *The Mask of Fu Manchu* an ideal MGM/UA video release. But they were long disappointed; mysteriously, *The Mask of Fu Manchu* failed, year after year, to appear on the video market. MGM/UA Home Video calmly denied that racism had anything to do with the film's failure to integrate into the video population. Instead, the company candidly claimed (to insiders) that such MGM horror classics as *Freaks, Mark of the Vampire,* and *The Devil-Doll* (as well as MGM/UA's releases of the Warner Bros. two-strip Technicolor classics *Doctor X* and *Mystery of the Wax Museum*) did such poor business (even after a price drop from $59.95 to $19.95) that marketing prospects for *The Mask of Fu Manchu* were simply bad business.

Yet this seemed cold, coming from a historic-minded company that released such noncommercial films as early Garbo "talkies" *(Romance, Inspiration)* and fare for Harlow fans like *The Girl from Missouri* and *Riffraff.* Some fans were skeptical, fearing that MGM was holding *The Mask of Fu Manchu* hostage due to the 60-year-old film's sociological naïveté.

Then, in the fall of 1992, MGM/UA sought to put all rumors to rest and, indeed, released *The Mask of Fu Manchu.* And the fans got a brand new shock.

In an age where Universal restored Lugosi's climactic groans as the stake is driven into his heart in *Dracula* and Little Maria's splash into the lake in *Frankenstein,* MGM/UA released a *cut* version of *The Mask of Fu Manchu.* The torture devices stayed in; the zingers came out. Tim Lucas, publisher/editor of *Video Watchdog,* reported that MGM/UA cut a total of one minute, five seconds from *The Mask of Fu Manchu.* The cuts included:

• Karloff's line to Starrett after the fake sword shrivels: "you accursed son of a white dog!"

• Some of Myrna Loy's "Faster! Faster! Faster!" cries as minions whip half-naked Starrett.

• The word "Christian" from Karloff's vow to Morley and Hersholt that they "and your compatriot, Sir Nayland Smith, will have the pleasure of entering your Christian heaven together."

• Karloff's promise to the heroes that they will "have the honor to be the first white martyrs to perish at the hands of the new Genghis Khan!"

• Karloff's raving, "Yes, this is only the beginning! I will wipe out your whole accursed white race!"

• The prepositional phrase "down on the white race," from Karloff's sacrificial rant, "...rain down on the white race and burn them!"

• And, perhaps inevitably, Karloff's apocalyptically delivered, "Would you all have maidens like this for your wives? Then conquer and breed! Kill the white man and take his women!"

A number of fans ran to MGM's defense. Some claimed these cuts were made way back in 1972, after the fracas with the Japanese-American Citizens League; some even professed the cuts were made *before* the film's 1972 theatrical rerelease. *Video Watchdog* reports, however, that all of these lines were in the '72 prints (rated "G" by the MPAA). Indeed, when I taped *The Mask of Fu Manchu* from Baltimore television in 1983, it was a complete version.

So the controversy goes on, at least in the world of movie fans. Many film buffs, oddly unoffended by a horde of garishly exploited freaks crawling through mud to mutilate a woman, still curl up their lip at the "racist" name of *The Mask of Fu Manchu.*

Times are still complex. And thus, we might expect *The Mask of Fu Manchu*, a funny, campy, almost endearingly naïve comic book of 1930s movie melodrama, to remain the sad, slant-eyed skeleton in MGM's horror movie closet.

An afterword: in March of 1993, a stage comedy called *Face Value*, described as "a farce about a white actor who steps into the role of Fu Manchu in a musical," began a pre–Broadway tryout in Boston. The script was by David Henry Hwang (who had written the enormously successful play *M. Butterfly*), the star was Mark Linn-Baker (of TV's "Perfect Strangers"), and the director was Jerry Zaks, who had won a Tony award for directing the 1992 revival of *Guys and Dolls*.

This talent force couldn't save *Face Value*, however; it closed in Boston on March 14, 1993, after only eight performances, bad reviews, and a loss of $2,000,000.

Boris Karloff would have sympathized.

Mark of the Vampire

Studio: Metro-Goldwyn-Mayer; Producer: Edward J. Mannix; Director: Tod Browning; Screenplay: Guy Endore and Bernard Schubert (based on Tod Browning's original story, "The Hypnotist"; fictionalized by Edwin V. Burkholder; additional dialogue by H. S. Kraft, Samuel Ornitz, and John L. Balderston); Cinematographer: James Wong Howe, A. S. C.; Art Director: Cedric Gibbons (Harry Oliver and Edwin B. Willis, Associates); Gowns: Adrian; Makeup: Jack Dawn (William Tuttle, Assistant); Film Editor: Ben Lewis; Recording Engineer: Douglas Shearer; First Assistant Director: Harry Sharrock; Running Time: 61 minutes; Premiere: Mayfair and Rialto Theatres, New York City, May 1, 1935.

The Players: Professor Zelen (Lionel Barrymore); Irena Borotyn (Elizabeth Allan); Count Mora (Bela Lugosi); Inspector Neumann (Lionel Atwill); Baron Otto Von Zinden (Jean Hersholt); Fedor (Henry Wadsworth); Dr. Doskil (Donald Meek); Midwife (Jessie Ralph); Jan, the Butler (Ivan F. Simpson); Chauffeur (Franklyn Ardell); Maria (Leila Bennett); Annie (June Gittelson); Luna Mora (Carroll Borland); Sir Karell Borotyn (Holmes Herbert); Innkeeper (Michael S. Visaroff); Innkeeper's Wife (Rosemary Glosz); Englishman (Guy Belis); Englishwoman (Claire Vedara); Old Woman at Inn (Mrs. Lesovosky); Bit Man (James Bradbury, Jr.); Coroner (Egon Brecher); Sick Woman (Eily Malyon)*; Grandmother (Zeffie Tilbury)*; Bus Driver (Baron Hesse)*; Deaf Man (Christian Rub)*; Fat Man (Robert Greig)*; Card Player (Torben Meyer)*.

●

The terrifying suspense of this picture demands that you be seated from beginning to end. Please don't tell your friends the thrilling climax!

—*Mark of the Vampire* publicity in the *New York Times,* on the film's premiere day, May 1, 1935

*These actors appeared in footage that was deleted.

The new year, 1935, was a wild, historic time for horror in Hollywood.

On January 2, 1935, below the mountains at Universal City, James Whale, Universal's "ace" of *Frankenstein, The Old Dark House,* and *The Invisible Man,* began shooting *The Return of Frankenstein*—which would be released as *Bride of Frankenstein.* Karloff was back as his "dear old monster," with Colin Clive reprising the Gothic monster maker and Elsa Lanchester playing Mary Shelley and the monster's mate; all the resources of erratic Universal were at Whale's elegant fingertips.

On January 12, 1935, far south on the flats of Culver City at the Metro-Goldwyn-Mayer studios, Tod Browning, director of *The Unknown, Dracula, Freaks,* and other famous melodramas, started directing *Vampires of Prague,* destined to be released as *Mark of the Vampire.* This remake of Browning's *London After Midnight* (which had starred Lon Chaney) boasted venerable, Oscar-winner Lionel Barrymore, classy starlet Elizabeth Allan, the redoubtable Lionel Atwill, and Bela Lugosi, who had made Hollywood history in Browning's *Dracula,* here once again donning the vampire cape. All the expertise of MGM, Hollywood's "most prodigal studio," was at Browning's disposal.

It was a grand chance for Whale and Karloff, Browning and Lugosi to flaunt just how much they had learned cinematically since the pioneering 1931 days of *Dracula* and *Frankenstein.*

Bride of Frankenstein, of course, became the baroque climax of Hollywood's Golden Age of Horror. *Mark of the Vampire* became something else again.

●

In the Golden Age of Greece, Gods and Goddesses disguised themselves as mortals and roamed the face of the earth. In the Golden Age of Hollywood, mortals disguised themselves as Gods and never left MGM.
—from Bob Thomas's book *Thalberg, Life and Legend*

In 1935 Metro-Goldwyn-Mayer Studios was a grand and gaudy 11-year-old, at the zenith of its power and glamour. The MGM of Mayer and Thalberg would win the Best Picture Oscar of 1935 for *Mutiny on the Bounty,* place three more contenders among the Academy's 12 nominees (*Broadway Melody of 1936, David Copperfield,* and *Naughty Marietta)*, and lead the studios with a dizzy $7.5 million Depression profit. A visitor to the lot could behold some of Hollywood's most sacred sights: Garbo's eyelashes, Harlow's platinum glory, Norma Shearer's patrician profile,

Clark Gable's wry grin. To the public, Metro was truly Hollywood's holy of holies.

Yet there was a grotesque aura behind the roaring Leo the Lion and his heavenly stars. Mayer seemed determined to live down the calumny that he had started his career as a junk dealer; Thalberg worked exhaustively, tending his weak heart, fearing the early death that indeed claimed him in 1936. The stars, in a sense, were grotesques too: "La Divina" Garbo, a morbid recluse (with false eyelashes) who once hid from fans by climbing up a palm tree beside her pool and roosting there all night; "Blonde Bombshell" Harlow, furtively sporting a platinum wig in 1935 to hide her bleach-ruined tresses and fated for a tragic death in 1937; "American Beauty Rose" Shearer (aka Mrs. Thalberg), requiring Metro's ace cameramen to hide the caste in her eye; and "King" Gable, with a mouth full of false teeth.

"In those days, we didn't just make movies," said Clarence Brown, veteran MGM director. "We made myths, and they had to be protected and helped." When MGM mythology clashed with the reality, the results (masterfully concealed by the studio) could be fascinating—and intriguing. Surely one of Metro's top private curiosities of 1935 occurred on *Mutiny on the Bounty,* when Clark Gable tried to break the ice with Charles Laughton by taking the homosexual star to a Catalina whorehouse.

"I think," wrote Elsa Lanchester, the long-patient Mrs. Laughton, "that Charles was flattered."

Metro was a "producer's studio," but there was still a very impressive roster of directors there in 1935: Victor Fleming, King Vidor, George Cukor, W. S. Van Dyke, Jack Conway, Clarence Brown. And curiously, still on the lot, adrift in the backlash of *Freaks,* was Tod Browning.

> American director remembered chiefly for his horror films of the twenties and early thirties; reevaluation has made them less striking than once was thought.
> —Leslie Halliwell, write-up on Tod Browning in *The Filmgoer's Companion* (Sixth Edition)

The early '90s are a lonely time to be a Tod Browning fan. This former carnival geek/circus ringmaster/blackface vaudevillian/D. W. Griffith assistant/Poe of the screen has been suffering some hard knocks for his stodgy cinema style and a pace as slow and scuttly as those armadillos that inexplicably upstage Lugosi's entrance in *Dracula.* When one learns of Browning's life, it is perhaps not surprising that many of his films unspool like an alcoholic's nightmare: confused, sick, sordid, muddled, populated by rats and bugs (and armadillos). Nor is it surprising that among film historians/critics, the armadillo hunt is on and has become an open season sport.

"More often than not," wrote David J. Skal in *Hollywood Gothic*, "the Browning end product is an unholy mess. There is no denying, however, the enduring fascination of his work, even if the fascination is akin to watching an auto wreck." In their 1990 tome *Universal Horrors*, Tom Weaver, Michael Brunas, and John Brunas (who coined the now-popular term "Browning-bashing") slap the Browning "rediscoveries" as "turgid, plotty bores, each representing one more nail in the once-fabled director's critical coffin." In 1974, famous critic/historian William K. Everson wrote in his *Classics of the Horror Film:*

> Apart from their plot lines, often unhealthy almost for the sake of it, Browning's films have usually had one major flaw: a dynamic and bizarre opening that is both disturbing and attention-getting ... and then a steady decline into stagy and talkative melodramatics, with no return to the motifs or suggested plot developments by which those opening shots held such promise.

Freaks, of course, had been one of the great disasters of MGM's history. Mortified, Mayer had demanded a vengeful pound of flesh from Tod Browning. He assigned the director to *Fast Workers,* yet another Mayer-concocted humiliation for John Gilbert, whom the producer despised, and whose infamous emasculation by sound in *His Glorious Night* (1929) delighted the vindictive "L. B." Leonard Maltin's *TV Movies and Video Guide,* rates the 1933 Browning curio "abysmal."

So in 1934, Tod Browning was a 54-year-old alcoholic with two recent flops, a reputation largely built on the dead Chaney and, apparently, an armadillo fetish. Only the success of *Dracula* buoyed his reputation. Mayer, whose favorite product would be the Andy Hardy and Lassie films, hated horror movies, but Thalberg was intrigued and Hollywood was virtually intimidating MGM into producing them. Warner Bros. had scored with *Doctor X* (1932) and *Mystery of the Wax Museum* (1933), both in two-strip Technicolor and both starring the superb Lionel Atwill. RKO had enjoyed one of its all-time hits with *King Kong;* Universal needed two Broadway theatres to accommodate the crowds for Whale's *The Invisible Man.*

Then, on May 3, 1934, Universal's *The Black Cat,* starring Karloff and Bela Lugosi, premiered at the Hollywood Pantages Theatre, becoming Universal's hit of the season. And in its wake came the announcement of Universal's long-promised sequel to *Frankenstein.*

MGM could resist no longer. It was time for a new Metro horror show. Much would be forgiven Tod Browning; if MGM was to make horror films, surely he was their man. Mayer had him proceed with *Vampires of Prague*, a remake of Browning's silent 1927 *London After Midnight*, which had starred Lon Chaney in the dual role of inspector and vampire. Browning would be on solid, previously trod ground, and vampires (unlike real circus freaks) were profit-proven Hollywood make-believe.

In the late summer of 1934, as Universal was counting the money from *The Black Cat*, MGM officially blueprinted *Vampires of Prague* on the shooting schedule. The project was labeled "Tod Browning's production."

●

> MGM was willing to rival Universal, if only because Tod Browning was on hand; but MGM's idea of a monster was nothing worse than Lionel Barrymore.
> —from *The Hollywood Studios,* by Ethan Mordden

The executive producer of *Mark of the Vampire* was E. J. "Eddie" Mannix, Mayer's top troubleshooter and Metro studio manager for half a century. The "bulldog-jawed" Mannix had been bodyguard for Metro president Nicholas Schenck back in the days when the Schenck Brothers owned the Palisades Amusement Park in New Jersey, where Mannix began his career as a laborer. Mannix was a great MGM power; no telegram entered or left the Metro lot without passing his eyes; he roistered with the legends and even mourned with them (when Carole Lombard perished in that plane crash in 1942, after selling war bonds, it was Mannix who stood by the grieving Clark Gable at the accident site in Nevada).

Eddie Mannix possibly occupies a much grimmer nook of Hollywood lore, however. In *Deadly Illusions: Jean Harlow and the Murder of Paul Bern* (Random House, 1990), the late Samuel Marx (story editor under Thalberg and later a Metro producer) and Joyce Vanderveen drop a Mannix bombshell. Marx claims that Howard Strickling (Metro's famed PR chief) late in life verified the long-whispered rumor that Mannix murdered George "Superman" Reeves, whose death in 1959 was long labeled suicide, after a messy scandal involving Mannix, Mrs. Mannix, and Reeves (who left his estate to Mrs. Mannix). Reeves's mother, who insisted his death was murder (and even had her son's body exhumed at one point) died before she could prove it.

It was rare for studio manager Mannix to play executive producer (he did again later in 1935 on Jack Benny's *It's in the Air*); but he supervised

Browning's *Freaks, Mark of the Vampire,* and, in 1936, *The Devil-Doll.* Mannix was Metro "family," as was Browning; perhaps Mayer felt Mannix could keep a sharp eye on Browning if he fell off the wagon or displayed unusually strange behavior.

Although *Vampires of Prague* would follow *London After Midnight* very closely in plot construction, MGM enlisted top writers for the production. First credit on the screenplay went to Guy Endore, young author of the novel *Werewolf of Paris.* Endore adapted Poe's *The Raven* for Karloff and Lugosi at Universal (his work was discarded before that film went into production in March of 1935 with a David Boehm script). Endore would share *Mark of the Vampire* credit with Bernard Schubert (who later in 1935 contributed to the screenplay of MGM's Basil Rathbone thriller *Kind Lady,* based on the Broadway play that had starred Henry Daniell).

It was Endore, reportedly, who contributed a fresh, gruesome folklore to Browning's original: the Gothic, decadent Count Mora and his slinky, depraved daughter Luna had committed incest, then suicide, and had arisen from the dead as vampires. The Count even sported a bloody hole in his temple as a talisman of this grisly fate.

Then came casting. While Chaney had indulged himself in the dual role of inspector and vampire in *London After Midnight, Vampires of Prague* divided the roles and metamorphosed Inspector Burke into Professor Zelen, a Van Helsing–like student of demonology. Browning presented the star part to Lionel Barrymore.

"Lionel was a stimulating man—a marvelous, a great man," said Boris Karloff, who acted with Barrymore in *The Bells* (1926) and was directed by him in MGM's *The Unholy Night* (1929). The eldest of the three legendary Barrymores, the 56-year-old Lionel was now in his thespic prime at Metro. He had won an Oscar as the lawyer who delivers a barnstorming speech to the jury (and then drops dead) in the Norma Shearer/Clark Gable *A Free Soul* (1931); was unforgettably touching as the dying Kringelein in the 1932 *Grand Hotel* (especially moving in scenes with John as the suave jewel thief), and was a resplendently evil, black-bearded Rasputin (with John and Ethel) in *Rasputin and the Empress* (1932). Louis B. Mayer adored Lionel; the producer, famous for acting emotionally toward his stars in his office (especially when he wanted them to do something they didn't want to do), proudly told friends that the "L. B." of his initials stood for "Lionel Barrymore."

Barrymore had acted for Browning already on two occasions at Metro. In *The Show* (1927), he played "The Greek," trying to snare Renee Adoree and attempting to kill John Gilbert by a poisonous gila monster

Opposite: **Poster for *Mark of the Vampire.***

and a carnival beheading act. In *West of Zanzibar* (1928), Barrymore played Crane, who steals the wife (Mary Nolan) of a magician (Lon Chaney) in this African jungle melodrama and tosses Chaney off a balcony, causing him to become "Dead Legs."

Winning the female lead of Irene Borotyn was 26-year-old Elizabeth Allan of Skegness, England, fresh from playing the doomed, frail mother of Freddie Bartholomew (and the terrified wife of wicked Basil Rathbone) in Metro's *David Copperfield*. The willowy, slightly pop-eyed redhead reached her Metro zenith later in 1935, winning the coveted role of Lucie (opposite Ronald Colman) in *A Tale of Two Cities*. Allan would make history (of sorts) at MGM. Mayer promised her the lead in *The Citadel* (1938), but gave the role instead to Rosalind Russell, so Elizabeth sued him. Mayer naturally blackballed Allan in Hollywood, and she returned to a distinguished stage/screen/television career in England. She was still a beauty in her mature years, with a silver streak through the front of her auburn hair; her last film, *The Haunted Strangler* (1958), saw her killed by Karloff. Elizabeth Allan retired after the 1977 death of her husband and agent, Wilfrid O'Bryen, to whom she was wed for 45 years; she died in 1990.

Lionel Atwill, clipped, cat-eyed, British horror great, who created such roles as wax-faced Ivan Igor of Warner's 1933 *Mystery of the Wax Museum* and one-armed Inspector Krogh of Universal's 1939 *Son of Frankenstein*, signed on *Mark of the Vampire* to play Inspector Neumann. The part came between two of "Pinky's" most famous performances: Henri Dumont, vile publisher beheaded by Claude Rains in Universal's *The Man Who Reclaimed His Head* (1934), and Spanish officer Pasqual, masochistically slaving after Dietrich in Paramount's *The Devil Is a Woman* (which opened on Broadway just after *Mark of the Vampire*). That Atwill had surrendered an outstanding career on the stage to "go Hollywood" still amazed many; it wasn't until his sensational 1940 Christmas "orgy," and all of its catastrophic legal repercussions, that the public gained insight into the incredibly complex personality of "Pinky" Atwill.

Jean Hersholt, a Metro regular in such fare as *Grand Hotel, Dinner at Eight,* and, of course, *The Mask of Fu Manchu,* filled the truly villainous role of Baron Otto von Zinden. Henry Wadsworth, of Maysville, Kentucky, took the male ingenue part of Fedor.

The true showmanship (and lasting appeal) of *Mark of the Vampire* would come, however, in the casting of the actor who would play the legendary vampire, Count Mora.

> Bela had an incredibly wonderful devilishness ... the sexiest
> man I ever knew ... a charming, wonderful person ... a friendly

Mark of the Vampire: **Lionel Barrymore and Carroll "Luna" Borland.**

panther . . . a playmate . . . I've never been out to Bela's grave.
I have a feeling somehow he isn't there.

—Carroll Borland

The old house at 2835 Westshire Drive, Hollywood Hills, is magnificent, a stone and brick Tudor castle sitting atop a cliff high in the hills

Henry Wadsworth, Elizabeth Allan, and Lionel Atwill in Mark of the Vampire.

under the old Hollywoodland sign. A great window looks out of the three-story fortress, surveying the movie capital; a high wire fence runs along the property, saving anyone who ventures a few yards outside the house from falling 70 feet down the steep cliff. On the Westshire Drive side, the short brick portals and black fence gate haven't changed in over half a century, and the garden is still lovely. It is one of Hollywood's old historic "star" homes—the house that Bela Lugosi enjoyed in 1935.

In 1935 Bela Lugosi, Hungary's classical stage actor turned glamorous Hollywood heavy, was at the climax of his career. Handsome, blue-eyed, several inches taller than most cinema leading men, the actor who had portrayed *Dracula* on Broadway in 1927 and had reprised his sensational performance in Universal's 1931 milestone, had then unleashed his passion in such now-legendary performances as Mirakle in *Murders in the Rue Morgue* (1932), Murder Legendre in *White Zombie* (1932), and vengeful Dr. Vitus Werdegast of *The Black Cat* (1934), who skinned top-billed Karloff alive (on Boris's "own embalming rack").

The appellation Lugosi had loved, "the male Garbo," quickly es-

Jean Hersholt, the "surprise" villain of *Mark of the Vampire*, with Elizabeth Allan on the set of the movie.

caped him. His going-rate was only $1000 per week (compared to Karloff's $2500), he squandered his talent on Poverty Row, and (catastrophically) he had rejected the monster role in *Frankenstein,* paving the way for Karloff. Nevertheless, Bela was savoring fame: enjoying his Westshire Drive domain, smoking his Havana cigars, indulging in his imported European delicacies, hosting parties where rich wine flowed and hired musicians played through dawn. The Hollywoodland sign (still featuring the last four letters in 1935) glowed through the night with 4000 light bulbs, and Bela's house glowed too, lights burning in every window in the great house atop the cliff.

Few people admired Lugosi or cared for him as much as a young, gifted actress, fascinated by horror and demonology, who was then attending Berkeley on a Shakespeare scholarship. She had first met Lugosi when he was playing onstage in *Dracula* in Oakland in the late 1920s; she later met him (with her mother) at his hotel to discuss her manuscript, *Countess Dracula*. Still later, she played Lucy to Bela's Count in a tour of *Dracula* and dated him. Her name was Carroll Borland and she later recalled:

> Lugosi had the charm, that quality of, any minute, "I will vanish in a puff of smoke" — *blue* smoke. I cannot convince people that Lugosi never wore false fangs. He didn't need them. His smile with his mouth closed was so much more terrifying than his successors gnashing their teeth — the wonderful quality of imagination.

Today, the actress glows as she shares her Bela memories: shivering at the sensation of an ice cube dropped down her back by a mischievous Bela during a passionate clinch in *Dracula;* dancing a Viennese waltz with her co-star at the Hollywood Roosevelt Hotel, feeling close to him, the reverberation through her body as he hummed along with the orchestra; privately playing Juliet to his Romeo, he reciting Shakespeare in Hungarian, she in English; window-shopping along Hollywood Boulevard with Bela ("hand in hand") at night at Christmas time, soothing his ego after they confronted Karloff's face among the wreathed star countenances that glowed on the boulevard at Yuletide. "Oh, I was a very fortunate teenager in having this fascinating, grown-up friend," she recalls, "we had a beautiful time together."

"Little Carroll," Bela called her, and Borland insists the magic time they shared was always platonic. On January 31, 1933, Bela married Lillian, his fourth wife, eloping to Las Vegas, while Carroll went on studying the Bard at Berkeley. Then, during the Christmas holidays of 1934, Carroll visited Hollywood and learned that Tod Browning was seeking a "woman beautiful enough to scare people" for *Vampires of Prague.* MGM had publicized its search for the "vampire girl," à la Paramount's 1932 search for "the panther woman," for *Island of Lost Souls,* and the result (if Metro PR is to be believed) was 18 pounds of photographs from all over the country of young ladies aspiring to play Luna (the role played by Edna Tichenor in *London After Midnight*). One of the contestants was teenager Rita Cansino, soon to be internationally known as Rita Hayworth.

Carroll Borland contacted her former "playmate." On December 27,

1934, Bela Lugosi had signed an MGM contract to play Count Mora in *Vampires of Prague* for $1000 per week on a three-week guarantee. Bela, however, counseled Carroll not to audition for the role. "If you do," prophesied the star, "you'll be stuck in that as I have been!"

Nevertheless, Carroll landed a test at MGM. Bela cooperated; the two played as if they had never met. Tall Bela scrunched in his Dracula cape, and "Little Carroll" wore her high heels. Browning was amazed at their chemistry.

The January 8, 1935, edition of *The Hollywood Reporter* announced that Tod Browning had a January 10 starting date for *Vampires of Prague*, but that his "beautiful hauntress" had not yet been named. Set changes caused a two-day delay. Finally, with usual showmanship, MGM announced on the eve of shooting the winner of the role of Luna: Carroll Borland. Metro's *Mark of the Vampire* pressbook would proclaim:

> A pair of dark, mysterious eyes won for Carroll Borland, University of California girl, one of the most sensational screen roles of the year. Her luminous orbs were the deciding factor.... "She has eyes," says Browning, "that glow with sinister mystery."

Meanwhile, one of Browning's great blessings was behind the camera—James Wong Howe (1899–1976), the Chinese cinematographer who would receive 16 Academy nominations for his outstanding camerawork and take home Oscars for *The Rose Tattoo* (1955) and *Hud* (1963). Finally, a production was all ready to go.

In the meantime, on January 2, 1935, James Whale had started filming *Bride of Frankenstein,* Universal affording him a budget of $293,750 and a shooting schedule of 36 days. MGM, for all its glory, wasn't so lavish for *Vampires of Prague,* which had a budget of $208,734.01 and a shooting schedule of 24 days.

This was $85,000 and two weeks less than Whale's *Bride.* Of course, it should be noted that Metro's *Vampires of Prague* budget was almost $8000 more than the Universal budgets for Karloff and Lugosi's *The Black Cat* and *The Raven* combined. But *Vampires of Prague*'s resources were still proverbial peanuts compared to Metro "A" films, as well as Browning's recent works (*Freaks* for MGM had cost $316,000 and taken 36 days to shoot; *Dracula* for Universal had cost $341,191.20 and taken 42 days to shoot).

On Saturday, January 12, 1935, Tod Browning began shooting *Vampires of Prague.*

●

The Cruelest Woman in Two Worlds!

A beauty from out of the shadow of doom . . . a dread temptress
who lured her victims to the hiding-place of her maniacal master! You will love each shivering, shuddering moment in the
strangest story ever told on the screen!
　　　　　　　　　　　　　　　　　—MGM Publicity, *Mark of the*
　　　　　　　　　　　　　　　　　Vampire

The words "Lionel Barrymore in *Mark of the Vampire*" lead off the
film's credits, as a musical score (already employed in Metro's Gable/
Harlow *Red Dust* in 1932) plays against a backdrop of tombstones.

The scene is Visoka, Czechoslovakia. A cross (anathema to all vampires) glows atop a steeple (spliced into *Mark of the Vampire* from Metro's
1933 *The White Sister*). In the night we see MGM peasants singing hauntingly, mournfully around a bonfire. A grotesque old woman hangs bat
thorn (Metro's equivalent of Universal's wolf's bane) on a horse (hungry
vampires); a couple fervently prays; a baby coos and plays with a sprig of
bat thorn (just as a baby had done in the opening of *Dracula*).

In the cemetery, an owl peers down from a gnarled branch as the old
witch (Jessie Ralph, 1876–1944, who had just played Nurse Peggoty in
David Copperfield) gathers herbs from the graveyard. A large bat frightens
her, and as she runs away, a gravedigger's rake (looking suspiciously like
a skeleton's hand) clutches the hem of her dress. Screaming, she scuttles
out of the scene and out of the picture, never to return.

In true Browning fashion, nothing else in *Mark of the Vampire* will
equal the macabre opening. And with the eighth-billed Ralph (then a
noted Hollywood character actress) disappearing so soon, *Mark of the
Vampire* presents the first of its many production mysteries.

In a village inn, the innkeeper warns a scoffing English couple to stay
in the inn that night. "The demons of the castle!" rasps Russian, mustached Michael Visaroff (1892–1951), who gave a similar eerie exposition
as the innkeeper in *Dracula*. Visaroff had also played the caretaker in
Browning's *Freaks* (lamenting about "the horrible, twisted things"). In
Dracula, Browning at least had given him close-ups.

Bald, little Donald Meek (1880–1946) timidly rushes into the inn as
Dr. Doskil. One of Hollywood's busiest character players (at least 21
feature releases in 1935), Meek was a delight in such roles as the whiskey
drummer of *Stagecoach,* but his comedy relief appears intrusive here.

"He can tut-tut all he likes about vampires," says the innkeeper's wife
(Rosemary Glosz), as Doskil hangs bat thorn in his room, "but I'd hate
to be on a farm needing his help tonight!"

And indeed, that wicked night in the old castle, Sir Karell Borotyn is
killed. Borotyn is played by Holmes Herbert (1882–1956), who acted in

Browning's 1929 *The Thirteenth Chair* (as well as the 1937 remake) and perhaps is best-remembered as Fredric March's priggish colleague Lanyon in *Dr. Jekyll and Mr. Hyde.* Sir Borotyn's body is drained of all its blood. The audience doesn't see the murder; it is announced the next day.

"Last night, your master, Sir Karell, was murdered," announces Sir Otto to the servants. Jean Hersholt (1886–1956) plays the role, looking like a mustached teddy bear; casting him as the villain was a stroke of subtlety—or stupidity, depending on your personal reaction.

"I'm not interested in your old wives' tales!" barks Inspector Neumann as Dr. Doskil announces "vampires" over Sir Karell's corpse. Lionel "Pinky" Atwill is razor-sharp in his double-breasted suit, polka-dot bow tie, and fresh lapel carnation; his Neumann is a fierce Doberman pinscher of an inspector, with nary a flicker of the aberrant kink who sewed a victim's lips together in *Murders in the Zoo.*

Browning introduces our ingenue: Elizabeth Allan, in her third year as a Metro lady, plays Irena in the traditional, corseted, wilting wallflower style of *Dracula;* in fact, she even bears a resemblance to Helen Chandler, leading femme of the 1931 classic. Our male romantic, Henry Wadsworth, fares badly. A stock Metro contractee who had played minor parts in movies like *The Thin Man* (1934), he virtually yodels his way into the movie as Fedor, greeting his bereaved fiancée with a marvelously mistimed: "Where have you been? I've been making enough noise to raise the dead!"

If Allan is an echo of Helen Chandler of *Dracula,* Wadsworth is a distortion of David Manners, lacking any of that actor's uniquely winning charm. Even Browning must have agreed. Before long, he has Wadsworth almost always upstaged by Miss Allan; by the film's finale, we have almost forgotten what he looks like.

The film tumbles into quick, almost blackout vignettes. A coroner (Egon Brecher, 1880–1946, who had just played the sinister majordomo in *The Black Cat*) attributes Sir Karell's death to "cause, or causes unknown." In a nice exterior episode, the peasants dance in the Tyrolean village for Irena as she takes a carriage ride with Fedor. Then, just before the couple can be married, Fedor staggers into the house one morning, claiming he collapsed at the castle the previous night and sporting two puncture wounds on his neck. "Vampires!" screams fat Annie (June Gittelson), a maid, running out of the room.

The next scene is set in Borotyn castle. Although only a year has passed, the formerly elegant estate is a disaster; there is a giant spider web, along with the usual Browning menagerie. And there, descending the staircase, with a candle in hand (just as he did in *Dracula*), watching a fluttering bat, is Bela Lugosi, as Count Mora. With him, in her shroud by Adrian, is Carroll Borland as Luna. The Gothic theatricality of the two players is

Gothic decadence: Carroll Borland and Bela Lugosi as the cursed Moras.

wonderful, and they look like the melancholy prince and mad Ophelia in the Hades company of *Hamlet*.

Browning marvelously captured what the *Vampires of Prague* shooting script described:

> Descending the stairs are two corpse-like creatures—Count Mora and Luna.... On Count Mora's forehead is plainly visible the frightful self-

inflicted wound by which he brought his life to an end. Luna, her pale beauty unmarred by the ravages of death, walks beside him—her soft gray shroud trailing behind her. The sound of scurrying claws and feet on the floor below indicates that everything with life and blood is fleeing from them to safety . . . across the floor scurry eight or ten large beetle-like insects and disappear in the cracks between the floor and wall.

Borland remembers creating the Luna look: the women's makeup department had claimed it "couldn't do anything" with Carroll's face, so they sent her to the men's makeup department. There they created an adaptation of Lugosi's face ("which was very much like mine, anyway," says Carroll). One day, as debates went on about what to do with Carroll's long, straight hair, she parted it in the middle.

"Bill Tuttle said, 'That's it!'" remembers Carroll. "'Part it in the middle and leave it down, hanging on either side of your face!' Well, now it's the classic vampire face, with the hair that way."

Tuttle later became head of MGM's makeup department and won an honorary Oscar for his work on Metro's *7 Faces of Dr. Lao* (1964).

The vampire father and daughter wander out of the castle; a servant couple, passing in a carriage, see Luna and the two are terrified. (The female servant, Maria, is played by Leila Bennett, a hard-faced, Brooklynese character actress who had also whined in Warner/First National's *Doctor X* and Paramount's *Terror Aboard.*) Then the father and daughter stalk the home of the heroine, who wanders out to the patio. . . . Luna wolfishly attacks her throat, as Count Mora grins in evil approval.

Enter Professor Zelen—Lionel Barrymore. "There's no more foul or relentless enemy of man in the occult world than this dead/alive creature spewed up from the grave!" hams the actor. When Barrymore suffered a disaster on Broadway as *Macbeth* in 1921, a critic for *The Forum* wrote that nothing could explain Lionel's performance "except that Mr. Barrymore not only believed Macbeth as Shakespeare conceived him insane, but Shakespeare and the audience insane as well." Perhaps Lionel felt the same way about Professor Zelen, Tod Browning, and the audience for *Mark of the Vampire.* Barrymore's venerable presence and hambone do enliven the endless dialogue as Zelen lectures the same three-credit course on vampirism that slowed down *Dracula*, ordering bat thorn hung around the house and wheezing his hoary dialogue. (Is Lionel better as Zelen than his brother John would have been? Probably. By 1935, the shockingly dissipated "Jack" would have probably delivered his vampire exposition with tooth-baring and sucking sounds.)

Meanwhile, Baron Otto discovers that the old castle has a new tenant—Sir Karell Borotyn! The baron believes it is Sir Karell's signature on the deed, and Baron Otto and Neumann set out for the graveyard to see if Sir Karell's corpse is still in its coffin.

The men peer into the tomb. It is empty. In a marvelous scripted touch, a large dog (or is it a wolf?) lopes behind the two men. And there, peering through the trees at them, is the almost luminous corpse of Sir Karell, flanked by Bela's Count Mora, the Count's face shining like a nightmarish harvest moon. On this ghoulish highlight, *Mark of the Vampire* has reached its midpoint.

And it will be no surprise to most readers that all these ghoulish antics, of course, are a hoax (as they were in *London After Midnight*), played out by actors contriving to trick Hersholt's murderous Baron Otto into revealing his guilt. Many film historians have analyzed this absurdity: actors masquerading all day and night in a decaying castle, never dropping character in hopes that somebody might peek in a window and see them spooking around, running up outrageous time and expense as they haunt a graveyard, stalk around the countryside, and even pounce on the in-on-the-joke heroine.

One of the most disturbing elements of *Mark of the Vampire* is Browning's desperate clinging to the flaccid mystery plot of *London After Midnight* and the fossilized drawing room style of *Dracula*. Not only had Endore and Schubert revamped the screenplay, but MGM had hired H. S. Kraft, Samuel Ornitz, and even the ubiquitous John L. Balderston (*Dracula, Frankenstein, The Mummy, Bride of Frankenstein*, et al.) to supply "additional dialogue." However, rather than taking the vampire into brave new territory, (as James Whale was doing with Karloff's monster in *Bride of Frankenstein*), Browning was lost in the shadows of previous works, too burnt-out to vitalize any new inspirations. Paying morbid homage to his previous works, draining the blood from his own earlier movies—Tod Browning, vampire.

And sadly, as *Mark of the Vampire* went on shooting, Browning adopted a catch-all phrase in dealing with any and all production problems—a barb that showed just how much this man was lost in his own past: "Mr. Chaney would have done it better."

●

> *Mark of the Vampire* is sort of my other life! I loved it. It's something that's not me anymore, a completely different person. My daughter says it was so strange for her to watch *Mark of the Vampire* and realize she was looking at me younger than she is now.
> —Carroll Borland

The adventure of playing Luna in *Mark of the Vampire*, acting with the great celebrities, enjoying the grand MGM ambience, is still vivid for Carroll Borland. She loved working every day with the stars:

So there I was with Barrymore, Atwill, Hersholt, and Lugosi—and it was like a little intellectual club that we had. I was reading Ludwig's *Napoleon* at the time, and these were European gentlemen, most of them, brought up on Napoleonic history. So we would have wonderful talks and arguments, and we had our own little clique. It was fun, because they didn't treat me as an impertinent young female. I was a *part* of this group, discussing things. It was a marvelous situation. And I learned a lot from them.

One of the most intriguing aspects of *Mark of the Vampire* was the new relationship between "Little Carroll" and her now-married "tame black panther." He had become her "Dutch uncle" whom Carroll now called "Mr. Lugosi":

> Still—on *Mark of the Vampire*, Bela was kind and friendly and helpful and indulgent to me. He also had a nice sense of humor. I remember we waited all day once as they put up a door we had to go through. I don't know what held it up, but after about two hours of sitting there, I said, "What do you think they're doing?" And Bela said, "Carroll, I think they're aging the door!" He was very avuncular, very formal, and always kept his eye on me. So it was very easy, and free—and a lot of fun.

Probably Carroll's most infamous memory of *Mark of the Vampire* is the night Lillian Lugosi drove her home, and Bela and Carroll, tired from a day of haunting MGM, kept on their makeup. A truck driver transporting a crate of chickens pulled up beside the Lugosi car and gazed over at Count Mora with his bullet wound in the head and Luna in the back seat. After performing "the most beautiful double take" Carroll has ever seen, the driver lost control of his truck and drove right up onto the sidewalk— the chickens screaming in terror.

Carroll remembers laughing so hard, "I couldn't stand it!" The vampire in the front seat, however, kept a straight face. "Why did he do that?" deadpanned Bela Lugosi.

At Universal, Jimmy Whale, elegant as ever with his cheroot and Byronic poses, was enjoying a mad, irreverent romp on *Bride of Frankenstein*—portraying Karloff's monster as a Christ symbol, encouraging Ernest Thesiger to play the evil Pretorius like a satanic old queen, mandating Valerie Hobson to wear her satin bridal gown with no lingerie beneath it, blueprinting a crazy, epic creation sequence for the bride, conferring with Franz Waxman about the epic musical score. Production candids show Whale in all his sartorial splendor grinning wickedly at his monster and having the skeleton's ball of his life as he blissfully ran over schedule and budget.

At MGM, *Mark of the Vampire* also ran over schedule and budget. The few production shots of Tod Browning show a crumpled, lethargic-looking man; Carroll Borland remembers him wearing loud clothes and smoking cigarettes, looking like a "race-track character."

In the second half of *Mark of the Vampire,* the butler Jan (Ivan Simpson, 1875–1951, the Scot who formerly ran Warners's acting school and was a friend of Karloff's, even sculpting a bust of "dear Boris") launches a flashback in which Lugosi's Count Mora invades the house, and Baron Otto sees the resurrected Sir Karell strolling in the night with Count Mora. Sir Karell begins playing the old organ in Castle Borotyn (where a new, wizened little ghoul, referred to in the script as "the other vampire," has joined the show). In the movie's most famous vignette Luna, with wondrous vampire wings, flies down from the castle rafters as Hersholt and Atwill peer in the window—a marvelously macabre shot that still enchants audiences. Says Carroll Borland:

> Well, to me, the main thing in *Mark of the Vampire* is the flying sequence. I love it! It happens so fast, if you drop your handkerchief and pick it up, it's over, but still, that's what people talk about. And of course, that wasn't trick photography—I was literally doing it.
>
> They hired a jockey as a stand-in for me, because to fix the lights exactly, someone had to be there. It was about the height of a telephone pole, with a special flying harness I wore, and the great big wings and all. But the man they hired got airsick—he couldn't stand it—so I took over. I said, "Well, I don't mind," and they would just hang me high up there and let me dangle until they got everything focused properly. I thought it was a terribly exciting thing to do—it was fun!
>
> But the landing—that really was funny. The men who were landing me—one was on the body part and the other was on the tail, so to speak—they didn't have sense enough to realize my feet had to come down first. So the two would land me together—right on my belly, and I'd go skidding. It was very uncomfortable. But finally they got the idea that even bats land feet-first, I guess.

"Surround the place! Set fire to it!" suggests the panicking Baron Otto back at the house.

"Search for them!" opts the professor. "Find their corpse-like bodies. . . . Their heads must be severed," leers Barrymore, his eyebrows going into a pagan mating dance, "with one clean stroke, and a sprig of bat thorn placed within the gaping wound!"

Luna lures Irena to the castle; Fedor, unaware of the charade, tries to save his beloved as Luna attacks her. The scene gave Borland her one vivid memory of Tod Browning.

"I want you to turn around and snarl like a wolf and growl," said Browning.

"Oh no, that's not the way it is at all!" said Carroll.

Today, she laughs at her impertinence, but she also knows she was right: she had read *Dracula,* she knew about the "Japanese mask" concept and the hiss. So Carroll formed the square mouth, and emitted the hiss. "That works," said the laconic Browning. Indeed, it has become part of the folklore of the movie vampire.

Finally, as the ghoulish Sir Karell plays the organ, Irena cracks. "He looks so much like Father!" she exclaims, now letting the audience in on the charade. The black cat's out of the bag for everyone but Fedor—and Otto, whom Zelen has been hypnotizing in the castle cellar. "Everything is getting cloudy.... It's one year ago."

The climax (or, actually, anticlimax) unfolds. Irena forces herself to cooperate, along with Jan the butler, as the hypnotized Baron Otto reenacts his crime. We learn of Sir Karell's approval of Irena's marriage to Fedor, Otto's desire to wed Irena himself, Otto's drugging of Sir Karell's wine, when he warmed a glass with a flame and took a pair of scissors, preparing to attack Sir Karell's jugular.

"Stop!" commands Barrymore's Zelen. Atwill's inspector apprehends the murderous Otto, whom the professor snaps out of his hypnotized state. "Sir Karell" drags off Jean Hersholt's baron, yet another horror film victim of mad, unrequited love.

"I don't get the idea of his heating the glass," questions Atwill's inspector.

"Why, to cup him with—to cup him of his blood," says Barrymore's professor, "that hot glass over the wound creates a powerful suction." He thus evocatively explains the mysterious draining of the blood.

"Hmm!" responds Atwill.

Allan's Irena apologizes to Wadsworth's Fedor for not having let him in on the game—"They were afraid that you wouldn't let me go through with it."

And now comes the infamous tag of *Mark of the Vampire.* There is Bela Lugosi, parading about with flourish; there is Carroll Borland, removing her Luna makeup. A theatrical trunk nearby bears the legend, *Luna, the Bat Woman.*

"This vampire business—it has given me a great idea for a new act. Luna, in the new act, I will be the vampire. Did you watch me? I gave *all* of me! I was greater than any *real* vampire!"

"Sure, sure," laughs Borland, "but get off your makeup!"

"Yes," sneers the unnamed ghoul, now in work clothes, "and help me with some of this packing!"

A zinger at the expense of the film's most demonic presence. There is no such thing as vampires, and Bela Lugosi is a hambone. On such a prosaic note, *Mark of the Vampire* ends with a few wisps of finale music.

"We had *believed* in it!" laments Carroll Borland of *Mark of the Vampire.* Apparently Browning had kept his plan to reuse the *London After*

Midnight denouement secret even from Guy Endore ("Guy was so furious!" remembers Miss Borland), as well as Lugosi, who shared Carroll's distaste for the trick finale. Indeed, most of the pages of the script detailing the ending are dated January 18, almost a full week after *Mark of the Vampire* began shooting, so it is very possible that the whole company of *Mark of the Vampire* were well into playing their roles before they became aware of the hoax.

Carroll desperately tried to persuade Browning to accept a variation. Why not have a telegram arrive from the vaudevillians apologizing for *not* arriving? Vampires after all! A trick to a trick ending, and one that would have respected the supernatural aspects of the film. Tod Browning, of course, would have none of it.

"We had done something in *Mark of the 'Vamp'* that had an 'otherworld' quality," Borland emotionally remembers, "and it was cut out from under us at the end."

In Charles Higham's 1970 book *Hollywood Cameramen,* James Wong Howe remembers *Mark of the Vampire:*

> Tod Browning, for whom I made *Mark of the Vampire,* was quite a character. . . . He was one of the old school who didn't know much about the camera. He had the actors play "at" the camera instead of moving around it, so the picture was very stagy, and he used cutting to get him through. . . . Bela Lugosi was funny; he lived the part of the vampire.

Bride of Frankenstein, which had started shooting ten days before *Mark of the Vampire,* was still merrily rolling along at Universal when Browning wrapped his Metro movie on February 20, 1935. The final cost for *Mark of the Vampire* was $305,177.90 ($96,443 over budget), and the number of shooting days was 34 (10 days over schedule).

Although MGM sold *Mark of the Vampire* as an "A" attraction, compare its production to Metro's most celebrated 1935 shows:

- *David Copperfield:* cost, $1,073,000; shooting days, 69.
- *A Tale of Two Cities:* cost, $1,232,000; shooting days, 70.
- *Mutiny on the Bounty:* cost, $1,905,000; shooting days, 88.

More tellingly, compare *Mark of the Vampire* to Universal's *Bride of Frankenstein,* which completed shooting March 7, 1935 (following a temporary shutdown to await the arrival of O. P. Heggie, who had been busy at RKO and would play the saintly blind hermit). *Bride's* cost: $397,023.79 ($103,273.79 over budget); shooting days, 46 (10 days over schedule).

Finally, *Bride of Frankenstein,* of course, boasted Franx Waxman's classic score, with its leitmoifs for the major characters and thrilling creation music. Curiously, the *Mark of the Vampire* pressbook features a story on the "music to scare people" that MGM orchestral director Herbert Stothart had devised for the film. The key players even reportedly had their own representative instruments (à la Prokoviev's *Peter and the Wolf*): the bassoon for Barrymore, violins for Elizabeth Allan, a French horn for Lugosi, a muted trumpet for Atwill, a cello for Hersholt, a flute for Carroll Borland—even a saxophone for Jessie Ralph's midwife! But this delightful idea never made it into the picture; save for the opening peasant ballad and the Tyrolean wedding dance, *Mark of the Vampire* would go into national release without any musical score at all.

There was one area, however, where *Mark of the Vampire* exceeded *Bride of Frankenstein* in expense: veteran director Browning earned $31,023.44, James Whale, $24,640.

> Let no one leave! . . . I hereby summon to this place next week every person within the sound of my voice. You shall be judges of this eerie conspiracy.
> —Bela Lugosi, narrating the trailer
> for *Mark of the Vampire*

By mid–March 1935 MGM was ready to preview *Mark of the Vampire*. More frightening for Metro than Count Mora and Luna was Universal's injunction to block the release of *Mark of the Vampire*—claiming it was a rip-off of the Laemmles' prized *Dracula*. Universal legally attacked, but Browning's stylistic repetitions went right by the lawyers, and the trick ending saved the day. MGM was free to release *Mark of the Vampire*. Bela Lugosi, still in a glow from his Metro engagement, returned to Universal for one of his greatest roles—Poe-obsessed Dr. Richard Vollin in Universal's Karloff and Lugosi chiller for 1935, *The Raven*.

"*Mark of Vampire* good," headlined *The Hollywood Reporter*, March 23, 1935:

> A medieval horror story that turns into a 1935 first rate murder mystery. While the horror is on, it's done with a capital "H," good for plenty of squeals and hysterical giggles. It's well-produced, well-acted, well-directed by that old master of the screaming thrill, Tod Browning. . . . Lionel Barrymore is sinisterly correct as the Professor. . . . Bela Lugosi is just elegant as Count Mora. Lionel Atwill is a demmed clever Inspector. Jean Hersholt, in a good, fat part, gives a good fat performance.

"Direction, first-rate. Photography, fine," reported *Film Daily* in its March 28, 1935, edition. It is here, however, that the greatest mystery of *Mark of the Vampire* looms: the trade reviews were seeing the *first cut* of the picture.

Over the years, the myth has blossomed that *Mark of the Vampire* was (in original form) Tod Browning's 85-minute masterpiece, so truly frightening that uptight MGM, paranoid after *Freaks,* desperately sliced nearly 25 minutes from the release print, including the incest lore of Count Mora and Luna. However, thanks to the shooting script (generously provided me by writer/historian Bill Littman), studio archival material (kindly made available to me by Karl Thiede and Buddy Barnett), surviving stills, and the Call Bureau Service cast list, it is possible to reconstruct what is missing from *Mark of the Vampire.*

First of all, the *Film Daily* trade review indeed records *Mark of the Vampire*'s running time at 85 minutes. This must have been a typo; MGM records list *Mark of the Vampire*'s first cut at 6800', which computes into 75 minutes. Studio records validate that, in preparing *Mark of the Vampire* for national release, the studio cut the film to 5570' — the 61-minute version that survives today. So, what was featured in the 14 minutes cut from *Mark of the Vampire?*

1. Originally, in the film's opening, old witch Jessie Ralph (last seen in the release print scuttling out of the cemetery after catching her skirt on the gravedigger's rake) rushes to her "crazy old tumbledown, weather beaten shack, with a sick fence reeling around it, to which is hung drunkenly a crooked sign reading: Midwife" (page 2 of the shooting script). Inside, sleeping when she should be watching her mother's bubbling cauldron, is the witch's daughter—an albino.

"You lazy heathen!" cries the witch, slapping the albino, who screams and "blinks at her mother out of frightened pink eyes." The witch blames her daughter for all her "good medicine" being ruined:

> Now if Politz' cow dies, it's me he'll blame—me, trudgin' the mountains searchin' for roots and herbs—to put a crust of bread in your mouth!

The witch's black cat arches its back, spits "venomously," and the vampire bat flutters outside the shack. "The saints protect us! A vampire! He's followed me!" shrieks the witch as she hangs bat thorn and the daughter crosses herself. "I'll teach you!" rants the witch. "Leavin' doors and windows unprotected at dark—when the fiends of the castle are out."

The witch has grabbed a hearth-broom, and as the scene ends, she is beating the daylights out of her poor albino daughter, "with good whacks." A still of Jessie Ralph, threatening the anonymous actress playing the albino, survives.

2. Shortly afterwards came a scene introducing Donald Meek's Dr. Doskil treating a sick woman (Eily Malyon) on a peasant farm. The grandmother of the household (Zeffie Tilbury, one of the eccentric English biddies in Universal's *Werewolf of London*) was "carrying a whining baby in

her arms (another older child dragging at her skirts) . . . hanging a sprig of wolf's-claw in the window."

"Don't go, Doctor!" pleads the sick woman. "We're alone here with the children. Please wait till my husband comes from the village!" Doskil nervously refuses to stay, and the grandmother says, "No daughter—don't delay him. Doctor Doskil is right. It's not safe to be out with the evils of darkness." Just then the peasant farmer arrives home ("his horses sweating as he dashes to home safely before darkness sets in").

The Call Bureau cast list sheet for the finished film notes the work of Malyon and Tilbury; a still of Tilbury, with a child, survives.

3. There was originally a musical comedy relief scene, outside in the courtyard of the village inn, where Prokop, "the fat man" (365 pound Robert Greig), tried to teach the boys and girls of the village to dance as they furtively snickered. "Look at that Prokop," said Meek's Doskil, "graceful like a hippopotamus! Still thinks he's the Ballet Master at the opera in Prague!" The villagers observing the scene include a deaf man with an ear trumpet (Christian Rub) and a card player (Torben Meyer, who appeared in such films as *Murders in the Rue Morgue*, *The Black Room*, *Frankenstein Meets the Wolf Man*, and *The Fly*). They discuss Miss Borotyn's marriage:

> DEAF MAN: Oh! Married in the morning.
> CARD PLAYER: No—no! Out of mourning—for her father. Dead a year—Wednesday.
> DEAF MAN: Dance till Wednesday? Long time.
> CARD PLAYER: No!—rehearsing dance for wedding—the *wedding*.
> DEAF MAN (chuckling): Oh!—bedding. Bedding—course they'll want bedding—

Considering that Tod Browning's "light comic touch" would have stunned an elephant, *Mark of the Vampire* must benefit from this excision. A long-shot of the singing, dancing villagers remains in the film in the carriage scene of Irena and Fedor (missing from the original script, this scene was presumably filmed at the last minute or during the retake days and originally dovetailed with the comic relief in the first-cut print).

The names of Mr. Greig, Mr. Meyer, and Mr. Rub all appear in the Call Bureau Service cast list.

4. In the first entrance of Count Mora and Luna at Borotyn Castle, *Mark of the Vampire* also originally introduced the little "other vampire" (identified in Richard Bojarski's *The Films of Bela Lugosi* as James Bradbury, Jr.). The script detailed:

> corpse-like man on couch—as the faint glow from the candle falls on his face, he seems to come to life. . . . Into the scene come Count Mora and Luna. Count Mora holds the candle closer to the figure on the couch,

who seems oblivious of their presence, still staring into space. He gets to his feet, and as if on a quest of his own—exits out of scene.

This was also an unfortunate cut, as the "corpse-like man's" sudden appearance in the latter half of the film seems to come entirely out of the blue. A still of the three players acting out the above-described action survives.

5. Also probably excised from the first cut were an introductory shot of Irena and Otto on the terrace of Borotyn castle, watching a peasant farmer (possibly the husband of the sick woman) cruelly lashing his horses to get home before dark; a scene of Fedor, choo-chooing like a train, intoning like a tour guide, and singing like a gondolier as he tries to cheer up Irena; a scene of Fedor running for his train, falling, and knocking himself unconscious near Borotyn castle; a shot of fat Annie, the maid, practicing dancing for the wedding and making the dishes and silverware rattle; a shopping trip to Prague, where Otto and Irena run into Inspector Neumann and discuss the case; and a scene in the castle, where Barrymore's Zelen studies a bat under his magnifying glass and professor and rodent eyeball each other.

6. Finally, many lines of dialogue were cut from the film, mostly trimmed from the opening and endings of scenes, which explains the rather choppy flow of the film; these excisions must have been made by MGM in a frantic try to improve the film's deadly pace. This action wiped out the role of the bus driver (Baron Hesse), originally seen conferring with the innkeeper; most of the cuts, however, abbreviated boring dialogue exchanges that still plague *Mark of the Vampire* today.

There was at least one unfortunate excision involving Count Mora and Luna. In the inquest scene, the coroner mentioned "Count Mora and his daughter—who had been dead and buried these three hundred years." A few lines later, asked to tell how his friends could identify the count and Luna, the innkeeper replied: "By the wound on his forehead—where he shot himself after he strangled his daughter!" At least this would have explained the hole in Bela's head!

So aside from the witch and her albino daughter, the atmospheric peasant farm scene, and the introduction of the other vampire, most of the cuts suffered by *Mark of the Vampire* actually were to its benefit, shearing it of silly comic relief and paring down the sort of static dialogue recitations that so notoriously crippled Browning's *Dracula*. Most disillusioning of all is the lack of any exciting episodes involving Count Mora and Luna, and the total absence of the infamous incest background. While this must have been hinted in Endore's scenario (and shared with the actors), there is no mention at all in the shooting script of this kinky legend; indeed,

Tod Browning (in beret) and James Wong Howe line up Lugosi, Carroll Borland, and James Bradbury, Jr., for one of the "cut" scenes from *Mark of the Vampire*.

Carroll Borland recalls that only in posing for a few stills did she and Bela manage to suggest this perversity.

One last curiosity: while Lugosi spoke one line in the script of *Mark of the Vampire,* he ironically narrated the trailer, running off at the mouth for the full minute the trailer ran. The trailer opens with a shot of Luna flying in the castle that is not in the release print, yet even this is a disappointment. Browning has her flying *away* from the camera, her face not seen. Charming as Luna's shrouded derriere might be, it is a bizarre angle from which to film a flying vampire.

"*Please!* Let your friends learn the thrilling climax for themselves!" pleaded the MGM ad copy as Metro landed a show business coup for the new Tod Browning shocker: at 6:00 P.M. on May 1, 1935, *Mark of the Vampire* enjoyed a world premiere on Broadway at *both* the 750-seat Rialto and the 1735-seat Mayfair theatres. "Too Much Horror for One Theatre" proclaimed the ad poster in the *New York Times,* which gave top-billing to "Bela (Dracula) Lugosi" (an honor that Lugosi was proud to report to the press). Frank S. Nugent of the *New York Times* critiqued:

[The film] manages, through use of every device seen in *Dracula* and one or two besides, to lay a sound foundation for childish nightmares. Even the adults in the audience may feel a bit skittery. . . . *Mark of the Vampire* should catch the beholder's attention and hold it, through chills and thrills. . . . Like most good ghost stories, it's a lot of fun, even though you don't believe a word of it.

Mark of the Vampire lured the crowds during a spring when Broadway was exalting horror. On May 9, 1935, Universal's *Werewolf of London* replaced the MGM film at the Rialto, although *Mark of the Vampire* carried on at the Mayfair. And that same night, three blocks north of the Mayfair, the 5886-seat Roxy Theatre on 50th Street hosted a special preview of a new Universal release: *Bride of Frankenstein*, which officially opened at the Roxy the next day.

Karloff's monster and Lugosi's vampire were competing on the Great White Way.

"On Broadway *Bride of Frankenstein* . . . is grabbing the business," reported *Variety*, "so far outdistancing everything else . . . there is no comparison."

Contrary to contemporary reports that *Mark of the Vampire* was a flop, the film earned a domestic gross of $339,000, plus a foreign gross of $224,000, tallying a world-wide gross of $563,000. When all was said, done, and paid for, *Mark of the Vampire* provided MGM a net profit of $54,000.

Carroll Borland discovered an ambivalent feeling toward the movie (and herself) at MGM, however, as she tried to perpetuate a career. She believes her bit as an Eurasian girl in the Gable and Harlow *China Seas* ended up on the cutting room floor; she auditioned for a part in *A Tale of Two Cities* but failed to win it. She reported to Universal to play a Russian countess in *Sutter's Gold,* but almost all her part was cut ("I recently saw *Sutter's Gold* for the first time, and there I am, at age 21, sitting in a corner, eating shish kebob!") After a bit in Universal's *Flash Gordon* serial, Carroll joined the Federal Theatre and toured Hollywood playhouses. The curse of *Mark of the Vampire* seemed to loom over her:

> Lugosi was right: even though I had played Shakespeare, and had been a staff artist on CBS Radio in San Francisco before *Mark of the Vampire,* I was seen as a slinky vamp who couldn't read lines and was good at haunting houses.

Tod Browning had slightly redeemed himself—*Mark of the Vampire,* at least, had made money—so MGM gave him a "go" for *The Devil-Doll,* to star Lionel Barrymore. The script, based on Abraham Merritt's 1933 novel *Burn Witch Burn!* would officially be credited to Garrett Fort (who had worked with Browning on the screenplay of *Dracula*), Erich von Stroheim, and Guy Endore (who had entertained such high hopes for *Mark of the Vampire*).

> Delightful, intriguing tale of vampires terrorizing rural village: Inspector Atwill, vampire expert Barrymore investigate. Beautifully done, with an incredible ending.
> —Leonard Maltin's review of *Mark of the Vampire,* in *TV Movies* (1988 edition)

> This'll either irk or delight you, depending on your reaction to its very controversial ending. I was irked.
> —Mike Clark's video review of *Mark of the Vampire, USA Today,* October 23, 1987

How can any devotee of Bela Lugosi, after enduring *The Ape Man, Bela Lugosi Meets a Brooklyn Gorilla,* and the inevitable *Plan 9 from Outer Space,* dislike *Mark of the Vampire?* The MGM gloss, the powerhouse cast, the atmospheric fancies of Browning all prove why this oft-bashed director still deserves a certain respect. *Mark of the Vampire* is in many ways a dazzler of a horror movie. Lugosi's Count Mora is wonderfully full of the Gothic glamour of Bela in his prime. And Carroll Borland's Luna, with those unholy eyes, that sexy stride, and that immortal hiss, created one of the classic images of the Golden Age of Horror—one that reportedly inspired Charles Addams' Morticia (and one ripped-off over the decades by Vampira through Elvira).

Indeed, the trouble with *Mark of the Vampire* is not in its Metro trappings or its ghoulish accoutrements; its sin is at its core. Any Broadway moviegoer who took in *Bride of Frankenstein* at the Roxy and *Mark of the Vampire* at the Mayfair the same week saw the vision of two legendary directors—each taking the horror genre down two wildly different paths.

In *Bride of Frankenstein,* Whale audaciously crucified Karloff's monster on a pole, had him laugh, smoke a cigar, drink wine, talk, cry— even heartbreakingly woo his horrific bride. Christ symbol, burlesque comic, tragic lover: the monster played them all in *Bride,* and miraculously—thanks to Karloff's genius—he played them all beautifully. In *Mark of the Vampire,* however, Browning not only refuses to break new haunting ground for Lugosi's vampire; he actually condemns Count Mora (and Carroll Borland's Luna) back to silent film. Only after breaking character can they break silence.

On *Bride,* Whale directs his whole cast on a crazy, stylized level: Clive's tormented Frankenstein, Thesiger's diabolically swishy Pretorius,

Lanchester's dainty Mary Shelley and horrifically vain monster's mate all remain memorable; even the ingenue, 17-year-old Valerie Hobson (as Frankenstein's pious Elizabeth), plays on such an arch, hysterical pitch that she becomes Gothic herself—a Colin Clive in drag. There's no uniformity in Browning's *Mark of the Vampire* company. Barrymore's wheezy Macbeth and Atwill's attack dog of an inspector collide with Elizabeth Allan's soignee poseuse and Henry Wadsworth's Kentucky little theatre hero—all smashing headlong into Lugosi and Borland's true Hollywood Gothic. And Browning's supporting cast—Ivan Simpson as Jan the butler, Leila Bennett as the maid, Michael Visaroff as the innkeeper—can't begin to compete with the glorious eccentricity of such *Bride* goblins (and Whale favorites) as screaming maid Una O'Connor, leering graverobber Dwight Frye, and pompous burgomaster E. E. Clive.

One of the comparisons between *Bride of Frankenstein* (which, incidentally, nicely survived about 15 minutes of prerelease cuts of its own) and *Mark of the Vampire* presents an awesome irony: Lugosi had rejected the monster role in *Frankenstein* (1931), claiming the mute role was a humiliating comedown after his success as *Dracula*. Now, in *Bride of Frankenstein*, Karloff's monster spoke his famous "44-word vocabulary," while in *Mark of the Vampire*, Lugosi's count spoke only at the fadeout.

The true difference between *Bride of Frankenstein* and *Mark of the Vampire*, however, is a profound one. In Whale's film, Karloff's monster has a *soul*. Humanity is the true monster as Whale bitterly scorns the real world and creates his own fantastic one. But in *Mark of the Vampire*, the vampires have no souls (not even lost ones); they are fakes. It is the sappy lovers who are real, while the children of the night are stripped of makeup, their ghoulish robes packed away with a wink and a fadeout laugh.

In *Bride of Frankenstein*, James Whale gleefully created his own "monster," merrily setting it loose to mock and challenge and shout "Boo!" at the conventions of 1935 Hollywood. In *Mark of the Vampire*, Tod Browning and MGM had the opportunity to unleash a movie that would become their own cinema "vampire," an alluring succubus that might have haunted the folklore of the terror genre, glamourously, seductively. But under the Metro cosmetics, the long-hair vampire wig, the false incisors, *Mark of the Vampire* is no succubus, but an aged, corseted flapper. And while she giggles self-consciously at her own exposure, we, the once-tantalized audience, can't help but feel deceived and cheated.

Via Tod Browning, MGM had cavalierly stripped away the mystique of the vampire, all the while vigilantly guarding the wig of Harlow and the dentures of Gable. Glamour, after all, is one of our most necessary illusions.

But then again, so is horror.

Tod Browning made two more films for MGM.

The Devil-Doll (1936), starred Lionel Barrymore, who played much of the role as an old lady, "Madame Mandelip," à la Chaney in *The Unholy Three,* and provided a terrific takeoff on his sister Ethel. The film offered marvelous miniature people special effects, and as a bonus, featured a score of *Bride of Frankenstein*'s Franz Waxman (who had left Universal to join the Metro fold). It proved to be Browning's most successful film of the 1930s, turning a modest profit of $68,000. Browning was still lost in the fog of his past, however. On May 20, 1939, Browning began shooting MGM's *Miracles for Sale,* a mystery about stage magicians starring Robert Young and Florence Rice, in which he planned to transform Henry Hull (Universal's *Werewolf of London*) into the "new Lon Chaney." The public, perfectly satisfied with its own Karloff and Lugosi, could not have cared less; *Miracles for Sale* lost $39,000 and was Browning's final work. Wealthy from real estate investments, the director retired to his lovely home, #31 of the famous Malibu colony.

"The Edgar Allan Poe of the Screen" would outlive Lionel Atwill (wasted by scandal and cancer in 1946), Lionel Barrymore (who died of a heart attack in 1954, terrified to the end that he would go to jail for delinquent taxes), and Bela Lugosi, whose heart attack was a merciful end in 1956 to final years of alcohol, drug addiction, and various other miseries (Lugosi was buried at Holy Cross Cemetery in his Dracula cape). Browning also survived his old boss Louis B. Mayer, who died October 29, 1957, and James Whale, who had drowned himself that spring.

Mysterious, obscure, totally forgotten by Hollywood, Browning finally died October 6, 1962, in Los Angeles. He was cremated at the Chapel of the Pacific in Santa Monica, and his ashes are interred in Rosedale Cemetery on Washington Boulevard, east of the old MGM lot.

Browning's death certificate revealed that he had contracted cancer of the larynx, had undergone a tracheotomy, and had died of stroke. The certificate also disclosed that the mystery man was 82 years old, had been a veteran of World War I, was a widower, and still owned his Malibu home, although at the time of his death, he was living with (and presumably cared for by) a Mrs. Harold Snow of 300 South Westgate Avenue, Los Angeles. Mrs. Snow apparently had only vague knowledge of the life's work of the Edgar Allan Poe of the screen. The informant for his death certificate, she listed his profession as "actor."

In later years, Carroll Borland gave up acting, wrote for radio, earned a doctorate in education, and taught at Pacific Oaks College. But she never forgot her "other life" of *Mark of the Vampire,* nor, of course, Bela Lugosi. She dressed up as Luna for the Hollywood premiere of Vincent Price's *Tomb of Ligeia* (1965), attending with Price, Vampira, and *Bride of Frankenstein* Elsa Lanchester. She was a devoted member of the Count Dracula Society, encouraged the founding of "The Bela Lugosi Society" in the late 1980s and even played a cameo as a college professor in the recent exploitation film *Scalps* so her daughter could have a film record of her in her 70s to go with *Mark of the Vampire,* showing her in her 20s.

And, of course, Carroll Borland still has, and cherishes, her memories of Bela Lugosi:

> Lugosi's charm was always there, his ability to project himself—and the rest of it was left to the audience. Once I went to a matinee of *Dracula,* in Oakland I think, and the house was only ⅔ full.
>
> If Lugosi were in his prime, and playing *Dracula* at a theatre here now, the line would go around the street twice for tickets!

Mad Love

Studio: MGM; Producer: John W. Considine, Jr.; Director: Karl Freund; Adaptation: Guy Endore (from Florence Crewe-Jones's translation/adaptation of Maurice Renard's novel, *Les Mains d'Orlac*); Screenplay: P. J. Wolfson and John L. Balderston; Cinematography: Chester Lyons and Gregg Toland; Music: Dimitri Tiomkin; Musical Director: Oscar Radin; Art Director: Cedric Gibbons (William A. Horning and Edwin B. Willis, Associates); Wardrobe: Dolly Tree; Recording Director: Douglas Shearer; Editor: Hugh Wynn; Running Time: 68 minutes.

Filmed at MGM Studios, Culver City, California, May 6–June 8, 1935. New York City premiere: Roxy Theatre, August 2, 1935.

The Players: Dr. Gogol (Peter Lorre); Yvonne Orlac (Frances Drake); Stephen Orlac (Colin Clive); Reagan (Ted Healy); Marie (Sarah Haden); Marianne (Isabel Jewell)*; Rollo (Edward Brophy); Prefect of Police Rosset (Henry Kolker); Thief (Harold Huber)*; Dr. Wong (Keye Luke); Henry Orlac (Ian Wolfe); Dr. Marbeau (Charles Trowbridge); Charles (Murray Kinnell); Francoise (Gogol's Housekeeper) (May Beatty); Endore (Rollo Lloyd); Nurse Suzanne (Nell Craig); Taxi Driver (Maurice Brierre); Nurse (Julie Carter); Detective (Christian Frank); Conductor (Hooper Atchley); Detectives (Sam Ash, Robert Graves); Chauffeur (George Davis); Blind Man (Otto Hoffman)*; Lavin (Frank Darien); Drunk (Robert Emmett Keane); Duke (Ramsey Hill); Notary (Carl Stockdale); Doorman (Al Borgato); Frenchman on train with dog (William [Billy] Gilbert); Station Master (Harvey Clark); Fingerprint Man (Alphonz Ethier); Piano Man (Clarence Hummel Wilson); Clerk (Edward Lippy); Detective (Roger Gray); Mother (Sarah Padden); Child Patient (Cora Sue Collins); Gendarme (Russ Powell); Detective (Earl M. Pingree); Policeman (Jacques Vanier); Prince (Mark Lubell); Newsboy (Matty Roubert); Horror Show Patron (Edward Norris); Gendarme Directing Traffic (Rolfe Sedan); Official at Guillotine (Michael Mark).

●

*These actors appeared in footage that was deleted.

First *The Hunchback of Notre Dame*.... Next *The Phantom of
the Opera*.... Then *Dracula* Chilled and Thrilled.... Finally
Frankenstein ... *and now*—The Greatest of Them *all*...
                                  —MGM ad copy for *Mad Love*
                                  (1935)

Mad Love is a virtual feast of joys for the horror film disciple. Indeed,
this 1935 MGM shocker offers so many tantalizing treats via its stars,
director, and cinematography, whips up so mad a brew of Grand Guignol
flourishes with the horror of modern surgical amputations, so indulges
itself in satirical homage to its fellow '30s horror classics, that it becomes
a movie that ultimately and deliriously overdoses itself.

The star trio is glorious: bald, egg-eyed Peter Lorre (in his U.S.
debut) as rhapsodically mad Dr. Gogol, tortured by the macabre credo
"Each man kills the thing he loves"; arch, lovely Frances Drake, the
Golden Age of Horror's most exotic heroine, as Yvonne, star screamer of
Paris's Theatre des Horreurs; gaunt, baroque Colin Clive, Hollywood's
Frankenstein, here as concert pianist Orlac, now a victim of science in a
perverse role reversal of monster maker, ranting of his new, stitched-on
hands (courtesy of a guillotined knife murderer), "they want to kill!"

The direction was by Karl Freund, cinematographer of *Metropolis*,
Dracula, and *Murders in the Rue Morgue* and director of Universal's *The
Mummy*. The adaptation was by Guy *(Mark of the Vampire)* Endore, with
an irreverent rewrite by John L. Balderston, of *Dracula*, *Frankenstein*, *The
Mummy*, *Mark of the Vampire*, and *Bride of Frankenstein*. The production
was MGM art deco gone madly Germanic.

Indeed, *Mad Love* plays almost like a sassy in-joke for horror fans,
paying mock homage to *Frankenstein*, *Freaks*, *Doctor X*, *The Mummy*,
Mystery of the Wax Museum, *The Black Cat*, perhaps even *Werewolf of London* (released days after *Mad Love* began shooting). Research proves the
satire was intentional; the final product shows the joke became so nasty
that it finally blew up in its own face. *Mad Love*'s satire was over the heads
of 1935 moviegoers; its stark horror mixture of Grand Guignol and
dismemberment drove audiences away. The biggest "box office" aspect of
the film—the U.S. debut of a little Hungarian actor who had scored
in Germany's *M* as a child murderer—was hardly irresistible to the
1935 Depression public in love with Shirley Temple. *Mad Love* fell
into Metro purgatory, didn't play television for many years, and only
came back into historical focus after Pauline Kael's vitriolic (if intriguing)
charge that Orson Welles copied *Mad Love* to create the look for *Citizen
Kane*.

Part sublime masterpiece, part incredible misfire, *Mad Love* survives
as one of the most striking horror films of the Golden Age, expressing a

few profound truths not only about the horror genre, but also about horror fans themselves.

●

Anyone can make a good cake if he has the right ingredients.
It all depends on cast, story and circumstances.
—Karl Freund

In 1926 all Europe was agog at the UFa movie *Variety,* directed by E. A. Dupont. The movie revolutionized the worldwide movie industry via its dazzling cinematography; in one bravura episode, the camera swung from a trapeze, showing how an audience looked from the dizzy perspective of a trapeze artist.

Karl Freund, measuring 5'8" and weighing 300 pounds, was not on the trapeze with the camera at the time. Born in Bohemia, January 16, 1890, Freund later claimed that his childish delight at the sight of a locomotive on a movie screen, seemingly roaring right into the audience, was the inspiration for his brilliant contributions to motion pictures. In the 1920s, Freund's cinematography was a legend thanks to such classics as *Der Golem* (co-photographed with Guido Seeber, 1920), *The Last Laugh* (1924), and *Metropolis* (1926); he also was the European producer of Fox's *Sunrise,* which won an Academy Award. By the time the 40-year-old Freund arrived in the U.S. with his wife, just before the '29 stock market crash, his reputation already was assured internationally.

Freund made a pilgrimage to Universal City, California, where fate was kind. "Junior" Laemmle was about to premiere his $1.45 million *All Quiet on the Western Front,* which was directed by Lewis Milestone and filmed by Arthur Edeson, but lacked a satisfactory ending. It was Freund who created the classic "butterfly" finale and shot it; the heartbreaking tag was edited into the film less than 48 hours before its premiere at Hollywood's Carthay Circle Theatre. It was the most unforgettable vignette of an unforgettable picture; *All Quiet on the Western Front* won the Best Picture Academy Award, and Freund, overnight, was Universal's ace cameraman.

After shooting such films as Tod Browning's *Dracula,* Robert Florey's *Murders in the Rue Morgue,* and John Ford's *Air Mail,* Freund won the promotion to movie director, making his debut via Karloff's *The Mummy* (1932). Totally in command of the show, Freund created (with cameraman Charles Stumar) *The Mummy's* dreamy, exotic, sensually nightmarish look, a perfect backdrop for Karloff's lovelorn Im-Ho-Tep. The Egyptian funeral scene, shot at night in California's Red Rock Canyon, was so exquisite that for years rumor claimed Universal had swiped the vignette from an old German silent.

Freund's nickname was "Papa," an odd soubriquet for a man full of the legendary Teutonic wrath and swagger. Perhaps the best bird's-eye view of "Papa" came via the late Zita Johann, magnificent as "Anck-es-en-amon" in *The Mummy*. Johann, who lived in a pre–Revolutionary War mansion near the Hudson River, was a gentle woman with deep religious beliefs and a history for working miracles with handicapped youths. At the mention of Karl Freund's name, 60 years after *The Mummy*, her glorious eyes sparked.

"Oh, that pig!"

Freund sadistically abused Johann on *The Mummy*—everything from threatening her with a nude scene to making sure she didn't get a chair with her name on it on the set to working her so cruelly that late one Saturday night, playing a scene with Karloff, she passed out cold. But Zita's sharpest image of Freund came on the last day of shooting. Universal had saved one of the famous, long-lost reincarnation episodes—Zita Johann as Christian martyr, devoured by lions—for the final day, in case any of the lions chewed not only the scenery, but the leading lady. Zita, in her Christian martyr rags, reported to the coliseum on the back lot. There were the lions. Barricades protected everyone (except Zita) from the beasts. And there, squeezed in a special, custom-built cage ("a very large one," smiled Zita), protected from the lions, raining down commands and abuse from his sanctuary, was Karl "Papa" Freund.

Freund directed several Universal films, such as the 1933 thriller *Madame Spy* (starring Fay Wray) and the 1934 musical *Gift of Gab* (with Karloff and Lugosi in guest star cameos). He returned to Universal cinematography only once (at the request of almighty James Whale) for *The Kiss Before the Mirror* (1933). The lot announced he would direct a lavishly budgeted remake of *Der Golem*, but so great was Freund's reputation that it was only a matter of time before he departed erratic Universal for richer pastures.

The richest beckoned. On Monday, February 4, 1935, *The Hollywood Reporter* announced that the newest director of Metro-Goldwyn-Mayer Studios was Karl Freund. "Starting today he will be attached to John Considine's unit," noted the *Reporter*, "and will specialize in unusual themes, his first probably being an original."

●

Each man kills the thing he loves.
                    —from *Mad Love* (and Oscar Wilde).

Producer John W. Considine, Jr., was quite new to Metro; he had been associate producer of the great hit *Dancing Lady* (1933), and had supervised three 1934 releases: the William Powell/Myrna Loy *Evelyn Prentice,* Carole Lombard's *The Gay Bride,* and the animal saga *Sequoia.* On March 7, 1935 (the day *Bride of Frankenstein* wrapped at Universal), *The Hollywood Reporter* announced Karl Freund's first MGM directing job in the Considine unit: *Mad Love.*

The original source material, of course, was Maurice Renard's novel *Les Mains D'Orlac;* Florence Crewe-Jones provided Metro with the original translation/adaptation. The story had already reached the screen as Austria's 1925 *Orlac Hande,* boasting *The Cabinet of Dr. Caligari*'s Conrad Veidt (as Orlac) and director, Robert Wiene. Considine recognized two bastions for horror fans. First was the legendary "Grand Guignol" Theatre des Horreurs, which had thrived in Rue Chapel, Montmartre, Paris, for many years. The little playhouse presented dramas of mass murder, mob vengeance, and amok hysteria, as actresses screamed on torture devices, "prop blood" poured over the stage, and grotesque heads and figures dangled from the rafters. It was all a toy store for sadists, of which there were presumably many in Paris during the Grand Guignol's little reign of popularity.*

More novel for 1935 audiences was the concept of medical transplants. Many passionately protested the concept, believing that the human soul did exist, after all, within the body. Hence, the grafting of one person's organs or limbs into/onto another person could sap away some of the soul of the donor and mix it with the existent soul of the recipient. To many people, the idea of Orlac becoming a knife murderer after receiving the hands of a convicted killer was not melodrama; it was metaphysics.

First to tackle the scenario for *Mad Love* was Guy Endore, author of the novel *Werewolf of Paris* and first-billed writer on Browning's *Mark of the Vampire.* He was also the source (or perhaps later inspiration) for one of *Mad Love*'s many in-jokes: in the final script, an assistant to the movie's prefect of police is named Endore. (Later studio material lists the character's name as Varsac.) According to the MGM collection at the University of Southern California, Freund worked with Endore on ideas for the early draft.

After receiving Endore's treatment, Considine strangely assigned the continuity and dialogue to P. J. Wolfson, a romance/comedy specialist whose previous MGM assignment had been the Harlow musical, *Reckless.* On Saturday, April 6, 1935, *The Hollywood Reporter* noted that Wolfson was to turn in his work that day, that Considine would read it over the

---

In 1979, the Grand Guignol came back with a vengeance in the Broadway musical Sweeney Todd, The Demon Barber of Fleet Street, which featured music by Stephen Sondheim and starred Angela Lansbury and Len Cariou. The show won a fleet of Tony awards, including Best Musical.

weekend, and that *Mad Love* "looms as a starter week after next, although the leads have not been determined."

Indeed, in MGM's pantheon of stars—Garbo, Gable, Harlow, Tracy, William Powell, Jeanette MacDonald, Nelson Eddy, Wallace Beery, Robert Taylor—who could play mad Dr. Gogol, madness-inspiring Yvonne, and hysterical Stephen Orlac?

The three stars finally selected were each ideal for their roles, and each, strangely, had a great personal irony in playing in *Mad Love*. The April 23, 1935, *Hollywood Reporter* broke major cinema colony news: MGM had engaged Peter Lorre (1904–1964) to make his U.S. bow as Gogol in *Mad Love*. The tiny, moon-faced, pop-eyed Lorre, born Ladislav Loewenstein in Rozsahegy, Hungary, was a veteran of the "Volksbuhne" ("People's Theatre") of Berlin, had won international notoriety in Fritz Lang's 1931 *M* as a pathetic child murderer, hoarding a closet-full of his victim's shoes. Lorre loved telling the story of how, one night after the release of *M*, a mob recognized him and pursued him down a Berlin street. Following playing the master criminal in UFa's science fiction spectacle *F.P.I. Antwortet Nicht* (1933) and starring in Alfred Hitchcock's British *The Man Who Knew Too Much* (1934), Lorre "went Hollywood" with actress wife Cecilia Lovsky, contracting with Columbia to star as Raskolnikov in von Sternberg's *Crime and Punishment*. The picture was delayed, so Lorre grabbed the Metro offer. Warped Dr. Gogol fascinated Lorre, and the young star agreed (reluctantly) to have his head shaved totally bald to play the bizarre part.

It was strange that Lorre should be cast as a surgeon; as Curt *(The Wolf Man)* Siodmak, who wrote *F.P.I. Antwortet Nicht*, remembered in a 1980 interview with the author:

> Peter *really* had a sadistic streak. He liked to go watch operations in the hospital. He really was a freak—he played the same part in life that he played in the pictures. He tried to live up to his screen standards . . . a great character.

"It is not conducive to sound sleep," *Time* magazine would write of Lorre in *Mad Love*, "to watch him operating on little girls."

For Yvonne, MGM had set blonde contractee Virginia Bruce, who had starred on loanout as Monogram's heroine in the 1934 *Jane Eyre* (opposite Colin Clive's Rochester). She was busy supporting Luise Rainer in *Escapade*, however, and rumor forecasted that the role of Yvonne would pass to the beautiful, moon-eyed Frances Drake. A Paramount contractee, Drake had already visited MGM for the Clark Gable/Joan Crawford/ Robert Montgomery *Forsaking All Others*, Metro's big Christmas special of 1934, playing the glamorous vamp who causes Montgomery to leave Crawford literally waiting at the altar.

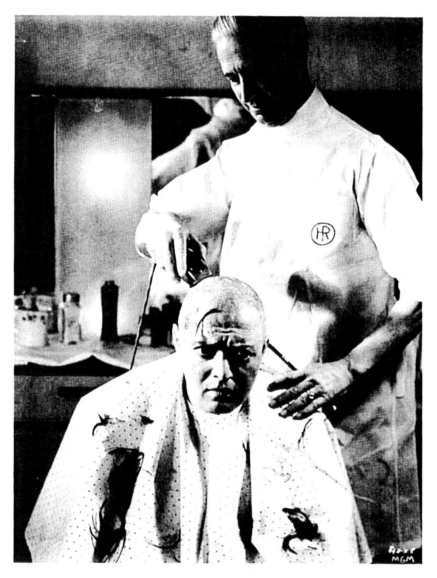

Peter Lorre reluctantly surrenders his hair for *Mad Love*.

"Oh, I'm such a *bitch* in that!" Miss Drake rejoices today.

MGM sent to Paramount for Frances—only to learn she'd been farmed out to Fox for *Orchids to You*. On April 26, 1935, Paramount recalled Drake and sent her to MGM for *Mad Love*. (Ruthelma Stevens inherited Miss Drake's part in *Orchids to You*.)

As for Frances Drake, *Mad Love,* and knives, on Paramount's *The*

Peter Lorre and Frances Drake with alternate title for *Mad Love*.

Trumpet Blows (1934) the adventurous actress had bravely agreed one day on location to pose for knife-thrower Steve Clemente (the "witch king" native of *King Kong*). "He wanted to do my profile," smiles Drake. Clemente was merrily outlining the actress's patrician profile with his knives just as director Stephen Roberts arrived, apoplectically stopping the sideshow. Only later did Drake learn why Clemente's circus and carnival act had ended: he had hit his wife with a knife and killed her.

"Of course, he didn't *mean* to," says Frances Drake.

Finally, to complete the star trio, MGM signed Colin Clive, Henry Frankenstein himself, to play Stephen Orlac. *Bride of Frankenstein* had just premiered at Hollywood's Pantages Theatre on April 20, 1935. The most frightening aspect of James Whale's outrageous fairy tale was Clive's closeups, showing the sad, terrible decay of the brilliant, chainsmoking, alcoholic Englishman. Colin Clive was officially on contract to Warner Bros. in 1935, and MGM borrowed him for the third-billed spot.

Clive's irony in *Mad Love* is the most chilling of all. The actor had trained at the Royal Military Academy to be a soldier—a dream destroyed when his horse fell one day and Clive broke his knee. The old leg injury grew progressively worse over the years, and a fall Clive suffered during *Bride of Frankenstein* didn't help. Not long after *Mad Love* completed shooting, Clive was horrified when doctors warned him they might have to amputate. It was the last demon to agonize this terribly sensitive man, who would drink himself to death less than two years after *Mad Love*'s release.

John Considine, P. J. Wolfson, Guy Endore, and Karl Freund had all met for script conferences in early April 1935. On April 24, 1935, the day after Metro's announcement of Lorre's casting, John L. Balderston reported to MGM to (in the words of the *Reporter*) "polish up dialogue" for *Mad Love*. "Revised by John L. Balderston" read page one after his polish job. The ubiquitous Balderston, with his incredible all-star credits ranging from the play *Dracula* to Hollywood's *Frankenstein*, *The Mummy*, *Mark of the Vampire*, and *Bride of Frankenstein*, mischievously made *Mad Love* a satire, incorporating bits and pieces from his previous adventures in the genre.* Balderston also revised the script with Lorre in mind—at one point calling for the star to employ "his *M* look."

MGM completed casting: Ted Healy, fast-talking, alcoholic vaudeville comic who had split from his backup boys, the Three Stooges, would play hotshot American reporter, Reagan. Isabel Jewell, then Metro's top supporting blonde floozie (probably best-remembered in Capra's *Lost Horizon* for Columbia, 1937), was signed for Marianne, a Parisienne voluptuary whose jewelry thefts intersect with Gogol's madness. May Beatty landed the part of Gogol's drunken old housekeeper, Francoise.

It was in MGM's seemingly Looney Tunes casting of Rollo—guillotined knife murderer whose hands become Orlac's—that the studio truly showed its hand in the fashioning of *Mad Love*.

"The features are malignant and brutal," noted the script about the

---

Balderston was definitely in the mood for satire that year. He had penned Bride of Frankenstein (William Hurlbut wrote the screenplay), but later bitterly disowned it—claiming he had written a satire and Junior Laemmle had transformed it back into a horror show.

circus knife thrower who killed a woman. "The mouth is agape, the eyes sinister." The role seemed to scream for a wild-eyed, frightening actor whose image and voice would haunt the rest of the film (wouldn't the young John Carradine have been ideal?). Instead, Metro hired Edward Brophy—round, bald, chubby character comic. It appeared as extreme a case of "casting against type" as could be imagined, but the reason, perhaps, was an in-joke that soared right over the heads of most horror fans. As film researcher Sally Stark has noted, MGM's *Freaks* had presented the Rollo brothers, a circus knife-throwing act, with the Rollos played by Matt McHugh—and Edward Brophy. The coincidence in name and casting seems too extreme to have been accidental (especially considering how Balderston stocked the script with other various in-jokes and homages). In a sense, the presence of Brophy as Rollo makes *Mad Love* an MGM sequel to *Freaks*. At any rate, nobody at MGM explained such casting, and *The Hollywood Reporter* of April 29 mysteriously claimed that "Eddie Brophy is being measured at MGM for an iron mask which will sheath his head during most of the production of *Mad Love*."

Mad Love's original budget was only slightly higher than that afforded *Mark of the Vampire,* as reported by Buddy Barnett and Karl Thiede: its budget was $217,176.53 and its shooting schedule was 24 days.

Chester Lyons, MGM cinematographer, was assigned to *Mad Love*—a rather precarious job, considering he would be working under the "great master" Freund. As things evolved, the obstreperous Freund would insist that MGM engage the famous Gregg Toland (who would win the Cinematography Oscar for *Wuthering Heights* [1939]), borrowing him from Goldwyn for what was reported as "8 days of additional photography" on *Mad Love*.

John L. Balderston was writing right up to *Mad Love*'s starting date and, indeed, would keep rewriting right into the third week of filming. *The Hollywood Reporter,* meanwhile, proclaimed that the "highlight and extra big kick" of *Mad Love* would be "the resuscitation of a dead man."

On May 6, 1935, Karl Freund began shooting *Mad Love* at MGM.

●

> Ladies and Gentlemen, Metro-Goldwyn-Mayer feels that it would be a little unkind to present this picture without just a word of friendly warning. We are about to unfold a story which we consider one of the strangest tales ever told. We think it will thrill you. It may shock you. It might even horrify you. So if any of you feel that you do not care to subject your nerves to such a strain, now is your chance to—well, we've warned you.
> —from *Mad Love*'s cutting continuity, July 5, 1935

Yes, that *is* almost the identical precurtain speech Edward Van Sloan delivers in Universal's 1931 *Frankenstein*—mischievously voiced over black frames in the opening of MGM's *Mad Love*. *Mad Love*'s horror homage #1, cut before the movie's original release.

Mad Love cleverly opens with a crash, literally. As the credits unspool against a glass pane, under the music of the great Dimitri Tiomkin (who would win Oscars for *High Noon* [1952], *The High and the Mighty* [1954], and *The Old Man and the Sea* [1958]), a fist rises (seemingly from the audience) and smashes the glass.

The first shot of the film is a cadaver hanging from a gallows rope. It is, of course, a dummy; we are at the Theatre des Horreurs, Paris, where a poster heralds the theatre's star attraction: Yvonne. *Mad Love* takes an immediate satirical jab at the audience. A pretty young lady is ranting at her date outside a theatre, words that must have been heard by many a young man who took his girlfriend to a horror movie:

> When I go out to a play, I want to have some fun. You bring me to a place like this, where they make you scream and faint. . . . If that's the kind of a man you are, you can take me home.

The camera shifts to backstage. There, in what the *Mad Love* script described as a "flimsy white dress in Italian 16th Century style," is a beautiful actress with long, flowing hair and magnificent eyes. She is Yvonne Orlac, played by Frances Drake.

In the Hollywood of the '30s, Frances Drake was one of the movies' great exotics. There seemed to be a sly, sexy secret in those giant hazel eyes, and her Victorian beauty sparked two of the best horror movies of the era: *Mad Love* and Universal's 1936 Karloff and Lugosi thriller *The Invisible Ray*.

Yvonne is reading a note: "Tonight I am sad, for no longer will I be able to watch you every evening from my lonely, shadowed box." Yvonne's wise-cracking maid Marie (Sarah Haden) makes jokes, but they both know the admirer who sends flowers every night: Dr. Gogol, the miracle-working surgeon, who cures "deformed children and mutilated soldiers." And outside, before the theatre, there drifts a little man in a fur-collared coat. He is Dr. Gogol, played by Peter Lorre.

"Peter was a face-maker," said Vincent Price in his eulogy for Lorre at his Hollywood funeral in 1964. It was the supreme compliment; Lorre always described his job as a "face-maker" in his offbeat career. He was one of the greatest character actors of the movies—and one of the movies' greatest characters. His top fame came as part of the late-lamented Warner Bros. world, via such classics as *The Maltese Falcon* (1941) and *Casablanca* (1943). Lorre was a great raconteur, drinker, Bogart crony, and practical joker. One of the most popular stories of Warner Bros. lore is about Lorre grabbing George Raft outside a soundstage one day, as a bus of tourists gaped, and kissing him right on the mouth. "I just thought we should give those poor creeps a little fun," explained Lorre.

Beloved in Hollywood, Lorre presumably never lost that sadistic streak. In an interview with *Filmfax*, Mrs. Lon Chaney, Jr., recalled once observing Lorre in a New York nightclub, putting out his cigarette on his wife's face.

Cut from the release print was an encounter outside the theatre between Gogol and a blind man (Otto Hoffman, 1879–1944) cured by Gogol's surgery, who nevertheless keeps begging. "Being blind is my trade!" explains the charlatan. Gogol's lovesick glances (under Tiomkin's lush music) at a wax statue of Yvonne survive, however. Drake stood in for her own wax dummy in closeups, just as Fay Wray had replaced the wax Marie Antoinette in Warners' 1933 *Mystery of the Wax Museum*. *Mad Love*'s horror homage #2.

"Take your hands off!" orders Gogol as a dandy drunk (Robert Emmett Keane, 1885–1981) in top hat and cape woozily flirts with and touches the statue. "She's not for either of us—she's only wax!" says the drunk. Gogol recovers and checks his hat and coat with a woman in a costume that makes it appear that she has no head.

In a nice touch, Yvonne, backstage in her horror heroine costume and hair, drags on a 1935 cigarette as she awaits her husband's radio broadcast. He is Stephen Orlac, the great concert pianist, performing at Fontainebleau; "slender figure, sombre, artistic face, his complete being immersed in his playing," notes the script.

Stephen Orlac was played by Colin Clive (1900–1937). Clive, remembered by *Frankenstein* leading lady Mae Clarke as having the "face of Christ," was Hollywood's patron saint of lost souls ever since he played the liquor-addicted Stanhope of James Whale's *Journey's End* (1930); *Mad Love* would be one of his most torturous cinema crucifixions. Many in the cinema colony cruelly regarded the sad, lonely actor as a freak, for alcohol had tragically transformed him into a real-life, pitiful Jekyll and Hyde. George Brent, who had co-starred with Clive and Josephine Hutchinson earlier in 1935 in Warners' *The Right to Live*, described the tragic Englishman as "a maniac who would cut off your head one night and stick it on the icebox!"

As Orlac plays his concert, Yvonne acts in a play called *Tortured*, moving center on the torchlit stage, the Tiomkin music rumbling ominously. The script offered this advice to the director:

> Little playlet that follows should not be played for gruesome or horrible values. Our audience should not be horrified, but should be inclined to laugh at the Paris audience for taking all this seriously.

"Sir, how dare you threaten your duchess with torture?" grandly demands Drake's Yvonne, arching those incredibly long, tapered eyebrows. Hooded ruffians tie Yvonne to the rack, and the hot, forked poker is prepared in the fire; we then see the audience, and there is a nurse on duty for the fainthearted. Balderston knew of the out-of-work bit actresses and chorus girls who had picked up Universal paychecks for posing as nurses in theatres showing *Frankenstein; Mad Love*'s horror homage #3.

Freund surveys the Grand Guignol audience. We might expect the same bizarre faces that beheld Karloff's satanic rites in *The Black Cat*. But no, these extras look like truck drivers. The duke demands to know the name of the lover who escaped from the duchess's balcony. When she refuses, the poker goes to work and we see a wonderful closeup of the terrified, wild-eyed Drake.

"Yes!" she screams wildly, confessing, climaxing her exquisite mock agony. "It was your *brother!*"

The script had wanted to have a man jump up in the audience, shout "Stop! Stop!" and faint, while a nurse ran to his aid. Of course, he was supposed to be a plant; later in the lobby, the "nurse" was to tell him, "Your scream was better than Yvonne's!" But this is missing from the film; instead, we see a bull-necked patron applauding brutally at the finale.

Dominating all, of course, is Lorre's Gogol—his bald head shining, his egg-eyes staring, looking like a kinky Humpty Dumpty as he sits up in his private box. Yvonne screams and he lowers his eyes in ecstasy.

Backstage, Gogol summons his courage to meet the lady who has obsessed him. The movie beautifully captures the moment. Gogol, all dressed up in his fur-collar coat, smiles timidly as he enters the dressing room; Yvonne, all prim in her street clothes, her long hair pinned up (or, more likely, taken off), is not at all the exotic of the stage but a no-nonsense actress who has finished a job.

"Every night I have watched you," purrs Gogol, shyly, "and tonight, the last night, I felt I must come and thank you for what you have meant to me." Yvonne is professionally polite, as Gogol expresses his plan to be in his box again every night when the theatre reopens. But she will not be there; she's on her way to England with her husband.

"Your . . . husband?" asks the heartbroken Gogol, the camera zooming in for a terrifically theatrical closeup of his crestfallen face.

Missing from the film (unfortunately) is a scene in which Yvonne shows Gogol a bust of Orlac's hands; "The Hands of Orlac," reads a metal plaque. "But I must see you again—I *must!*" pleads Gogol.

Charles (Murray Kinnell), of the theatre management, calls them to the party. There is a huge cake with a guillotine atop it; an actor hands Yvonne a headsman's axe with which to cut the cake. As the actors laugh about Yvonne finally going on her honeymoon, the players line up, each getting a kiss and a piece of cake. Gogol, forgotten, leans forlornly against a set.

"What, doctor?" asks Charles, "no champagne, no cake, and no kiss?" He propels Gogol to the cake. A moment's hesitation, and then Gogol grabs Yvonne and plants a terrific kiss on her, to the cries of the party. "A flash of horror in her face," noted the script, "but she's an actress, and quickly recovers and laughs."

In this scene, Lorre brilliantly displays Gogol's mad obsession for Yvonne, while Miss Drake delicately hints Yvonne's natural revulsion for her admirer. And as Gogol leaves the theatre, he buys the wax figure of Yvonne, which was en route to the melting pot for its 50 francs worth of wax. Gogol pays 100 francs for it.

"Did you ever hear of Galatea?" says Lorre's Gogol. "Pygmalion formed her out of marble . . . she came to life *in his arms.*"

On the night train from Fontainebleau to Paris, Clive's Orlac sits in his compartment, making music notes with a fountain pen. "Fountain pen has a long, tapering end," notes the script, prophetically, "making it easy to throw as a missile." A "fat, bourgeois Frenchman" (Billy Gilbert, 1894–1971, the great comic sneezer) in spectacles joins Orlac, smuggling his dog onto the train to save 20 francs. In a nice touch, Orlac sells his "confidence" for a piece of the Frenchman's bologna, then gives it to the dog—much to the fat man's disgust.

The train stops. Clive's haunted face looks out the window into the night; he wipes the frost off the pane as the train steam rises out on the platform, like smoke from Hades. Freund's vision is wonderful; Orlac is a passenger en route to hell but doesn't know it. Orlac sees two men escorting Rollo (Edward Brophy, 1895–1960) onto the train en route to the guillotine.

"Rollo!" exclaims the Frenchman, as Orlac lights a cigarette. "The American threw knives in a circus . . . stuck one in his father's back because of a woman."

Taking Orlac's pen, the Frenchman runs for an autograph; Billy Gilbert meets Edward Brophy. It's quite a sight, these two future models for Walt Disney, babbling away in a horror movie. "For once I got top-billing," boasts Rollo of his murder trial. "Boy, I bet it burned those guys in the circus!" Brophy's Rollo, glimpsed insulting Hans the midget in *Freaks* just three years before, just might be *Mad Love*'s most audacious in-joke—a very big #4. Clive, chasing the escaped dog, arrives at Rollo's compartment just as the talk turns ugly.

"Hey, you can't talk about her like that!" says Rollo. "I loved that dame, even if she did two-time me!"

Retreating, the Frenchman asks for the fountain pen back, and Rollo (despite his handcuffs) throws it like a knife; it narrowly misses the

Frenchman's fat face as it sticks into the wooden door frame. "This happens to be my pen," says the shocked Orlac.

Meanwhile, in Paris, we meet Reagan (Ted Healy, 1896–1937), American newspaper reporter à la Hildy Johnson of *The Front Page*. "Ted Healy, a highly amusing comedian, has gotten into the wrong picture," the *New York Times* would critique; indeed, Healy's brash, fast-talking performance (his comic timing is excellent) only makes sense in the Germanic texture of *Mad Love* when one remembers Lee Tracy in *Doctor X*. Healy even sports the same type of long coat and porkpie hat that Tracy wore in that 1932 Warner Bros. release; horror homage #5.

In a scene scripted May 13, one week after *Mad Love* began shooting, the prefect of police (Henry Kolker, 1874–1947, who was playing almost simultaneously the baronial father of the Karloff twins in Columbia's *The Black Room*) gives Reagan a press pass—he will be the first American press member to witness a guillotine execution. The prefect also telephones Gogol, who never misses a guillotining. "Of course, I'll be there," says Gogol; "His eyes shine," notes the script.

Later in the night, Orlac's train crashes cataclysmically. Yvonne, Marie, and Reagan ride out to the accident site and find that Orlac has been mutilated. In a nice touch, Marie takes care of the dog Stephen had befriended.

"Amputate?" shrieks Yvonne as Dr. Marbeau (Charles Trowbridge) issues his verdict: Stephen's crushed hands must be cut off.

"Can you get me an ambulance to take my husband to Dr. Gogol's house immediately?" pleads Yvonne, as Miss Drake gives her tempted angel look.

In a scene set at dawn, we see Dr. Gogol's house and his housekeeper, Francoise (May Beatty, 1882–1945)—a wonderful comic grotesque, seemingly Freund's drunken, blowsy answer to Whale's Una O'Connor (homage #6). Francoise has a white cockatoo on her shoulder, à la Lugosi's vulture in *White Zombie* (homage #7); she's trying to persuade the bird to join in a draught of liquor. As Francoise answers a telephone call for Gogol, Freund focuses on her shadow (and the cockatoo's) on the wall. "If you want to know, he's visitin' Madame Guillotine," guffaws Francoise. "He never misses one of those head-choppin's."

The script lovingly details the execution: the blade's test run on the bundle of hay; "the little old black van, which looks like a Punch and Judy wagon, with iron-rimmed wheels and one horse," standing by to carry away the decapitated body; the horsemen of the Garde Républican; even a reminder that a guillotine is 15' high. The death march begins. One of the officials, in derby and mustache, is Michael Mark (1889–1975), "Little Maria's" bereaved father of *Frankenstein* and famous bit player of so many classic horror films. His mute presence here seems almost like an homage in itself—#8, to be precise.

"Boy," marvels Rollo, smoking his final cigarette, looking up at all 15' of Madame Guillotine. "Ain't that somethin'!"

Once again, however, the real star of the scene is Lorre's Gogol—clinically and morbidly keeping an eye squinted on the offscreen guillotine as it severs Rollo's head. Reagan, however, becomes ill at the spectacle ("I'm as sick as a bedbug").

"How dare you let people turn my clinic into a public hospital?" Gogol demands of his nurse, Suzanne, only to learn the patient is Orlac and that Yvonne has brought him to Gogol's house herself. "There are other outlets for musical talent besides playing," Gogol comforts Yvonne after examining Orlac's hopelessly crushed hands. "He is also a composer."

"And I believed you could save them," says Yvonne bitterly, "believed you would help *me*."

"If it would help, I'd gladly give my own two hands!" vows Gogol.

The amputation surgery begins, with Gogol's assistant, Dr. Wong, participating. (Dr. Wong was played by veteran Chinese actor Keye Luke, 1904–1991. Luke was then very popular at Metro, having provided the studio a great service: he had saved Garbo from falling off a treadmill on *The Painted Veil* [1934].)

"Impossible, professor," says Wong, regarding the saving of Orlac's mutilated hands.

"Impossible?" exults Gogol, his eyes bulging, an unholy idea forming. *"Napoleon said that word is not French!"*

There followed the scene that *The Hollywood Reporter* had promised to be the "extra big kick" of *Mad Love*, a scene that if found in the MGM vaults, might be a major rediscovery.

The "Punch and Judy" van arrives at Gogol's clinic, delivering, per his request to the prefect, Rollo's body. In an episode dated May 22, Balderston's script described the outrageously mad laboratory scene, fated never to appear in the release print:

> [The room is] fitted up with glass pipes, tubes, wires, coils, all the appliances of scientific experiment. Camera pans slowly around until it catches Gogol and Wong in center of room. In front of them, on table propped against wall, is body of Rollo. His head is fastened by means of straps and iron braces to trunk.
>
> A glass tube is in his neck. This is attached by long rubber tube to beaker which holds blood fluid, under which gas flame is burning.

"Ah, but the great artery!" said Gogol. "That is the crux. Now if I can pump blood through the severed artery, what will that prove, Wong?"

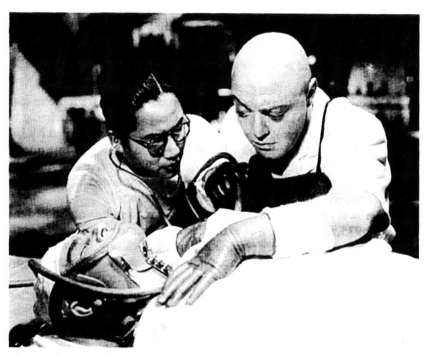

The promised highlight of *Mad Love*, later cut: Keye Luke and Peter Lorre strap on the head of decapitated Edward Brophy to restore him to life.

"That you have done the impossible," Wong replied.

"Why?" demanded Gogol. "It's been done with rabbits, with dogs."*

This horribly graphic episode, featuring Rollo's body with its decapitated head strapped back on, a glass tube replacing his guillotined neck artery, his life temporarily restored to make his hands transplantable, was a nasty little paean to *Frankenstein* (homage #9); it also yielded some metaphysical debate between Gogol and Wong, as Bach played on the record player:

> WONG (smiling): How foolish you Occidentals are! Life is only a preparation for death.

This must have been a reference to the famous Dr. Robert E. Cornish experiment that restored life to a dog; it had inspired Universal's Life Returns (1935), which was so bad that Universal never released it through regular channels, but finally sold it to an independent producer (just as MGM eventually had done with Freaks). Freund asked to see Life Returns while preparing Mad Love, and Dr. Eugene Frenke, who directed and co-scripted Life Returns (and who wed actress Anna Sten), was so delighted by Freund's request, hoping it might lead to big things, that he spent $100 of his own money to strike Freund a new print. Only after the showing did Frenke learn that "Papa" simply wanted to see the technique used on the dead dog in Life Returns as homework for Mad Love.

GOGOL: The day will come when man can stay alive as long as he wills!
WONG (Gently, with a remote sort of pity): Then he will learn to *will*
death. For what is life? We seek and do not find—power—riches—we
seek love, and are left with empty arms.

Of course, this entire vignette was doomed to be cut from the release
print of *Mad Love*. Making the long-lost scene even more tantalizing to
historians is *The Hollywood Reporter* blurb of May 29 that noted that MGM
had borrowed an ultraviolet ray diffuser from the California Institute of
Technology for this scene. The diffuser reportedly emitted a 200° flash on
the set, while all microphones and the camera were shielded from the light,
and "all players with gold teeth warned out of range."

"Series of *dissolves* to be inserted here showing her dreams," noted the
May 22, 1935, script page. We see the sleeping Yvonne dreaming of a smiling Stephen, the sky, hands playing a piano, a flock of sheep, a speeding
train heading right for the audience (which must have delighted Freund),
the train's revolving wheel, and Gogol's obsessed face.

The operation is a success, and *Mad Love* has presented a superbly
horrific scenario: Lorre's Gogol is Frankenstein and Clive's Orlac, husband of the woman Gogol adores, has become his monster. Spike this with
the surgical dismemberment (easily interpreted as a symbolic castration),
the concept of Orlac's body being violated by the man who desires his wife,
and one intuits why *Mad Love* repulsed more audiences that it attracted
in 1935.

In Gogol's study, Francoise, with cockatoo, is combing the hair of the
wax figure of Yvonne. "There's never been any woman in this house but
me," she grouses to the waxwork. "If he must have them here, I prefer *live*
ones to *dead* ones!" The words remind one of Karloff's nocturnal slinking
through the cellars of *The Black Cat*, ogling the preserved bodies of his
satanic sacrifices as he cradles the title feline; horror homage #10. And as
the exhausted Gogol goes to his study, in the great tradition of Karloff in
The Black Cat, (as well as Chaney in *The Phantom of the Opera*, March in
Dr. Jekyll and Mr. Hyde, Lugosi in *The Raven*, et al.), Lorre's Gogol triumphantly plays the organ (horror homage #11) and serenades his wax
statue of Yvonne. "Galatea," he lovingly sighs.

Stephen Orlac survives, with "hands." Clive and Drake play a love
scene by a lake under a tree, she in pretty dress and magnificent bonnet,
he all smiles. He starts to embrace her, then notices his huge, splinted, grotesque bandaged hands. The sickly funny scene seems a puncture of the
pastoral love scene halfway through *Frankenstein* between Clive and Mae
Clarke (homage #12); only here, when hero goes to clasp heroine, he has
the monster's hands. At any rate, the love scene continues, and Clive kisses
Miss Drake far more passionately than he did Mae Clarke.

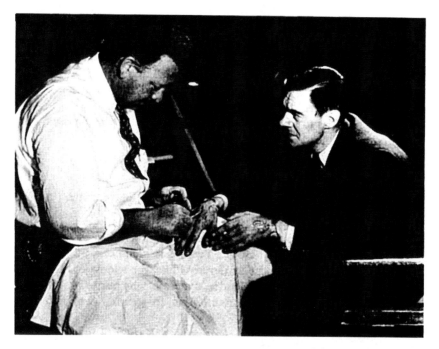

Colin Clive submits his hands for makeup scars on *Mad Love*.

"They feel dead. . . . They don't look like mine," laments Orlac when Gogol removes the bandages. The *Frankenstein* role reversal is complete: Clive now appears to have the same, scarred, stitched-on hands Karloff's monster had raised to the skylight. The recovery of massages and ultraviolet treatments is long and expensive. A new montage shows the treatments, the bills, Yvonne selling her jewelry as Tiomkin's music plays desperately. Finally, all that remains in the sparsely furnished room is the bust of Orlac's hands and the grand piano. Stephen has been unable to play it. One day, Yvonne hears the music Stephen flamboyantly played on the radio that night in Fontainebleau and rushes into his study.

"Wonderful invention, the phonograph," ruefully laughs Orlac. "Keeps a man alive, long after he is dead."

Yvonne comforts Stephen, but in breaks the piano man—none other than Clarence Hummel Wilson (1877–1941), a crabby little character player best remembered as the shyster of W. C. Fields's *Tillie and Gus* (1933). "I want my money!" whines the piano man. Stephen hears Yvonne and Marie fighting him off. He picks up his fountain pen, the same pen Rollo had thrown that night on the train.

Clive's anguished face is wild, magnificent; he looks like he's turning into Mr. Hyde before our very eyes. Suddenly, Orlac's scarred hands aim his pen, and like a professional knife-thrower, he demonically throws it through the air, nearly slicing the piano man's bald head.

"The angle of camera, the door jamb, should be *identical* with the shot of pen in railway door jamb" noted the script. The piano man runs out. Yvonne and Marie look at Stephen in shock. Dazed, the pianist walks over to the door frame and removes the weapon.

"This happens to be my pen, gentlemen," Clive's Orlac reprises, with a frightening sadness.

●

> I enjoyed the Hollywood scene. There were lots of parties,
> and I liked most of the picture people that I met.
> Frances Drake

Frances Drake, the foxy, Gothic Yvonne of *Mad Love,* lives today in a beautiful mountaintop house in Beverly Hills, the widow of the son of the Countess of Suffolk. She is slender, dynamic, very attractive; with her white hair, she looks like Yvonne Orlac in gentle, very flattering age-makeup.

In her Hollywood days, she acted with Karloff, Lugosi, March, Laughton, Lorre, and Clive. Her beautiful eyes are still luminous, and they flash, spark, and charm as she remembers *Mad Love:*

> Little Peter Lorre was charming, and so cute. . . . He had to meet me before he had his head shaved, to show me that he had hair. And lots of it. . . . But he was rather naughty. If your scene was going very well, he'd suddenly say, "Don't you know me? I'm your little Peter." You know, he didn't want you to be *too* good.

Drake remembers the *Mad Love* set as being fun; one day Colin Clive brought to the stage a young lady who wanted to meet Frances and took her up to the wax statue. Frances Drake also remembers the film as being "A bit difficult," however, primarily due to the director:

> Director Karl Freund kept wanting to be the cinematographer at the same time. And Gregg Toland was a marvelous cameraman. And he was such a dear little man, sort of slender, and he looked rather hunted when this wretched big fat man would say, "Now, now, we'll do it this way!"
>
> You never knew who was directing. The producer was dying to, to tell you the truth, and of course he had no idea of directing. Finally I did say, "Look here, we've got to have one director, because we're all going mad."
>
> That Englishman would go to sleep. He'd pay no attention to anybody—it was too sweet! Colin Clive—he just went to sleep. He didn't care who was directing, he didn't give a damn. He was such a good actor that he didn't need it, perhaps.

Drake recalls that Clive was "Jekyll" on the *Mad Love* stage: "No problem on the set; he always knew his lines, and everything was fine." It was at a Hollywood party one evening, however, that the actress sadly saw Clive's "Hyde":

> I remember once we were at a party, about six or seven in the evening, and he was in the garden and he was sitting on a little straight-backed chair.... And we were all having a drink ... the back of the chair sank slowly down, and he lay there with his head in a flower bed, drinking his drink—and nothing phased him! Absolutely amazing.

All in all, Frances Drake loved the role of Yvonne Orlac; she enjoyed playing melodrama and would do so again that fall, joining Karloff and Lugosi ("they were both totally darling") at Universal for *The Invisible Ray*.

With a deep love for animals, Drake happily runs off the names of various creatures—raccoon, deer, coyotes—who romp around her mountain home. Fifty years after her last picture (MGM's 1942 *The Affairs of Martha*), the glamour is still there.

●

Mad Love's second half moves like lightning.

Orlac takes Yvonne's advice and reluctantly seeks the help of his stepfather, jeweler Henry Orlac. "Not a sou!" sneers Orlac (played with lip-smacking relish by veteran character player Ian Wolfe). "For years I wanted you in business with me. But being a tradesman wasn't good enough for you. Now that your hands are smashed up, you can't thump a piano any longer, you come crawling back to me."

Stephen is hypertense.

"And that actress you married," leers Wolfe wonderfully. "Why don't you let *her* help you now? Her pay may be small, but she could *supplement* her earnings, eh?"

Once again, Clive's face chillingly convulses, and Stephen throws a knife, narrowly missing his evil stepfather.

"Your thoughts are only for him," muses Gogol in Yvonne's drawing room. "Is there no room in your heart—even pity—for a man who has never known the love of a woman—but who has worshipped you since the day he first walked by that absurd little theatre?"

"Yes!" says Yvonne. "I knew of your feeling for me—I traded on it.... But I can give you nothing else in return. ... Even if I didn't love him—there's something about you that...."

"Repulses you?" volunteers Gogol.

"Frightens me," replies Yvonne.

"You are cruel!" cries Lorre, almost out of control with emotion. "But only to be kind."

Back at Gogol's house, the doctor has bought his waxwork of Yvonne a new negligee, which the drunken Francoise unwraps. When Healy's Reagan shows up and knocks at the door, Francoise mumbles her way down the staircase, just like Dwight Frye's hunchbacked Fritz scuttled down the tower staircase in *Frankenstein* (horror homage #13). Reagan bribes his way in with cognac.

"You know, I used to go with a girl like you," quips Healy. "Only she drank."

The two players have a fun scene; he is looking for Rollo's body and she thinks he is discussing the wax statue of Yvonne:

> FRANCOISE: You said it had no head.... I look at it every day—he makes me brush its hair every evening.
> REAGAN: Where does he keep it?
> FRANCOISE: Upstairs in his drawing room, just like it was alive. He sits at his organ and plays music to it every night.

Reagan runs upstairs, sees the statue of Yvonne, thinks it is the real thing, and gets tossed out of the house by an apoplectic Gogol.

Meanwhile, Orlac arrives at Gogol's house. "What have you done to me?" cries Clive, masterfully, holding his hands out before him. "You and your black magic ... *whose hands are these?* ... They feel for knives ... they want to throw them—and they know how to. *Watch!*"

Orlac takes two scalpels and throws them expertly into the wall.

"They want to kill!"

Lorre smoothly delivers a bogus speech on "wish fulfillment" to calm the hysterical Orlac, claiming the problem stems from some childhood trauma. Stephen departs and Gogol sends for Yvonne.

"I didn't dare to tell him his hands were those of a murderer," says Gogol to Wong. "That would probably drive him..." Lorre's face is priceless as the evil idea flickers, "to commit murder himself." Gogol's voice quivers in excitement as he considers the possibility.

Gogol and Yvonne have a showdown. The scene is sublime: Lorre, squat in surgeon smock and cap, Drake, tres chic in suit and cocked chapeau; his Cabbage Patch Kid sideview vs. her beautiful left profile:

"The shock has affected his mind. ... His life is ruined already. Yvonne, get away from him before he ruins your life as well!"

"Now I understand," sniffs Drake, her eyes flashing.

"I, a poor peasant, have conquered science," rants Lorre's Gogol. "*Why can't I conquer love?* Don't you understand? You *must* be mine!"

Drake snarls like a glamorous cat, and as Lorre lunges for her, she claws him away.

"Liar!" shrieks Yvonne. *"Hypocrite! You disgust me!"*

She sashays out. Devastated, Gogol prepares for surgery on a little girl (Cora Sue Collins). "Liar! Hypocrite! You disgust me!" taunts the haunting voice of Yvonne; the demented doctor sways, his eyes bulging above his surgical mask. Gasping for air, he leaves his surgery, as Wong takes over. (In the original script, Gogol's breakdown resulted in the child dying; fortunately, the film has Wong save her through his own surgery.) In the other room, Gogol's spectres taunt him.

"Nothing matters to you but one thing—Yvonne, Yvonne, in your arms!" The various Gogol phantoms who mock the doctor are truly frightening; the bald, bug-eyed Lorre is now horrible, looking like a tarantula after chemotherapy, lovingly, sadistically tormenting himself.

The scene has a curious tag. As the evil idea of driving Orlac to madness percolates in his head, Gogol goes into his study and dilates his eyes as he sees a fly-eating plant enjoying a snack. Such a fly-eater had just added to the atmosphere of Universal's *Werewolf of London,* as part of Henry Hull's botanical wonders. *Werewolf of London* had opened on Broadway May 9, 1935—three days after *Mad Love* began shooting. It tempts one to believe that the *Mad Love* company, catching the latest horror film from the Universal lot, tossed in the plant as yet another horror homage (#14) of shameless *Mad Love.*

The original script followed with a scene of the wandering Orlac visiting a carnival one night, where he is tempted to step up to the knife-throwing booth. This probably was not shot; the Call Bureau cast sheet of July 15, 1935, lists none of the carnival types described in the script.

Definitely filmed, however (but doomed to the cutting room floor) was the entrance of a street girl, Marianne (Isabel Jewell, 1910–1972), who has picked up none other than old Henry Orlac. "I've got the prettiest little bracelet in my safe!" promises Orlac, tempting the blonde into his shop. She flirtatiously pretends to demur—all the while having an Apache thief (Harold Huber, screen heavy who played Fu Manchu on CBS's radio show of 1933) in the street, prepared to help her knock out the jeweler and steal his trinkets. But before the thief can strike, a mysterious figure sneaks into the shop and hurls a knife into Orlac's back.

Suspicion, of course, falls on Stephen Orlac, who receives a message: if he will come that night to a certain address, he will learn the truth about his hands.... The pianist makes his way through a dark street. Inside a foul lodging, he sees a man seated behind a desk, wearing a cloak, dark glasses, and a large-brimmed hat.

It is one of the best, most frightening, unforgettable scenes of horror films.

"You said you'd tell me the truth about my hands," pleads Orlac.

"I have no hands," hisses the stranger, revealing prosthetic fingers of shining steel. They look horrible, obscene—a macabre testimonial against the wonders of medical science. "Yours—they were mine once ... and so—when you knifed your father in the back last night, you killed him with *my* hands!"

Orlac fights the thought he might have killed his father. The stranger sticks a large knife into the table. "Use it when they try to arrest you."

"Who are you?" asks Orlac.

"I am Rollo, the knife thrower."

"No, no! Rollo died in the guillotine."

"Yes," says the stranger, slowly rising. "They cut off my head. *But that Gogol—he put it back, here.*"

The steel fingers rip away the coat collar. Orlac sees the head, the eyes masqueraded by dark glasses, the lips curled back, and, of course, the horrible steel and leather harness joining the head to the neck. As the stranger explodes with horrible laughter, the sickened Orlac runs away.

The hissed lines, the bared teeth, the maniacal laughter—Lorre's cruel, wickedly mad masquerade is grimly, horribly magnificent. Of course, before the film was cut for national release, the scene was all the more frightening and ambiguous. "This is the same steel brace," noted the script, "we saw on Rollo during the experiment in Gogol's lab." Although there's no real suspense that the figure might be Rollo (we fully suspect that it is Gogol), the fact that it truly is the doctor, going to such horrid lengths to drive a man crazy, makes the scene all the more sinister and horrific.

The frazzled Orlac returns to Yvonne's boudoir. "It wasn't I who did it," says Orlac. "It was Rollo's hands.... You remember Rollo. They cut off his head—but Gogol put it back on." Orlac reveals to his wife how he can throw a knife, tossing one right through the heart of a portrait on the wall, and he announces he will turn himself in to the police for the murder of his father. The police take him away. And the hysterical Yvonne, in a gown, her hair down, looking almost as exotic as she did at the Grand Guignol, rushes to Gogol's house.

Francoise, drunk as usual, sees Yvonne and thinks she's the statue come to life. "It's come alive!" she shrieks—an obvious salute to Clive's classic cackle in *Frankenstein* (horror homage #15). Then, out in the street, the spooked housekeeper drunkenly rants, "It went out for a little walk."—*Mad Love*'s most famous in-joke, echoing the famous line Bramwell Fletcher laughed when Karloff's mummy came alive in the 1932 classic *The Mummy* (directed by Freund, scripted by Balderston). Horror homage #16. Police escort Francoise away, while Yvonne takes the place of her own wax statue.

Dr. Gogol (Peter Lorre) speaks to his "statue" of Yvonne Orlac (Frances Drake) in *Mad Love*.

For the rest of *Mad Love*, Lorre plays Gogol on a crazy note of bravura madness. *"The fool,"* laughs Gogol, grunting, wheezing, stripping away his neck harness like some fat, horrible witch removing her corset, as Yvonne (and the cockatoo) watch in horror. Snarling, stretching, laughing triumphantly and demonically, Lorre's Gogol is gloriously, horrifically mad. Freund, too, is his most inspired now; he adds to the horror, making

Gogol's house appear even more Germanic, twisted, and macabre than it did in the earlier footage; the whole house seems to be warping in accordance with Gogol's rapturous madness.

"He—he shall be shut up in the house where they keep the mad," says Gogol to his waxwork Galatea. "I, Gogol, will do that. He shall be shut up—when it's I who am mad!"

Gogol serenades Galatea at the organ. Yvonne stands terribly still. Finally terrified beyond control, Yvonne runs, frightening the cockatoo. The bird scratches her face and she screams.

"Galatea!" marvels Gogol, seeing the blood. "I am Pygmalion! You came to life in my arms ... Galatea! Give me your lips!"

The madman insanely caresses Yvonne, as Drake writhes wonderfully. However, as he slavers over her and she screams, a phantom voice suddenly booms over the room, "Liar! Hypocrite! You disgust me!" and then, Gogol's own voice—"Each man kills the thing he loves. ... *Each man kills the thing he loves.*"

This ominous line also is related to *Werewolf of London;* in that film, Warner Oland tells Henry Hull, "the werewolf instinctively seeks to kill the thing it loves best." Even if coincidental, the line works as *Mad Love's* horror homage #17.

Gogol carries his Galatea to the couch and with a horrible smile, begins strangling her with her own hair, reciting:

> In one long raven string I wind,
> Three times her little throat around
> And strangle her ... No pain feels she.
> I am quite sure she feels no pain.

Screeching to the rescue are the prefect of police, Reagan, and Orlac. In a cut scene, the hysterical Marianne, caught pawning Henry Orlac's jewels, has insisted she was innocent of his murder; through fingerprints, the police have realized that Orlac does have Rollo's hands. Reagan tells the police that he saw Yvonne (or so he thought) in Gogol's house. They run upstairs and peer through the barred door.

"He's killing her!" cries Orlac. And, expertly, Clive's Orlac, the knife-throwing monster created by Gogol, throws a knife right into his "creator's" back.

Gogol falls to the floor, and Orlac embraces his wife. "Oh, Stephen," soulfully sighs Yvonne, and Gogol hears her. The dying Gogol rolls over and sees his Galatea embracing the freak he created. Lorre's Gogol rolls his egg-eyes up in his head and quietly, sadly dies—the "great peace in his face" called for in the script registering strangely and powerfully in the final fade-out.

An early script treatment had called for a happy ending:

> Yvonne and Stephen recover from the weeks of horror and Stephen becomes master of his hands once more. He gets a position as conductor of a great orchestra and he and Yvonne live in happiness.

Balderston removed the happy ending tag. And as Dimitri Tiomkin's music (strangely mute through the second half of *Mad Love*) swells for the end, one wonders if Clive's Orlac might, indeed, "kill the thing he loves."

●

Mad Love wrapped June 8, 1935, one week over schedule. The negative cost was $257,562.14, putting the show more than $40,000 over budget. Still, *Mad Love* proved an MGM economy product: about $48,000 less than *Mark of the Vampire*, about $53,000 less than *Freaks*, and about $70,000 less than *The Mask of Fu Manchu*.

On May 22, 1935, MGM had announced that the definite title for the new melodrama would be *The Hands of Orlac;* the studio had also toyed with the title, *The Mad Doctor of Paris*. However, amid the postshooting rumors that Karl Freund would move to Paramount to direct a film or go abroad to direct Chevalier, MGM prepared to preview their little thriller under the original title of *Mad Love*.

> The climax, while neatly disposing of the villain, does tend to gloss over the fact that the hero is still left with a plethora of personal problems—debts, inability to perform as a pianist—the only profession he knows—and most of all, the rather embarrassing ownership of hands that insist on throwing knives at people!
>
> —William K. Everson, *Classics of the Horror Film* (Citadel, 1974)

In late June 1935 MGM hosted a Hollywood preview of *Mad Love*. The June 27, 1935, *Hollywood Reporter* threw bouquets to Lorre, calling *Mad Love* his "personal triumph":

> Peter Lorre's first American production. That he is a distinct and distinguished addition to the fan roster of this country, there can be no doubt. Lorre triumphs superbly in a characterization that is sheer horror.... There is perhaps no one who can be so repulsive and so utterly wicked. No one who can smile so disarmingly and still sneer. His face is his fortune.

The *Reporter* was reserved about *Mad Love* itself ("neither important nor particularly compelling"), claiming the movie "falls right in the middle between Art and Box Office" and giving little space to either Miss Drake ("manages to be one of the more attractive horror victims") or Clive ("jitters his way through").

As with *Mark of the Vampire*, MGM decided to trim its new horror release. When previewed in Hollywood, *Mad Love* ran 83 minutes; the national release print ran 68 minutes. The 15 minutes of cuts included, of course, the lavish, centerpiece laboratory sequence reviving the decapitated Rollo; it is hard to believe that MGM ever imagined that the sight of a corpse, the decapitated head held on by straps and harnesses, a glass tube inserted in its neck, being brought back to life by a God-defying scientist, would ever get by local censor boards—not to mention getting by Louis B. Mayer.

Also cut were the precredit warning stolen from *Frankenstein*, scenes of the bogus blind man, various flourishes of the Grand Guignol showmanship, and Isabel Jewell's entire performance as Marianne.*

On Friday, August 2, 1935, *Mad Love* opened at New York City's Roxy Theatre, where Universal's *Bride of Frankenstein* and *The Raven* had played earlier in the year. "The Screen's Strangest Sensation!" proclaimed the ads; "The Star of *M* and *The Man Who Knew Too Much* in His Most Amazing Portrayal!" Trying to help *Mad Love* attract crowds into the air-conditioned Roxy was a "joyous new revue" featuring the Roxy's Gae Foster Girls and a variety of acts. *Time* magazine heralded *Mad Love* as "one of the most completely horrible stories of the year," waxing eloquent about Lorre:

> Lorre, perfectly cast, uses the technique popularized by Charles Laughton of suggesting the most unspeakable obsession by the roll of a protuberant eyeball, an almost feminine mildness of tone, an occasional quiver of thick lips set flat in his cretinous, ellipsoidal face.

Aside from Fredric March's Academy Award–winning *Dr. Jekyll and Mr. Hyde*, Lorre's Dr. Gogol was the critic's darling of horror grotesques; Charlie Chaplin, after seeing *Mad Love*, praised him as "the greatest living actor." *Mad Love* proved all too much for poor *Variety;* the show business Bible reported that Rollo "choked his victim" (hence missing the whole concept of the knives) and summed up the proceedings with "Thus, the pianist husband finally kills his stepfather." *Variety* noted the film's need

---

*Jewell's name appeared on poster work for the British release of Mad Love, *entitled* The Hands of Orlac, *so it is possible that the longer version played in England. However, considering the censorship guidelines there, it is more likely that MGM forgot to delete the actress's name in advertising.*

for "exploitation," forecasting *Mad Love* "probably will do fair biz on the whole."

Even in its box office forecast, *Variety* was way off. *Mad Love* earned a puny domestic gross of only $170,000, almost $120,000 less than the domestic take on MGM's *Freaks*. While Browning's 1932 disaster had been a "freakish" hit in such locales as Cincinatti, Buffalo, and even Boston, nobody stood in line to see *Mad Love*. The overall response was outrage at so "sick" a picture. William A. Levee, manager of the Suffolk Theatre of Riverhead, Long Island, New York, reported to the *Motion Picture Herald:*

> The producers must have been mad to even attempt such a piece as this. This is certainly a black eye for MGM.... *Mad Love* is the picture that makes a manager want to hide from view when the cash customers leave the theatre. To have to face an audience on a bank night after subjecting intelligent people to sit through *Mad Love* is enough to turn one's hair gray.... *Mad Love* is the type of picture that brought about censorship.

Mad Love's foreign gross (probably due to Lorre's name) was actually better; it took in $194,000 abroad, tallying total world receipts of $364,000. The final net loss: $39,000.

The box office debacle of *Mad Love* was intriguing. Lorre's bravura insanity, Miss Drake's exotica, Clive's painful anguish, Freund's Germanic stylistics, the wicked pace, and the exciting (but queerly unresolved) ending, almost made *Mad Love* appear to be MGM's stylish mea culpa for Browning's cop-out *Mark of the Vampire* (which opened on Broadway the week before *Mad Love* began shooting). Draping itself in horror "homage," pioneering the future shocks of amok surgery and amputations, *Mad Love* seemed the studio's sick, slick reminder that it was MGM, after all, that produced the sinister Chaney silents, the shocking *Freaks*, and the joyously sadistic *The Mask of Fu Manchu*.

Mark of the Vampire was too slow and staid, but *Mad Love*, for 1935, was too audacious. As *Time* had reported, it was "completely horrible," and the public rejected it.

MGM quickly forgot *Mad Love*. By late August 1935 its producer, John Considine, was already redeeming himself, previewing *Broadway Melody of 1936*, starring tap-dancing Eleanor Powell; the musical was one of Hollywood's top-grossers of the year, winning a Best Picture Oscar nomination. A big year for Metro-Goldwyn-Mayer was 1935, with such giant hits as the Gable/Harlow *China Seas*, MacDonald and Eddy's *Naughty Marietta*, Garbo's *Anna Karenina*, and the Best Picture Oscar winner *Mutiny on the Bounty*. *Mad Love*, as far as the front office was concerned, was an aberration best forgotten. MGM tossed *Mad Love* into the limbo of the vaults, where it would burn for its erotic, sadistic, stylistic sins for over three decades. Its eventual "ascension" would prove almost as bizarre as *Mad Love* itself.

> I don't want to go down in history as a monster. I've never
> played a frog that swallowed a city, or something like that.
> —Peter Lorre, 1963

Colin Clive lived less than two years after *Mad Love*'s release. In late 1935, Clive returned to Broadway in *Libel!* as a shell-shocked amnesia victim; the courtroom thriller was a hit, but Clive's declining health forced him out of the play and into a sanatorium in only two-and-a-half months. The final curtain fell tragically in Hollywood: on *History Is Made at Night* (UA, 1937), Clive, as Jean Arthur's satanically jealous spouse, had a frightening breakdown during one of his scenes, bursting into hysterical sobs. On *The Woman I Love* (RKO, 1937), starring Paul Muni and Miriam Hopkins, Clive, as a captain of the LaFayette Escadrille, was so hellishly drunk by noon that he had to be held up for "over-the-shoulder" shots.

The actor holed up in his house, 2520 Nottingham Avenue, in the Los Feliz colony high in the Hollywood Hills, near the Griffith Observatory; "Hyde" had escaped and would never be subdued again. The medical threat of amputating his long-damaged leg, which perhaps gave Clive true nightmares about *Mad Love,* was the final demon to taunt this sad, brilliant actor.

Colin Clive died of consumption on the morning of June 25, 1937, at Cedars of Lebanon Hospital, Hollywood. The Edwards Brothers Colonial Mortuary hosted the wake, and the public could pass a great funeral bed, on which Clive's body lay. One of those who visited the mortuary was 20-year-old Forrest J Ackerman, fated to become legendary editor of *Famous Monsters of Filmland;* he recalls the scene:

> Do you remember in the beginning of *Bride of Frankenstein,* when Clive's recuperating, and he's sitting up in bed, with a nice dressing gown on? Well, in those days, it was possible to walk into a funeral parlor, and there was a room where he was just lying in bed—and he looked very much like that scene in *Bride.* As I recall, he had a dressing gown on, and he was calmly lying there. I just stood by his side, and thought my thoughts about him—I liked him immensely.

The funeral of June 29, 1937, was a Hollywood carnival, with 300 "mourners" showing up for a lonely soul who had died alone. One of the pallbearers was Peter Lorre.

Before 1937 ended, another *Mad Love* alumnus died, under bizarre circumstances. In December of 1937, Ted Healy's 23-year-old wife gave birth to a son, and the alcoholic comic celebrated by going on what the *New York Times* described as "a lone round of film colony cafes." Late on the night of December 20, Healy showed up roaring drunk at the Trocadero nightclub, where the management ordered the waiters not to sell him any liquor. According to Trocadero employees, Healy got into a fight in the parking lot with an unidentified foe. The next day, December 21, 1937, the 41-year-old Healy died at his Hollywood home.

At first, it was announced that Healy had died from a heart attack. Then coroner Frank Nance, noting "evidence of heavy blows about the head which had necessitated surgical sutures," demanded an autopsy, believing a fist fight had contributed to his death. On December 22, autopsy surgeon Dr. A. F. Wagner announced death was due to natural causes, arguing that the facial wounds were "entirely superficial in nature" and that Healy's celebration "might have been a contributory factor" in his demise. It was divulged quickly that Healy's death was due to acute toxic nephritis, induced by acute and chronic alcoholism.

Naturally, this all became big Hollywood gossip. Healy's wife was still in the hospital with her baby. Then came the news that Healy, despite his $1750 per week salary, was penniless. Friends paid for his requiem High Mass funeral at St. Augustine's Catholic Church (where MGM producers Eddie Mannix and Harry Rapf were among the pallbearers), and for the burial at Calvary Cemetery. As the scandal erupted, a reporter (à la Healy's Reagan of *Mad Love*) managed to get a mortuary shot of the dead actor's facial wounds; a copy of the picture still survives in a Hollywood still shop.

Then on Christmas Eve, Healy's first wife and ex-vaudeville partner, Mrs. Betty Healy (who had played Stan Laurel's wife in *Our Relations* [1936]), demanded a complete D.A. investigation of her ex-husband's death. "I am convinced there was foul play in connection with Teddy's death," she told the press, implying that the D.A. was protecting somebody—possibly somebody famous. The second Mrs. Healy, still in the hospital with her infant son, made a Christmas Day appeal to the first Mrs. Healy not to proceed, arguing that such sensational charges "would do no one any good" and labeling Betty Healy's claims "entirely preposterous." Nevertheless, Healy's first wife protested throughout the holidays, promising to give the D.A. the names of the men (plural) who supposedly beat Healy to death. She also claimed that she was told the reportedly destitute actor actually owned Hollywood real estate and ranch property and a $100,000 life insurance policy protecting her and his new family. No will was reported, the headlines faded, and the *New York Times* quietly explained Healy's impecunious nature by writing he "gave freely for years to friends in poor circumstances." Nevertheless, rumors ran wild, and the Hollywood grapevine whispered for years that the man primarily responsible for beating Healy to death was none other than Healy's MGM co-worker, Wallace Beery.

The ironic title of Healy's final, posthumously released film: *Love Is a Headache* (1938).

And, as for Peter Lorre, he followed *Mad Love* with Hitchcock's British *Secret Agent* (1935) and Columbia's *Crime and Punishment* (1935), before signing with 20th Century–Fox. The studio so wasted the great actor in the *Mr. Moto* potboilers that Lorre reportedly had a nervous breakdown. Departing Fox, Lorre joined Karloff and Lugosi (receiving the best salary of the trio) in the Kay Kyser comedy *You'll Find Out* (RKO, 1940), had a horror success in Robert Florey's *The Face Behind the Mask* (Columbia, 1941), and began his triumphant Warner Bros. years as swishy Joel Cairo in *The Maltese Falcon* (1941). One of Lorre's best WB performances was Dr. Einstein, the drunken plastic surgeon who made Raymond Massey resemble Boris Karloff in the 1944 *Arsenic and Old Lace* (Lorre reprised the role with Karloff on a 1955 telecast of the classic comedy). Lorre nicely teamed with massive Sydney Greenstreet in several Warner melodramas; the party-loving, hard-drinking, raconteur Lorre upset his obese co-star with his increasing tendency to paraphrase lines.

In 1946 Lorre had one of his richest Warner roles, evocative of *Mad Love;* it was *The Beast with Five Fingers,* directed by Robert Florey and scripted by Curt Siodmak, with Lorre as a madman tormented by a dismembered hand that plays the piano.

The 1950s were an odd era for Lorre. He directed, co-wrote, and starred in the European *The Lost One* (1951), a great curiosity among film buffs; became ill and gained 100 pounds; suffered health problems; and, more and more, played himself in such films as Jerry Lewis's *The Sad Sack* (1957), seemingly reveling in his own pop-eyed, bedroom-voice mannerisms. Of course, by the 1960s, these mannerisms had hit icon status. Lorre enjoyed a comeback via the American-International hits *Tales of Terror* (1962), *The Raven* (1963), and *The Comedy of Terrors* (1964). Another curiosity of this era was his appearance with Karloff and Chaney, Jr., on the famous 1962 Halloween episode, "Lizard's Leg and Owlet's Wing," of "Route 66." He was heavy, ill, still ad-libbing, and (according to several sources), probably on drugs to ease his pains; but he still had his powers.

"Peter Lorre was wonderful," Hazel Court, the beautiful, red-haired "lost Lenore" of *The Raven,* told me in 1991. "A great intellectual—he was so bright.... He had a wonderful twinkle."

Peter Lorre died of a stroke March 23, 1964. Vincent Price delivered the eulogy at the Hollywood funeral, which drew an overflow crowd. Lorre is buried at Hollywood Memorial Park with his third wife, who at the time of Lorre's death had separated from him and had filed for divorce.

And, as for Karl Freund, *Mad Love* was his final film as a director.

Mad Love production shot: left to right Ted Healy, Henry Kolker, Peter Lorre, and Karl Freund (seated in dark glasses).

He returned to cinematography, winning the Oscar for MGM's 1937 *The Good Earth*. His obstreperous ways remained; Hume Cronyn, who acted in Fred Zinnemann's first film, *The Seventh Cross* (MGM, 1944), remembered Freund as "an absolute bastard" who made life miserable for novice director Zinnemann. Freund left MGM for Warners in the late 1950s; in 1951 he began a long tenure as cameraman of Desilu's "I Love Lucy" show, pioneering the three-camera technique for TV. He eventually supervised the photography of all Desilu products, made major contributions to light meters used in aviation, and finally retired, well fed by his Desilu residuals.

In November 1968 Freund was guest of honor at Universal City, as the studio prepared theatrical reissues (again) of *Dracula* and *Frankenstein*. "They're so young to be interested in these pictures!" marveled Freund, who had mellowed (according to writer Bill Warren, who knew him well) into "a great big teddy bear" in his final years. Karl Freund died May 3, 1969, and is buried at Mt. Sinai Cemetery in Los Angeles.

So Freund, Lorre, Clive, and most of the creative forces of *Mad Love* were dead by 1971, when Pauline Kael published *Raising Kane*. The book accused Orson Welles of copying *Mad Love* in the visual style of his 1941 milestone, *Citizen Kane.* Her ammunition included the facts that both Gogol and the old Kane are bald; that Gogol's house and Welles's "Xanadu" are similar; that both Gogol and Kane have a pet cockatoo. Gregg Toland, who had provided the eight days of additional photography on *Mad Love,* was Welles's cinematographer on *Citizen Kane,* and Miss Kael opined that Toland "had passed on Freund's technique to Welles."

The Kael attack was intriguing, but cruel and self-serving; she failed to interview any of the dynamic forces of *Citizen Kane,* and her argument (later disproved) that Welles failed to write any of the final screenplay (which she credited totally to his billed co-writer, Herman Mankiewicz) seemed more character assassination than cinema history.

At any rate, director Peter Bogdanovich published a hot rebuttal in *Esquire* magazine (October 1972) calling Miss Kael's account "malicious nonsense." Both writers, strangely, panned *Mad Love;* Kael called it "a dismal, static horror movie," while Bogdanovich claimed it was "one of the worst movies I've ever seen." All of this, of course, was to *Mad Love's* benefit; critics who never would have deigned to examine the old shocker now watched it, and MGM's forsaken horror movie came back into its rightful place as one of Hollywood's most disturbing, exciting, and fascinating melodramas.

In the fall of 1992, MGM officially made peace with its notorious, money-losing horror of 1935 and released *Mad Love* on MGM/UA video cassette.*

●

> The cinematic image of the surgeon daring and sinister enough to experiment with transplants is fading; today severed hands are sewn back on without a second's thought. Of course, *Mad Love* is concerned not with hands but with souls, and whether some of a murderer's strength and character and evil can be grafted onto another. And it explores an even more traditional theme, one that is curiously satisfying; that even wise men can be driven mad by love.
>
> —*Cinema of the Fantastic,* by Chris Steinbrunner and Burt Goldblatt, 1972

---

*The Hands of Orlac, *meanwhile, had seen many incarnations since* Mad Love. *To mention just three: the French-British 1960* The Hands of Orlac, *with Mel Ferrer as the pianist, Donald Wolfit as the surgeon, and Christopher Lee tossed in as a magician; the London play,* Duet for Two Hands, *in which John Mills scored a success; and the 1961 episode of Karloff's NBC TV series* "Thriller," *"The Terror in Teakwood," starring Guy Rolfe as a pianist so madly jealous of his dead rival that he dismembers the corpse's hands, wears them like gloves as he triumphs performing the rival's "impossible-to-play" composition, and, predictably, is killed by them as they take on a vengeful life of their own. Hazel Court screamed as Rolfe's wife; Paul Henreid directed.*

Due to the cuts, the report of Freund's (non)direction, and the power of the three stars to transcend production idiosyncrasies, assessing *Mad Love* critically is maddeningly tricky.

In addition to his cinematography of *Der Golem, Metropolis, Dracula,* and *Murders in the Rue Morgue,* Karl Freund deservedly holds a special place in horror's pantheon as director of two horror classics: the moody, romantic *The Mummy,* with its aura of evil, ancient Egypt, and the exotic, perverse *Mad Love,* with its wild Germanic flourishes. As a cinematographer, Freund might well have believed that his only real job as director of these two films was to create the "look"; indeed, in *Mad Love,* he had all the proper ingredients for his macabre cake: two powerhouse stars, a beautiful, dramatic leading lady, and a supercharged script (stuffed with Balderston's little jokes and touches that some historians have attributed to Freund's on-the-set inspirations).

A "more perfect" *Mad Love* required the personality of a more obsessed director, however. *Bride of Frankenstein* sparks with James Whale's inspired sympathy for Karloff's monster, along with his mad, operatic theatricality; *The Black Cat* so spits and arches with Edgar G. Ulmer's own sexual/religious hangups that he creates an evil, almost alive backdrop for the Boris vs. Bela championship. Even poor Tod Browning, "bashed" though he might be, manages through his sickly loving perusals of bats and bugs and armadillos to supply a sinister, personal, "D.T.'s" sense of horror to his films.

Mad Love craved but lacked the passion of a Poe-esque director; instead, in Karl Freund, we get General Electric. The movie is fastidious in its sleek, brilliant style, but, as with *The Mummy,* in which Karloff and Zita Johann provide the movie's true passion, *Mad Love* had to look to its stars for its essence.

Of course, Lorre, Clive, and Frances Drake are all wonderful. They give the movie its soul. For all of Freund's bravura craftsmanship, *Mad Love* is its most compelling when the camera simply focuses on the eyes of the star trio, for it is there that the madness, fear, and demons of *Mad Love* truly shine, and they transform what might have been Freund's mere stylistic exercise into a true movie nightmare.

Enjoying *Mad Love* gives a viewer two wishes. One is that MGM might discover the approximately 15 missing minutes and restore *Mad Love* for a video rerelease, so all could behold Rollo's harnessed-on head with the glass tube in his neck, mean old Henry Orlac's death scene, Isabel Jewell's hysteria, and the missing excesses of the Theatre des Horreurs.

The second wish is totally fanciful. One imagines that *Mad Love,* upon its summer, 1935, release, was a big hit and MGM produced a sequel. Colin Clive and Frances Drake, naturally, reprised their roles, and we learn if knife-craving Orlac eventually "killed the thing he loved."

Adding to Orlac's torment is a mysterious figure haunting his path (à la the 1991 horror hit, *Body Parts*), a squat shadow with no hands and a strapped-on head.

It is, of course, the resurrected Rollo, escaped from Gogol's mad laboratory and hellbent on getting back his own infamous hands.

The Black Room

Studio: Columbia; Producer: Robert North; Director: Roy William Neill; Cinematographer: Al Siegler; Screenplay: Henry Meyers and Arthur Strawn (from a story by Arthur Strawn); Editor: Richard Cahoon; Art Director: Stephen Goosson; Musical Director: Louis Silvers; Costumes: Murray Mayer; Sound Technician: Edward Bernds; Assistant Cameraman: Gert "Andie" Anderson; Prop Man: George Rhein; Electrician: Homer Planette; Running Time: 67 minutes.

Filmed at Columbia Studios and the Pathé Studios, Hollywood, May 6–June 1935. Opened at the Fox Theatre, Brooklyn, New York, August 16, 1935.

The Players: Baron Gregor de Berghman/Baron Anton de Berghman (Boris Karloff); Thea (Marian Marsh); Lieutenant Lussan (Robert Allen); Colonel Hassel (Thurston Hall); Mashka (Katherine DeMille); Beran (John Buckler); De Berghman (Henry Kolker); Lieutenant Hassel (Colin Tapley); Peter (Torben Meyer); Karl (Egon Brecher); Franz (John M. Bleifer); Josef (Fredrik Vogeding); Doctor (Edward Van Sloan); Bridesmaids (Lois Lindsey, Phyllis Fraser); Major-domo (George Burr McCannon); Archbishop (John Maurice Sullivan); Tailor (Reginald Pasch); Prosecuting Attorney (Robert Middlemass); Marie (Marion Lessing); Chief Justice (George MacQuarrie); Court Women (Edith Kingdon, Carrie Daumery, Grace Goodall); Court Men (Eric Mayne, Edwards Davis, Count de Stefini, Wilfrid North); Bit Gentleman (Richard Lancaster); Hairdresser (Sidney Bracy); Housekeeper (Helena Grant); Raoul (Joseph Singer); Michael (Victor DeLinsky); Peasants (Paul Weigel, Bert Sprott, Michael Mark); Gentlemen (James Gordon, Bert Howard); Bit Servant (Hans Von Morhart); Gatemen (Ivan Linow, Abe Dinovitch); Anton and Gregor as Boys (The Bleifer Twins); Court Clerk (John Beck); Judges (Alexander Melesh, E. Acosta); Double for Karloff (Herbert Evans); Double for Fall in Pit (George DeNormand); Thor the Dog (Von).

●

Karloff, the Terrible! Karloff, the Fiend! Karloff, the Monster!

—from Columbia's pressbook for *The Black Room*, 1935

157

In the fall of 1957, television offered its own black magic. The phenomena was "Shock Theatre," which invaded the Friday or Saturday late shows of over 90 cities nationwide. Lugosi in *Dracula*, Karloff in *Frankenstein*, Rains in *The Invisible Man*, Chaney, Jr., as *The Wolf Man*—like witches on broomsticks, they flew over the airwaves, into the homes of I-like-Ike America. Providing work for local actors as horror hosts (most infamously "cool ghoul" Zacherley), winning surviving actors new legions of fans (with "poor Bela" tragically not living to bask in the glory), the great goblins of Universal mythology enchanted a new generation of fans, many of whom have retained a love for these films and actors to this day.

The 52 Universal films ran over and over again, and Screen Gems, the enterprising distributor, rushed out *Son of Shock!* The new batch not only offered such hitherto unreleased classics from Universal's vaults as *Bride of Frankenstein* and the *House of Frankenstein* and *House of Dracula* "monster rallys," but to pad out the package, Screen Gems added Columbia horror shows. Television stations eventually sent back some of the Universal titles that were hardly horror films (e.g., *Nightmare* [1942], a spy yarn with Diana Barrymore and Brian Donlevy), kept the best of the bunch, and the films played on and on. At WTOP, Channel 9, in Washington, D.C., the *Shock!* package played for over a decade after the Saturday late show, almost ritualistically followed by the faithful who had survived the short-lived sensation of the late '50s.

Interspersed with the Universals, the Columbia films were a strange mixed bag. The most famous films, perhaps, were Karloff's popular "Mad Doctor" series: *The Man They Could Not Hang* (1939), *The Man with Nine Lives* (1940), *Before I Hang* (1940), *The Devil Commands* (1941), and the 1942 farce *The Boogie Man Will Get You*, which teamed Karloff with Peter Lorre. There were curiosities, like *Behind the Mask* (1932), a gangster yarn featuring the spectacle of Karloff with a black derby and a cigar that was sold on the actor's post–*Frankenstein* glory and *Night of Terror* (1933), with Lugosi as a red herring in a turban. There were losers, like *The Soul of a Monster* (1944), with Rose Hobart, and the 1944 *Cry of the Werewolf* (in which a German shepherd played the werewolf) And there were winners, such as *The Return of the Vampire* (1943), one of Lugosi's finest vampire turns, the star assisted by a werewolf servant (Matt Willis), a lovely victim (Nina Foch), and atmospheric direction (Lew Landers).

For most purists, however, Columbia's finest horror was *The Black Room* (1935). It is an enchanting Gothic melodrama that seems to have come to life off the engraved pages of a beautiful old storybook; it offers more charm, artistry, and flair in its 67 minutes than all the other Columbias combined. Its blessings are many: Karloff's virtuoso triple performance as evil Count Gregor, his kindly brother Anton, and Gregor-

Karloff and Katherine DeMille in *The Black Room.*

posing-as-Anton; the beauty of heroine Marian Marsh; and (perhaps most overlooked) the incredibly sensitive, atmospheric, and exciting direction of Roy William Neill, whose handling of this film (and *Frankenstein Meets the Wolf Man*) might qualify him as the most unsung of Hollywood's horror directors.

The Black Room has won a devoted following ever since its revival of *Shock!* over 30 years ago. Perhaps its finest compliment is that it not only looks like a '30s Universal film, it looks like a James Whale '30s Universal film. The recognition it enjoys today is particularly satisfying, for no horror film of the 1930s ever received so unfair, ignorant, and cruel a fate from the trade journals as did *The Black Room*.

> One day Harry Cohn—he was the president of Columbia and a very, very crude man—said to me, "Go up to wardrobe and they'll dress you. There's an Italian artist who's going to paint your picture." . . . I was a stock contract player, and for $75 a week we did everything but sweep the floor. . . . I remember it was very hot, mid-summer, and I was wearing this little pink one-piece bathing suit I always wore to interviews. . . . One girl

said, "No wonder you got the job, coming here in a bathing suit!" Anyway, for the painting, the Columbia people draped me in a big black velvet robe that hung all the way down in front. . . . I posed for three days—seven, eight hours a day. I got a Coke and a break for lunch. The torch was made out of light material, plaster or papier-mache, but my arm got so tired from holding it up in the air that I told the artist it was going to fall off. So he got the prop man to drop a wire down from the ceiling, and they hung the torch from the wire. I just sort of held onto it, and it helped. . . . I didn't know until I saw it on the screen that it was going to be the Columbia Pictures symbol. . . . Nobody told me. Residuals, are you kidding?

> —Amelia Batchler, model for the
> Columbia logo, in a *People*'s "The
> 100th Birthday of Hollywood" issue,
> February 9, 1987

"It beats being a pimp," was the famous reflection of Harry Cohn on the wonders of being production chief of Columbia Pictures, 1438 N. Gower Street, Hollywood. "King Cohn" (as Bob Thomas titled his 1967 biography of the man) was perhaps the most feared and despised mogul of them all. When he died in 1958, after over 30 years as Columbia's power, 2000 people came to the funeral held at Columbia Studios—a record for a Hollywood wake—and Red Skelton cracked the notorious joke: "Well, it only proves what they always say—give the public something they want to see, and they'll come out for it."

In 1935 Harry Cohn was top of his heap. On February 27, 1935, at the Biltmore Bowl in Los Angeles, *It Happened One Night* won an Oscar sweep (à la *One Flew Over the Cuckoo's Nest* and *The Silence of the Lambs*)—Best Picture, Best Actor (Clark Gable), Best Actress (Claudette Colbert), Best Director (Frank Capra), and Best Writer (Robert Riskin). The Gable/Colbert hitchhiking scene, with La Colbert stopping traffic by revealing her black-stockinged thigh, became one of the classic vignettes of Hollywood; after years as a bush-league studio majoring in action yarns and potboilers, Columbia Studios had arrived with a vengeance.

Meanwhile, Universal's Karloff was restless. Completing *The Black Cat* with Lugosi, awaiting the long-ballyhooed *The Return of Frankenstein*, Karloff wisely sought a pasture away from the crazy, precariously erratic Universal City and signed an outside, one-picture star contract with Columbia. On May 28, 1934, the Los Angeles *Examiner*, domain of Louella Parsons, published this notice:

> Columbia has just signed Mr. Karloff for *The Black Room Mystery* by Joseph W. Newell. The story was purchased by Harry Cohn in New York and it has to do with the decoding of enemy communications. Karloff plays a spy and you can guess the rest.

While one might wonder where Louella got her information, there is some understanding of Karloff's attraction to Columbia. It was there, after all, that Boris had reprised his Los Angeles stage role of Galloway, the jailbird murderer of *The Criminal Code* (1931), starring Walter Huston and directed by Howard Hawks. That prison melodrama launched the career impetus that led to *Frankenstein* later that year and Karloff's extraordinary international fame.

One man on the set of *The Criminal Code* was Edward Bernds, who spent 30 years on the Columbia lot—first as a sound technician, later as a sound effects man for the Three Stooges, and still later as a resourceful director. He recalled in an interview with the author:

> I had observed Karloff on Columbia's *The Criminal Code,* 1931, directed by Howard Hawks. We did something then, for a short while, that was unique: we did a complete Spanish version—photography, recording, and all—on the more important Columbia pictures. I was assigned to the Spanish *The Criminal Code.* When Hawks shot during the day there was a script clerk who meticulously took down every camera move, diagrammed the staging so that when we, the Spanish crew, came in at night, all we had to do was follow exactly what Hawks had done with the actors. We were called in early, in case Hawks finished early, so we could pick right up, so I spent a lot of time on the English-speaking version of *The Criminal Code.*
>
> So I saw Karloff in action, with no hint of the unique contributions to the horror films that were to come in the future. He struck me as a strong, dominating actor who played the killer Galloway with terrific menace. That dark face of his could be sinister like no other in cinema history!
>
> Shooting the Spanish version of *The Criminal Code* was a pleasant enough job. ... One thing I remember is that the Spanish actor who played Karloff's part spent time on the set, watching Karloff. And he succeeded in looking like and sounding like Karloff. A really great performance.

The June 22, 1934, *Hollywood Reporter* noted that Columbia had assigned Robert Wexley to concoct the Karloff vehicle (still unnamed). Meanwhile, Karloff played a cameo in Universal's *Gift of Gab*, along with such Universal stars as Paul Lukas, Binnie Barnes, and Bela Lugosi—who soon reported (with *Gift of Gab* star Edmund Lowe) to Columbia for *The Best Man Wins.*

As fate decreed, Karloff would star at Universal in *Bride of Frankenstein* (which began shooting January 2, 1935) and rejoin Lugosi in *The Raven* (which began shooting March 20, 1935) as the Columbia property waxed and waned. It was to everybody's benefit: *Bride of Frankenstein* shot Karloff to the peak of his stardom, and Columbia vowed to provide a proper vehicle.

The result, in fact, was an actor's dream. The property was *The Black Room Mystery*, a medieval horror tale; it offered a dual role for Karloff—twin barons—the devilishly evil Gregor and the charmingly noble Anton. Arthur Strawn (who later scripted Columbia's 1936 thriller *The Man Who Lived Twice*) wrote the story, collaborating on the screenplay with Henry Meyers. The Karloff vehicle became part of the 1935 Columbia program of Associate Producer Robert North, who would supervise six releases that year, a hectic schedule averaging two months to prepare, shoot, and edit a film for release. North's three 1935 projects prior to *The Black Room Mystery* were *Mills of the Gods*, starring May Robson, Fay Wray, and Victor Jory; *Let's Live Tonight*, starring Lilian Harvey; and *Party Wire*, starring Jean Arthur and Jory.

North naturally selected directors from the Columbia contract roster. And to give *The Black Room Mystery* the touch of class Columbia desired for this Karloff show, the producer selected Roy William Neill.

Edward Bernds remembers Neill:

> Roy Neill was an unlikely-looking Irishman—he was dark, had jet-black hair, and a lot of it. His speech was that of an educated Irishman, and, incidentally, he had a couple of fingers of his right hand missing. . . .
> According to information I have about Neill from the Academy library . . . he was born in Dublin in 1890, and attended St. Mary's College there. In 1911 he was in San Francisco (all this according to Academy records) and went as a correspondent to cover a Chinese war. By the way, Halliwell's *Filmgoer's Companion* gives Neill's real name as Roland de Gostrie. (What's a French name doing with an Irishman? I guess he could have been a born-and-bred Irishman of French ancestry.)

Neill reportedly made his acting debut in San Francisco in 1911 and later toured Europe and the Orient on the stage. He became a stage manager for the illustrious David Belasco and manager/director of San Francisco's Alcazar Theatre. Neill joined the Thomas Ince Studios in Hollywood in 1915 as a director; he had worked for Paramount, Pathé, FBO, and Fox by the time he joined Columbia in 1930. Neill directed a variety of Columbia products and had a distinct style on the lot, both as a director and as a gentleman. Edward Bernds recalls:

> Roy Neill was soft-spoken and gentlemanly, unlike most of the "loud-speaker" directors at Columbia—Lew Landers, Lambert Hillyer, Ross Lederman, Al Rogell, C. C. Coleman, and the like. And this made him an ideal director for Karloff. . . .
> I recall a Karloff quickie for Columbia—1932's *Behind the Mask*, directed by John Francis Dillon. . . . I didn't like Dillon, and he didn't like me. Dillon was a loud, sometimes abusive, rough-spoken man; he had one of the reddest faces I've ever seen—looked as though if you

touched a piece of paper to it, it would burst into flame. It must have taken gallons, maybe barrels, of whiskey to produce that bourbon blush of his. He was rough-spoken, and I'm quite sure that Karloff, the gentleman, couldn't have been too comfortable with that—and would have been much happier with the gentlemanly Roy Neill.

But there was one thing about Roy Neill—I didn't like to work with him for one very good reason. On the Columbia "quickies," we always worked long, dreary hours. In the morning, Roy was a meticulous, artistic director, taking pains with every scene—so, we'd fall behind schedule for the day's work. The production office would get on him, tell him to get the scheduled day's work or else, and Roy was too gentle and submissive to argue. So he'd try to speed up. But he was genuinely incapable of shooting anything really sloppy—and we'd often work far into the night. We knew him—not in his presence—as "rocking chair" Neill. That was because he had to have a rocking chair on the set, and the prop man always provided one for him. He sat there and rocked, and we worked far into the night—that was Roy Neill.

Columbia's brainstorm of two Karloffs followed hot on the heels of the studio's *The Whole Town's Talking*, which had starred Edward G. Robinson as a meek clerk and a snarling gangster. Directed by John Ford, co-starring Jean Arthur, the film had opened in New York in February of 1935, just in time to inspire Columbia to employ the same trick photography for *The Black Room Mystery*. Unusually fine production was lined up in everything from sets to costumes; "My recollection is that *The Black Room* was treated considerably better than the typical Columbia 'B,'" says Edward Bernds, who joined the movie as sound technician, "and I guess it shows in the film."

One of the blessings of *The Black Room* mystery was the leading lady. Marian Marsh had won stardom at the age of 17 as Trilby to John Barrymore's *Svengali* (1931); the little blonde also scored as a Warner contractee in melodrama *(Five Star Final)* and comedy *(Under Eighteen)*. After working in Europe, Marsh returned to the U.S. and found Columbia's Harry Cohn interested in rekindling her Hollywood stardom. In 1983, Marian Marsh told this writer at her Palm Desert home:

> I had returned from making European films, and there was a lot of publicity about it—I was one of the first stars to go abroad to make films. Columbia didn't want anyone to know they were negotiating with me for a contract, because other producers might too. I had just been back for three or four days, and a director named Eddie Buzzell made the arrangement for the meeting with Harry Cohn. At an appointed time, we drove around in a car, stopped in front of the studio; Harry Cohn came out and got in the car with us. We drove around and around the block—around Columbia Studio, Gower Street, Hollywood Boulevard, down the little side alley—and talked about the contract. So that was a very happy time, for me, at Columbia Studio.

On Monday, May 6, 1935, the same day that MGM began shooting *Mad Love,* Columbia began shooting *The Black Room Mystery.*

●

Horror stories were probably the first forms of fiction. Although we have no records to prove it, it is more than likely that the tales about the fire in the caves of prehistoric man were horror stories. To him the outside world must have seemed filled with monsters whose manifestations were thunder, lightning, tempest, earthquake and other natural phenomena. Fear was an ever-present emotion. Even among the primitive people of the world today—the Eskimo of the Arctic, the savages of the African equatorial districts, and the Bushmen of Australia—the monster is the predominating character of their folklore.

Homer knew the appeal of the horrible. His *Odyssey* is crammed with creatures which menaced the adventurers. Early Greek mythology tells of the chimera, of the gorgon, of Medusa, Hydra; the dragon is part of Chinese folklore—as it was of the early Saxon. Tales of monsters in human form and tales of the supernatural have always been a part of the written word. Bluebeard with his slain wives; Poe's grisly tales, *The Tell-Tale Heart, The Fall of the House of Usher, The Pit and the Pendulum,* are horror stories. Vampires, werewolves, ghosts, giants, ogres, witches have been folklore and fiction devices to inspire fear in the minds of the listener or reader.

Why do people enjoy horror tales? For the same reason they flock to accidents or to the scene of a disaster, some psychologists claim. Others state that the reaction inspired by a really hair-raising horror tale transcends any human emotion. In other words, horror stories furnish a "kick" that a real experience rarely does.

> —Boris Karloff, in Columbia's *The Black Room* pressbook

The Black Room opens with a lush overture; the title credits are on a medieval scroll, instantly setting up the storybook style of the movie. As the beautiful music plays (sadly uncredited), we see a castle tower; it is clearly a momentous day, as a parade of peasants brings gifts of wheat to the fortress, where they are blessed by an ancient priest. The tower was a familiar sight to moviegoers; it had been the wicked castle of Jerusalem in DeMille's 1927 *The King of Kings,* standing on the old Pathé back lot. Late in 1938, the set would burn down (along with the *King Kong* walls) as firewood for the burning of Atlanta in *Gone with the Wind.*

Inside the castle, a group of beautifully costumed aristocrats look fervently up through the foyer toward a closed, second story door. A nun

Karloff and Thurston Hall take a stroll with Katherine DeMille (Cecil B.'s daughter) during the filming of *The Black Room*.

prays on the balcony. Neill's atmospherics are brilliant; within less than a minute, he has fastidiously captured a medieval world of Catholic belief and ritual. Edward Bernds remembers:

> The religious atmosphere in *The Black Room*—that was Roy Neill all the way, not the cameraman, Al Siegler. It's not the cameraman's job to create, but to execute what the director wants. As for Roy Neill creating

the Catholic atmosphere, he was Irish born-and-raised, so he was probably exposed to Catholicism, but that doesn't necessarily mean he did that out of conviction. I never saw any signs of religious preoccupation. A director uses and should use anything to make a scene or picture work for him, and it needn't be conviction at all.

Most fervent of the group is Baron de Berghman (Henry Kolker, who took this Columbia job at virtually the same time he was playing the prefect of police in Metro's *Mad Love*). The door opens and out steps the doctor, Edward Van Sloan. While the role of the doctor who delivers the cursed de Berghman twins is a significant one, it seems almost a bit part for the man who played Van Helsing of *Dracula*, Dr. Waldman of *Frankenstein*, and Muller of *The Mummy*; still Van Sloan plays it with customary dignity. He descends the staircase.

"An heir, my Lord," announces Van Sloan's doctor. "And a brother for him. Twins."

The young Lt. Hassel (Colin Tapley) proposes a toast, but the baron gravely stops him — "Don't toast this birth!" The music ominously interjects, and we see the coat of arms of the de Berghmans.

"Do you all know how our family began?" the baron asks. "With twins. Brand and Wolfram. And it will end with twins. Brand the younger murdered his brother. This house began with murder — it will end the same way." He gravely acknowledges the massive coat of arms that hangs on the castle wall:

"Principio et Finem Similia," reads the Baron, translating, "I end, as I began."

The baron directs the young Lt. Hassel to read the old Latin curse, believed for hundreds of years: how Brand had slain his brother in the Black Room; how the older brother inherits the title and lands, while the younger will be fated to be bitter and violent.

"The younger will have greater reason than that for bitterness, my Lord," says Van Sloan's doctor. "His right arm is paralyzed."

The old baron is fanatic in his fear, so Lt. Hassel proposes a simple solution: "Seal it up. There won't be any Black Room!" The baron takes his suggestion.

The Black Room shows its passage of time worthy of a horror movie via the cemetery. We see the little de Berghman brothers (played by the Bleifer twins) standing by their mother's grave; later, as young men, by their father's. And it is in the cemetery, 20 years later, that we first see Baron Gregor de Berghman — the evil one.

"If you'll permit me to say so, your Lordship," says Hassel, now a colonel, and now played by Thurston Hall (1883–1958) in a fine, floridly hearty performance, "your parents' graves are in a disgraceful condition."

"I know, I know," says Gregor, in his cloak and hat, standing amidst cemetery statuary that looks as if it were rented from Universal City. "But now that my brother's returning, we can take care of it together." There have been so many assassination attempts on Gregor that he won't venture into town to meet his brother after a ten-year absence; Col. Hassel must take the coach and meet him. And as they leave the graveyard, we see a large raven sitting on the fence—a touch that director Neill would repeat in the marvelous graveyard opening of Universal's *Frankenstein Meets the Wolf Man*.

Gregor will be one of Karloff's most striking portrayals, acted with a rich, Byronic depravity. For followers of the actor's career, there is an oddity: Karloff's Gregor, in growl and leers, seems an ancestor of the Grinch of the animated 1966 Dr. Seuss special, *How the Grinch Stole Christmas*, for which Karloff, of course, supplied the Grinch's voice—and the narration. One might guess the creators of that classic special (today a holiday tradition) studied Karloff's Gregor in animating the Grinch. It's a touch that adds to the enjoyment of Karloff's powerhouse performance, rather than detracting from it.

The village is in the Tyrolean, gingerbread style of *Frankenstein* and *Bride of Frankenstein*. In the inn, a glockenspiel plays and the peasants are restless. In their ranks will be some faces familiar to horror fans. First there is Egon Brecher, who had played the major domo in *The Black Cat* and the coroner in *Mark of the Vampire*. "What does he have to do to us before we strike back?" demands Brecher, as the coach from Budapest arrives. Out steps Baron Anton, fastidious in his top hat and cloak, holding on a leash a magnificent Great Dane named Thor (played by "Von," who, according to *The Black Room* pressbook, devoured four-and-a-half pounds of raw meat per day on the picture).

"Has the baron's coach arrived?" he asks a terrified barmaid, who obviously mistakes him for his notorious sibling. "Oh. Some sherry, please." He sits, and smiles at the horrified peasants who think he is his brother.

If Gregor is "the Grinch," Anton is the real-life, gentle "dear Boris," just as we might imagine him entering the 1935 Universal (or Columbia) commissary for lunch, while the awestruck looks of the peasants are probably just the kind of glances the star had to tolerate whenever he appeared in public.

The coach rides up into the mountains, as Anton recalls why he left: not because of the legend, but "Because of what hearing so much about it did to me. I began to believe in the prophecy, in spite of myself. Every time I looked at Gregor—my own brother—he seemed to expect me to kill him." A shot blasts through the coach window. "That was meant for your brother, Gregor," says Col. Hassel.

Awaiting Anton at the castle is Peter, the loyal family servant, played by Torben Meyer, latest member of the "all-star peasant cast" of *The Black Room*. Bald, Slavic Meyer had played the Dane in *Murders in the Rue Morgue,* been cut from *Mark of the Vampire* (he appears to be looming in long shots), but had a nice bit as the Gypsy companion of Maria Ouspenskaya in Neill's *Frankenstein Meets the Wolf Man.* Anton warmly greets him. Back inside Anton warily eyes the coat-of-arms.

Thor barks viciously. He sees Gregor, slouched in his study, as he smokes a pipe. Here we see the wonderful nuances of Karloff's performance—slouchy, loose-limbed, tousle-haired Gregor and courtly, fastidious, classically polite Anton.

"If my subjects hadn't been so unruly, I would have proclaimed a great festival in your honor," says Gregor. "But they don't deserve a feast—much as you do!"

The trick photography varies: at first, Neill relies on a double for Karloff (actor Herbert Evans), with back angled to camera as the scene focuses. Quickly, however, Al Siegler's camera captures the movie magic of two Karloffs in the same scene—slickly captured, and still impressive today. Edward Bernds says:

> The trick photography . . . My guess is that it was the standard split-screen done in the camera, rather than the optical printer. Dupe negatives were of poor quality then, and if the double–Karloff scenes are good quality, they probably were done in the camera. The time-consuming nature of the split screen is that the camera must be fastened down solidly, not the slightest movement permitted—all this while the actor takes time to change his costume or makeup, or both.

Peter brings wine from the south vineyards, but fearful of poison, Gregor makes *him* drink it. Gregor denies the peasants' charges against him, mocks the Black Room, and vows friendship—only to have Thor bark. A squad of peasants has attacked the castle.

The de Berghman brothers leap into action. Anton grabs a sword and Thor pins down a peasant named Franz. Gregor watches in glee, and Neill gives him a chilling closeup as the villain leers, "Kill him, Thor!"

"Ask him what became of my sister," hisses Franz after Anton saves him from Thor, "and the other women. Ask him what becomes of *all* the women. Why are they never seen again?"

Gregor orders the assailant taken away; when Anton intercedes, Gregor freezes his brother with a murderous glance.

That night, the twins pay a call on Col. Hassel and his beautiful blonde niece, Thea. Marian Marsh looks properly ethereal as she plays the harp and sings the haunting "Love Is Like Music," while Anton smiles and sways his eyepiece, and Gregor slouches—and then ebulliently claps his hands as she finishes.

"Lovely. Lovely!" says Anton.

"Yes," leers Gregor, grabbing Thea's hand to kiss it. "She's a lovely child!"

"I think your Lordship's brother was referring to the music!" snaps Columbia's young workhorse leading man, Robert Allen. As the soldier leaves, the young people have a scene beneath a religious statue; he warns her that Gregor is a monster and never to be alone with him.

"You know, my dear, if I ever decide to marry, I can think of no one who would make a more charming baroness than you," says Gregor, as Thea rejoins the group. The offer chills Thea, nor does it sit well with Mashka, the servant girl who is Gregor's mistress of the moment (played by Cecil B. DeMille's talented adopted daughter, Katherine, for many years the first wife of Anthony Quinn).

Late that night, Mashka moves through the cemetery to meet her wicked lover at the castle. Beran, the village leader, follows and stops her. "You used to want to be with me all the time," says Beran, a character well played by John Buckler. He was an English stage actor with the looks and voice of a matinee idol and is perhaps best remembered as the evil Captain Fry of MGM's *Tarzan Escapes* (1936). (Buckler met an early, tragic end. On Halloween morning, 1936, residents of the Lake Malibu colony awoke to see the wheels of Buckler's automobile floating over the lake's surface. A storm in the night presumably had swept Buckler's car off the road and into Lake Malibu, drowning Buckler and his 66-year-old actor-father Hugh Buckler; both were found dead inside the car.)

Mashka eludes her erstwhile suitor and arrives at the castle for one of *The Black Room*'s finest scenes. As she plays a mandolin and sings "Love Is Like Music," Karloff's Gregor sits with his leg thrown over his chair's arm and devours a pear. Mashka jealously tirades the baron and the dialogue is delightfully double-meaning:

"Don't you want to kiss me?" pleads Mashka.

"A pear's the *best* fruit," sneers Gregor.

"Every time you see her, you want to be rid of me!"

"Lots of juice in a pear!"

"Well, I won't be got rid of so easy. Do you hear what I say?"

"Adam should have chosen a pear!"

"You've got it all planned, haven't you? You're going to marry her? You're going to make *her* your wife, your baronness!"

"I like the feel of a pear. And when you're through with it . . ." Gregor violently throws the pear core across the room.

Mashka promises to put an end to the marriage plans. "Who would you choose?" she demands. "A sweet little innocent who plays the harp or someone who knows the other door to the Black Room? Someone who's seen you carry heavy things in there late at night?"

Roy William Neill's flair for atmosphere is evident in this still from *The Black Room* (note Katherine DeMille in the mirror).

Within a moment, Mashka is whimpering for her life; before the night is over, she is the latest heavy thing Gregor is carrying through the secret door to the Black Room.

The disappearance of Mashka is all the peasants need to become violent. Back in the village, we see the townspeople; there, perhaps inevitably, is Michael Mark, father of Little Maria in *Frankenstein,* familiar of such horror shows as *The Black Cat, Mad Love, Son of Frankenstein, The Mummy's Hand, The Ghost of Frankenstein, House of Frankenstein,* and, later in 1960, Roger Corman's *The Wasp Woman.* "The baron was there!" is his sole line. The men drag in Peter, who has found Mashka's shawl in the castle; it is all they need to storm the castle.

"Have you ever seen a man torn to pieces by a mob, Your Lordship?" Hassel warns Gregor as the peasants climb the mountains. Thor sounds the alarm as the mob storms into the castle, and Beran unfolds Mashka's shawl. "That butchering brother of yours has carried off our women before you ever came here!" says Beran, assuring Anton of their respect. "It ends right now!" But Gregor has a surprise.

"I renounce my title in favor of my brother ... in fact, that's why I brought my brother back. I knew you were dissatisfied, I knew you wanted somebody else to govern you. Well, you have it. My brother, Anton!"

Anton is as shocked as everyone, but reluctantly agrees. Hassel is delighted. So are the peasants. "Your worries are over too," growls Gregor to Thea. "Now you won't have to be the baroness after all."

That evening, Gregor merrily turns over the title to a worried Anton, who sits petting Thor. And he has a new surprise—a secret entrance, through the fireplace, into the Black Room.

"It's nothing—centuries of fear for nothing!" smiles Gregor. "Come in. Still worried about that stupid legend? Don't be foolish! According to the legend, *you're* supposed to kill *me!*"

"The Black Room," sighs Anton inside. "It *is* black."

Like a tour guide, Gregor cranks open a medieval floor covering.

"The pit," announces Gregor. "Our ancestors used to throw their enemies there and left them until they rotted and died. That's where Brand killed Wolfram—and the legend began."

"Why, there are bodies there," gasps Anton, seeing Mashka's atop the pile.

"Yes," says Gregor.

"And this knife, there's blood on it."

"Yes."

"Is that a woman?"

"Yes. Mashka."

"Then the horrible things they say about you are true."

"Yes!"

And Gregor kicks Anton, who tumbles way down into the pit. He lands on his back, the knife he had discovered wedged in his paralyzed arm—and facing upward.

"Did you really think I meant to turn the title over to you? I've been getting ready for this for months. I knew they wanted to be rid of me. Now when I appear before them as the kindly Anton, no one will oppose me— not even Thea. Good-bye brother. There's nothing to fear now—the prophecy can't be fulfilled."

"It *will* be fulfilled," the dying Anton gasps.

"Perhaps you'll come back from the dead to kill me?"

"Even from the dead."

Gregor lowers the covering on the pit. He stares at himself in the black, onyx wall. And in a tour de force, Karloff's Gregor pushes back his tousled hair, dramatically draws up his right arm as if paralyzed, and smiles mockingly, terribly, at his reflected masquerade as he lampoons his late brother:

"Will you announce Baron Anton? Good evening, Col. Hassel. My *dear* Thea."

●

Blood-Curdler Karloff Man of Refinement in Real Life But
His Character in *The Black Room* Would Frighten a Regiment
—A headline in Columbia's press-
book for *The Black Room.*

The Black Room was a happy production, as Karloff and Neill enjoyed
a great rapport. As Bernds says:

> Karloff liked and respected Roy Neill. I think Karloff recognized the
> "try-for-quality" that Neill made. There was another factor in their rap-
> port. Roy Neill, although he was Irish-born-raised-and-educated, had
> the accent and some of the reserve of the upper-crust Englishmen. I
> believe Karloff was comfortable with that. I don't mean that Karloff was
> snobbish; it was just that his reserve was part of his personality. The crew
> respected that reserve, and his professionalism—which was exemplary.
> The man was always prepared, always working to make scenes as good
> as he could make them.

Marian Marsh enjoyed working with Karloff too. The actress soon
found herself a guest at the Karloff house, an old Mexican farmhouse high
in the mountains of Coldwater Canyon. It was there that Boris—in favored
attire of top hat and swim trunks—enjoyed his roses, his pool, and his bevy
of pets. Marsh remembers one pet particularly well.

"Boris had a pet pig, whose name was Violet," says Miss Marsh. "She
was the cleanest, pinkest pig I've ever seen, and always wore a violet bow.
And the pig had a playpen, with little rails, and a spread over the floor, inside the house."

Marsh was often a guest at the Karloff hacienda for dinner, and
sometimes Boris would be late coming home from the studio. When Violet
heard Boris's car, she would start bouncing forward and back, squealing
away for her beloved master.

"Well, what's the matter with Violet?" the dinner guests would
playfully ask. "Is Boris coming home?"

The more Violet heard the name "Boris," the more desperate she
became; the squealing got more passionate, and as Marsh says, "its little
eyes would be just *huge.*"

Finally dear Boris would make his entrance—"How's my little Violet
today?" he'd inquire—then climb into the playpen to romp with his pig.

"It was really a sight to be seen," says Marian Marsh. "But the funny
thing was, my name at birth had been Violet—and I never did tell Boris,
because I was afraid it might upset him."

The cast had fun. According to *The Black Room* pressbook, Neill was
"disappointed and irritated" when a coachman reported for a scene with

a "lively and prancing" quartet of horses. Wanting the horses to appear as if they had been driven a long distance, Neill told the coachman to go driving for hours to wear down the horses. "But Karloff had a better idea," noted the pressbook. "He made the happy suggestion that the cast wear out the horses and have a good time to boot." So Boris and the various cast members all took turns taking long rides in the coach—with everyone (according to the PR) having "a very merry time."

Finally, there was a relaxed atmosphere on *The Black Room*. Due to Karloff's prestige, with *Bride of Frankenstein* in its first run, and with the post–Oscar-sweep euphoria of Columbia's *It Happened One Night*, "rocking chair Neill" didn't have to work late into the night to create his atmosphere and pace. While information about the exact budget and the number of shooting days remains elusive, it is clear that *The Black Room* was getting the time and resources to be an exceptional melodrama.

Everyone held high hopes for its success.

●

Gregor's masquerade as Anton proceeds. It is actually Karloff's third performance of the movie: he impersonates his charming brother persuasively, but with a sly, evil glee, as if he's enjoying the fakery and laughing at those fooled by it.

Gregor/Anton and Col. Hassel play chess one stormy day; the baron suggests a marriage to Thea, to bring the houses together. The young lieutenant has other ideas; he threatens to "put a foot of steel" through anyone who tries to take Thea from him. Even in the love scenes, Neill manages to decorate the story and festoon its mood. The young lovers have a scene by the door; Marsh takes the soldier's high military hat, cocks it on her head, and flirtatiously refuses to return it: "Because if I give you your hat and you go out wearing it in this storm, you won't catch cold or get pneumonia and I won't be able to bring flowers to the hospital or wear beautiful black clothes to your funeral!" Then she laughs and gives him a little salute, still wearing the hat; it is a decorative, doll-like touch that suits this Gothic fairy tale and remains Marsh's most memorable image of the movie. Later, the young people watch a charming old music box play. Under Neill's sure hand, the young lovers never seem obnoxious or silly; rather, they perfectly fit the medieval mood, while exuding a genuine likability.

Meanwhile, that stormy nightHassel suggests a marriage agreement to the baron that offers him complete control of the Hassel family fortune. One problem: the hitherto right-handed Gregor must sign it. He sends Hassel across the room for some celebratory liquor and while the Colonel's back is turned, rapidly signs it with his "paralyzed" right hand. Hassel sees

his action in the mirror and confronts him. In a marvelous moment, "Anton" relaxes his arm, gives a Grinchy grin and sneers, in Gregor's old tones: "Why don't you notify the authorities?"

Hassel plans to do so—and within seconds, he has a knife in his back.

The discovery of Hassel's body the next morning also shows what an inspired director can do. A little blonde housemaid, Marie (Marion Lessing), coy and vain, comes to tidy up. She is full of herself, enjoying her reflection in the mirror, sashaying about like a little popinjay; indeed, Neill has the twitter of birds on the soundtrack. She enters the room where the body lies and runs out screaming, totally hysterical, all her vanity forgotten as she shrieks her way up the stairs.

Naturally, the baron engineers guilt to fall on Lieutenant Lussan. The courtroom comes complete with a large cross; Lussan is found guilty, stripped of his epaulets, and sentenced to be shot to death one month from that day.

Thea begins staying in the cemetery. The baron calls on her there and says Lussan doesn't want to see her. She breaks into tears, and as her head lowers, we see Karloff's face light up with a sadistic grin, which naturally vanishes as she looks back up at him. He proposes she marry him.

"I wish I loved you," Thea says.

"Won't you try?" asks the baron.

To the sound of wedding bells, the village is celebrating, with garland wreaths and dancing peasants; it looks like Colin Clive's wedding day from *Frankenstein.* In a nice scene, ladies tend to Thea in her bridal gown a magnificent, pink satin creation inspired by an 1840 Viennese gown, complete with tiny seed pearls and pink lace, the memory of which still thrills Marian Marsh to this day. One of her attendants says she's beautiful, "even for a baroness."

"When I used to dream of being married," says Thea, with a tender sadness, "it was never as a baroness."

Tailors are fluttering about the baron, too, in his own wedding finery. "Never use your right arm again," he advises himself after the tailors bow themselves out of the room. "Never stretch it out. Never embrace Thea. Never even defend yourself with it. It's paralyzed—to death." With his left hand, he cocks his top hat in place, throws on his cape—and then feels the temptation to visit the Black Room. He raises up the massive lid and shines a candle far down at Anton's body.

"Yes, you're dead, Anton. Good and dead. You're going to be married today—but you won't be there."

There's an interruption—the barking of Thor. The Great Dane attacks Gregor, who viciously whips it.

Opposite: **The wedding feast in** *The Black Room.*

"Poison him! Drown him! Do anything, but get rid of him!" orders Gregor/Anton with a chilling leer at a servant. He leaves to be married.

The final act of *The Black Room* is a spectacle, almost out of an operetta, that is handled by Neill and his cast with a wonderfully exciting flair. The bride's coach arrives at the church. Later, the groom arrives too. The peasants shower him with cheers and flowers. At first, the villain grimaces, then he recovers and gives an "Anton" smile—a marvelous moment for Karloff.

Inside the church, a choir sings hymns. In the bride's chamber, Lussan—let free by Beran—has come to say good-bye to Thea. They kiss, he escapes through the window, and the weeping bride prepares to meet her bridegroom at the altar.

Of course, the film's true hero has also escaped—Thor, the Great Dane, who is running to the church. As the choir sings and the baron and Thea meet for their vows, the priest asks if anyone knows any reason why they should not be joined as man and wife.

In lunges Thor.

"I remember that big dog," says Edward Bernds. "We had the usual trouble that we had with dogs on movie sets—the hot lights made the dog lazy. It was a task just to get him to his feet. And he panted, and slobbered, and the dog trainer had to cool him off and 'de-slobber' him for every scene!"

When the dog attacks the baron, he raises his right arm to defend himself, and Lussan, who has stayed to watch the ceremony from the back of the church, springs into action. "Look, he moved his right arm! It's the man who murdered Col. Hassel!"

Hysteria breaks out. Karloff's baron escapes from the church, looking at the give-away right arm as if he'd like to rip it from its socket. Leaping atop a coach, he whips his horses as he races away into the mountains. Of course, the whole village follows, on foot, Thor in the lead, as the music plays in wonderful agitato style. They race past the religious monuments to the castle, where Gregor has naturally taken sanctuary in the Black Room. In a grand moment, we see the frightened villain looking in the direction of at his pursuers; he darts his tongue out of his mouth like a lizard. Lussan and the peasants find the secret passage, thanks to Thor who rushes into the Black Room, lunges at Gregor, and knocks him into the pit, where he falls down and lands on the knife wedged in Anton's right arm. The villagers gather around the pit.

"The older brother—killed by the younger brother's knife," says Lussan. "The prophecy has been fulfilled!"

The "Love Is Like Music" theme swells as the movie ends.

●

Karloff and Marian Marsh in *The Black Room*.

Karloff as Super Bluebeard
in Film, *The Black Room*
Screen's Ace Horror-Man Seen as a Human
Devil with a Private Graveyard
—Columbia publicity for *The Black
Room*

Finally, Columbia placed the finishing touches on *The Black Room*. It was a horror movie that seemed to have everything: a bravura performance from Karloff, a lovely leading lady in Marian Marsh, a fine supporting cast, a beautiful score, and, of course, all of Neill's sensitive directorial flair. The studio prepared the pressbook for *The Black Room*, invoking the name Karloff just as Universal was doing, and offering a bevy of promotional ideas:

• There was, of course, the usual "street ballyhoo," suggesting the hiring of a man made up ("face chalk-white ... darken his eyebrows heavily") to walk around town with a banner bearing the legend "See Karloff in *The Black Room*," with the name of the theatre pinned on by a knife. The pressbook gave tips on how to create the illusion, with the advice, "Knife blade should be dulled by grinding to prevent possible injuries."

• The pressbook suggested a contest in which newspaper readers would send in their own family superstitions, in 150–200 words or less. "Award cash prizes and tickets for best letters contributed!" hawked the pressbook.

• Columbia suggested a "Have You Hair Like Marian Marsh?" beauty contest, with local beauty parlors to provide judges and courtesy manicures and beauty treatments for prizes. "Runners-up should be given tickets to see the picture," noted the pressbook.

• There was even a national promotion that trumpeted Karloff and Dodge cars. "Karloff enthusiastically endorses the new Dodge automobile!" announced the pressbook. "And Dodge is reciprocating by planning a national advertising campaign that will directly help its dealers and exhibitors featuring *The Black Room!*" The pressbook even hinted an upcoming "Dodge-Karloff" parade.

"Every penny spent and every moment devoted to thought will pay dividends when you play *The Black Room!*" hawked the pressbook. "Karloff will bring many dollars to your Box Office . . . the picture will do its part! Do yours!"

Meanwhile, Columbia proudly previewed this new Karloff chiller for *The Hollywood Reporter.* The July 17, 1935, review was a "pan" that must have shocked Columbia, Karloff, and Neill:

> Four people are killed without any excitement and certainly no mystery. Since it is perfectly obvious that this was made as a filler and tossed to the nearest producer, it is equally obvious that there's no sense in playing it unless you have to. . . . Mr. Karloff muggs at himself throughout the picture. Marian Marsh looks very, very beautiful and is called upon to do no more. . . . The script was bad to begin with and Neill couldn't do much to help in the way of direction. Al Siegler's photography is top-notch—too bad it's wasted.

And this from *The Hollywood Reporter,* which had praised *Mark of the Vampire* and Tod Browning's flaccid direction.

Trade reviews could be devastating; if *The Black Room* had any chance for a Broadway opening, the *Reporter* killed it. On the Thursday night of August 15, 1935, the 4088-seat Fox Theatre—the biggest movie house of Brooklyn, New York—hosted a preview of *The Black Room.* The new Karloff film officially opened there the next day. The *New York Times* ignored it. *Variety,* of course, paid a call and once again provided a review so obtuse as to be embarrassing:

> Karloff fans get a load of their favorite to the saturation point here, but the picture will not get much at the box office. . . . Just a dualer . . . Roy

Wm. Neill has directed as well as possible a tawdry and obvious story, but the only kudos attaching to the affair must go to Al Siegler for his beautiful camera work and to the makeup man who produced the numerous character types.... As for Karloff, he is his usual self in practically every sequence of the lengthy, dull proceedings. The rest of the cast are so unimportant its membership is hardly worth mentioning.

At the same time, *The Black Room* opened at Hollywood's Warner Theatre on a double bill with RKO's *Jalna*. Karloff's box office power sold the picture, but *The Black Room* hardly claimed its just desserts, and one wonders why. Surely there was something wildly askew in the critical eye of Hollywood trade papers when the critics missed the wonders of Karloff's dual role, the atmospherics of Neill, the sets, the costumes—even the uncredited musical score. And there was a wicked injustice in a business in which "experts" hailed directors like Karl Freund (who, according to Frances Drake, made no attempt to direct *Mad Love*, preferring to toy with the camera) or Tod Browning (who, by the time of *Mark of the Vampire*, was reportedly doing little more than calling "action" and "cut") while Neill, who worked painstakingly on performance, atmospherics, and pace, was dismissed routinely.

Perhaps the problem was timing. In 1935 *Mark of the Vampire*, *Werewolf of London*, *Bride of Frankenstein*, *The Raven*, and *Mad Love* were all released. The latter two had appalled many critics; *The Raven*, in fact, was such an embarrassment in Britain that it helped inspire the horror ban. The production of these films had more knowing movie followers whispering words like incest, necrophilia, sadism, and masochism. It was, perhaps, politically correct by midsummer of 1935 to chastise horror films, and Hollywood journals took it out on *The Black Room*—the most charming horror film, ironically, of the lot.

Life went on in the wake of *The Black Room*. Boris returned to Universal for *The Invisible Ray* (1936), third of the Karloff and Lugosi vehicles, and signed a star contract with Warner Bros. He would revisit Columbia in 1939 (following his third and final feature appearance as the monster in Universal's 1939 *Son of Frankenstein*) to commence the popular "mad doctor" series. Edward Bernds met the star again on the set of *The Man with Nine Lives* in 1940 and recalls:

> I remember the picture well, because the idea of deep-freezing people for medical purposes was a new and somewhat startling idea at the time. My diary tells me we shot scenes in the famous icehouse in Los Angeles, where Capra had shot the mountain scenes for *Lost Horizon*, so you could see the actors' breath. This big cold storage place was pretty much empty, because home refrigerators had taken care of manufactured ice, but one thing I do remember—there were huge piles of frozen tuna, great big tuna

weighing about 100 pounds each—stacked up, frozen solid, like cord wood.

As for Karloff on *The Man with Nine Lives* . . . I think Karloff was just as professional, but just a little more reserved; he didn't have the rapport with director Nick Grinde that he had with Roy Neill those years earlier. Karloff was professional, of course, but he didn't confer with Grinde as much. Grinde was not a bad director—I think he was a cut above a lot of the Columbia directors—but he was more preoccupied with getting it done on budget, on schedule, satisfying the bosses, getting another assignment. Roy Neill somehow created the impression that he was really trying to do it a little better than it was really in the cards to be.

The Black Room proved a perennial moneymaker for Columbia. As early as 1943, it was playing a rerelease double-bill with Lugosi's 1932 *White Zombie* and was still visiting theatres right into the 1950s.

And as for Roy William Neill, he departed Columbia in 1936. He directed *Dr. Syn* (1937) for General Film Distributors, served a '38–'39 stint at Warners as a director and writer, and in 1942 joined Universal, where he won great acclaim (much of it retrospectively) as director of the Basil Rathbone/Nigel Bruce Sherlock Holmes series. John Rawlins directed the first Holmes melodrama of the Universal series, *Sherlock Holmes and the Voice of Terror* (1942), but Neill directed all of the subsequent 11, from *Sherlock Holmes and the Secret Weapon* (1942) through *Dressed to Kill* (1946). Neill's atmospherics were so fine one could almost imagine the smell of Holmes's pipe; he had the distinction of helming the villainous performances in the series of Lionel Atwill, George Zucco, Henry Daniell, Evelyn Ankers, Gale Sondergaard, Patricia Morison, et al.; and Rathbone, in his long out-of-print memoir *In and Out of Character,* saluted Neill as the true heart and soul of the series.

Neill's most famous credit, however, is certainly Universal's *Frankenstein Meets the Wolf Man* (1943). Long dismissed because of Lugosi's Waterloo portrayal of the monster, this fifth entry of the monster saga has become over the years one of the most popular of all horror films, and Neill's work is wonderful, from the opening robbery of the wolf man's grave (arguably the most frightening episode of all Universal horror films) to the marvelous Festival of the New Wine (complete with the "Faro-La, Faro-Li" song) to the climactic battle of wolf man vs. monster. While Neill could do little to help "poor Bela" (whose performance was destroyed by the notorious editing of his dialogue and references to the monster's blindness), he focuses sumptuously on Ilona Massey's beauty, allows Lionel Atwill (as village mayor) to chew the scenery, showcases the kitschy mystique of Maria Ouspenskaya, and gets the best horror performance ever out of Lon Chaney.

During the Universal sojourn, Neill also directed *Madame Spy*

Director Roy William Neill (in light shirt to right of camera) sets up a scene with Karloff and Marian Marsh in *The Black Room*.

(1942), *Eyes of the Underworld* (1943, featuring Chaney as an imbecile), *Rhythm of the Islands* (1943), the Maria Montez *Gypsy Wildcat* (1944), and both directed and co-produced *Black Angel* (1946). He died in London, England (where he was negotiating for a film project), on December 14, 1946—reportedly from a cerebral hemorrhage (some sources say a heart attack). The 59-year-old artist was survived by his wife Elizabeth and daughters Patricia and Barbara.

●

> *The Black Room* is a curious one-shot horror film for Colum-
> bia. . . . With its traditionally Victorian story of prophecy, sealed
> rooms, and family curses, and effectively Gothic pictorial castle,
> church and cemetery scenes, it is the kind of (serious) melo-
> drama that has virtually disappeared from the screen. . . . Kar-
> loff turns in an excellent performance. . . . The musical themes
> throughout are first-rate.
>
> —William K. Everson, *Classics of the
> Horror Film* (1974)

For most followers of the horror scene, *The Black Room* reigns as Columbia's top terror show and as time goes by, gains in its appeal as one of
the favorite Karloff films of the '30s. The impetus it picked up on *Shock!*
over 30 years ago has built steadily since. In his famous tome *An Illustrated
History of the Horror Film,* the late Carlos Clarens praised Karloff's "barnstorming" performance; happily, the film became one of the first horror
video releases in the early 1980s, transferred to tape from an exquisite
35mm print. Showcasing Karloff the virtuoso, supported by Neill the
stylist, *The Black Room* wins honors as one of the Golden Age's finest films
and makes one wish that star and director had worked together again.

Columbia Studios won a new place in horror in the 1950s, when it released the English-made *Curse of the Demon* (1958), the William Castle
novelty *The Tingler* (1959) and several of Sam Katzman's budget chillers.

Finally, a sad, ironic footnote to Karloff and Columbia. Following his
magnificent performance in Paramount's *Targets* (1967), Karloff, wealthy
but still passionate to work, signed to star in four Mexican horror films—a
deal consummated by Mexican producer Luis Vergara and Hollywood's
Columbia Pictures. The 80-year-old Karloff, in a wheelchair, crippled by
emphysema and arthritis, reported to an infernally hot soundstage on
Santa Monica Boulevard, inspiring everyone as he rose from his wheelchair to star in four movies in five weeks. The Hollywood shooting was a
nightmare: many of the actors promised by Vergara never showed up;
some of those who did were never on time; the U.S. crew and Mexican
crew clashed; so did Columbia and Vergara. As the battles waged, Karloff
sat serenely in his wheelchair, breathing from his oxygen tank, perhaps
remembering the camaraderie and wonderful studio efficiency of the
Hollywood of old.

Karloff perhaps came to suspect that these films, fated to be reedited
into near-pornographic atrocities back in Mexico, would be the nadir of
his career; mercifully, all four films—*Isle of the Snake People, The Incredible
Invasion, The Fear Chamber,* and *House of Evil* would be released posthumously, featuring such awful scenes as Karloff laughing at the prospect of a

female victim awakening to find herself covered with maggots and leeches. When Karloff died in his beloved England February 2, 1969, his fee for the four films—a reported $375,000—was still on depost in a Mexican bank; the shooting had apparently been so unpleasant that the very well-off Karloff had yet to pursue claiming his money.

But on his final day of shooting, Boris Karloff rose to the occasion. Standing from his wheelchair, he addressed the company of what were to be his final movies, expressing his pleasure at having completed four films, and having worked with everyone on the set. He was a sincere, grateful star, happy to be acting after 60 years, and there were tears in his eyes.

The Walking Dead

Studio: Warner Bros./First National; Producer: Jack L. Warner; Executive Producer: Hal Wallis; Director: Michael Curtiz; Screenplay: Ewart Adamson, Peter Milne, Robert Andrews, and Lillie Hayward (from a story by Ewart Adamson and Joseph Fields); Camera: Hal Mohr; Art Director: Hugh Reticker; Set Designer: Anton Grot; Film Editor: Tommy Pratt; Costumes: Cary Odell; Assistant Director: Russ Saunders; Dialogue Director: Irving Rapper; Production Supervisor: Lou Edelman; Gowns: Orry-Kelly; Running Time: 66 minutes.

Filmed at Warner Bros. Studios and Griffith Park, California, November 23– December 1935. Premiere, Strand Theatre, New York City, February 29, 1936.

The Players: John Ellman (Boris Karloff); Nolan (Ricardo Cortez); Dr. Evan Beaumont (Edmund Gwenn); Nancy (Marguerite Churchill); Jimmy (Warren Hull); Loder (Barton MacLane); Werner (Henry O'Neill); Betcha (Eddie Acuff); Warden (Addison Richards); Blackstone (Paul Harvey); Merritt (Robert Strange); Trigger (Joseph Sawyer); Judge Shaw (Joe King); Mrs. Shaw (Ruth Robinson); Martin (Kenneth Harlan); Sako (Miki Morita); Reporters (Earl Hodgins, Eddie Shubert, Larry Kent, Milton Kibbee, Charles Marsh); Sob Sister (Isabelle LeMal); Tough Girl in Court Room (Lucille Collins); Broadway Type (Charles Sherlock); Copy Boy (Spec O'Donnell); Bailiffs (Lee Phelps, Tom Brower, Harry Hollingsworth, Lee Prather); Servant (George Andre Beranger); Guard (Wade Boteler); Convict (Nick Moro); Guard (Edward Gargan); Trusty (William Wayne); Priest (Edgar Cherrod); Black Prisoner (Cris Corporal); Prisoners (Tom Schamp, Ed Carli, Jim Pierce); Announcer (Gordon "Wild Bill" Elliott); British Doctor (Boyd Irwin); French Doctor (Jean Perry); Russian Doctor (Nicholas Kobliansky); English Doctor (Harrington Reynolds); Guests (Paul Irving, Brandon Beach, Malcolm Graham); Female Physician (Sarah Edwards); Train Engineer (Edward Peil, Sr.); Florist (Alphonse Martell); Joe (John Kelly); Second Guard (James P. Burtis); Watchman (Frank Darien).

●

Boris
Karloff

The Master of Horror
Achieves His Masterpiece!
—Publicity for Warner Bros.' *The
Walking Dead*, February 29, 1936

It is an irony that the horror genre, despite its accent on violence and mayhem, frequently is the most religious of genres—often profound in its dramatized relationship between the Almighty and mortals.

Universal City's classic horror films of the 1930s were offering a virtual catechism to moviegoers: Colin Clive's Frankenstein paid dearly for his blasphemy, as Karloff's monster tossed him from the fiery windmill; he survived, of course, only to twitch in angst in the hysterically religious *Bride of Frankenstein* as well. Lugosi's Dracula, a creature of the devil, cringed at the sight of the crucifix. The title character in *The Mummy* implied that God had supernatural relatives from the Egyptian glory days, still potent in the hills of the Valley of Kings, while Claude Rains in the title role in *The Invisible Man* intoned on his deathbed, "I meddled in things that man must leave alone." Elsa Lanchester, as *Frankenstein* authoress Mary Shelley, perhaps put it best in the fanciful prologue to *Bride of Frankenstein:* "My purpose was to write a moral lesson—the punishment that befell a mortal man who dared to emulate God."

Even in Universal's less sophisticated second wave of horror, this theology was apparent, as in *The Wolf Man* (1941), with Maria Ouspenskaya browbeating a priest for not recognizing the blessings of death, following the death of her werewolf son, Bela (Bela Lugosi): "Bela has entered a much better world than this—at least so your ministers always say, sir."

Universal, of course, was not alone in its piety. Religious overtones popped up in horror films everywhere—from Paramount, where Fredric March's Jekyll gave up Rose Hobart's Muriel as penance for his crimes, to Columbia, where Karloff's castle containing *The Black Room* was packed with Catholic icons, statues, and shrines.

An irony amidst this irony is one of the most religiously thematic horror films of the classic era: *The Walking Dead* (1936). On its surface, the film is a horror picture built around the Karloff star persona (brought back from the dead in a laboratory sequence strikingly similar to *Frankenstein*) and mated with Warner Bros. gangster melodramatics. It comes complete with an electric chair, racy deaths for the hoodlums, and all the slick pace Michael Curtiz later gave to WB's *Angels with Dirty Faces*.

Yet this horror/gangster morality tale dares to be different by making Karloff's monster Heaven's avenging angel. The remarkable sensitivity of

Karloff's bravura performance, the solid direction by Curtiz, and a script that insists on delivering more than expected all create one of the most surprising, moving, and truly spiritual horror movies of the time.

Indeed, *The Walking Dead* suggests what might have evolved if God had done a rewrite on *Frankenstein.*

It was the summer of 1935, and the big parade of Karloff hits kept marching through theatres. The year had seen Boris reprise the monster in *Bride of Frankenstein* and team again with Lugosi in *The Raven,* both from Universal, while he visited Columbia to have an actor's feast day as the good/evil barons of *The Black Room.* Come September, Karloff teamed once more with Lugosi in *The Invisible Ray* at Universal, which had no qualm about now promoting its legendary bogeyman as "The Great Karloff."

"It was always a happy lot," reminisced Karloff about Universal City late in his life. But it also was a crazy, seemingly doomed lot, under the guidance of physically/emotionally wracked Junior Laemmle and his almost absurdly nepotistic father. Loyal to the studio that made *Frankenstein* and had packaged his stardom so powerfully, Karloff maintained his commitment to the lot, while nevertheless negotiating for outside contracts with other studios. (It was a wise move; the Laemmle Universal would topple in March of 1936 and fall into the hands of antihorror management.)

One such outside contract Karloff was happy to sign was a star contract with Warner Bros./First National, right over the Burbank hills from Universal City.*

"San Quentin" was the nickname of the Warner Bros. Studio and the "warden" was Jack L. Warner. "This is exactly the look he had when he fired you," quipped Julius Epstein, co-author of the script for *Casablanca,* observing a giant portrait of a smiling Warner at a dinner honoring the memory of the late great producer after his 1978 death. With his flashy smile, slicked-down, thinning hair, and flashy clothes, Warner epitomized the word *mogul,* though he professed to hate the word ("It reminds me of some bad Turkish cigarettes I used to smoke"). Warner was a shameless, ruthless showman—suspending stars like Bogart, chasing Bette Davis to British courts in 1936 when she walked off the lot, taking to the Warner Bros. radio airwaves (KFWB) to croon "When the Red Red Robin Comes Bob Bob Bobbin' Along" under the name of Leon Zuardo, to cheers from the audience (mostly Warner relatives). Warner was the producer of such milestones as John Barrymore's *The Sea Beast* (1925) and Jolson's "talkie"

*The Hollywood Reporter *had revealed in March of 1935 that Warners was considering buying Universal City for a price of $9,000,000—$5,500,000 of which was to go to Laemmle, Sr., and the rest was to cover Universal's outstanding debts. The deal reportedly collapsed when "Uncle Carl"—a nepotist to the end—demanded long-term WB contracts for Junior, son-in-law Stanley Bergerman, and other relatives.*

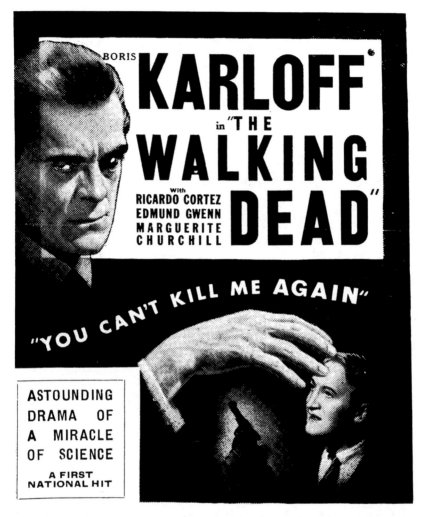

No. 401   A Powerful D/c. Advertising Block   Price 6/-

THE TRAILER'S TERRIFIC!

Trade advertisement for Karloff's *The Walking Dead*, picturing Karloff and Joseph Sawyer.

The Jazz Singer (1927), the wild and racy "Blood-and-Beer" gangster
sagas of the early '30s like Edward G. Robinson's *Little Caesar* and James
Cagney's *Public Enemy*, "socially conscious" sagas like *I Am a Fugitive from
a Chain Gang*, Busby Berkeley terpsichorean madness like *42nd Street*, and
in late 1935, the Errol Flynn/Olivia de Havilland swashbuckler, *Captain
Blood*.

The true dynamo of the Warner lot, however, was Hal Wallis—
successor to Darryl F. Zanuck as Warner's executive producer and the
man who truly styled the Warner product. It was Wallis who wrote this
memo to production supervisor Lou Edelman on August 16, 1935 (the day
The Black Room opened in New York):

> I am sending you herewith a six-page outline of an original idea entitled
> *The Walking Dead*, on which we have an option. Ewart Adamson will
> report to you Monday morning to develop this story as a vehicle for Boris
> Karloff.

Karloff completed *The Invisible Ray* at Universal on October 25,
1935. One week later, on November 2, 1935, Wallis received for his approval Karloff's contract for *The Walking Dead*. Myron Selznick had arranged the deal, calling for $3750 per week on a four-week guarantee, with
this proviso:

> Artist's name shall be accorded first billing on the screen and in adver-
> tising and publicity under the control of the Producer, and the name of
> no other member of the cast may appear in larger size type, and only the
> name of one female member of the cast may appear in the same size type,
> as that used to display artist's name.

As of this date, *The Walking Dead* was still very much a gleam in the
Warner corporate eye. Next to the word "Part" on the Karloff contract,
there is not the name "John Elman" (as he's listed in the film's credits),
nor "John Ellman" (as he's named in the newspaper montage sequence),
but simply the name "Creepy."

The one-picture deal and the "Creepy" contract was enough for
Warner Bros. The studio proudly placed a full-page collage of nearly two
dozen star portraits in the 1936 *Film Daily Yearbook*, and there was Boris
Karloff, along with Cagney, Davis, Muni, Robinson, Flynn, de Havilland,
Kay Francis, Joe E. Brown, Claude Rains, and the other "Triumphant
Warner Bros. Stars."

Everything fell into place quickly. On November 1, 1935, Wallis had
sent a draft for *The Walking Dead* to Michael Curtiz (1888–1962),
Warner's legendary director, then between *Captain Blood* and *The Charge
of the Light Brigade*. Curtiz had directed three of Warner's four famous

horrors of the 1930s: Barrymore's *The Mad Genius* (1931) and the Lionel Atwill/Fay Wray two-strip Technicolor classics *Doctor X* (1932) and *Mystery of the Wax Museum* (1933).* Workhorse Curtiz has become famous for his Hungarian distortions of the English language, from "Bring on the Empty Horses" (hence the title of David Niven's best-seller, based on Curtiz's command during *The Charge of the Light Brigade*) to my personal favorite, "The next time I send a no-good rotten son-of-a-bitch to do something, I go myself!" The remuneration for this awesomely versatile director on *The Walking Dead* would total $17,600.

Most of the supporting cast came right off the Warner Bros. contract roster. Hal Mohr (1894–1974), who would win the 1935 Best Cinematography Oscar for his work on WB's *A Midsummer Night's Dream* (and later win a Best Color Cinematography Oscar for Universal's 1943 *Phantom of the Opera*), was cameraman for *The Walking Dead*. Anton Grot, set supervisor of Warner's classic horror movies, was in his element for *The Walking Dead*, with its miracle laboratory and rain-swept cemetery.

The Walking Dead featured one scientific "miracle" from the headlines: the Lindbergh heart. Col. Charles A. Lindbergh had sacrificed his career as a pilot to assist Nobel Prize winner Dr. Alexis Carrel, famed for his work in the prolongation of life in human and animal organs. Carrel and Lindbergh had kept the Lindbergh heart, a germ-proof mechanical circulating system, pumping for an extended time in their research lab at the Rockefeller Institute.

And, finally, *The Walking Dead* featured one rather notorious name from movie/science history: Dr. Robert E. Cornish, whose experimental revival of dead dogs was performed (by Cornish himself) in Universal's 1934 *Life Returns*. Cornish had hoped for a credit on MGM's *Mad Love* (see that chapter); now Warner Bros. allowed him to get in on the action of *The Walking Dead* by basing the tilting operating table that would carry Karloff on those tables Cornish had used with his resurrected canines.

As the shooting date approached, there was only one problem: the script.

The original story was by Ewart Adamson and Joseph Fields, who had just concocted the story for RKO's *Annie Oakley* (1935), starring Barbara Stanwyck. Adamson had developed the original treatment for *The Walking Dead*, dated November 19, 1935. The role fashioned for Karloff was "Dopey" Ellman—described as "a nervous wreck" and "terribly nervous and twitchy" due to a dope and booze addiction. After his frame-up, execution, and restoration to life, Karloff's "Dopey" was a far cry from the John Ellman that ultimately haunted *The Walking Dead*. "He is a

---

**The other Warner/First National horror classic: Barrymore's* Svengali *(1931), directed by Archie Mayo.*

repulsive, vicious thing," noted Adamson's original, "still without the power of speech, which makes one recoil in horror."

Thereafter, the script has a field day describing "Dopey" as horribly as possible: "snarling," an "awful thing," "a bestial horror," "more like a monkey than a man," "the hideous thing," and so on. He has "a savage roar." To kill the gangsters, Dopey scales apartment buildings; he climbs 12 stories above an alley to kill Trigger and with "a savage leap," dares a 200 foot drop to pursue Merritt. While doing so, in the original script, he sees Mrs. Merritt, a "sleeping woman in a revealing nightgown. His mouth hangs open as his hands itch to touch her."

The first script also offered an episode in which one of the gangsters, Blackstone, disguised himself as a bearded, bespectacled professor ("with a deep, gutteral accent") to get to "Dopey" (safe on hospital grounds) and kill him with a poison gumdrop. Dopey, sprawled on the ground like a dog, "sniffs the air . . . his nostrils quiver, a look of snarling ferocity comes over his features" as Beaumont brings the disguised Blackstone to see him. Dopey sniffs around Blackstone like a dog and manages to foil Blackstone with his own poisoned gumdrop.

Karloff was aghast. With the shooting date only days away, the star expressed his problems with the script, citing Ellman's Tarzan-like agility (which, he believed, would have the audience in hysterical laughter), his lack of speech (which Karloff saw as too similar to his role in *Frankenstein*), and the accent on sensational violence. Hal Wallis rushed in three new writers — Peter Milne (who had just worked at Warner/First National on the script of Busby Berkeley's *Gold Diggers of 1935* and would later contribute to the script for WB's 1937 *San Quentin*), Robert Andrews (fresh from WB's 1935 *Little Big Shot*, directed by Curtiz), and the prolific Lillie Hayward (who had just contributed to the WB 1935 Bette Davis vehicle *Front Page Woman*, directed by Curtiz, and who much later worked on Disney's 1959 *The Shaggy Dog* and 1960 *Toby Tyler*).

Out came the nickname "Dopey," his alcohol and dope problem, the "bestial" mannerisms, the "savage leap," Mrs. Merritt and her revealing nightgown.

As the script was refined, so was the makeup concept. Karloff had been undergoing makeup tests, and on November 19, 1935, Hal Wallis sent this memo to Michael Curtiz and makeup artist Perc Westmore:

> In the Karloff test where he is photographed with Mike Curtiz, I don't like the white tucks of hair . . . anywhere. What he should have is a streak of white hair, running from the forehead back, in one narrow streak of white hair, and the rest of it should be the natural color of hair. Don't have those little white tucks; it looks like some kind of an animal.
>
> I'm not crazy about the makeup, either . . . the silvery effect. It looks a little too phoney. It looks exactly like what it is: A silver metallic paint

of some kind put on his face.... You'll have to make another test.... I don't think you're going to get anything out of this silver paint.

The overall final vision of Karloff in *The Walking Dead* would move light years from the original concept as the production progressed.

On November 23, 1935—Boris Karloff's 48th birthday—production began on *The Walking Dead.* Early "Daily Production and Progress Report" sheets would note that the script was unfinished.

●

> When I made my recent picture, *The Walking Dead,* directed by that grand fellow, Michael Curtiz, I discovered it was my name and not so much my ability that helped me.... A few months before Mervyn LeRoy chose me for a double-faced newspaper reporter in *Five Star Final,* I was called in for an interview with Michael Curtiz. Seeing me, he at once hesitated, and then said: "Well, I called you over, so I suppose I shall have to use you." I didn't understand what he meant. He gave me the role of a Russian, however, in *The Mad Genius,* the John Barrymore picture he was directing for Warners. The other day I was talking to Mike and he asked me if I remembered working for him previously. "The reason I called you in," he explained, "was because I thought you actually were a Russian. Your name is Karloff—it certainly sounds Russian. When you came in you seemed so anxious to get the job that I decided to let you have it!"
>
> —Boris Karloff, in a 1936 interview
> with Jonah Maurice Ruddy

The scene is set in a packed tense courtroom—as only Warner Bros. could present one. Reporters swamp the courthouse, awaiting the verdict of Judge Roger Shaw (Joe King) in the sensational case of Stephen Martin (Kenneth Harlan)—accused of stealing $350,000 from the city treasury. During a recess in the judge's chambers, Mrs. Shaw (Ruth Robinson) cries to her husband. She tells him of the latest telephone death threat from the infamous Loder gang, of which Martin is a notorious member.

Loder himself sits in the courtroom, like Old King Cole, with his top henchmen, confidently waiting for the decision. Beefy-faced Barton MacLane (1900–1969), WB's bulldog character heavy (best described by William K. Everson as "never speaking when shouting would do") is perfectly cast as Loder. Finally, Judge Shaw enters.

"Dinner at my house at eight," smirks Nolan, Martin's lawyer and the brains of the Loder gang, to his sweating client. "We'll celebrate!" Ricardo Cortez (1899–1977) is tailor-made for the sleazy lawyer. Once considered a Latin lover rival to Valentino, billed above Garbo in her first U.S. film (MGM's *The Torrent*, 1926), Cortez was eventually revealed to be Austrian-born Jack Kranze from Brooklyn. Thereafter, he became a splendid character actor. A Warner familiar, he would play Sam Spade in *The Maltese Falcon* (1931) and Perry Mason in *The Case of the Black Cat* (1936), but was at his best as a heel like Dolores del Rio's gigolo dance partner of *Wonder Bar* (1934).

But there's no cause for celebration; Shaw sentences Martin to ten years in the state penitentiary. The court is in an uproar, and Nolan plots a foolproof way to murder the crusading judge.

A tall, gaunt caller comes to Loder's house that night. "My name is John Ellman," he says. "A man told me to come and see you. He said you're always happy to help a fellow." Karloff, long-haired, melancholy, has a strange, almost heartbreaking gentleness in the role.

"Ellman, eh?" says Loder (who has been told by Nolan to expect his visit). "Oh yeah. I remember. Judge Shaw sent you up for second degree murder."

"Yes—for ten years."

"Some woman in the case, wasn't it?"

"It was my wife. I struck a man, but I didn't mean to kill him."

"Sure, sure. Well, what can I do for you?"

"I want a job, Mr. Loder. I'm a musician, and a good one, too. Look, I'll show you!"

Ellman sits at the piano and begins sensitively playing his favorite composition, Rubinstein's "Kammenoi-Ostrow." Loder stops him, insults him, and has his Oriental houseboy throw the humiliated man out of the house.

Out in the cold Depression streets, Trigger Smith, the gang's "hit man," moves into action. Blond, flint-nosed Joe Sawyer (1901–1982), fresh from playing Bogart's henchman in WB's *The Petrified Forest,* was one of Warner's repertory character players—perfect in fare like *San Quentin* (1937) and *The Roaring Twenties* (1939), later turning up in films like *It Came from Outer Space* (1953) and the "Rin-Tin-Tin" teleseries. Sawyer's Trigger pretends to recognize the distraught Ellman by chance, buys him a cup of coffee, and offers him a job watching each night the house of Judge Shaw—the very man who had sent Ellman to prison.

"You see, he's been playing around a little," smooth-talks Trigger, "and his wife wants some evidence." Desperate, Ellman accepts the job.

Ellman is haunting the grounds of the Shaw estate the night Trigger Smith kills the judge. Late that night, a speeding car careens and smacks the automobile of a young engaged couple, Jimmy and Nancy, who work as assistants to the distinguished scientist, Dr. Evan Beaumont (Edmund Gwenn, 1875–1959). "Just my luck—my insurance ran out yesterday!"

says the outraged Jimmy, played by Warren Hull (1903–1974), hero of the radio serials "Mandrake the Magician" and "The Spider" and later host of the "Strike It Rich" TV game show. As Nancy, Marguerite Churchill is just as likable; a couple of months after *The Walking Dead* she played the heroine of Universal's *Dracula's Daughter.*

Jimmy speeds after the car. He and Nancy see the gangsters stop at the Shaw home and watch as they place the judge's corpse in the back of Ellman's rented car.

"Listen you two!" barks a gang member. "You haven't heard or seen a thing. Keep your traps shut, understand. Now beat it!"

Ellman appears from the shadows and looks innocently at the young couple. As they drive away, Ellman finds the cadaver of Judge Shaw in his automobile.

The charge is first-degree murder. District Attorney Werner, played by silver-haired WB hanger-on Henry O'Neill (1891–1964) prosecutes Ellman; Nolan "defends" him. The contrived evidence is overwhelming, and Ellman's one hope—that the young couple will appear and prove him innocent—withers because Nancy fears the vengeance of the Loder gang on herself and Jimmy.

The verdict: guilty. Death in the electric chair.

The night of the execution arrives. The prison warden (Addison Richards, 1887–1964) calls at Ellman's cell. "Well, Ellman, it's within my power to grant any last request you care to make."

"You take away my life and offer me a favor in return," says Karloff's Ellman, with wonderful irony. "That's what I call a *bargain.*"

"Anything you want, within reason."

"Anything I want. I'll give you something easy, Warden. I'd like music. Have you anyone here who can play a violin, or a cello? ... I'd like him to play my favorite piece, as I walk out there. It'll make it easier. Is it such a strange request, Warden? I always think of heaven like that."

Meanwhile, Jimmy and Nancy can live with themselves no longer. They tell Dr. Beaumont of Ellman's innocence. It's great fun to see Gwenn (who would win an Oscar as Kris Kringle in Fox's 1947 *Miracle on 34th Street*) as the determined Beaumont—Santa Claus in a horror movie. The British actor plays his miracle-working scientist/seeker of divine truth with mustache and goatee, and without a single hackneyed gesture and inflection. "Teddy" Gwenn was one of Karloff's dearest friends, and "dear Boris" loved working with him on *The Walking Dead.*

The scientist telephones Nolan, who slyly continues his dinner and takes his time before contacting D.A. Werner and the governor.

Ellman walks the Warner Bros. "last mile" as a cello plays "Kammenoi-Ostrow." He stops before the room where the electric chair awaits him (just as it awaited such Warner alumni as Cagney and Bogart) and looks upward.

"*He'll* believe me," says Ellman.

The governor's call comes as two guards debate baseball; by the time one responds to the phone, the first jolt of electricity has hit Ellman.

"Werner, get the governor back," orders Dr. Beaumont. "Tell him to call off the autopsy. . . . Never mind why! Don't ask questions! There's no time to lose! *Call him!*"

In Beaumont's laboratory, the body of Ellman lies strapped to an operating table, which rocks under awesome arcs of electricity. Great vials of chemicals boil furiously, machinery flashes, and a Lindbergh heart pumps in a glass case as Beaumont, assisted by Jimmy and Nancy, attempts the modern miracle of bringing a dead man back to life. Curtiz and cameraman Hal Mohr bring terrific excitement to this "mad laboratory" scene, capturing it all from a variety of unusual angles reminiscent of (though not as spectacular or eccentric as) Whale's work on *Bride of Frankenstein*); the (uncredited) musical score helps too. As steam rises from a great dynamo in the midst of the laboratory, an X-ray machine signals the presence of a heartbeat.

"He's alive," sighs triumphant Beaumont in a quiet, relieved voice that is a far cry from Colin Clive's mad blasphemy in *Frankenstein*. "He will live."

A very celebrated guest beheld this laboratory sequence, H. G. Wells. On December 5, 1935, Wells paid a visit to Warner Bros. and visited *The Walking Dead* set, posing for pictures with Karloff and the cast, Jack L. Warner, and Curtiz. He also looked over the seventeenth century ships from *Captain Blood*, watched work on *Anthony Adverse*, and lunched with Warner, Hal Wallis, Will Hays, and Olivia de Havilland.

Beaumont's success awes the world. Ellman does not share his joy, however. Karloff's risen Ellman is strikingly macabre—a strange, remote being with a deep, pleading "evil" eye, a renegade white streak through his hair, a twisted body that eloquently conveys the tortures of his spirit, and a terrible melancholy. There's a quiet anguish in Karloff's performance that will totally transcend the melodrama.

There is also a blood clot at the base of Ellman's brain, which Beaumont believes is the cause of the man's professed lack of memory. Nevertheless, Beaumont has his doubts. "There are times when I feel that man knows everything," he says.

District Attorney Werner agrees. When Ellman had looked at him with those tragic eyes and denied that the man who prosecuted him was his enemy, he felt, too, that Ellman possessed some supernatural knowledge.

"All I know is that, for a short time, the spirit of life left his body," says Beaumont. "Now what happened during that transition? What effect did the experience of death have on his subconscious mind?"

In the sitting room, Nancy is playing "Kammenoi-Ostrow." When Ellman hears the music from his room, he limps to the piano and starts playing his beloved piece.

Beaumont runs to the room. So does Nolan, who had swaggered in with the news that the state has awarded the resurrected man $500,000 and named Nolan as Ellman's guardian. Ellman sees his guardian, rises, and stalks slowly toward him.

"Get out," commands Ellman. *"Get out!"*

Beaumont asks Nolan to wait in his office, then proceeds to question Ellman about his reaction to his erstwhile lawyer. "He's the best friend you have."

"No," insists Ellman. "He's my enemy."

"Why do you say Nolan is your enemy? Tell me."

"I don't know," answers Ellman, his eyes pleading.

"He seems to be driven by strange impulses," says the fascinated Beaumont to Werner. "As if he were the instrument of some supernatural power." Werner admits that he never believed Nolan was Ellman's friend and that the trial convinced him that the Loder gang had framed Ellman for Judge Shaw's murder. And this gives Beaumont an idea, "If Ellman shows antagonism towards Nolan without apparent cause, would he react in the same way to...."

Loder and Nolan accept invitations to join Beaumont, his board of trustees, and some distinguished doctors and scientists at a soiree. So do gang lieutenants Merritt (mouse-faced Robert Strange, 1881–1952) and Blackstone (Paul Harvey, 1884–1955, who had just played in WB's *The Petrified Forest*). The purpose: to introduce John Ellman. The gangsters join the celebrated guests in a concert room.

"Rather than embarrass him by putting him on exhibition as the man who returned from the dead," says Beaumont, setting up a scene Mel Brooks would satirize in his 1974 *Young Frankenstein* (when Gene Wilder's Frankenstein and Peter Boyle's monster performed "Puttin' on the Ritz"), "I prefer to present him to you as a pianist."

Ellman, a carnation in his lapel, enters the room, aided by Nancy, who feels a strange sympathy and affection for him. Ellman sits at the piano. He begins playing "Kammenoi-Ostrow." As he plays, beautifully, a tear forms in his eye. Ellman's face turns to the audience, and he glares at each of the men who plotted his death: Merritt, Blackstone, Loder, Nolan.

The gaunt face, the magnificent eyes, the white streak through the hair; never has Boris Karloff looked so ... well, Karloffian. This showcase for the star becomes, in the words of Jeffrey Richards in *Focus on Film*, a "classic paean to Karloff." Here, Karloff's eyes are truly "the windows of the soul," and they glare right into the evil spirits of the gangsters not only with a melodramatic ire, but with pain, pathos, and a terrible sorrow.

The true power of this wonderful scene, however, is in the realization that Karloff's gaunt, frightening, back-from-the-dead Ellman is not a monster, not a bogeyman, not a zombie, but an angel.

Merritt can take no more and rushes from the hall. So does Blackstone. Loder and Nolan soon join them. And so does Werner.

"Don't you appreciate music?" smiles Werner.

"Why sure we do—when it's good," snarls Loder.

"I don't need the aid of the supernatural to read the guilt that's written all over your faces," volleys Werner. He accuses the gang of the frame-up. In a panic, Blackstone puts in another call to Trigger Smith, who agrees— at triple his usual rate—to assassinate Ellman.

The scene is Trigger's room. As the hit man prepares to leave, a caller enters his apartment—it is Ellman.

"Why did you kill Judge Shaw?" asks Ellman. "That night I thought you were my friend. You took my life."

"Well, I'm gonna take it again!" snaps Trigger. "Unless you got cat blood in ya' no one's gonna bring you back this time. Put 'em up!"

"You can't kill me again," says Ellman, raising his arms, moving ominously toward Trigger. "You can't use that gun. . . . You can't escape what you've done."

Cowering away, Trigger falls over a table and shoots himself. There is no joy of vengeance in Ellman's face, however, just sorrow. Blackstone, arriving with the money, finds the body and sees the shadow of Ellman moving down the hallway steps.

At a train station, Blackstone nervously prepares to leave town on the late train, when suddenly he hears a voice:

"Blackstone . . . Why did you have me killed?"

"You're mad!" gasps the hysterical Blackstone, running away from the twisted figure, ignoring Ellman's warning as he flees directly into the locomotive of a top-speed train.

The next scene is set in Merritt's hotel room. A terrible storm rages in the night, and the hoodlum's bodyguards have left. Merritt has arranged to change rooms with Betcha (Eddie Acuff, the gang's comic chauffeur), but before the change can be made, he too hears a voice.

"Merritt . . . Why did you have me killed?"

The terrified gangster gapes at the cadaverous Ellman. "Don't look at me like that! Keep away!" A heart attack strikes the horrified Merritt, and he crashes backward through a plate glass window, falling to the sidewalk below.

The Walking Dead has created, in Karloff's playing and in these three death scenes, a striking variation on Mary Shelley's "man-creates-arti-

H. G. Wells visits the laboratory set of *The Walking Dead:* Warren Hull, a dapper Karloff, Edmund Gwenn, Wells, Jack L. Warner, an unidentified woman, and Michael Curtiz.

ficial-life-in-defiance-of-God" theme. Here, the major power behind Ellman's new life *is* God—a righteous, vengeful, moral God who blesses Beaumont's efforts to restore life to the dead man, then motivates the resurrected Ellman to confront his murderers and terrify them to self-destruction. And the stage is set for a dramatic, exciting, and very moving finale.

A watchman finds Ellman peacefully wandering the grounds of Jackson Memorial Cemetery. Beaumont decides to operate on the blood clot, freeing Ellman's mind in order to learn of the "secrets from beyond" that he believes Ellman must know. Nolan and Loder, fearful for their lives, meanwhile obtain a court order committing Ellman to an institution. Before either the scientist or the gangsters can take action, however, Ellman escapes again. Nancy, guessing he has returned to the cemetery, drives off to find him, and Nolan and Loder follow.

Nancy finds Ellman walking through the rainy cemetery in the night. "It's quiet," Ellman tells the girl. "I belong here." As Nancy calls Dr. Beaumont, Ellman suddenly senses that his final enemies are near and walks into the storm to meet them.

Boris Karloff as the pre-electrocuted John Ellman of *The Walking Dead*.

As Ellman walks through the graveyard, Nolan and Loder fire at him. Finally, a bullet strikes him. The gangsters escape, but as they speed over the wet roads, Loder loses control of the car and it violently smashes into a telephone pole, as wires fall and electrocute the men who masterminded Ellman's trip to the electric chair—a spectacular and ironic demise for our chief villains.

Karloff and Marguerite Churchill in the stormy climax of *The Walking Dead*.

Dr. Beaumont, Werner, and Jimmy soon join Nancy at the cemetery, where Ellman lies dying in the caretaker's cottage. Before the end arrives, Beaumont desperately tries one more time to learn from Ellman what he experienced in death.

"It's so strange, remembering," says Ellman. "All the things you wanted to know. How I knew I had been framed."

"But how did you find out?" demands Beaumont. "You knew nothing before your execution. How do you know *now*?"

"It's hard to explain."

"Try, John, try!" begs Beaumont. "That's why I brought you back from death."

"Leave the dead to their Maker," speaks Karloff's Ellman. "The Lord our God is a jealous God."

"But John, what *is* death? Can't you put it into words? Tell me . . . what is death?"

"I think I can," sighs Ellman. "After the shock . . . I seemed . . . to feel . . . peace, and . . . and. . . ."

Ellman dies. The divine mission is over: the Almighty has reclaimed Ellman's soul before he can reveal any of death's mysteries to the God-emulating Beaumont. The scientist closes the dead man's eyes.

"He's happier now," says Jimmy, comforting the weeping Nancy.

"It will never be known" says Dr. Beaumont, looking out into the night at the rain-slashed tombstones.

"The Lord our God *is* a jealous God."

The "Kammenoi-Ostrow" music swells. And, as the movie ends, there is a final, Christian touch: behind the words "The End," the fallen shadow of Ellman slowly, dramatically, resurrects.

●

At 8:00 P.M. on December 20, 1935, Karloff reported to Griffith Park for his final work on *The Walking Dead*. The scene being shot: Ellman prowling Judge Shaw's estate and the discovery of Shaw's body in his car. The star completed work at 2:30 A.M.; Curtiz worked Warren Hull and Marguerite Churchill until 3:05 A.M. The year of 1935 had been Karloff's greatest year in the movies, and he finished *The Walking Dead* just in time to enjoy the Christmas holidays.

Also on December 20, with *The Walking Dead* in its final stages, the Warner budget department prepared a cost sheet for the film. Even with Karloff's star salary of $18,750, plus the film running about a week past its 18-day schedule, *The Walking Dead* came in for a cost of $217,000.

On Saturday, December 21, 1935, Hal Wallis, after watching the "dailies" on *The Walking Dead,* shot off this memo to supervisor Edelman:

> In the dailies on *The Walking Dead* I did not see a take in which Edmund Gwynn [sic] spoke the line: "The Lord our God is a jealous God," after Karloff dies. Did Curtiz make this? If not, I want him to make it.

Presumably, Curtiz had left the line out in his shooting—a line that underscores the whole theme of the film. (Wallis would get after Curtiz for not shooting important scenes in *Casablanca* seven years later.) An adjustment was made: in the finished *The Walking Dead*, Gwenn's voice is heard offscreen (probably a case of simple dubbing), intoning the Old Testament theology as the camera pans the cemetery.

●

Sh-h-h-h-h!!!
Karloff
Is Coming from Beyond the Grave
to strike down . . . one by one . . . his own murderers . . . and
strike terror to your heart with the dreadful tread of
The Walking Dead
—Warner Publicity

On February 20, 1936, *The Hollywood Reporter* announced that Karloff had signed a new two-picture deal with Warners the day before. "Karloff Scores in Remarkable Role," headlined the *Reporter* in the February 24, 1936, edition, reviewing *The Walking Dead:*

> Here's excellent spookery for those who can take their crime fare seasoned with the supernatural. It is a well-made picture; avoids the stock props of the chiller formula, and steers away on a fresh and less gruesome course.... Karloff is impressive as the strangely-possessed one, his distinctive diction and those eyes helping to build an unearthly portrait hard to forget.... The direction of Michael Curtiz is admirable in its restraint and its unhurried building of suspense. The photography of Hal Mohr yields all that such a story should have in the way of odd lightings for spooky effects and is especially good in the Karloff closeups and the night exteriors ... the musical score, uncredited, is highly effective in enhancing the drama.

Warner Bros. sold *The Walking Dead* as wicked melodrama, with no concern for (and considerable defiance of) the PTA's, women's federations, etc., then chanting for an end to horror movies in the wake of *The Raven* and *Mad Love.* Some posters displayed Karloff as a hulking monster, with bald dome and skeletal hands; the film's trailer, via perverse editing, transformed Karloff's gentle Ellman into a stalking fiend, terrifying Marguerite Churchill (his great friend in the movie) into hysterics.

The Walking Dead premiered at Broadway's 2758-seat Strand Theatre on February 29 of the leap year 1936. Frank S. Nugent, respected drama sage of the *New York Times,* was impressed:

> Mr. Karloff, who must be getting pretty tired of having to be the human guinea pig for all these outlandish scientific experiments, is being brought back from the dead at the Strand this week....
>
> There is no denying that he makes an impressive zombie. With a blaze of white streaking his hair, with sunken mournful eyes, hollow cheeks ... Karloff is something to haunt your sleep at nights. We didn't even dare laugh when he sat down to play the piano; and all through the picture we were congratulating ourselves that we were not among the racketeering band, led by Ricardo Cortez, who had him convicted....
>
> Horror pictures are a staple commodity, and this one was taken from one of the better shelves.

Once again, poor *Variety* blew it, sniffing at "the trite and pseudo-scientific vaporings" and then referring to the film as *The Living Dead.* Nevertheless, *The Walking Dead* was a hit; 1936 was a big year for Warner Bros. and the studio's profit tallied a very impressive $3.2 million.

Karloff followed *The Walking Dead* at Warner Bros. with four more films: *West of Shanghai* (1937, as a Chinese warlord named Fang); *The*

Invisible Menace, (1938, as an aged red herring); *Devil's Island* (1940, actually shot in 1938, as an unjustly imprisoned doctor), and *British Intelligence* (1940, as a scarfaced Teutonic spy). Karloff might have returned to Warner Bros. in glory late in 1941, to repeat his Broadway smash as mad Jonathan Brewster in *Arsenic and Old Lace,* but the stage producers refused him a leave of absence (as they had given "old aunts" Josephine Hull and Jean Adair, and "Teddy" John Alexander), fearing a box office slump. (In his 1992 book *Frank Capra: The Catastrophe of Success,* Joseph McBride reveals that *Arsenic's* producers, Howard Lindsay and Russell Crouse, were willing to provide Karloff to WB if WB would loan them Humphrey Bogart to fill in for Karloff; it all came to naught.) Warners made up Raymond Massey to look like the screen's top bogeyman and intone the famous line, "He said I looked like Boris Karloff."

There would be no more horror movies for Michael Curtiz, who went on to direct such Warner products as *The Adventures of Robin Hood* (co-directed with William Keighley), *Yankee Doodle Dandy,* and *Casablanca*—the last winning him an Oscar. The late Hal Wallis, in his 1980 memoir *Starmaker* (written with Charles Higham), quoted Curtiz's acceptance speech: "So many times I have a speech ready, but no dice. Always a bridesmaid, never a mother. Now I win, I have no speech."

Warner Bros. did very little else in the horror genre during the "Golden Years." The studio's one other horror show of the '30s was *The Return of Doctor X* (1939), which was actually not a sequel at all to the 1932 *Doctor X,* which had starred Atwill and had been directed by Curtiz. WB announced the movie as a vehicle for Karloff, then reported negotiations with Lugosi after Karloff bailed out, and finally cast no less than Bogart as the blood-seeking, rabbit-petting grotesque (with a white streak through his hair, à la Karloff's John Ellman). Vincent Sherman directed. Forgotten B chillers (*The Gorilla Man, The Mysterious Doctor,* etc.) lowered the studio's batting average until *The Beast with Five Fingers,* starring Peter Lorre and a dismembered hand, directed by Robert Florey, and scripted by Curt Siodmak. It was released in December of 1946, the final curtain on horror's most celebrated era.

Warner Bros. came on strong in horror in the 1950s, however, with the 3-D smash *House of Wax,* the 1953 remake of Curtiz's *Mystery of the Wax Museum,* with Vincent Price inheriting the Atwill role, and such science fiction fare as *Them!* (1954), which featured *The Walking Dead's* Edmund Gwenn as a distinguished scientist battling giant ants. (WB made sport of *The Walking Dead* in *Ensign Pulver* [1964], using clips from the 1936 film in this sequel to *Mr. Roberts* and referring to it as *Frankenstein Meets Young Dr. Jekyll.*)

Finally, a word on how *The Walking Dead's* "Dr. Evan Beaumont" faced his own demise. Gwenn, of course, won a Best Supporting Actor

Leading players of *The Walking Dead* line up for a shot: Ricardo Cortez, Marguerite Churchill, Karloff, Henry O'Neill, Barton MacLane, and Warren Hull.

Oscar for his beloved performance as Kris Kringle in 20th Century–Fox's *Miracle on 34th Street* (1947). It was not an easy role for him to play; director George Seaton worked very closely with the actor, who rarely played comedy. "Nothing is so hard as comedy!" Gwenn would lament on the set. Then, in 1959, when the 84-year-old Gwenn was dying at the Motion Picture Hospital, Seaton came to visit him.

"Dying is hard, George," Gwenn sadly spoke to Seaton. Then a Kris Kringle–like twinkle came into his eye.

"But," said Gwenn, "not as hard as playing comedy."

●

> The horror of the film is generated not by a rampaging monster or physical action, but by a consistent mood — a strange eeriness created by Karloff's virtuoso performance and a combination of Curtiz's expressionistic direction and Hal Mohr's shadowy cinematography . . . unlike earlier films in which some type of religion operates in order to *destroy* a monster (The Christian God in *Dracula* and the Egyptian Isis in *The Mummy*),

God actually works through John Ellman—the deity *becomes*
part of the monster in order to punish sinners . . . Ellman is not
a vindictive monster bent on revenge, but an "avenging angel"
from the Christian heaven.

—Scott Allen Nollen, *Boris Karloff: A
Critical Account of His Screen, Stage,
Radio, Television and Recording Work*
(McFarland, 1991)

The Walking Dead has long reigned as one of Karloff's most popular
non–Universal horror films, and John Ellman was one of his most beloved
performances. The role takes backseat only to the Frankenstein monster
as a showcase for what James Whale had called the "queer, penetrating
personality" of Karloff. Many of the star's fans admit to weeping at the
film's powerful finale, but one need not be a Karloff disciple (nor even a
melodrama fan) to be moved by *The Walking Dead.* This "Astounding
Drama of a Miracle of Science" featured not only a "miracle" star performance, but a miracle in its own sensitivity, passion, and transcendence of
its original packaging.

Karloff's Frankenstein monster with angel wings and Curtiz's punch
bowl mix of Germanic expressionism with Depression gangster melodrama make *The Walking Dead* much more than a horror/gangster movie,
creating what one might describe as God's own answer to the Frankenstein
mythos.

In the years following *The Walking Dead,* religion would find its place
more in fantasy than in horror in films such as Columbia's *Here Comes Mr.
Jordan* (1941), with heavenly Claude Rains bringing Robert Montgomery
back to Earth (and to a new body), and MGM's *A Guy Named Joe* (1943),
with angelic Spencer Tracy returning to earth to guide Van Johnson in his
fighter pilot traumas. MGM, which had stayed clear of religion in its
wicked '30s shockers, placed a heavy hand on the Bible and metaphysics
for its 1941 *Dr. Jekyll and Mr. Hyde* and its 1945 *The Picture of Dorian Gray,*
stockpiling each with the concept of the good and evil in each man's soul.
At 20th Century–Fox, Laird Cregar's Jack the Ripper cherished his Bible
in *The Lodger.* And at RKO, Val Lewton was deep into the topic: In *Cat
People,* Kent Smith and Jane Randolph fend off cat woman Simone Simon
by holding a drafting tool like a cross and saying, "In the name of God,
. . . leave us in peace" and in *The Seventh Victim,* our heroes defuse a coven
of devil worshippers by reciting the Lord's Prayer.

Perhaps the most powerful, exploitative melding of religion and horror came in 1973 from Warner Bros., 37 years after the studio's *The Walking Dead:* it was *The Exorcist.*

A final word on religion in the cinema and one oddly reminiscent of
the theme of *The Walking Dead.* One of the most famous cuts of all movies

was Colin Clive's dementia in the creation scene of *Frankenstein*. "O, in the name of God!" screamed Clive after Karloff's stitched monster hand moved, and the rhapsodic "It's alive!" cries followed. "Now I know what it feels like to *be* God!" The "blasphemous" line was cut early after *Frankenstein*'s premiere engagements leaving the famous jump-cut. In 1986 there was excitement when MCA/Universal promised to restore the long-lost line, along with the hypodermic needle of Edward Van Sloan's Dr. Waldman, the closeups of Dwight Frye's Fritz torturing the monster, and, of course, Karloff's lake episode with Marilyn "Little Maria" Harris.

Yet a bizarre thing happened. On the restored laser disc and cassette, Clive's line only goes, "O, in the name of God! Now I know what it . . ." — the remainder of the oath strangely nonrestorable, and drowned out by vindictive thunder from on high. It was a weirdly perpetuated censorship — one of which Karloff's John Ellman, and the "jealous God" from *The Walking Dead*, would most surely have approved.

Cat People

Studio: RKO-Radio; Producer: Val Lewton; Executive Producer: Lew Ostrow; Director: Jacques Tourneur; Screenplay: DeWitt Bodeen; Cinematographer: Nicholas Musuraca; Music: Roy Webb; Musical Director: C. Bakaleinikoff; Editor: Mark Robson; Art Directors: Albert S. D'Agostino and Walter E. Keller; Set Decorators: Darrell Silvera and Al Fields; Gowns: Renie; Sound Recordist: John L. Cass; Assistant Director: Doran Cox; Photographic Effects: Vernon L. Walker and Linwood G. Dunn; Orchestrations: Leonid Raab and John Liepold; Russian Lyrics: Andrei Tolstoi; Dialogue Director: DeWitt Bodeen; Animal Trainer: Mel Koontz; Running Time: 74 minutes.

Filmed at RKO Studios, Hollywood, July 28–August 21, 1942. New York City premiere: December 7, 1942.

The Players Irena Dubrovna (Simone Simon); Oliver Reed (Kent Smith); Dr. Judd (Tom Conway); Alice Moore (Jane Randolph); The Commodore (Jack Holt); Carver (Alan Napier); Miss Plunkett (Elizabeth Dunne); Cat Woman (Elizabeth Russell); Blondie (Mary Halsey); Zoo Keeper (Alec Craig); Mrs. Agnew (Dot Farley); Hotel Attendant (Terry Walker); Minnie (Teresa Harris); Bus Driver (Charles Jordan); Shepherd (Murdoch MacQuarrie); Organ Grinder (Steve Soldi); Taxi Driver (Don Kerr); Whistling Cop (George Ford); Mrs. Hansen (Betty Roadman); Woman (Connie Leon); Second Woman (Henrietta Burnside); Patient (Lida Nicova); Cafe Proprietor (John Piffle); Mounted Policeman (Bud Geary); Street Policeman (Eddie Dew); The Panther (Dynamite); Stunt Man (Louis Roth); Cat Sounds (Dorothy Lloyd).

●

In case of an air raid, report to RKO Studios. They haven't had a hit in years.
—Hollywood joke attributed to Bing Crosby, 1940s

"Showmanship in place of genius."

It was RKO's desperate, bitter motto for 1942. The studio at 780 Gower Street, Hollywood, was suffering the wicked backlash of brilliant, money-losing "oeuvres" of wunderkind Orson Welles. *Citizen Kane* had stylishly, dramatically, and thrillingly lampooned William Randolph Hearst and his mistress Marion Davies. The 25-year-old producer/director/star/co-writer even dared to drag in "Rosebud"—in the movie, Kane's childhood sled; in life (as was learned decades later), the term was "W. R."'s private nickname for Davies's vagina. Hearst's wrath had been almighty—a pullout of RKO advertising in all Hearst papers—and the lot was still reeling from the blow.

Welles's followup, *The Magnificent Ambersons*, was another shocker for the studio, so frightening RKO with its dashes of brilliance that the studio was cutting it extensively while Welles was in South America.

How could RKO have seen decades down the cinema history path and realized how posterity would cheer the late studio's stand to release *Citizen Kane* in defiance of Hearst, L. B. Mayer, Louella Parsons, Samuel Goldwyn, and so many sacred Hollywood cows? All RKO knew was that when Welles and Herman Mankiewicz won *Kane*'s sole Oscar for screenplay, boos and hisses sounded through the Biltmore Bowl for both absentee winners. Hollywood was always a tough town for a genius.

The indulgences of enfant terrible Welles, along with musical chairs leadership in the front office, had terrified RKO. Many employees were laid off; the studio grasped onto an economy kick. Had RKO stopped to review its 13-year history, it might have taken heart. This was the studio where *King Kong* (all 18" of the furry little doll) had pounded his chest in 1933, the studio where Fred Astaire had cut a rug (and worn one) while dancing through those terrific musicals with Ginger Rogers (who, incidentally, had been 1940's Best Actress Oscar winner for *Kitty Foyle*—an RKO picture). In 1939, the cinema's evergreen season, RKO had provided such super-hits as the Charles Boyer/Irene Dunne *Love Affair, Gunga Din,* and Laughton's *The Hunchback of Notre Dame,* which proved to be one of the biggest money-makers in that greatest of movie years. And it was RKO, in those days, who had released such beloved Walt Disney films as *Snow White and the Seven Dwarfs, Dumbo,* and *Bambi.*

But RKO was running scared. George Schaefer, RKO's president and Welles's champion, was dethroned. A scourging of "genius" took place; Welles would be given a few hours to clear off the lot, like some saloon cowboy given till sundown to get out of town. Welles's familiars were fired too or vindictively cast into the "B" unit; the studio loudly, sadly, proclaimed its glorious new destiny to attract the philistines, to woo the unwashed. For whatever major 1942 releases RKO had in the offing, the studio seemed sadly hell-bent on proving itself the studio for lowbrow entertainment. The studio's favorite preview theatre was the RKO-Hillstreet, in downtown Los Angeles, favored by delinquents and drunks.

So RKO cast its lot for financial salvation through "series." There were the *Falcon* programmers, first with George Sanders (available whenever Zanuck felt like temporarily tossing the irreverent actor off the Fox lot), later with George's brother, Tom Conway. There were the *Mexican Spitfire* comedies, raucous thigh-slappers with Lupe Velez and Leon Errol. In fact, when RKO finally did release its butchered version of Welles's *The Magnificent Ambersons,* it shared the double bill with *Mexican Spitfire Sees a Ghost.*

Taking a cue from Universal, Monogram, and PRC, RKO now planned its own series of horror films. The chosen one to lead RKO's horror hit parade was a big bearlike man with beautiful eyes. He was a sensitive, neurotic poet with a Hemingway complex, who always carried a Boy Scout knife; a sophisticate who was devoted to his family and named his yacht after his mother; a man who would produce the most personal, subtle, disturbing, and intelligent horror shows of the era, and perhaps in all Hollywood history.

Although it was the last thing the studio wanted, RKO, in signing Val Lewton, had contracted another genius.

●

How did I meet Val? I was thirteen years old, and my family happened to live on the same street as his family in Worcester, New York. My sister, who was crazy about the theatre, went to the same high school as Val's sister, and somehow she got an invitation to tea at "Who-Torok," the "lady's farm" of Val's aunt, Nazimova, the great actress. I was dragged along. Well, I was a shy New England girl, and I remember sitting very quietly and listening to everything going on, and suddenly this guy walked in, and was introduced—it was Val. I had never seen anyone or anything so handsome—he really was something.

A couple of years passed before I met him again, at a block party. And later I received a letter from him; he was then going to New York Military Academy, and asked permission to write to me—very, very polite.

I was about sixteen—and really fell madly in love with him.

Well, my family *didn't* consider him good husband material. He wasn't head of a top corporation; Val was a poet and a writer, who had come from Russia as a boy—"Who knows what kind of background he has?" my family would say. But we both persevered, and in 1929, at the Old Episcopal Church in New York City, we were married. Very happy years . . .

Val was very romantic; it fulfilled my particular need. He had a pretty wild imagination. Once, before we were married, Val got up at a basketball game, and began reciting from *Cyrano de Bergerac.* They had to drag him off the floor. After we were married, Val's mother, whom I adored, said to me, "Well, I'm glad you married him. At least you kept him out of jail!"

Val was a very stressed individual—partly because of his own imaginative powers; and I always felt life was just difficult for him. But we had a very loving relationship.

—Mrs. Ruth Lewton, in an interview
with the author, March 1993

"My nephew is 28, married four years, has a baby," wrote Alla Nazimova of Val Lewton (in a letter quoted in Joel E. Siegel's excellent 1973 book, *The Reality of Terror*). "Fell in love at 16 with a school friend and married her. Knows nothing about 'life.' Writes 'hot' books for a living. That's life too, isn't it?" Despite his credentials—newspaper reporting, novels, poetry, radio serials, even pornography—Val Lewton never quite got proper respect, at least in his own mind. He was one of those attractive, sensitive, creative souls whose personality and intellect won him as much resentment as it did idolatry; it was a problem, tragically, with which he never came to peaceful terms. Even his own mother, Nina Lewton, for years head of MGM's New York story department, was dismissive of her son's accomplishments, even as he began his associate producer RKO contract in March 1942.

The RKO offer seemed a climax to the colorful life of 38-year-old Lewton. Born in Yalta, Russia, on May 7, 1904, Vladimir Ivan Lewton was the victim of an early unsettled life. His father, a gambler and womanizer, so hurt his mother, Nina, that she took six-year-old Lucy and two-year-old Val away; he never really knew his father. Lewton's widow Ruth told me:

> Val never liked to travel; it frightened him to be away from home. He was a fairly insecure person, but I think it was because he was uprooted from his early childhood home in Russia. They went to Berlin to live for a year with Mrs. Lewton's brother, and then they came to the United States in 1910 to live with Nazimova, whose life was full of excitement and people from the stage.

These strong women who raised him had an influence on Lewton's films. His son, Val Lewton, Jr., an artist with the Smithsonian Institution, recently told me:

> One of the things that strikes me about his movies is that there are a lot of strong female characters. Many of the men in his films aren't all that interesting. And I think that came from his being raised by women—they were a strong influence in his life.

Val Lewton wrote for several New York newspapers, covering such topics as the cosmetics industry and stigmatas; he later noted in his résumé that he was fired from all reporter posts for "inaccuracy"; "impudence," he boasted, "ran a close second." He penned a 1923 book of verse *(Panther*

Skin and Grapes); wrote many features for such magazines as *Redbook,* *Adventure,* and *Romance;* did MGM publicity work; wrote the scripts for the early 1930s radio serial "The Luck of Joan Christopher"; and produced nine novels. The 1932 novel *No Bed of Her Own* (filmed by Paramount and totally revamped as the Clark Gable/Carole Lombard *No Man of Her Own)* and the 1933 novel *Yearly Lease* are Val Lewton, Jr.'s, choices as his father's best books. Lewton, Sr., even dabbled in pornography: *Yasmine* ("said to be one of the most beautifully illustrated books ever published, and retails for $75 a copy," noted his résumé) and a translation of the Russian *Grushenskaya.*

"I have a beautiful picture of this book," noted Lewton in his résumé, "taken from the *New York Daily Mirror,* showing it being shovelled into the police department furnace."

It was a good life for Val Lewton and his wife Ruth, who adored him. "Val was a person who attracted attention," she says today, over 60 years after they were wed (and over 40 years after his death). "I used to walk with him down Fifth Avenue, and women would turn and look at him. He was so handsome, especially when he was young."

> When I became pregnant, I said, "I'm not going to have a baby in New York City"—so we moved to Rye, New York, and Val would commute to New York City. Then we decided to move to Old Greenwich, Connecticut—Val became interested in boats and wanted to learn to sail. We had a charming little place, a renovated chicken house, and it was just a delight to be there on Long Island Sound. I had a lovely, wonderful baby, Nina, named after my mother-in-law. Very happy years, even though I can remember times we were strapped for money; *very* happy.

The segue to Hollywood was offbeat:

> Val's mother was head of the story department of Metro-Goldwyn-Mayer in New York. She received requests from various producers, especially MGM men, to do screenplays based on various books; one was by Gogol, the Russian. So Mother Lewton, who was a pretty wise lady, added my husband's name to the list of proposed writers. We went out expecting to stay only a couple of months, but Val and David Selznick liked each other very much. We took a wonderful house, which we loved dearly, in the Pacific Palisades, and Val was Selznick's story editor for nine years.

It wasn't always a picnic working for David O. Selznick. Alan Napier, the wonderful 6'5" English character player (who died in 1988), became one of Lewton's best friends. In 1983, relaxing in his house on a cliff above the ocean in Pacific Palisades, Napier remembered:

Val was a darling. . . . Selznick gave him some deplorable, demeaning jobs to do. It was Val, for example, who had to sit at previews of *Gone with the Wind* and count how many people got up during the four-hour movie to visit the bathroom. Val provided other services, too. One day, on *Gone with the Wind,* director Victor Fleming had lined up a shot of Vivien Leigh at a dining table, and had positioned two cantaloupes right in front of her breasts. It was Val who persuaded him otherwise.

When the RKO offer came, Lewton—basically insecure, worried about providing long-range security for Ruth, daughter Nina, and his little boy, Val, Jr., and terrified at the thought of leaving the powerful Selznick—almost rejected it. Ruth Lewton explains:

> When Val went to RKO, he thought other people might think that he had deserted Selznick. I was the one who said, "If Selznick really likes you," which he really did, "he's going to *want* you to progress. He's going to *want* you to further your career." And that proved to be true.

So Val Lewton, of all people, joined the militantly lowbrow RKO Studios. The task: to produce audience-tested horror titles for under $150,000 apiece. The salary: $250 per week. And Lewton's listing in the RKO directory (much to his own amusement): "Ass. Prod."

Charles Koerner, new RKO production chief, welcomed Lewton to RKO by giving him the short story "Ancient Sorceries," by Algernon Blackwood; it was to serve as a model of the type of film RKO wanted Lewton to produce.

A man like Lewton could only function with a simpatico talent force. One of the first to join the band was DeWitt Bodeen, a reader in RKO's story department, whose play on the Brontës, *Embers at Haworth,* had impressed Lewton. Years later, Bodeen became the cinema's foremost historian; he died in 1988.

"I have a kind of affection for only two of the screenplays I wrote that were produced, *Cat People* and *I Remember Mama* (I have affection for all the ones that weren't)," the Fresno-born Bodeen told me in his cottage at the Motion Picture Country House in 1980. It was Bodeen who had accompanied Lewton to the office of RKO's Charles Koerner the day Lewton learned about his first production:

> I was with Val in Koerner's office when he first suggested the title *Cat People.* Koerner had managed a lot of first-class movie theatres and was brought into RKO to manage the studio because his sense of exploitation was so acute. He believed in the value of audience reaction and audience-researched every title brought to his attention as an original. He had already got reaction to the title *Cat People* when he faced Val and me with it that day in his office, and was testing it on us. It did pique my interest,

but Val was really horrified that he, Val Lewton, should be asked to make
a picture called *Cat People*. He wasn't his mother's son for nothing.

The offer was also ironic: Val Lewton himself had a cat phobia. Ruth
Lewton says:

> Val hated cats! Oh gosh, I remember once, I was in bed, and he was
> writing—he used to like to write late in the night. There was a catfight
> outside, and the next thing I knew, he was up at the foot of my bed, ner-
> vous and frightened. He was very unhappy about cats. I think it stemmed
> from an old folk tale he remembered from Russia—that cats were pe-
> culiar creatures that you couldn't trust.

Lewton petulantly offered Bodeen a chance to bail out of the lurid production Koerner had decreed, but Bodeen was intrigued.

"No one has done much with cats," Koerner had said, and he was
right. In Universal's *The Mummy*, Karloff's pet cat "Bast," a vain, white,
puffed-up creature, slays heroine Zita Johann's German Shepherd dog,
Wolfram. Universal's Karloff and Lugosi *The Black Cat* (1934) flirted with
the evil of felines; who can forget Lugosi's fits of horror whenever he
glimpses a black cat and Karloff's evil smile and laughing eyes as he
sadistically lisps of Bela, "He has an intense and all-consuming horror—of
cats!"

Cats were usually friendly creatures in the classic horror films,
however. Marilyn Harris, as "Little Maria" in *Frankenstein,* was playing
with her kitty when Karloff's monster met her by the mountain lake; a cat
screeched in horror as Henry Hull went lycanthrope in Universal's 1935
Werewolf of London. And in Dwain Esper's infamous 1934 exploitation film
Maniac, cat is victim, not menace, as Bill Woods gouges out the eye of a
black cat and—with relish—eats it.

In *The Cinema of Adventure, Romance & Terror,* the book's editor
George E. Turner (editor of *American Cinematographer* magazine) reported
on the evolution of *Cat People*'s script:

> Searching for a story basis, Lewton considered Ambrose Bierce's "The
> Eyes of the Panther," but decided its premise of pre-natal influence
> would not be convincing in a movie. He then turned to a story by
> Margaret Irwin, "Monsieur Seeks a Wife," which he noted down as "a
> fetching little tale about a man who meets two sisters who are not really
> women, but cats." He recommended Cornell Woolrich's "Black Alibi"
> to Koerner as a good cat story; Koerner bought the rights, but it became
> the basis of Lewton's third production, *The Leopard Man*.

The late Arch Oboler, creator of radio's "Lights Out!" later claimed
Val Lewton had told him that *Cat People* owed inspiration to "Cat Wife,"

Cat People poster (1942).

one of the "Lights Out!" radio shows in which Boris Karloff had starred during his five-show visit to the Chicago-based program in March/April, 1938. The famous show is a wild half-hour; Karloff, as John, fights with his slatternly, money-lusting wife, Linda, who vows to leave him and take all his money.

"You . . . you cat!" raves a wildly over-the-top Karloff. "That's what you are—a cat! A big, white, heartless cat! You think like one, you screech like one, you claw like one."

Linda laughs mockingly.

"You even *look* like one! . . . I didn't marry a woman—I married a cat . . . a stinking, yowling cat . . . a cat . . . *a cat!*"

The suggestion works and Linda begins transforming. "John, what's happening to me? John, my head . . . John, help me. . . . What are you staring at? What are you. . . ?

"Meow!"

"Linda!" shrieks Karloff. *"Linda, Ooooh, Linda!"*

Linda transforms further and further into a horrible cat woman, as the screaming, howling Karloff tends to her. "Meow," purrs Linda as Boris shoots the doctor who wants to expose Linda to science; he gets her plenty of milk and cream, buys her fresh liver at the butcher, and screams as Linda eats their pet canary and sounds a mating call to the alley cats. Karloff eventually shoots a nosy neighbor; Linda attacks the corpse and then claws out Karloff's eyes. For a finale, Karloff kills his "cat wife," laughing insanely all the while, and then remorsefully shoots himself.

"Wait for me Linda, my beloved—wait," says Karloff, and we hear him fall.

If Lewton saluted Oboler and "Cat Wife" as an inspiration for *Cat People*, one imagines he was being polite. Indeed, Lewton and Bodeen truly created *Cat People* by tapping the producer's own personal phobias: not only a fear of cats, but a dread of being touched. A series of French fashion designs (of all things) provided additional inspiration. The fortuitous result: Irena Dubrovna, fashion designer from Serbia, who fears that if a man makes love to her, she'll turn into a raving cat.

Here was the hook. Suddenly, *Cat People* wasn't just a horror movie anymore, but a sex drama that could go in any number of kinky, wildly imaginative and dramatic directions. Val Lewton now had enthusiasm for *Cat People*.

●

We tossed away the horror formula right from the start. No masklike faces hardly human, with gnashing teeth and hair standing on end. . . . But take a sweet love story, or a story of sexual antagonisms, about people like the rest of us, not freaks, and cut in your horror here and there, by suggestion, and you've got something. Anyhow, we think you have.

—Val Lewton, interviewed by the *Los Angeles Times*

Lewton assembled his *Cat People* task force. There was director Jacques Tourneur (1904–1977), son of the great French director Maurice Tourneur (whose credits included the 1923 *Trilby*). Lewton was comfortable with Tourneur; together they had supervised the second unit "Storming of the Bastille" for Selznick's 1935 MGM show *A Tale of Two Cities*. Tourneur had been directing MGM "B" films like *Phantom Raiders* (1940) and had also directed Republic's *Doctors Don't Tell* (1941); he was very happy to join his friend at RKO.

There was Mark Robson (1913–1978), who had edited Welles's *Citizen Kane* and *The Magnificent Ambersons* and had been punished for his Welles connection by being exiled to the "B" unit. Robson was one of Lewton's great protégés and soon made his directorial debut for him.

Finally, there was Jessie Ponitz, Lewton's young, attractive, well-read secretary, who appreciated her boss's almost feminine sensitivity and became fiercely protective of Lewton in his battles with the RKO brass.

Over Russian tea and strawberry jam, the congenial group shared concepts for *Cat People*. An early idea was to begin the tale in a snowy Balkan village, where a Nazi Panzer division has invaded. By night, the villagers turn into cats and attack the Germans. Our leading lady escapes the village and goes to New York, where her evil heritage follows her. The topical war connection was soon cut.

Lewton screened for Bodeen a number of Universal shockers—not as inspiration, but as examples of what he did not want. They used Carl Van Vechten's *Tiger in the House,* all about cats throughout history, as a resource reference. Bodeen finished *Cat People,* first as a 50-page short story, then as a screenplay. He was having great fun, as were all the forces of the Lewton unit, as *Cat People* took final form.

Meanwhile, the front office passed down the budget: $141,659. The sum was about $40,000 less than Universal's original budget for *The Wolf Man.* Casting, as such, had to be very economy-minded. Yet Lewton felt he needed one very special star for the role of Irena Dubrovna.

●

I'd like to have the girl a little kitten-face like Simone Simon, cute and soft and cuddly and seemingly not at all dangerous.
—Val Lewton, in a memo to RKO
executive Lew Ostrow, April 1942

The ooh-la-la legend and lore of Simone Simon fascinated Val Lewton. With her bedroom eyes, pouty mouth, and baby-talk voice, the French actress had arrived in Hollywood in 1935 for 20th Century–Fox. Her illnesses and notorious temperament soon cost her some top roles (Claudette Colbert replaced her as "Cigarette" in *Under Two Flags*). Simon also became the star of a major Hollywood sex scandal in which she allegedly gave out gold keys to her home to male admirers. During this brouhaha, her secretary (accused of embezzling from the actress) threatened to blackmail Simone with a recording made at a Hollywood party, where the French star could be heard carrying on in wild and wicked fashion. The scandal was spectacular, and at its peak, a 17-year-old boy, overly titillated by the publicity about La Simon, tried to crash through the window of her second story boudoir in the middle of the night.

"The actress coolly summoned her butler," reported a typical press account, "and sat up in bed clad only in a silk nightie."

Accompanying the scandal came nasty rumors about Simone (she was truly from Salem, Oregon, she walked a panther on a leash, she was really 45 years old, etc.). She did manage to star in a few Fox films—*Girls Dormitory* (1936), *Seventh Heaven* (1937), *Josette* (1938) among them—but the studio dumped the controversial lady in 1938. Her departure for Paris was not without incident. In New York harbor, IRS agents demanded to see her income tax receipts and passport before allowing her to sail away, and a gaggle of autograph seekers (whom Simone had eluded) jeered catcalls. I think I *never* come back here!" cried Simone.

La Simone landed on her feet in Paris, scoring in *La Bête Humaine*. Her new prestige allowed her to escape the war in Europe and return to the U.S., first to the stage and eventually to Hollywood, where she played the witch girl from "over the mountain" in RKO's 1941 *The Devil and Daniel Webster*. Val Lewton found her absolutely stunning and had DeWitt Bodeen fashion the role of Irena with Simone in mind.

Finding Simone was an adventure; after *The Devil and Daniel Webster*, she had taken off again and was traveling—enjoying her notorious reputation as an international playgirl. RKO began a search, finally locating her in Chicago, where she was appearing in a stage production. The exotic role tantalized Simon; she cabled her acceptance quickly.

"I think Val was intrigued with Simone Simon," says Mrs. Lewton. "She was an intriguing lady. So French, so different. And she was awfully nice to me—she really was."

Economy forced Lewton to cast the other roles almost exclusively from the RKO contract roster. He found himself fully dependent on the various departments of the RKO lot to achieve the vision he was developing.

Nicholas Musuraca, who had created the "look" of a superb noir "B"

for RKO, Peter Lorre's *Stranger on the Third Floor* (1940), would be cine-matographer. Lewton retained DeWitt Bodeen as dialogue director. And he entrusted his friend Jacques Tourneur to work wonders with the $141,000 budget, leftover sets, and three-week shooting schedule.
Cat People began shooting July 28, 1942.

> Originally, I had the cat woman appear several times—once, I remember, right at the beginning, when the wind blows, that sketch which Simone had made of the leopard pierced with a sword over to the restaurant; it is stabbed by the parasol of a lady, who rescues it, and examines it with an enigmatic smile; it was to have been our first glimpse of the Cat Woman. I had visions of Jetta Goudal playing the part. But Elizabeth Russell was perfect, and Val was very right in limiting her part to that one scene.
> —DeWitt Bodeen, 1980

The credits began against an art deco backdrop of a magnificent leopard—a folding screen that, we shall see, dominates Irena's apartment. And for a prelude, there's a fanciful quote attributed to the film's psychiatrist, Dr. Louis Judd, from his (supposed) book, *The Anatomy of Atavism:* "Even as fog continues to lie in the valleys, so does ancient sin cling to the low places, the depressions in the world consciousness."

Cat People instantly mixes Lewton creativity with RKO expediency. A calliope plays, and we see Irena Dubrovna, Serbia-born fashion designer, sketching the panther in the Central Park Zoo. A horror heroine with artistic talent is Lewton's contribution; the set—a hangover from an Astaire/Rogers musical—is RKO's. Irena's sketch depicts a great cat pierced through with a sword.

Simone Simon, attractively feline, is a captivating Irena. The actress has that "I'm-undressing-you-with-my-eyes look," along with a Daddy-I-want-a-kiss voice; she uses both on our hero, Oliver Reed, played by Kent Smith. Lewton had noticed the young actor bicycling to the RKO lot one day; he is effective as the sweet, stolid ship designer (a far cry from the lusty actor Oliver Reed of the contemporary movies). They talk and Oliver walks Irena home to her New York brownstone apartment, on an RKO street in the same neighborhood where Robert Armstrong discovered Fay Wray in *King Kong*. Inside is one of *Cat People*'s most notorious sights: the old staircase left over from *The Magnificent Ambersons*. RKO even seems to be punishing Welles's set by tossing it into a "B" horror film.

In the dark apartment, Irena hums a lullaby. The apartment is strange; it is so near the zoo that one can hear the lions roaring. Some nights, says Irena, she can hear the panther screaming "like a woman."

Oliver notices Irena's "warm, living" scent that fills the apartment (along with the many feline objects that were the delight of Lewton's set designers). He also notices the sculpture of King John of Serbia slaying a great cat. Irena explains the violent scene in a masterfully written (and delivered) monologue:

> You see, the Marmalukes came to Serbia long ago, and they made the people slaves. Well, at first, the people were good, and worshipped God, in a true, Christian way. But little by little, the people changed. When King John drove out the Marmalukes, and came to our village, he found dreadful things. People bowed down to Satan, and said their masses to him. They had become witches.... King John put some of them to the sword, and some—the wisest, and the most wicked—escaped into the mountains.... Those who escaped, the wicked ones—their legend haunts the village where I was born.

This speech puts *Cat People* over. Simon's delivery, Musuraca's shadowy camera work, Roy Webb's softly sinister music make one imagine there's a Marmaluke lurking in the shadows of Irena's apartment. The film's famous hypnosis is at work; it will rarely falter.

We shift to Oliver's shipping design office. The commodore appears; he is Jack Holt, once Paramount's #1 box office star, (and the inspiration for Al Capp's "Fearless Fosdick"). Bodeen remembered how Holt ended up in a supporting role in *Cat People*:

> Jack Holt did the picture because his scenes were no more than two or three days' work. I know he was paid $5000 for the part, because RKO had a commitment with him for several pictures, for which he was to be paid that sum apiece. They were quickies, and had he not played the part, the studio wouldn't have given him the money, his final obligation on an old contract. This studio procedure was known to Val, and that's how he later got Richard Dix to play in *The Ghost Ship*, Dennis O'Keefe to play in *The Leopard Man*, and James Ellison to play in *I Walked with a Zombie*. Val simply got a name of some value because the actor had one unfulfilled film to do on an old contract.

Not long after *Cat People*, Holt, fearing a Japanese invasion, sold his Pacific Palisades house and property to Lewton for the bargain war years price of only $15,000. Lewton, his wife Ruth, and his daughter and son would live there the rest of Lewton's life, near the ocean, where Lewton kept his yacht, the *Nina*.

Also in the high-rise office, looming over the squat Commodore Holt, is 6'5" Englishman Alan Napier as "Doc" Carver. "There was nothing in this part that called for a British actor," said Napier in 1983. "Val gave me the part simply because we were friends." Also in the office is Jane Randolph as Alice.

No love lost: Simone Simon and Jane Randolph clash on *Cat People*.

And here we have one of the great joys of *Cat People:* Irena the cat vs. Alice the fox.

In her large, black 1940s chapeau, her long beige coat, and those black high heels that would click so memorably in her famous nocturnal flight through Central Park, Jane Randolph created one of the most chic heroines of horror: a sophisticate with a dry, sexy voice, a cigarette habit, a job and—in the classic swimming pool episode—a terrific scream. An alluring, leggy blonde from Youngstown, Ohio, who had trained in Shakespeare with Max Reinhardt and studied at Warner Bros. Young Talent School (making her film debut there as a nightclub chanteuse in *Manpower* [1941]), Jane had joined RKO in 1942, starring in *Highways by Night* when Dorothy *(Citizen Kane)* Comingore failed to report for a screen test. Jane's Alice Moore would be a perfect foil for Irena's eerie maladjustment.

Jane Randolph retired after playing the sexy insurance investigator in Universal-International's 1948 classic *Abbott and Costello Meet Franken-stein;* she wed wealthy Spaniard Jaime del Amo and has spent most of her life since then in Europe. Today a widow, Randolph discussed her RKO adventures with me during her 1989 visit to Los Angeles:

I was very busy, because the publicity department liked me; I was very fortunate, and they kept me busy doing something all the time. The people were so nice in publicity. The girl who was head of the wardrobe department was marvelous, and I would say the camera crews, everybody at RKO, were just exceptional. And so nice always to me—and that's a big help....

Oh sure, I saw Val Lewton every day. He couldn't have been nicer.... I was always sorry when I moved to Spain and wasn't here for so many years that I never saw him. He always had a lot of things to talk about.

Oliver is courting Irena earnestly. He buys her a kitten that is terrified of her; "cats don't seem to like me," says Irena. They go to a pet shop to exchange it for a canary; as Irena enters, the animals begin screaming. "The last time they did that," marvels the pet shop proprietress, "was when an alley cat got in and ate up one of my nice white finches!"

Nevertheless, Oliver falls deeply in love with Irena. They have never kissed, but he proposes marriage. She hesitates, referring to her weird ancestry, but Oliver refuses to take seriously King John or the Marmalukes. "Those fairy tales," he says, "you can tell them to our children. They'll love them."

Irena's hold in *Cat People* now is not only over Oliver, but over the audience. She also captivated the producer. Family man sophisticate Lewton, always on the set to supervise meticulously, found Simone delightful; he saw her as a globe-trotting siren and loved her worldly humor, her risqué high spirits, and her jokes about the "falsies" she professionally affected.

During the filming of *Cat People,* a curious thing developed: Simone and Randolph, rivals in the movie, produced their own jealousy on the set. As Jane Randolph remembers:

I think Jacques Tourneur was a marvelous director, but he had a lot of trouble with Simone Simon, because she's a very difficult girl. Terrible! If I was in makeup in the morning, and she walked in, she was furious, because she didn't want to wait one second for anybody. I hadn't done very many movies—doing a play is different—and she was always upstaging me. So Jacques Tourneur really bawled her out—in French—and she didn't like that either. She was very difficult with everyone.

Irena and Oliver are married. On a snowy night, the bride and groom celebrate at the Belgrade Cafe with their wedding party, including the commodore, Carver, and Alice. The episode presents one of *Cat People*'s little masterpieces—the introduction of the cat woman.

Elizabeth Russell was one of the most electrifying presences of horror movies of the 1940s; she looked like an evil Dietrich. She had first won

Elizabeth Russell, "the cat woman," greets her "sister," Simone Simon, in the wedding celebration scene from *Cat People*.

fame by modeling Paris fashions in a New York City rotogravure; after modeling for hats, cigarettes, and stockings, she had a brief fling at Paramount in 1936 before returning to the East for stock. Now back in Hollywood, Russell had just played Lugosi's evil, ancient spouse, Countess Lorenz, restored to beauty via the fluids of kidnapped brides in Monogram's *The Corpse Vanishes* (1942).

"We wanted a woman who looked like a cat," said Jacques Tourneuer, "and we searched and searched until we found this very thin model." In 1990, Elizabeth Russell, a grandmother, living in Washington, D.C., remembered being cast in *Cat People:*

> I was on a double date with Maria Montez, and one of the men was Peter Viertel, a writer, who later married Deborah Kerr. He said, "You know, I have a friend at RKO who needs a woman for his new movie who looks like a cat. Why don't you go see him?"
> "You mean you think I look like a *cat?*" I asked.
> "Well," he said (trying to get out of it!), "They'll talk about you looking like a cat, so the audience will accept it." So I went to see Val, and that was that. We became good friends; I'd go to his house for dinner, and I played in lots of his movies.

"Look at that woman," says Holt's commodore, eyeing the glamorous woman across the cafe. "Isn't *she* something."

"Looks like a cat," says Napier's Carver.

The cat woman slinks across the cafe to the wedding table, and grins almost lewdly at Irena.

"Moya Sestra," purrs the cat woman (Simone Simon dubbing the voice). "Moya Sestra!"

Irena blesses herself. The cat woman sashays out into the snow.

"She called me sister!" gasps Irena to Oliver as the wedding party tries to laugh off the chill. "You saw her, Oliver! You saw what she looked like!"

It's one of the great moments of 1940s horror, one remembered vividly by several of the talents who helped create it:

> ELIZABETH RUSSELL: They used Simone's voice for "Moya Sestra." And do you know, later, Val Lewton told me that was the biggest mistake he ever made—letting her dub my line.
>
> JANE RANDOLPH: We were all sitting at a table in a cafe, and Simone *deliberately* took her drink—and just spilled it down the front of her pale blue silk suit. Well, that stopped production—they had to send the suit out to be cleaned, they had to shift to another set—it cost a lot of money. She'd do things like that.
>
> DEWITT BODEEN: Although the cafe meeting of Simone and Elizabeth Russell was very brief, some audience members read a lesbian meaning into the action. I was aware that could happen with the cafe scene, and Val got several letters after *Cat People* was released, congratulating him for his boldness in introducing lesbiana to films in Hollywood. He was indignant when he called me to his office, demanding to know if I had deliberately written the scene with that meaning. I saved myself by saying, "Val, if you write a scene between two strange women and one says to the other in a foreign language, 'My sister,' you can bet your ass that there will be those who will say, 'ah, lesbians.'" He cooled down then and laughed. Actually, I rather liked the insinuation and thought it added a neat bit of interpretation to the scene. Irena's fears about destroying a lover if she kissed him could be because she was really a lesbian who loathed being kissed by a man.

(Perhaps Lewton mellowed or Bodeen got bolder, or both: in Lewton's 1943 *The Seventh Victim*, co-scripted by Bodeen and Charles O'Neal, several of the major characters are obviously lesbians.)

That wedding night the marriage fails to be consummated. "Oliver, be kind, be patient. Let me have time—time to get over that feeling there's something evil in me," says the bride. Oliver agrees and bride and groom decide to sleep in separate rooms that night. Irena impulsively begins to leave her room to go to her husband but then hears a cat screaming in the zoo.

A month passes and things do not improve. Irena visits the zoo, fascinated by the leopard, whom the zoo attendant reminds her is "an evil critter," referring to the Beast described in the Book of Revelations. And then one day on a strange impulse, Irena reaches for her pet canary. She queerly paws at it, a strange little grin on her face. Then the expression changes to one of guilt and horror, as Irena realizes what she has done.

She has frightened the canary to death.

Impulsively, Irena runs to the zoo and tosses the dead canary to the panther.

●

> Although I was only about three when *Cat People* was made, I certainly knew about my father's movies—although I wasn't allowed to see them until later. You couldn't avoid them. I used to listen to the radio, and they would advertise his movies—I'd hear shrieks and screams, and my father being referred to as "The Sultan of Shudders!" And also, a good deal of his conversation and stories at home were about what was going on in the studio.
>
> My father was very entertaining, a lot of fun, and very kind to the people who worked for him. I think the main thing I remember about my father was that he was a great storyteller. He would sit at the dinner table at our house in Pacific Palisades, and he would tell stories—stories about his growing up, stories about his days in New York as a newspaper reporter, and, of course, stories about making his movies. My father's grandfather had a reputation as a great storyteller in Yalta, and my father would tell very colorful, embroidered stories. He was great.
>
> When I see my father's movies today, I see his sense of detail and history, his focus, and his sense of drama.
>
> —Val Lewton, Jr., in an interview
> with the author, March 17, 1993

In the horror genre (indeed, in most genres), the producer was in general not only the least creative element, he was frequently the antagonist of creativity.

Universal's Junior Laemmle, who produced Hollywood's most legendary horror classics in his 1929–1936 power reign, had indulged his child's primer attraction to horror movies, but ultimately turned over the vision to James Whale, Edgar Ulmer, Karl Freund, or some powerhouse director who worked miracles while Junior placed a race track bet.

At MGM, Louis B. Mayer and Irving Thalberg had given the green light to Tod Browning and Lon Chaney for their legendary silents; Thalberg had entrusted Tod Browning with the disastrous 1932 *Freaks*. But horror was simply a business commodity at MGM, and Mayer later grimly tolerated such films as Karloff's *The Mask of Fu Manchu*, Peter Lorre's *Mad Love,* and Browning's *Mark of the Vampire* and *The Devil-Doll,* while caring only for the profits they might achieve for Hollywood's top money-making studio.

At the barrel bottom, there was Sam Katzman, horror king of the yahoos, raking in the bucks via his "Banner Productions," based at Monogram. Katzman seemed to delight not only in producing junk but in debasing fine actors—starring Lugosi as *The Ape Man,* or, in *Voodoo Man,* casting John Carradine as a moronic geek while dressing up George Zucco in feathers and warpaint as a voodoo high priest.

Then came Val Lewton. "Everybody that worked with Val, and for Val, loved him dearly," says Ruth Lewton. Indeed they did. "A nice, nice man," says Jane Randolph. "A lovely man, and too good to fight with the hucksters at RKO," said Alan Napier. "He was one of the great men of the motion picture industry," says Elizabeth Russell. "Val was a wonderful person," said Jacques Tourneur. "He had Russian background, and he was a dreamer and an idealist. I am a realist: I always brought him back to earth." Editor Mark Robson was so under the spell of Lewton that, as friends remembered, he even began dressing and talking like him.

The adoration was justified. On *Cat People,* Lewton was the inspiration, the spark. It was Lewton who developed the style of the story, worked closely with Bodeen on the screenplay, personally engaged the director, approved all casting, and meticulously oversaw every aspect of production. It was the agony of a perfectionist sophisticate at work and doomed to crash into the philistines-forever credo of 1942 RKO.

As Jacques Tourneur told Charles Higham and Joel Greenberg in their 1969 book, *The Celluloid Muse:*

> Val was so conscientious! I'd go to a film or a theatre downtown, and my wife and I would be driving back to the San Fernando Valley at half-past-one or two in the morning. And always, as we passed the studio, we'd see a light in that corner office of his, and he'd be alone working, correcting what the writer had written; he could only work at that time of night. Next day he'd hand the work to us. That conscientiousness killed him; he was overly wrought up; he was one of those people with a very calm exterior, rather stout, but seething inside. And that killed him, I think.

"Val cared too much about his work," says Elizabeth Russell today, who played in four more films for Lewton. "He worried himself into a state—and it finally killed him."

Lewton had his first crisis on *Cat People* just four days after shooting began. Lewton's direct supervisor was Lew Ostrow, whose background included supervising the very popular *Andy Hardy* films at MGM. While

Mark Robson claimed that it was Ostrow who directly engaged Lewton for RKO, it is certainly true that Ostrow was light years away from Lewton's sensitivity and sophistication. On the fourth morning of shooting, Ostrow called Lewton to his office and announced he was firing Jacques Tourneur—the first three days' shooting had hardly impressed Ostrow as the peak in lurid horror. Lewton begged Ostrow to allow Tourneur to remain on the film that fourth day, until Charles Koerner got back and could see the rushes for himself. Ostrow reluctantly agreed, and Koerner, looking at the rushes the next day, approved Tourneur's work and allowed Lewton to retain his friend. It was a victory for Lewton, but the first of many bitter battles that tormented the highly strung producer during his legendary RKO stay.

To be fair, for all its corporate desperation, RKO was a happy, wonderfully efficient lot. In the studio archives (once open to researchers, now locked away by Ted Turner), personnel files feature warm, personal notes from Charles Koerner, who took the time to write to actors and talent forces on their first day of shooting to wish them his best.

"At RKO everybody was exactly fitted to his job," said Jacques Tourneur, "each man was a specialist." It was this great talent force that allowed Lewton to indulge his perfectionism, his creativity, in virtually every area. For example, Lewton wanted Irena to hum throughout the picture a tune "with a catlike feeling . . . a sinister note of menace," preferably a lullaby with "a haunting, memorable quality." After considering such classical pieces as the music from the Puss in Boots scene from Tchaikovsky's *The Sleeping Beauty,* Lewton heard the high-spirited Simone Simon sing her childhood lullaby, "Do, Do, Baby Do," on the *Cat People* set one day. Lewton took her to musical director Roy Webb, had her sing the song, and Webb transformed the lullaby into Irena's leitmotif. RKO even engaged a Russian writer, Andrei Tolstoi, to translate the lullaby into Russian lyrics and tutor Simon in singing it (although she only hums it in the release print).

It was RKO efficiency and craftsmanship that gave Lewton the tools to create his little masterpieces, but the inspiration was all his own.

The incredibly complex Lewton came to hate his bosses; he was basically too shy and gentlemanly, however, to tell them what he thought. Hence, Lewton's mauve paisley "dog puke" tie, worn as a private way of thumbing his nose at any superior whose acumen he questioned. "Anyone who looks at this tie and doesn't realize that I'm insulting him is a fool anyway," Lewton would argue.

One enjoys the idea of a meeting-of-the-minds of horror producers, circa 1945, that would have taken place in a seminar featuring Junior Laemmle, Louis B. Mayer, Sam Katzman, and Val Lewton. How funny (and incredibly sad) it would have been to have heard the first three gentlemen try to talk about the horror genre—and then to have Val Lewton deliver his wonderfully creative, visionary ideas and ideals. One thing for certain—in meeting his "peers," Lewton, most assuredly, would have worn his "dog puke" tie.

●

> I recall that after a horror sequence we always tried to give the audience relief by going to something very beautiful, lyrical if possible. We tried to make the films visually interesting. We didn't have anything else, you see.
>
> —Mark Robson, editor of *Cat People*

"I envy every woman I see on the street," Irena tells the very patient Oliver. "They're happy, and they make their husbands happy.... They're free." Oliver, realizing Irena's sexual neuroses are more complex than he had believed, arranges for her to visit a psychiatrist, Dr. Judd.

Lewton had envisioned Fritz Kortner playing the smoothly sinister Judd; he also considered Edgar Barrier and Vladimir Sokoloff before finally casting RKO's own Tom Conway (1904–1967). George Sanders's real-life brother, Conway was known inside Hollywood as "the nice George Sanders"; he replaced his brother as RKO's Falcon. The transition film, featuring both gentlemen, was appropriately dubbed *The Falcon's Brother* (1942), and the leading lady was Jane Randolph, who recalls her work with Conway:

> Tom Conway was just an angel—a dear, sweet person, so nice, so polite, so charming. Everybody just adored him. But *George* wasn't very nice. I first met him on *The Falcon's Brother*, when we were doing stills, and George was always "on-the-make" for every girl that he ever worked with. We had a lot of models from New York on that movie, and George was always after every one of them.
>
> Well, he tried it with me, and Tom said to George, "Look—leave this girl alone. She's a nice girl." George didn't like that—so he was very mean to me the whole picture. And George upstaged his brother whenever he could, and tried to outact him, and everything—it was hard for Tom.
>
> Years later, I learned that Tom was ill, at the Motion Picture Home. I asked George, "Do you go out to see him?" and he said, "No." I think that's terrible.

Under hypnosis, her face in a pool of light, Irena tells suave Dr. Judd about her village in Serbia and her childhood there: how her father died in a strange accident in the woods, and the children teased her, claiming her mother was a cat woman. Irena tells how these cat women, in jealousy or anger, change into great cats like panthers.

"And," says Dr. Judd after Irena awakes, "if one of these women were to fall in love and if her lover were to kiss her, take her into his embrace, she would be driven by her own evil to kill him."

Dr. Judd assures Irena he can help her, but Irena is humiliated to learn that Oliver has discussed her frigidity with Alice (who, in fact, suggested Dr. Judd). She stops seeing Dr. Judd and starts visiting the panther cage at the zoo at night. Meanwhile, Oliver admits his unhappiness to Alice in the office, and his co-worker begins to cry.

"I just can't help it," says Alice. "I can't bear to see you unhappy. I love you too darn much, and I don't care if you do know it, Ollie. I love you."

And Irena senses it.

One night Alice walks home through a Central Park transverse. (More economy was at play here; the Central Park stone wall was actually on the RKO ranch, where it had been used in *The Hunchback of Notre Dame* [1939].)

The scene is one of the most famous vignettes of 1940s horror: Randolph, in a long beige coat and a terrific '40s hat, tingles with the sensation that a large cat is following her. She's terrified. The staccato of her high heels grows faster and faster.

Suddenly a bus stops, releasing a loud shriek of brakes.

"You look as if you'd seen a ghost!" cracks the bus driver.

"Did *you* see it?" gasps Alice.

Hence, the famous Lewton "bus," which Mark Robson explained in *The Celluloid Muse:*

> In each of these films we had what we called the "bus," an editing device I had invented by accident, or possibly by design, on *Cat People* that was calculated to terrify people and make them jump out of their seats.
>
> It derived from a sequence in *Cat People* . . . this girl backed away from the mysterious sound, ready to accept anything that might jump on her. From the other side of the park a bus came by, and I put a big, solid sound of air brakes on it, cutting it in at the decisive moment so that it knocked viewers out of their seats. This became the "bus," and we used the same principle in every film.

In the tag of this classic episode, a shepherd in Central Park finds some of his lambs slaughtered. Nearby are the tracks of a great cat, which change into the prints of high heel shoes. Irena returns home; in a macabre cheesecake scene, Simon strips off her stockings and later sits weeping in her bathtub—obviously cleansing herself of the lambs' blood.

Cat People picks up intensity. There's Irena's dream sequence, in which cats prowl and Conway's Dr. Judd appears—glistening in armor, like Serbia's King John.

And then comes the swimming pool episode.

Alice visits the pool in her hotel. In the low, dark room, she hears a bloodthirsty growl and dives into the water. The growling becomes more ferocious, and on the wall, Alice sees the shadow of an enormous cat. She screams wildly.

Suddenly, Irena steps out of the shadows. "What is the matter?" she innocently asks. Irena leaves with a contented grin, and a shaken Alice asks a hotel girl (who had come at the sound of her screams) to hand her the robe.

"Gee whiz, honey," says the girl, holding up the tattered robe. "It's torn to ribbons!"

It is *Cat People*'s most famous episode, and one of the most frightening scenes of Hollywood terror: the shadow on the wall, the rising, savage growl, and most effectively, the sight and sound of Randolph's Alice, once our cool, chic heroine, now a wild, screaming hysteric as she bobs helplessly in the pool.

"We had to go downtown and find a pool," says Jane Randolph. "To get the right feeling of claustrophobia," says Tourneur, "we purposely selected a pool in an existing apartment building here that was like the inside of a shoebox: white walls and low ceiling, with powerful light reflections from the water." The site was the Royal Palms Hotel in downtown Los Angeles, and DeWitt Bodeen remembers:

> The swimming pool scene was shot at a one-time elegant apartment house on Alvarado in an area near Westlake Park that had once been fashionable; in fact, it was near the bungalow court where William Desmond Taylor had been murdered, and that had once been a bit elite and expensive. It's very run-down now. That bungalow court is gone long ago, and a big market stands there now. The apartment house, with the swimming pool in the basement, is probably long gone, too.

Tourneur shot the scene at one morning; the cat shadow on the wall, he said, was actually the shadow of his fist. In later years there was some controversy about the true inspiration for this classic moment. Tourneur said it was based on his personal experience of swimming in a friend's pool alone in the San Fernando Valley one hot day; one of the friend's two pet cheetahs escaped from its cage and growled at him as he swam "in circles in the nude." Bodeen refuted this: "The whole swimming pool sequence was my creation," he stated in 1980, explaining he had based the episode on his experience of having fallen into a pool from a swing rope. Alone, he had almost drowned.

Lewton saw the potential of the pool sequence, and it became the source of another battle with the RKO front office. Lewton dispatched John Cass, and his sound crew spent one day at Gay's Lion Farm, recording various growls and roars, plus two days at the Royal Palms, experimenting with reverberating sound effects, hoping to create the optimum spine-tingling roars. Lewton even engaged actress Dorothy Lloyd to dub in her vocal impersonations of a shrieking cat, to mix with the growls of the lions. All this fun appalled the studio chiefs, who were outraged at the time devoted to such caprice in what they perceived, after all, to be just a "B" potboiler.

Alice now believes Irena's cat fears, as she tells Dr. Judd. He sneers and asks if he should arm himself against the supernatural—"a gun, perhaps, with a silver bullet?" This, of course, was a Lewton swipe at Universal's *The Wolf Man* (1941); as it is, Judd carries a sword cane.

"I'm no longer afraid," Irena tells Oliver. She is ready to make love; there's a subtle tinge of suggestion that her stalking and terrifying Alice has sexually charged her. But it's too late; Oliver loves Alice, and he tells Irena he wants a divorce. In perhaps Simon's finest moment in *Cat People,* she falls on the couch, her eyes hauntingly peering over the sofa back, at the audience, and she rambles bitterly, hysterically: "I love loneliness!" Her dementia frightens Oliver, who leaves at her command.

As he does so, Irena's fingernails slit open the sofa.

Dr. Judd counsels Oliver and Alice to plan to annul Oliver's marriage to Irena (because the law will not allow a spouse to divorce a mate declared legally insane). Oliver and Alice put aside wedding plans, however, feeling bound to place Irena in a hospital where she will receive care. Judd agrees to this plan. They make a date to meet Irena at her apartment at 6:00 P.M. to discuss the situation with her.

When Irena doesn't arrive, Oliver and Alice leave for the office to complete some work. There they see in the shadows a growling panther stalking them.

"Irena!" cries Oliver finally, pulling a drafting tool off the wall and holding it up like a cross. "In the name of God—leave us in peace!" The invocation works; the satanic presence goes away. Outside the office, they smell the scent of Irena's "strong and sweet" perfume.

This famous scene was another battlefield between Lewton and Ostrow. The supervisor, forecasting the panther scene to be *Cat People*'s big climax of conventional horror, was shocked to see the panther's presence merely suggested. Ultimately, he ordered the scene reshot. In the retake, the panther is definitely seen—but only in shadows, and only for split seconds. Once again, Lewton had the last laugh.

Fighting the front office, the budget, and his own terrible stress, Val Lewton still found time to indulge his company. As Jane Randolph recalls:

> One night, Jacques Tourneur, and Val Lewton, and Bodeen, and all—
> we were going home, and we were all in a room, talking. And Simone

**Simone Simon in a publicity pose for *Cat People*, gruesomely accoutre-
mented by a studio artist.**

came in and said, "Oh, my car doesn't start." I said, "Do the lights go
on?"—and she looked at me, frightened, you know, because she hadn't
thought of that. We all went out to the car, and DeWitt or Val started the
car—it started right away.

Then Simone said, "Well, I'm hungry."

These men want to get home to their wives and have dinner. Anyway,

**Jane Randolph, Tom Conway, and Kent Smith on a staircase in *Cat People*
left over from Orson Welles's *The Magnificent Ambersons*.**

we all piled her in a car and went up to the drive-in on Sunset Boulevard
and ordered something to eat.

Then she didn't eat it—she picked at it.

So, we finally took her back to the studio and left. But she would do
things like that. All day long.

Hoping to warn Dr. Judd, Oliver and Alice call the psychiatrist, who
has returned to Irena's apartment. He hangs up as Irena enters. It is in this
scene where, perhaps, we feel the deepest sympathy for Irena; this tragic,
lonely woman, who, after all, loved her husband too much to subject him
to possible death, now finds herself cruelly seduced by the arrogant,
suavely menacing Judd. "Don't be afraid of me, Irena," says Judd, and he
kisses her. Irena moves toward him, and as she does so, her face (in an op-
tical effect mastered by Linwood Dunn) seems to be growing darker, to
be distorting; the eyes glow.

Judd attacks the panther with his sword cane, but he's no match for
her; Oliver and Alice find his slaughtered body. They trail Irena, who is
seriously wounded by Judd's sword (King John had put the Marmalukes
to the sword). The miserable woman is at the Central Park Zoo, where she
unlocks the door of the panther cage. The beast leaps upon her and then
runs off into the night where it is hit by a car.

Roy Webb's beautiful music grows soft and sad. Oliver and Alice see a body near the empty cage. Is it Irena, or some horrible hybrid of woman and panther? Musuraca's camera leaves it ambiguous, but the final, understated line seems to clarify the shadow.

"She never lied to us," says Oliver.

DeWitt Bodeen recalled a final touch of class that Val Lewton wanted to add to *Cat People:*

> Val asked me, when the screenplay of *Cat People* was finished, if I could find a poetic verse that validated the strange plot. I spent an evening going through the Bible and Shakespeare, and then thought of John Donne, because of *For Whom the Bell Tolls*. Right away I found the quote in *Holy Sonnets V,* in one of the Modern Library editions. It fits as if it had been written for it:
>
> > "But black sin hath betrayed
> > to endless night
> > My world, both parts, and
> > both parts must die."

●

> You'll Shiver.... You'll Shake.... You'll Shudder and Shrivel!
>
> —RKO promotional copy for *Cat People*

On August 21, 1942, *Cat People* completed shooting. It was ahead of schedule; the final cost would tally $134,959—almost $7000 under budget.

"Getting damned hard to please these 'B' producers," memoed RKO veteran technician artist Al Simpson after Lewton requested a change in a matte painting. The producer despaired about everything—even the title credits. He appealed to the Screen Writers Guild to bill Bodeen's work as "written by" instead of "original screenplay" (arguing the latter had a "rather dismal look and sound"). When RKO's title department goofed and billed the director as "Jack Tourneur," the appalled Lewton corrected it to "Jacques"—at a cost of $25.

Roy Webb, meanwhile, was composing a very effective, moody, romantic musical score that used Simone Simon's lullaby as a major leitmotif. Both major shock sequences had *no* music; Jane Randolph's high heels and the bus brakes had "scored" the Central Park walk, while the rippling pool water and cat growls had put over the pool scene. Lewton's brilliant use of sound would be one of his top gifts as a producer.

Finally came the day when Charles Koerner, Lew Ostrow, and various RKO pooh-bahs filed into a studio projection room to see *Cat People*. The men sat stonefaced, oblivious to such feline touches as the statue of Bubastis in the museum, the cats in the Goya painting over Irena's mantle, the cat claws on the bathtub base where Irena cleanses herself after slaying the lambs. The superiors had little reaction to the "bus" or the swimming pool sequence. As the film ended and a John Donne quote filled the screen, Koerner and company marched right out of the screening room. They wouldn't even talk to Lewton. Only Ostrow lingered, to blast Lewton for ignoring *Cat People*'s potential for crass melodrama.

On Tuesday night, October 6, 1942, a terrified Val Lewton and his creative force all attended the first public preview of *Cat People*, hosted, naturally, at RKO's 2916-seat RKO Hillstreet Theatre (one of the biggest movie houses in L.A.). Lewton noticed that the project that had consumed so much of his energy, creativity, and passion over the past months would play to a crowd primarily of juvenile delinquents and drunks. The lights dimmed. RKO warmed up the house with a Disney cartoon about a pussy cat, and the crowd began to "meow."

"Oh God!" gasped the perspiring Lewton.

On came *Cat People*. Now the "meows" grew monstrous as the crowd laughed and catcalled at the sight of the movie's title. But as the movie unreeled, the catcalls stopped. The audience became still. In the big fright moments, screams filled the giant theatre.

"The audience accepted and believed our story," said DeWitt Bodeen, "and was enchanted."

Val Lewton had given the Hillstreet audience a movie stocked with frigidity, lesbiana, and even John Donne—and they had loved it.

On November 12, 1942, RKO hosted *Cat People* for a trade audience. The next day, Friday the 13th, *Variety* published a favorable (and actually incisive) review:

> Fans of horror subjects will find *Cat People* a distinctive piece of entertainment. Its marrow-chilling potentialities for lovers of the eerie build to believable peaks of spine-tingling, hair-raising suspense without once resorting to fake melodramatics or overstaging. As a production bow [for] Val Lewton in the chiller field at RKO, the picture gives him a top mark to shoot at in subjects to follow and is marked by careful development under his supervision.

On December 7, 1942 (the first anniversary of Pearl Harbor), *Cat People* opened at New York City's Rialto Theatre, Manhattan's horror house. John T. McManus, in his popular, sophisticated *PM Reviews*, couldn't resist titling his critique "See the Pretty Panther Woman," but saluted the picture as "the most original idea in a coon's age" and called it Holly-

wood's best fantasy film since Columbia's 1941 *Here Comes Mr. Jordan.*
Most other Manhattan critics were aghast, however.

Despite the critical barbs, *Cat People* became a "hold-over" hit at the
Rialto, playing week after week and building into one of the biggest
"sleepers" and greatest popular successes in Hollywood history. In his
book *B Movies,* the late Don Miller remembers the phenomenon of *Cat
People* at the Rialto:

> It was with a sense of elation that one sat in the back row of the Rialto
> and watched the sequence of Jane Randolph walking through Central
> Park at night ... something ... behind ... her ... and the concerted
> scream of the packed house when a bus pulls alongside the girl wih a hiss
> of airbrakes. An optical illusion perhaps, but it seems that the entire
> theatre audience rose and fell in one rippling wave of fear, startled by
> Lewton's use of sudden sound after silence. These were not impres-
> sionable patrons either, but hardened horror addicts who were more
> likely to show scorn and disdain than register any other reaction.

RKO gave *Cat People* its Hollywood premiere in January 1943, at the
Hawaii Theatre (supported by Warner Bros.' *The Gorilla Man* as second
feature), and business was astounding. *Cat People* broke the Hawaii atten-
dance record, playing 13 weeks (*Citizen Kane* had played 12). The movie
repeated its success all over the country and internationally; just as *Dracula*
and *Frankenstein* had saved Universal a decade previous, so did *Cat People*
(and *Hitler's Children* [1943], another Koerner pet project) prove the salvation of RKO. DeWitt Bodeen estimated *Cat People*'s international gross at
an incredible $4,000,000.

Val Lewton was the talk of Hollywood; David O. Selznick bombarded
RKO with telegrams, saluting his ex-employee's giant hit. Yet *Cat People,*
for all its glory, couldn't escape the shackles of being a horror movie.
Lewton's own mother wouldn't even go see it. And the RKO office—at
least in Lewton's eyes—never appreciated the revolutionary tactics he had
bequeathed Hollywood Gothic.

"Val and Koerner were not buddy-buddy," said DeWitt Bodeen,
"but actually, Koerner was really proud of the success of *Cat People.* After
all, the picture had been his baby. It was he who had suggested the title,
and he who had been proved right."

●

A variation on the werewolf theme, the case history of an
obsession, a study in frigidity (or possibly repressed lesbianism), *Cat People* benefits from this ambiguity and keeps us
guessing until the end. To an audience surfeited with puttied,

gruesome creatures, Lewton was to bring in this and subsequent
films a low-keyed and ominous mood, well-dosed moments of
shock, and nearly subliminal hints of something almost too evil
to be put into words and images.

—Carlos Clarens, *An Illustrated History of the Horror Film*

Cat People survives today as Val Lewton's most famous (if not his best)
production; it remains a fascinating film, a superbly crafted chiller, so
different from the rival horror shows of the time that one perhaps must
study it in historical context to appreciate it fully. Curiously, in December
of 1942, weeks after *Cat People*'s popular trade previews, Universal began
shooting its long-in-the-works *Captive Wild Woman* (1943); if RKO had
a "cat woman," Universal would have a "gorilla girl." Examining the films
as a double feature gives an awesome indication of the genius of Val
Lewton.

In *Captive Wild Woman*, a gorilla becomes a beautiful woman (Acquanetta) via the surgical machination of a mad scientist, played with leers
by John Carradine. In *Cat People*, Simone Simon becomes a cat (or doesn't
she?) through her own neurotic fears.

In Universal's picture, Acquanetta reverts to her simian self when she
sees her lion-taming heartthrob, Milburn Stone, give the overworked
Evelyn Ankers a hug. In the RKO film, Simone Simon never sees Smith
embrace Randolph; the mere imagining of it, the mental conjurings of
their making love, bring on her transformation.

And, of course, in *Captive Wild Woman*, poor Acquanetta suffers
through a complete Jack P. Pierce gorilla girl makeup. In *Cat People*, the
far more frightening Simon never fully reveals her bestial self; thanks to
Lewton's artistry, she tempts and baits the audience, hiding in the black
shadows with which cinematographer Nicholas Musuraca so effectively
paints the film.

There are other similarities; while *Cat People* offers the pet shop visit,
where Irena's presence disturbs the animals, *Captive Wild Woman* has Acquanetta visit the circus and spook the camels, zebras, and lions. Indeed,
one wonders if Universal caught a preview of *Cat People* and quickly plotted a rip-off, but no matter: while *Captive Wild Woman* is sheer hokum,
Cat People transcends being a horror film and becomes a true tragedy.

Most film buffs are familiar with the tragedy of Val Lewton. In his
meteoric rise and fall, he was stuck making audience-title-tested horror
movies, but was at the same time provided the artistic freedom (more or
less) and awesome RKO efficiency to make them fascinating, personal,
poetic works.

There was the visually beautiful *I Walked with a Zombie* (directed by
Tourneur); the sadistic, voyeuristic *The Leopard Man* (also directed by

Tourneur); the satanic, exquisitely morbid *The Seventh Victim* (directed by Mark Robson, photographed by Nicholas Musuraca, scripted by DeWitt Bodeen and Charles O'Neal);* and the long-lost (due to a plagiarism suit), recently rediscovered *The Ghost Ship* (directed by Robson, filmed by Musuraca). All these films appeared in 1943.

Perhaps inevitably, there came *The Curse of the Cat People* (1944). The sequel found Kent Smith and Jane Randolph, reprising their roles, now married and living in Tarrytown, the locale of Washington Irving's "The Headless Horseman" (and near "Who-Torok," Nazimova's country cottage where Lewton played as a boy). The couple have a little girl, Amy (Ann Carter), who lives in a dream world; she sees a picture of the dead Irena, whose spirit (Simone Simon) begins visiting her. Also in the story, living in an old mansion, are elderly actress Julia Farren (Julia Dean) and her neurotic daughter, Barbara (Elizabeth Russell). DeWitt Bodeen wrote the script, and the original director was Gunther Von Fritsch, whose "too slow" work caused his replacement by an increasingly dynamic force of Lewton's unit: editor Robert Wise.

As it was, *The Curse of the Cat People* turned into an enchanting film, a sensitive story of child psychology, whose only real moments of horror were old actress Julia telling the tale of the headless horseman and mad Barbara stalking Amy up the stairs of the old mansion in the snowy night climax. James Agee, critic for *Time* and *The Nation,* who praised Lewton's work, hailed the movie as being "full of the poetry and danger of childhood." Bodeen, however, always resented the fact that Lewton himself rewrote the final part of the film, shifting it from the supernatural to psychology; he saw the producer's act as a manifestation of his increasingly obsessive, finally fatal self-pressure to be creative.

Lewton dabbled with a juvenile delinquency movie, *Youth Runs Wild* (1944, directed by Robson), and a costumer, *Mademoiselle Fifi* (1944, directed by Wise, and awarding Simone Simon the starring role) before returning to horror. Despite Lewton's track record, RKO brought in Jack Gross, formerly of Universal, where he had supervised such films as *The Wolf Man* and the 1943 *Phantom of the Opera,* to oversee Lewton's work. Gross's key plan—to sign Boris Karloff to a two-picture contract—appalled Lewton, but the happy result produced *The Body Snatcher, Isle of the Dead,* and (as Karloff extended his contract) *Bedlam.*

It was a happy and brilliant collaboration, but for more on that, and on Lewton's tragic downfall, see the later chapter on *Bedlam.*

An example of RKO's power: DeWitt Bodeen, researching The Seventh Victim *in New York City, slyly asked the studio office to arrange a meeting for him with a devil-worshipping cult. The appointment was made. Bodeen attended the meeting on the West Side under an alias and described the satanists primarily as elderly sophisticates, drinking tea and casting spells against Hitler.*

●

Cat People is basically a very good B-movie with one or two
brilliant sequences. I certainly don't feel I was trying to stand
on top of a mountain. I mean, we're not talking about a real
classic, like *Stagecoach* or *Scarface.*
                                    —Paul Schrader, director of the 1982
                                    remake of *Cat People*

"Erotic" was the word for *Cat People* (1982), remade by director Paul
Schrader, starring Nastassia Kinski and Malcolm McDowell, with screenplay by Alan Ormsby, makeup by Tom and Ellis Burman, and released
by Universal Pictures. *Cinefantastique*'s Stephen Rebello described the
remake as "a high-ticket amalgam of Krafft-Ebing sexual kinks and mythology—laced with a soupcon of French avant-garde cinema à la Jean
Cocteau." The film worked hard to strike its own novelties, but did contain one homage to the 1942 film: the swimming pool scene, with Alice
(played by Annette O'Toole) threatened by the snarling Irena. There was
a notable difference, however: in the 1982 film, O'Toole's Alice is topless.

●

In his first film, Val Lewton had displayed the battle of faith vs.
despair that would wage in his best work—and in his own mind. "Let me
have time," Irena asks Oliver in *Cat People,* "time to get over that feeling
there's something evil in me." In retrospect, this pitiful plea seems Val
Lewton's own request of his audiences, who would watch the producer's
war of light vs. darkness wage in his incredible body of work.

Just as *Cat People*'s Irena lacked the power to denounce her evil side,
Val Lewton ultimately would lack the confidence to overcome his own
natural despair. Over 40 years after her husband's death, Ruth Lewton
says:

> In *Cat People,* there was the weird quality of cats that had intrigued Val;
> even though cats made Val uneasy, they struck a note in his own psyche
> that was scared of the unknown. I don't think Val thought as highly of
> his films as he should have. He injected something into them that was so
> bizarre, thoughtful, sensitive—you could pick out a lot of sensitivity, I
> think, in the films of this romantic, poetic man.
>
> I'm very pleased and thrilled with all the attention Val and his films
> have gotten. I wish he knew about it.

The Lodger

Studio: 20th Century–Fox; Producer: Robert Bassler; Director: John Brahm; Screenplay: Barre Lyndon (from Mrs. Marie Belloc Lowndes's novel, *The Lodger*); Cinematographer: Lucien Ballard; Special Photographic Effects: Fred Sersen; Art Directors: James Basevi and John Ewing; Set Decorator: Thomas Little (Walter M. Scott, Associate); Film Editor: J. Watson Webb, Jr.; Sound: E. Clayton Ward and Roger Heman; Costumes: Rene Hubert; Makeup Artists: Guy Pearce and Allan Snyder; Music: Hugo W. Friedhofer; Musical Director: Emil Newman; Dance Director: Kenny Williams; First Assistant Director: Sam Schneider; Assistant Director: George Schaefer, Jr.; Production Manager: Max Golden; Unit Manager: Sam Wurtzel; Script Clerk: Marie Halvey; Dialogue Director: Craig Noel; Camera Operator: Lloyd Ahearn; Camera Assistants: Ray Mala, Vincent Barlotti; Sound Mixer: E. C. Ward; Prop Man: Ed Jones; Wardrobe Man: Earl Leas; Wardrobe Woman: Louise Knapp; Hairdresser: Lilian Meyer; Grip: Leo McCreary; Gaffer: Eddie Petzoldt; Best Boy: Bobby Petzoldt; Secretary to Mr. Brahm: Chalmers Traw; Running Time: 84 minutes.

Filmed at 20th Century–Studios, California, August 9–October 8, 1943. Premiere, Roxy Theatre, New York City, January 19, 1944.

The Players: Kitty Langley (Merle Oberon); John Warwick (George Sanders); The Lodger (Laird Cregar); Robert Burton (Sir Cedric Hardwicke); Ellen Burton (Sara Allgood); Supt. Sutherland (Aubrey Mather); Daisy (Queenie Leonard); Jennie (Doris Lloyd); Sergeant Bates (David Clyde); Annie Rowley (Helena Pickard); Dr. Sheridan (Lumsden Hare); Sir Edward (Frederic Worlock); Harris (Olaf Hytten); Harold (Colin Campbell); Charlie (Harold de Becker); Wiggy (Anita Bolster); Publican (Billy Bevan); Cobbler (Forrester Harvey); Comedian (Charles Hall); Costermonger (Skelton Knaggs); Manager (Edmond Breon); Conductor (Harry Allen); Bit Boy (Raymond Severn); Bit Girl (Heather Wilde); Plainclothesmen (Colin Kenny, Clive Morgan); Aides (Craufud Kent, Frank Elliott); King Edward (Stuart Holmes); Call Boy (Walter Tetley); English Policeman (Boyd Irwin); Conductor (Herbert Clifton); Cab Driver (Jimmy Aubrey); Newsboy (Will Stanton); Milkman (Gerald Hamer); Plainclothesmen (Bob Stephenson, Les Sketchley); Stage Manager (Montague Shaw); Stage Hand (Cyril Delevanti); Bit Woman (Connie Leon); Mounted Inspector (Kenneth Hunter); Concertina Player (Donald Stuart); Down-and-Outer (John Rogers); Vigilante (Wilson Benge); Conductor (Alec Harford); Policeman (Yorke Sherwood);

Sergeant (Dave Thursby); Mounted Policeman (John Rice); Constable (Herbert Evans); Vigilante (Charles Knight); Policeman (Colin Hunter); Porter (Douglas Gerrard); Hairdresser (Ruth Clifford).

●

> I am down on whores and I shan't quit ripping them till I do get buckled. Grand work the last job was. I gave the lady no time to squeal.... You will soon hear of me and my funny little games.... The next job I do I shall clip the lady's ears off and send them to the police, just for jolly, wouldn't you? ... My knife's so nice and sharp, I want to get to work right away....
>
> Yours truly,
> Jack the Ripper
> —letter, written in red ink, delivered at the Central News Agency, Fleet Street, London, September 27, 1888, believed to have been posted by Jack the Ripper

> Men will not look at you again as they did tonight!
> —Laird Cregar, as Jack the Ripper in *The Lodger* (1944)

In the history of real-life horror, five Whitechapel prostitutes—Mary Ann Nicholls, "Dark Annie" Chapman, "Long Liz" Stride, Catherine Eddowes, and "Black Mary" Kelly—have won a warped, pathetic immortality. These diseased doxies have the sad infamy of being the slaughtered victims of Jack the Ripper. While this most infamous of murderers butchered only five women throughout his reign of terror, August 31 to November 9, 1888 (Stride and Eddowes were mutilated the same evening), the Ripper has perpetuated his bloodlust via the fascinated cinema.

Jack the Ripper has slashed his knife through the expressionistic sets of the German 1924 *Waxworks,* escaped unpunished in Hitchcock's British 1926 *The Lodger* (in which prime suspect Ivor Novello, in a wicked irony, was an innocent Christ symbol), slaughtered a voluptuary (Louise Brooks) and her lesbian lover on Christmas Eve in G. W. Pabst's German 1928 *Pandora's Box,* and struck terror in *The Phantom Fiend* (1932).

Easily the most celebrated of the Jack the Ripper movies is 20th Century–Fox's *The Lodger,* of 1944. This flamboyant, fiery, chilling, exquisitely theatrical costume melodrama is the most lavishly mounted of the Ripper screen sagas—magnificent in its atmosphere, pioneering in its sexual tension, and wickedly audacious in the brilliant, quirky, outlandishly perverse performance by Laird Cregar as the most haunted and haunting of screen Rippers.

It is the only film to capture not only the madness of the maniac, but the shadowy, Victorian alleys of his Whitechapel world as well. And it is one of the only Hollywood movies ever to contribute—directly, tragically, catastrophically—to the pathetic downfall and demise of its star.

●

From hell, Mr. Lusk, sir, I send you half the kidne I took from one woman, prasarved for you, tother piece I fried and ate it; it was very nice.

—letter to George Lusk, leader of the Whitechapel Vigilance Committee, received October 16, 1888, containing a human kidney and signed, Jack the Ripper

When the police found the disembowled body of "Long Liz" Stride on September 30, 1888, three nights after the first quoted letter in this chapter was received, there was a macabre oddity about the body: a portion of the right ear was missing. Jack the Ripper, who had promised to "clip the lady's ears off" in his not-yet-publicized letter, had apparently attempted to do just that, before being forced to retreat from the scene of his crime. The second letter featured a shock even more grisly: it contained a human kidney. Police discovered that the kidney, posted "from hell," was indeed the human kidney missing from the body of Catherine Eddowes.

A study of the Ripper's grotesque humor, as well as the intentional grammar and spelling errors made to baffle his pursuers, adds an even greater aura of the demonic to this never-apprehended criminal. Indeed, Jack the Ripper had a sick touch of insane theatrics and would have been delighted by posterity's fascination. In 1913, twenty-five years after the Ripper murders, Mrs. Marie Belloc Lowndes wrote *The Lodger,* which titillated readers by placing the Ripper as the lodging guest of a respectable (and increasingly jittery) London family. Naturally, the role of Jack the Ripper was a rich fantasy for a dramatic actor, and *The Lodger* quickly became a play. In fact, Lionel Atwill, later the great Hollywood villain of *Mystery of the Wax Museum* and *Murders in the Zoo,* made his Broadway debut as *The Lodger,* which premiered at the Maxine Elliott Theatre January 8, 1917. (It should be noted, however, that the play had permutted into a comedy, with Atwill's lodger no Ripper, but a handsome, lovesick fool.)

While the German and British cinema dramatized the Ripper, Hollywood, strangely, steered clear of his story. After all, the Ripper had been *real;* the Phantom of the Opera, Dracula, Frankenstein's monster,

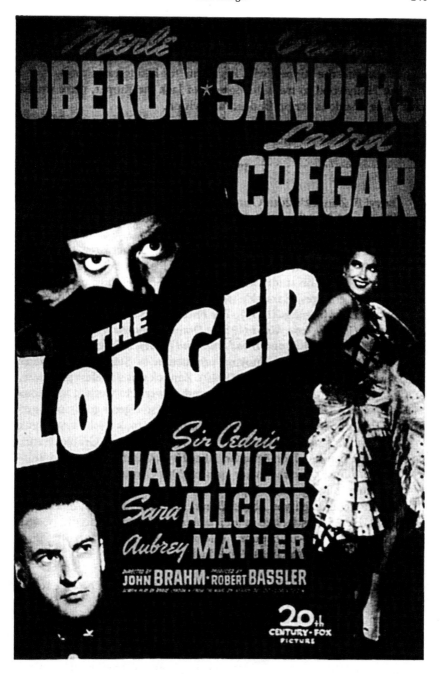

A poster for *The Lodger*.

King Kong, the wolf man and so on were just out of literature and folklore. They had not shed real blood, massacred real whores, nor deluded all the powers of Scotland Yard. Also, there was the very real, sinister undercurrent of sex with the Ripper, with his mania for killing prostitutes.

For Hollywood to treat the horrors of Jack the Ripper, there would have to be a serious script, budget, and vision.

> Don't say yes until I finish talking!
> —line attributed to Darryl F. Zanuck
> (1902–1979)

Darryl F. Zanuck's 20th Century–Fox Studio, 10201 W. Pico Boulevard, Westwood, had been thriving since 1935. The small, buck-toothed, polo club swinging Zanuck, of Wahoo, Nebraska, was a dynamo; he had progressed from writing Rin-Tin-Tin movies for Warner Bros. to becoming Warner's production supervisor to forming his own 20th Century Productions to merging his studio with Fox to create one of the most powerful of Hollywood empires. Zanuck's trademark was epic costume spectacle fare such as *Les Misérables* (1935), *The Prisoner of Shark Island* (1936), *In Old Chicago* (1937), *Jesse James* (1939), *Drums Along the Mohawk* (1939), *The Mark of Zorro* (1940), and *Blood and Sand* (1941), although his greatest achievement was his gutsy, moving production of Steinbeck's Pulitzer Prize winning *The Grapes of Wrath* (1940). Zanuck was a tireless producer, ruling over Fox with frightening force and power. He worked a furious pace, screened his films well into the night, and (so legend goes) indulged a huge sexual appetite: each day, Zanuck reputedly took a 4:00 P.M. break to "relax" with his starlet of the hour. Tyrone Power, Betty Grable, Henry Fonda, Linda Darnell, Don Ameche, Alice Faye, Gene Tierney, and Shirley Temple—these were the major stars of 20th Century–Fox, and many of them came to loath their despotic and ruthless boss.

"What I could tell you about Darryl Zanuck!" swoons Alice Faye, cryptically. Henry Fonda, late in life, habitually referred to his old boss as "Darryl F-for-Fuck-it-all Zanuck." Glenn Langan, who had a brief fling as a Fox contractee in the 1940s (and died in 1991), perhaps expressed his wrath most cleverly.

"Regardless of what Darryl had to say," laughed Langan, "due to my inbred love of animals, I have always liked him!"

Twentieth Century–Fox had dabbled very little in the horror genre, even though Zanuck had signed several of Hollywood's greatest screen villains to Fox contracts. While John Carradine, at the lot from 1935 to 1942, committed some of his most evil deeds in Fox spectacles, he made no horror films in his long sojourn there (unless one counts *The Hound of the Baskervilles* [1939], first of the Basil Rathbone and Nigel Bruce

Sherlock Holmes films with Carradine as a red-herring butler). Lionel At-will, who was under contract to Zanuck in 1939 and 1940, came closest to horror in the old chestnut *The Gorilla* (1939), a vehicle for the Ritz brothers, which also employed Bela Lugosi (and wasted Bela and Lionel again as red herrings). Peter Lorre, a Fox player from 1936 through 1939, spent his time primarily in *Mr. Moto* potboilers and made no terror films at all. Finally, in 1942, Fox churned out two low-budget horror "B" films: *Dr. Renault's Secret* (in which George Zucco turned a simian into J. Carrol Naish) and *The Undying Monster* (a sublime werewolf melodrama).

In 1943, however, Zanuck had powerful reasons to seek a solid "A" horror project. There was a young actor on contract to 20th Century–Fox, a 6'3", 260-pound giant who, in only a few years, had become one of the great villains of the screen, with a strange flair for illuminating tortured souls. His name was Laird Cregar.

> I realized that I would have to find my own parts. I am, after all, a grotesque. That is, an actor who doesn't fit readily into parts. I needed special roles. I am too big, too tall, too heavy. I don't look like an actor. If I wanted to act, I would have to find plays I *could* act.
> —Laird Cregar

At 4:30 A.M. on July 28, 1913, at the Cregar home, 6705 Cresheim Road, in the fashionable Mt. Airy region of Philadelphia, Dr. Josephus T. Ullom delivered the sixth son of Edward Matthews Cregar, a tailor, and his wife, Elizabeth Bloomfield Smith Cregar, of Philadelphia society. The baby's name would be Samuel Laird Cregar, and years later he would say:

> From my first day of consciousness, I wanted to be an actor. Maybe the quirk, the fact that villainy is my special forte—although I hate to be symbolized as such—comes from being a direct descendant of John Wilkes Booth. He was a "Ham," and so am I.

Whether John Wilkes Booth was an ancestor of Laird Cregar isn't certain; Laird had a tendency to embroider the truth (insisting, for example, he was born in 1916). But it is true that from his earliest memory of his early childhood days in Philadelphia, where he practiced his "trapped rat" face before a mirror, through his days at the Winchester Academy in London, the death of his father and the loss of the Cregar fortune, his vagabond days as a dishwasher in Miami, a uniformed usher at the Paramount Theatre in New York, an arrested vagrant in Hollywood, to his 1936 scholarship to the Pasadena Playhouse and his meteoric rise in the movies, Laird Cregar passionately wanted to be an actor.

Zanuck took note of Laird Cregar (as did all major producers) when the young player starred in *Oscar Wilde* at Hollywood's El Capitan Theatre in the spring of 1940. Cregar had mounted the production as a vehicle to showcase himself, and he was a sensation. John Barrymore, Laird's idol, intoxicated the young actor by sending him a fan letter, hailing him as the greatest actor to come out of Hollywood in 20 years.

"Sammy was a genius," said the late Henry Brandon, "Barnaby" of Laurel and Hardy's 1934 *Babes in Toyland*, referring to the actor by his Christian name. "But he had that selfishness that goes with genius . . . an incredible selfishness, self-centeredness." Brandon, who several times watched Laird's "brilliant" Oscar Wilde, remembered visiting the arrogant Laird in his dressing room after the show:

> I remember that, at the end of *Oscar Wilde,* he was wearing a monk's cowl, which he kept on as people crowded into his dressing room. And he sat there, so gracious, so grateful for every word of praise, seemingly so humble. It was even a greater performance than he had given on the stage!

At 6'3', weighing 300 pounds, Laird Cregar signed with 20th Century–Fox, making his studio bow as "Gooseberry," Paul Muni's boisterous, bearded, scene-stealing sidekick in *Hudson's Bay* (1941). Laird's first screen villain followed—Curro, the fickle critic of matadors in the sumptuous, Technicolor *Blood and Sand,* starring Tyrone Power, Linda Darnell, and Rita Hayworth. It's a fascinating, kinky, amazingly effeminate performance, typical of the sly Laird; as his Curro basks in the ringside sun like a gay iguana, gaudy in his sun bonnet, director Rouben Mamoulian cuts repeatedly from femme fatale Hayworth to Laird—each eyeballing bullfighter Power with passion. As Power finally drives his sword into the bull, Laird hysterically screams, "I tell you he is the greatest of the great! The first man of the world!"—giving the impression of a sexual climax.

It was *I Wake Up Screaming* (1941), a Fox sex melodrama with Betty Grable, Victor Mature, and Carole Landis, that catapulted Laird Cregar to stardom. The actor played Ed Cornell, a mad detective with a satanic smile, a silky voice, and a grotesque love for the dead Landis. "I'll follow you into your grave! I'll write my name on your tombstone!" purrs Laird to Mature, upon whom he's trying to pin Landis's murder. Laird haunted the film with a terrific theatricality—leering at Landis in flashback, showing up in the middle of the night in the boudoirs of Grable and Mature, seeming to lurk everywhere (save the indoor pool scene in which Betty and Victor flaunted their physiques; 300-pound Laird was mercifully spared from mingling among the trunked participants). Come the climax, we find Laird's apartment a macabre temple to the dead blonde, and in comes

Laird, like a shy eunuch, tenderly placing flowers beneath Landis's giant framed portrait—brilliantly shifting Cornell from hateful heavy to pathetic lovelorn.

Upstaging even Betty Grable's legs, Laird Cregar was a sensation in *I Wake Up Screaming* and talked of life as a Hollywood nightmare:

> The trouble with being a consistent screen villain is that your villainy hounds you wherever you go. I get into elevators in a perfectly normal frame of mind, wanting only to be taken up or down, with no thoughts of murder or violence. The elevator girl invariably recognizes me and quakes with fear until we reach my floor.

Cregar's colorful parade of villains continued: the Gestapo chief who slaps Michele Morgan's face in RKO's *Joan of Paris;* the sissy fifth columnist who endangers Veronica Lake in Paramount's *This Gun for Hire;* the legendary Captain Henry Morgan in Fox's Technicolor pirate romp, *The Black Swan.* In Fox's *Heaven Can Wait* (1943), directed by Ernst Lubitsch, Laird was ideally cast as the devil.

Laird Cregar lived in a little cottage at 9510 Cherokee Lane, back in a lemon grove, high in the mountains of Coldwater Canyon. He was popular in Hollywood—a champion of "The Game" (a form of charades), a favorite at costume parties (usually attending in drag), reciting Byronic verse at parties. The actor savored his success, and a favorite pastime was performing wonderfully graceful cartwheels as he made his happy way across the Fox lot.

"Laird was frenetic," said Henry Brandon. "I think he knew somehow he wasn't going to live very long, and was determined to live as fully as he could in the time he had."

There was a dangerous seesaw of genius in Cregar, however. That there was a strange garnish of sexual aberration in some of his performances was not surprising; a gay man himself, he was torn between acknowledging his sexual preference and hiding it. His "camping it up" even created one Hollywood legend (of sorts).

After the 1942 Academy Awards ceremony was held at the Coconut Grove on March 4, 1943, Danny Kaye and his wife Sylvia Fine hosted a big party and presented mock Oscars. Laird Cregar's "Oscar": Best Female Impersonation of the Year.

Greer Garson had just won the Oscar for *Mrs. Miniver;* "I am practically unprepared," she had begun, then had given an acceptance speech five-and-a-half minutes long. When Laird Cregar got his female impersonation "Oscar" at Kaye's party, he launched into a wicked lampoon of Greer Garson, described in Mason Wiley and Damien Bona's book, *Inside Oscar:*

> [Cregar] mimicked Garson's polite English and said, "I am practically unprepared." Cregar then went on to parody Garson's entire acceptance speech by dragging it out to ludicrous length. In no time, Hollywoodites started "remembering" that Garson bored everyone for over an hour and her speech became a Hollywood legend.

"Please clear up this myth," Greer Garson asked the authors of *Inside Oscar*. "It was funny for two weeks, but now I'm quite tired of it."

Sadly, Cregar's own sexual identity caused him much anguish. As it happened, 20th Century–Fox was preparing a role that would be a dramatic release and an ultimately disturbing showcase for Laird Cregar and his private demons.

> She is rigid from horror, and staring. We know that Jack the Ripper has come into the room, although we cannot see him. Jennie realizes who he is, and she knows why he is there. She starts slowly to back away.... We see the dread in her eyes, and hear her gasping voice as she pleads in terror.... She is so afraid that she cannot find her voice. She is looking into our eyes as she looks into the eyes of Jack the Ripper.
> —from Barre Lyndon's screenplay
> for *The Lodger*, July 12, 1943

Robert Bassler, who produced such Fox hits as the Rita Hayworth musical *My Gal Sal* (1942), the mental illness milestone *The Snake Pit* (1948), and Marine paean *The Halls of Montezuma* (1951), prepared *The Lodger* while Zanuck was serving in the Signal Corps. For the screenplay, Fox selected Barre Lyndon (1896–1972), a British author who wrote the play *The Amazing Dr. Clitterhouse*. The psychological melodrama of a doctor who studies the criminal mind, only to become a criminal himself, proved a great success for Sir Ralph Richardson on the London stage, for Sir Cedric Hardwicke on Broadway, and for Edward G. Robinson in the Warner Bros. 1938 version. Lyndon would pen the screenplays for such exceptional thrillers as *The House on 92nd Street* (Fox, 1945) and *The War of the Worlds* (Paramount, 1953). In a 1971 interview with Joel Greenberg, published in *Focus on Film* (Summer, 1975), Lyndon remembered the challenge of dramatizing the lodger:

> The first problem with him was to get him sympathetic, because he was in it all the way through; he was really the leading man. You couldn't have just a plain and simple murderer. That's one of the reasons I had him quote the Bible. He read it constantly. I liked that touch; though a maniac, he wasn't thoroughly wicked, which could well be. He had the feeling that he should punish people.

Lyndon had visited the Black Museum at Scotland Yard and had seen a letter supposedly written in blood by Jack the Ripper. He also researched the Ripper murder at the Huntington Library, studying the London *Times* accounts ("The reports were very restrained, but it was all in there"). He completed his first draft script July 12, 1943.* Meanwhile, Zanuck returned from his stint in the Signal Corps, and Lyndon received a telegram to report to Zanuck's office one morning for an audience:

> When I turned up I found Bassler there and an executive producer, Bryan Foy. I was a bit nervous about it, and presently we went in to see Zanuck. He had his amaneunsis Molly Mandaville there. His was a big office, and near the end of it was an archway, and his desk was at the far end of the office behind the archway, and you didn't go through, you sat outside.

Ensconced in his archway like a great statue in a cathedral niche, Zanuck announced that the script was "about 85 to 100 percent right" and then demanded a new ending. The original script had climaxed with a mob chasing the Ripper through the streets, shoving him into an excavation pit (and falling on top of him) and still following as the Ripper miraculously escaped, at last casting himself off in a dinghy to perish in his beloved "dark and deep" waters of the Thames. Lyndon remembered Zanuck coming out of his sacred arch and acting out his concept of a new ending.

From the conception of the project, Zanuck wanted to star Laird Cregar as the lodger. Now he turned his energy to selecting a director.

> I have been called many things by many people — stubborn, difficult, temperamental, overexacting. Maybe they are all true. I know I will do a scene 100 times if necessary to get what I want on the screen. I know I cannot have my actors dominate me or my judgement, lest my bird's-eye view of the picture as a whole be distorted by so much as one false note. An artist painting a portrait knows just where the highlights must be. The subject cannot have the same perspective.
> —John Brahm, *Motion Picture* magazine

Today, John Brahm (1893–1982) enjoys a posthumous recognition from aficionados of film terror, primarily for his work on *The Lodger* and *Hangover Square* and his later television work on such shows as "Thriller,"

Ironically, Robert Bloch's famous short story "Yours Truly, Jack the Ripper" was appearing simultaneously in the July 1943 edition of Weird Tales.

"The Twilight Zone," and "Alfred Hitchcock Presents." Nephew of the legendary German producer Otto Brahm, John Brahm had begun his career as a light comedian on the stage in Germany, before fighting in World War I and receiving the Iron Cross. Afterwards he was artistic director of Vienna's Burg Theatre, where he staged the world premieres of several Schnitzler and Molnar plays. Later, he opened his own theatre in Berlin and wed the famous actress, Dolly Haas.

After the Nazi rise to power in 1933, Brahm and his wife fled to Paris, then London, where he was production supervisor of *Scrooge* (1935). His direction of the 1937 remake of D. W. Griffith's *Broken Blossoms* for the Twickenham Studios won him passage to Hollywood and a contract with Columbia. After such Columbia films as *Penitentiary* (1938) and *Let Us Live* (with Henry Fonda, 1938), and a fine melodrama for Universal, *Rio* (1939, starring Basil Rathbone), Brahm signed with Fox, directing *Wild Geese Calling* (1941, also starring Fonda).

The independent Brahm had almost defied himself off the Fox lot: he had objected to directing *Orchestra Wives,* a musical built around Glenn Miller's Band. The result was an ugly fracas in which Zanuck yanked Brahm off the film, replaced him with Archie Mayo, and almost blackballed the German director into Hollywood limbo. Brahm's atmospheric direction of the Fox "B" *The Undying Monster* saved his career, however. It was a moody werewolf saga, set at an old manor house atop a cliff by the sea, with terrific atmosphere and a memorable limerick:

> When stars are bright, on a frosty night,
> Beware the bane, on the rocky lane.

Most memorable in *The Undying Monster* was a scene in which a girl is killed on the cliffs by the werewolf and the camera becomes the lycanthrope, twitching and jerking insanely as it closes in on the wildly screaming girl.

"I was a fallen angel, a black sheep," Brahm boasted. "Then Zanuck . . . remembering *The Undying Monster,* gave me *The Lodger* to do."

The bald, good-natured Brahm (who resembled a benign Otto Preminger) had an unusual habit as a director: he explained his scenes for the actors and crew at a blackboard, like a geometry teacher or a football coach. He also lightened his independence streak with a quick and caustic wit. Once an unwelcome guest sought Brahm's secluded Pacific Palisades house, especially designed by the director to accommodate his European furniture.

"I went to a lot of trouble to find this place," huffed the guest.

"Not half as much trouble as I went to hide it," shot back Brahm.

Fox prepared *The Lodger* in its usual epic costume style; as such, top billing went to Merle Oberon (1911–1979), as Kitty Langley, toast of London music halls for her "Parisian Trot" and the Ripper's alluring nemesis. Best-remembered for her magnificent death scene as Cathy in Goldwyn's *Wuthering Heights* (1939), Oberon was at that time Lady Alexander Korda. Sir Korda had cast her as Anne Boleyn in the 1933 milestone *The Private Life of Henry VIII* and wed her in 1939. In a posthumously published interview with Al Kilgore and Roi Frumkes in *Films in Review* (February 1982), the legendary beauty cavalierly recalled *The Lodger:*

> I had been very ill during that period and I didn't want to work anymore. I hadn't worked for a long time, and Zanuck almost forced me into doing this. He said, "You're so silly. You've got to work." And the war and everything had gotten to me. So I rather blindly took it—I thought also it was less taxing on me because there wasn't very much to do. But I mean I wouldn't choose that part, you know.

As will be seen, Oberon, whose casting in *The Lodger* was announced in *The Hollywood Reporter* July 21, 1943, would have artistic and personal reasons for remembering *The Lodger* less than fondly. The offer certainly was flattering, however. Because Sir Korda was flying to Hollywood in late August to escort his wife back to England, Zanuck moved *The Lodger* up from a late–September starting date to August 9, 1943, to accommodate the leading lady.

As John Warwick, Scotland Yard inspector, Zanuck cast George Sanders (1906–1972), Fox's most irreverent and troublesome star, then campaigning for romantic assignments following his loan-out to UA for *The Moon and Sixpence* (1942). Sanders, incidentally, had taken a Fox suspension for refusing to star in Brahm's *The Undying Monster.*

"The only thing that keeps me from killing half the people in Hollywood," purred Sanders, "is the thought of being jailed."

Laird Cregar, winning the title role, took third star billing under his more experienced compatriots; it was the first time at Fox that the Cregar name would receive star billing.

A bonus for *The Lodger* came in the casting of the landlords. Playing Robert Burton was Sir Cedric Hardwicke (1893–1964), a superb actor, most memorable in Hollywood as Death, chased up a tree by Lionel Barrymore in MGM's 1939 *On Borrowed Time* (his favorite screen role), and the evil justice, tossed off Notre Dame cathedral by Laughton's Quasimodo in RKO's 1939 *The Hunchback of Notre Dame.* Hardwicke also won a certain celebrity in the Universal horrors, starring in *The Invisible Man Returns* (1940), *Invisible Agent* (1942), and, of course, as the "second son" of the monster maker in *The Ghost of Frankenstein* (1942). Sara Allgood (1883–1950), an Irish actress Oscar-nominated for Fox's 1941 *How Green Was My Valley,* played his wife, Ellen.

One of the real stars of *The Lodger* was the set. In 1937, Fox recreated the nineteenth century "Windy City" for *In Old Chicago,* covering nearly six acres atop a hill northeast of the Fox main gate. For *The Lodger,* Fox transformed about a quarter of "Old Chicago" into London's sooty Whitechapel, adding cobblestone streets, bay windows, twisty archways—thereby creating a marvelously sinister set worthy of the Ripper. (Fox's back lot was destroyed to make way for "Century City" nearly 30 years ago, and executive buildings, apartments, and stores now stand where Laird Cregar's Ripper haunted the Whitechapel alleys.)

Lucien Ballard, who had been Brahm's cinematographer on *The Undying Monster,* was behind the camera for *The Lodger.*

The Lodger attracted a curious amount of censorship innuendo before it began shooting. *The Hollywood Reporter* of July 30, 1943, assured the movie colony that this would be a free adaptation of the Ripper murders and that Ripper's victims would be actresses, not prostitutes. Then the Hays Office objected, protesting the can-can dance "Kitty Langley and her girls" were to perform; the censor noted that the can-can dancers usually affected garters, stockings, and lacy underwear. In a battle that must have delighted fetishists everywhere, the Hays Office solemnly ordered Fox that Miss Oberon would have to wear opera hosiery when she kicked her can-can.

On Monday, August 9, 1943, *The Lodger* began shooting.

While debating lingerie, the Hays Office had totally overlooked the imagination of the true star of *The Lodger.*

●

> This is an essential point: in all the killings, we must get over the fact that when these women find themselves face-to-face with the Ripper, and know that they are to be murdered, their great fear of what is about to happen paralyzes their vocal cords, so although they try desperately to scream, they can't do it. Then we'll have a great situation at the end with Kitty, when we see her open her mouth to scream, and no sound come out. Finally she manages to cry "John!" but there should be a great moment of suspense before she does so, when we believe that she, too, may meet the fate of the other victims of the Ripper.
> —from Darryl F. Zanuck's conference notes, August 2, 1943

The scene is set in the foul streets of Whitechapel, autumn, 1888. The backlot set is magnificent, looking like the slums of hell itself, with twisted archways and black alleys and so much fog from the smoke pots that the company ran between scenes to a parking lot for fresh air. This is Jack the

Ripper's world; it is his evil that seems to be warping the buildings and producing that spectral fog. It's expressionistic, Germanic cinema, and Lucien Ballard recalled in Leonard Maltin's book, *Behind the Camera:*

> I'd always wanted to do fog the way I did it in *The Lodger.* Before then it was always a gray haze. I did it with the fog in spots, with black and white definition still coming through. And when they ran the rushes, I got hell for it; the producer said, "I've lived in London, and fog doesn't look like that." I said, "You may have lived in London, and fog doesn't look like that—but that's how it *should* look."

To the sound of cackling laughter, a hag, drunk and waving a bottle, departs the lights of a tavern. Her raggedy cronies, dancing about, cry their good nights after her, their voices echoing eerily down the cobblestone street.

"Look out for Jack the Ripper!"

"Don't let him catch ya', dearie!"

She passes a mounted policeman and stumbles around a corner into the darkness. There is a terrible scream, and, in one of the great moments of Hollywood horror, her murderer screams too.

Far from the poverty-stricken Whitechapel, we see fashionable, gaslit Montague Square. Sir Robert Burton leaves his house, #18, to buy the latest newspaper: "Jack the Ripper Seen!" hawks the headline. Sir Cedric Hardwicke, in pince-nez, beard, ruffled toupee, and cigar, is a delightfully eccentric character. Fascinated, Burton turns to a mammoth stranger who has appeared from the fog.

"Amazing," exclaims Burton. "Another murder in the same district ... throat cut from behind. Extraordinary!"

The stranger seems oblivious. He has read that Burton has a room to rent, and Ellen Burton, Robert's wife, played somberly by Sara Allgood, tends to his concern.

"My name," says Laird Cregar's lodger, remembering a street sign, "is Slade."

Ellen shows him the rooms. To her surprise, the lodger prefers to take the attic as a lodging, with its skylight and sparse furnishings. The polite, dulcet-voiced stranger explains that he is a pathologist who simply needs a place to study, although at times he does require "great heat." Ellen explains that she doesn't normally rent rooms, but a business mishap of Robert's has shattered his career and their finances, and she hopes the money from a lodger might help put him back in business. "He'll break up, with nothing to do," says Ellen of her spouse. "In a way, these dreadful Jack the Ripper murders are a God-send ... he thinks and argues about them instead of moping."

Indeed, one of the delights of *The Lodger* is Hardwicke's eccentric

Sara Allgood and Laird Cregar in *The Lodger*.

performance. "Mr. Zanuck thinks it is important that we plant a certain amount of suspicion on Robert," noted a Fox memo. "However, we shouldn't have any clues that point to him as a possible murderer, or anything like that . . . so that we plant in the minds of the audience that here is a man who could be guilty of a crime." Hardwicke suggests that abnormality. It's sad that Hardwicke himself faced a financial embarrassment late in his life, following a divorce from his young second wife; when he died in 1964, the distinguished, knighted gentleman was terrified of ending his life in an actors home.

"This is like a refuge," sighs the lodger. He pays a month's rent, 20 pounds, in advance, and shyly apologizes, "I'm afraid that my habits are . . . irregular. I often need to be out quite late at night. But I'd use the back door. . . . Just regard me as a lodger . . . not as a guest. Then you'll hardly know that I'm in the house." The lodger is especially pleased by the beautiful old Bible, which he implores Ellen to leave in the attic. "Mine, too, are the problems of Life . . . and Death," he says.

Ellen descends the staircase and informs Robert that the lodger will be moving into the attic. She returns upstairs with supper and finds the lodger has slammed the paintings on the wall—paintings of Victorian belles—around backwards.

"Wherever you went in this room," he says with a barely controlled ferocity, "the eyes of those *women* seemed to follow you about!" Besides, he states, they are pictures of actresses.

Ellen hopes the lodger isn't prejudiced against actresses, for there's one in the house: her niece, Kitty Langley, whose saucy and daring Parisian Trot has made her the rage of the provincial music halls.

"Behold," quotes the lodger, "there met him a woman subtle of heart."

Cregar's lodger is fascinating; in his posing and posturing, he seems like a nineteenth century Shakespearean actor, as he plays Jack the Ripper the way his "ancestor" John Wilkes Booth might have acted the role. But added to this style, however, are a hint of demonic mania and a touch of feyness that become incredibly audacious as Cregar develops his performance.

Kitty Langley—beautiful, sophisticated, charming—meets the lodger on the night of her premiere, as she prepares to leave Montague Square for the theatre. Merle Oberon is quite perfect in the part, all gussied up like a peacock, painted, coiffed, and tightly corseted; one finds oneself wondering how she'd look after somebody squirted her with a hose. Merle Oberon was a fascinating lady; as was revealed after her death, she was born in India (she claimed Tasmania), beginning life as Queenie Thompson, the daughter of an Indian mother who, as Merle Oberon ascended in her fame, posed as her maid. Plastic surgery, ambition, and her marriage to Sir Alexander Korda made the metamorphosis complete. Oberon nicely douses her role of Kitty with an aura of sweetness and kindness, and the artificiality of her appearance is actually just right for unhinging the Ripper, who hates the painted ladies of the stage.*

The lodger politely turns down the offer of a pass to the theatre. He has work to do and will be out very late. Kitty listens as the lodger soliloquizes:

"I enjoy the streets at night ... when they're empty.... Sometimes I go down to the Thames.... Have you ever held your face close to the water ... and let it wash against your hands as you look down into it? Deep water is dark, and restful—and full of peace."

"You fascinated him, you know," Burton tells Kitty later. "He couldn't take his eyes off you."

The lodger steps out into the fog. A double-decker bus stops for him. Although there's plenty of room below, the lodger climbs up to the top, sitting alone on the top deck, and heads toward Whitechapel.

---

*Korda's nephew Michael wrote a best-selling "roman-à-clef" novel about Merle Oberon, Queenie, which became a two-part 1987 made-for-television movie with Mia Sara as Merle Oberon and Kirk Douglas as the Korda character.

At the Royal Piccadilly Theatre, Kitty makes up in her dressing room and has a caller—Annie Rowley, once "La Belle Anne," now a poor, forgotten drudge. Annie was a plum part for a character actress, and Fox seriously considered Elsa Lanchester, Doris Lloyd, and Helga Moray for the tragic role. All three ladies lost out to Helena Pickard, who might have had an edge over her competitors: she was married at the time to Sir Cedric Hardwicke. Annie wishes Kitty luck; Kitty presents her with a golden sovereign, which the has-been actress later uses to send Kitty flowers.

That night Kitty performs her Parisian Trot to the cheers of a packed theatre (and royalty itself). Oberon displays beautiful legs as she sings (in dubbed voice) her "Tinc-Tinc-A-Tinc-Tinc-Tinc" song, striking ooh-lah-lah poses and performing (with her "girls") her can-can. "So the lady can kick," telegrammed Cole Porter to Oberon after he saw *The Lodger;* a less appreciative critic noted that the star's can-can might better have been dubbed the "Can't-Can't." All in all, Kitty's "Parisian Trot" provides *The Lodger* with a nice vignette of costume spectacle.

However, as Kitty Langley scores a triumph, Jack the Ripper mutilates Annie Rowley in an alley.

Kitty and her girls and the Burtons are celebrating at the Piccadilly when Inspector John Warwick of Scotland Yard arrives. There's instant attraction between Kitty and Warwick, despite his morbid mission: to inform her of the slaughter of Annie Rowley.* Since starring as the Gauguin-like painter of *The Moon and Sixpence* (UA, 1942), the suave screen villain Sanders had demanded Fox provide him with romantic roles. He delighted in being Fox's most recalcitrant actor; "George was a first-class shit," said Alan Napier, the veteran British actor who died in 1988 and was one of Sanders' few close friends. But Napier admired Sanders's dry wit, inventions, and irreverence toward Hollywood potentates:

> As an example of George's humor—I worked with him on an aerodynamic project, since I was good with my hands and he wasn't. I produced many ingenious little balsa wood gliders we would fly over the beach at Laguna. He once called me on the phone at one in the morning—thus demonstrating his complete disregard of other people's comfort or convenience. What he said was this: "Nape ... [pause] ... It's just occurred to me that Darryl Zanuck is worth his weight in *balsa.*" I've been laughing at it ever since.

---

*Although we learn of Annie's death through George Sanders' dialogue, we have seen it—in The Lodger's opening. Zanuck felt Brahm's handling of this murder was so dramatic and would serve so well as an opening for the melodrama, that he cut the episode from where it originally appeared (right after Kitty's performance), splicing it into the Whitechapel opening. The producer ordered new dialogue dubbed in (e.g., "Good night, Katy" instead of "Good night, Annie"), used only long shots of Miss Pickard, and gambled confidently that no one would recognize her as the victim later in the film.

Warwick notes that all of the madman's victims were (at one time) actresses and that the maniac was glimpsed carrying a satchel.

Meanwhile, the lodger gives the Burtons (and the audience) cause for
suspicion. He burns his satchel, after reading that the Ripper was seen with
one; later, he awakens Kitty in the middle of the night when he burns his
bloody coat, claiming it was contaminated during his pathological work.

The truly startling episode, however, occurs when Cregar's lodger
shows Ellen a self-portrait of his dead brother. "I can show you something
more beautiful than a beautiful woman," says the lodger, becoming almost
hysterical as he stares lovingly at the man's handsome features.

"Isn't that a marvelous piece of work to come from the hands of a man
... a young man?" demands the lodger, looking almost lustfully at the
cameo picture. The actor's performance has taken another audacious
jump: as Charles Higham wrote of *The Lodger* in his biography of Merle
Oberon, *Princess Merle*, Cregar's "obsession with his dead brother offers
more than a hint of incestuous homosexuality." Yet Cregar caps the
episode with true pathos, as he tenderly cries.

"He need not have died," the lodger weeps. "He need not have died."

●

> Laird Cregar was a quiet, sad, aloof sort of man who saved
> it all for the camera. . . . Cregar saw himself 100% in these char-
> acters, being a Victorian at heart, and because he brought so
> much subtlety and shading that came from deep within.
> —John Brahm, in an interview with
> David Del Valle, July 1979 pub-
> lished in *Video Watchdog* (1992)

As *The Lodger* went on shooting, word spread that Laird Cregar was
giving the performance of his life. Joel Greenberg wrote in *Focus on Film*
(Summer, 1975), Cregar "found in the role of the Ripper an almost thera-
peutic alleviation of his private Angst, the misogyny of a tormented
homosexual." Cregar's homosexuality was popular gossip on the Fox lot,
and Henry Brandon remembered:

> Sammy had a little boyfriend who was a dancer in a musical in
> Hollywood. One night, the boyfriend was sick, so Sammy went on for
> him, and was in the chorus—and he was a star at the time! I happened
> to be in the theatre that night, and I couldn't believe my eyes! And he was
> incredibly graceful, floating like a balloon; still, it was incongruous to see
> this great fat man among those little chorus boys. Well, Zanuck found out
> about it, and put his foot down with a *bang!*

As Cregar slyly spiked his role with homosexuality, incest, and even hints of necrophilia, John Brahm allowed the performance. He suspected (rightly, as it turned out) that most audiences wouldn't detect the Krafft-Ebing neuroses with which Cregar mischievously embellished the performance.

The Lodger became Cregar's film, which reportedly upset Merle Oberon; Charles Higham wrote in *Princess Merle* that Oberon was so upset by Cregar's domination of the movie that she invited a carpenter youth to her Bel Air house for dinner and tried to seduce him; when he honorably resisted, he was missing from the crew the next day. Be that as it may, Oberon did begin a romance with Lucien Ballard, who so lusciously photographed her in *The Lodger;* she eventually divorced the mighty Korda and wed Ballard on June 26, 1946. Marrying a cinematographer was considered social suicide by Merle's society friends; the Ballards divorced three years later.

Oberon did admire Laird Cregar and feel sympathy for his plight, as Higham wrote in *Princess Merle:*

> Merle tried hard to establish some kind of friendship with this difficult, unhappy man, and in order to cheer him up she told him that he was basically very handsome and if he would lose forty pounds in a diet she recommended of vegetables, light proteins, and no fats, he would look wonderful and still be acceptable in leading character roles. As a result, Cregar suddenly became convinced he could turn from the gloomy restricted life of the homosexual to the more optimistic world of the heterosexual and perhaps could attract a woman and find fulfillment with her. . . .

Such encouragement, tragically, proved the beginning-of-the-end for Laird Cregar. Meanwhile, he kept up his incredible performance as *The Lodger.*

●

Perhaps the most famous episode of *The Lodger* is the Ripper's murder of the Whitechapel hag, Jennie. Red-haired, blue-eyed Doris Lloyd, the British character actress who played in such films as Monogram's 1933 *Oliver Twist* (as Nancy), as well as such Universal horror fare as *The Wolf Man* (1941) and *Frankenstein Meets the Wolf Man* (1943), missed out on the part of Annie Rowley, but actually did better for herself in this unforgettable cameo. We first see old Jennie in a Whitechapel pub, singing a Kitty Langley song, even ending with a derriere thrust à la Kitty to the delight of her friends. She lends her old accordion to Wiggy (Anita Bolster, who beat out Una O'Connor and Eily Malyon for the part) and returns through the streets, past policemen and plainclothesmen, as Wiggy plays her hymn on the accordion. Jennie enters her hovel and sits down to undress. Then she hears a creaking and the lamp goes out.

The execution is a cinema masterpiece. Just as Lyndon's script dictated, the camera (and the audience) becomes the Ripper, shaking and jerking insanely as he attacks Lloyd, horribly, fatally trapped—and unable to scream as Friedhofer's music brilliantly swells. Brahm staged it superbly, just as he had staged the lycanthrope attack in *The Undying Monster*. It is one of the most frightening tour de forces of the horror film, and one that won notoriety for Lloyd. The veteran actress, who died in Santa Barbara in 1968 (she was remembered in the will of legendary horror director James Whale), told Joel Greenberg that a fan serenaded her with a letter, claiming he had watched *The Lodger* 13 times because her nightmarish death scene "gave him a tingle."

Police search Whitechapel. And in the night, by the Thames, a giant man crouches over the side of a rowboat and bathes his hands in the dark water.

In a July 1979 interview with historian David Del Valle, Brahm, bathing in the sun outside his cottage high above Malibu Beach, remembered how deeply Cregar felt about this ritualistic touch:

> Laird Cregar, you'd be pleased to know, said the Ripper would do this as a religious ceremony, to ease his conscience. . . . Laird was magic to direct in this, to say the least.

Later, back at Montague Square, Kitty and the lodger have a conversation. "It's one thing if a woman is beautiful merely for herself," he says. "But when she exhibits the loveliness of her body upon the stage as a lure . . . leading men on. . . ."

"You are prejudiced against actresses, aren't you?" laughs Kitty, nervously.

"You wouldn't think that anyone could hate a thing, and love it too. . . . You can . . . and it's a problem then. . . . I take my problems to the river. . . . I also know that there is evil in beauty . . . and if the evil is *cut out.* . . ."

Warwick (who, naturally, has fallen deeply in love with Kitty—a convention Brahm and Lyndon make novel by having him take her on a tour of Scotland Yard's Black Museum) has employed fingerprints to ascertain that Slade is, indeed, Jack the Ripper. He has also found a small painting of the lodger's brother at the body of the Ripper's first victim—a morbid, degenerate self-portrait of the man after a heartless actress had ruined his life. He suspects Slade, and as Warwick prepares to trap the maniac, Kitty and her girls perform the Parisian Trot in a Whitechapel theatre.

Merle Oberon as Kitty Langley, together with her girls in *The Lodger*.

In the audience is the lodger. And as Kitty strikes her poses, flaunts her lingerie, and kicks to the saucy music, the lodger's eyes burn and his face contorts.... Brahm wickedly cuts back and forth from Oberon's legs and lacy panties to Cregar's anguished face.

Kitty returns to her dressing room. The lodger is there.

"You are so exquisite," gasps Jack the Ripper, embracing the terrified Kitty, who is too paralyzed to scream, "more wonderful than anything I have ever known.... You corrupt and destroy men, as my brother was destroyed."

He draws his knife.

"But, isn't it the life in a thing that makes it beautiful?" gasps Kitty. "If you take away the life, then...."

"Then it is still," insists the lodger. "Then it is even *more* beautiful! ... I have never known such beauty as yours—nor such evil in such beauty.

"Men will not look at you again as they did tonight!"

Cregar's face begins twitching magnificently—he looks ready to explode. Oberon's Kitty splendidly performs her agonized attempt to scream—so painfully, the audience wants to scream for her. At long last

"When the evil is cut out of a beautiful thing . . ."—Laird Cregar and Merle Oberon in *The Lodger*.

comes the scream, and Warwick and company break down the door, shooting at the Ripper. Wounded in the neck, the madman surrenders his prey and runs away, the police in pursuit as he ascends into the eaves of the theatre.

The Ripper runs like some horrible monster. In a brilliant shot, Cregar's Ripper runs across a catwalk, the shadows below flickering up and down his body. This is grand, Germanic cinema now, complete with Friedhofer's thrilling music and bravura cinematography, and—dominating all—Cregar's dynamite performance.

As Kitty recovers below, the Ripper makes another mad attempt to kill her: he cuts heavy sand bags from the rafter pulleys, which fall and land just inches from the terrified actress.

Finally, Warwick and his men corner the Ripper high in the theatre attic. As the men slowly move in, the Ripper's face, streaked with blood and sweat, glares at them. His panting builds monstrously. Friedhofer's music has stopped; the only sound is the Ripper's breathing.

Cregar's face, as Brahm slowly, almost sadistically advances the camera on him, is a spectacle. It's all there: the "trapped-rat" face Cregar had practiced as a boy; the insanity of one of the world's most horrible murderers; the flamboyance and imagination of a genius, doomed actor in what would be his greatest role.

Suddenly, the Ripper whirls about; music crashes back onto the soundtrack as he crashes through a window and falls far below, into the waters of the Thames.

Later in the night, the Burtons, Warwick, and Kitty arrive near the river.

"A river sweeps a city clean," says Warwick.

"It carries things out to sea—and they sink, in deep water," says Kitty.

And, in the dark, peaceful waters of the Thames, we see a shred of the Lodger's ulster, floating out to sea.

●

> The most-sensational picture of its kind from 20th Century–Fox!
>
> —PR for *The Lodger,* January 19, 1944

John Brahm completed *The Lodger* Friday, October 8, 1943; on October 27, 1943, Brahm began added scenes. Soon the picture was ready for preview, and Barre Lyndon remembered the night vividly:

> I saw it at what was then the Paramount Theatre. I remember that very well because the theatre was full and we had to sit at the back among the college crowd. To my astonishment they were all excited and they loved it. When George Sanders came on they applauded and laughed before he said anything at all. They really were with it.

Preview audiences hailed *The Lodger,* and Laird Cregar enthusiastically began plugging the picture. On Friday night, January 7, 1944, Cregar guest-starred on CBS Radio's "The Kate Smith Show," in a dramatization of Robert Bloch's "Yours Truly, Jack the Ripper."

On Wednesday, January 19, 1944, 20th Century–Fox treated the melodrama to a deluxe premiere at New York's Roxy Theatre. "No $4.40 Broadway show ever had such stars, tunes, laughs, thrills and girls!" proclaimed the huge poster in the *New York Times. The Lodger* stage show boasted radio's Chamber Music Society of Lower Basin Street, Jack Durant, Hal Le Roy, Maurice Rocco, the Gae Foster Roxyettes, and "The Voice of Over 10,000,000 Records," Helen Forrest. Tucked in a corner of the advertisement was a bonus:

"In Person! *Laird Cregar Today Only!* All Performances!"

Although he had seen three previews of *The Lodger,* Cregar was sitting in the first balcony of the Roxy, thrilled to see the movie with an audience and sitting right next to *New York Times* critic Thomas Pryor. The critic reported that the star "obviously was not prepared for the ripples of laughter which greeted his more ominous movements on the screen. 'Interesting reaction,' he mumbled at least three times." The *Times* critic confessed in his review that he might have laughed too, "if Mr. Cregar weren't quite so big and hadn't happened to occupy the next seat"; he also opined that *The Lodger* might have been "a good deal more interesting, if Mr. Cregar's character were less that of a posturer and if he didn't continually go around trying to scare the daylights out of everyone."

The *Times* was largely alone in its reservations, however: *The Lodger* became an instant popular and (for the most part) critical smash hit. John T. McManus, Manhattan's most sophisticated critic, reported in his *PM* review:

> *The Lodger* is undoubtedly the best Jack-the-Ripper movie ever made. Its casting is bound to satisfy the most discriminating Crime Clubber, both as to villain (Laird Cregar), Scotland Yardsman (George Sanders) and imperilled heroine (Merle Oberon). Its Whitechapel setting is storybook London to the Queen's taste—bowlered Bobbies materializing in fog-shrouded by-ways, glistening cobblestones and clopping cabs, toffs and slatterns slinking in and out of pubs, and finally an Old Vic interior of backdrops, high-spiraling stairways, and lofty catwalks for the final closing-in.

PM praised Oberon's "remarkable frontview can-can," while Howard Barnes of the *New York Herald-Tribune* noted *The Lodger* became "something of a Krafft-Ebing case history of a sex maniac," hailing Brahm's "expert direction." The true star of the show, of course, was Laird Cregar, and the *New York Journal-American* reported:

> Mr. Cregar has gone to town as never before. Which is by way of saying that in his newest film Mr. Cregar is scarcely any, if at all, short of being terrific. This psychological story of the maniacal killer . . . was made to order for Cregar. . . . It just goes to show what Hollywood can do with a whodunit when it really wants to. And what Mr. Cregar can do, when given half a chance.

The *New York Post* gave perhaps the best evidence of Laird Cregar's success as *The Lodger:*

> This department simply must report that, while Scotland Yard's finest were feverishly scouting the on-screen theatre for the Ripper, the affable Mr. Cregar was seated in the press section, calmly enjoying the picture.

A little while later, the popular actor made a personal appearance on the stage — and took a five minute ovation before he finally made his exit.

The Lodger became a monster hit. Cregar, thrilled by his reception, stayed with the Roxy stage show for the whole run of the movie; his showboat performance, with its quirky spices (that fascinated even those audiences who didn't understand his motivation), fully crowned him a movie star, and no actor had achieved so great a success in a horror role since Lon Chaney, Jr., in Universal's 1941 The Wolf Man.

The Lodger was, however, a more significant film (at the time of release) than The Wolf Man. It was a pioneering horror film, paving the way for sexual neuroses in the cinema of terror. The sight of Cregar's face, twisting and leering as Merle Oberon flaunted her lacy panties and seamed opera hosiery and kicked the can-can, was much more novel and sensational to 1944 audiences than a man growing a face full of special effects hair. Costume spectacle, sexual melodrama, and showcase for a young, brilliant actor who made Jack the Ripper his masterpiece performance, The Lodger was one of the most memorable movies of the 1940s. As the New York World-Telegram perceptively noted:

> This is a horror picture that will reach 'way beyond the specialized audience that follows the claptrap to which Hollywood has reduced this style. The Lodger is a magnificent example of its type and a magnificent picture as well.

●

All the dramatizations of the Ripper saga would be a book in themselves.* On May 19, 1946, Vincent Price played "The Lodger" on CBS radio's "Hollywood Star Time," with Cathy Lewis. Fox remade The Lodger as Man in the Attic (1953), with Jack Palance twitching as the Ripper; the film was a virtual facsimile of the 1944 hit, with Constance Smith as the showgirl. Palance, often criticized for overacting, is subdued here, hardly a match for Cregar's mad bravado. Hugo Fregonese directed. There was Jack the Ripper (1959), with the maniac climactically squashed under an elevator; A Study in Terror (1965), with Jack (John Fraser) waging battle with Sherlock Holmes (John Neville); another battle of Holmes (Christopher Plummer) and Watson (James Mason) vs. the Ripper in Murder by Decree (1979); Time After Time (1979), in which the Ripper (David Warner) took a ride in the time machine of H. G. Wells (Malcolm

---

*For a comprehensive assessment, see "Jack the Ripper: His Life and Crimes in Popular Entertainment" in Filmfax #31.

McDowell) and found the savagery of contemporary society much to his liking. There was even a highly touted $9.5 million 1988 television miniseries, "Jack the Ripper," produced by CBS, Lorimar, and Britain's Thames Television and starring Michael Caine as the Scotland Yard inspector. Televised on the 100th anniversary of the Ripper murders, the program promised to reveal the identity of Jack the Ripper (or, at least, make a stab at it by selecting one of Scotland Yard's finalists). Its choice, incidentally, was at odds with that of a rival documentary television show that selected a different Ripper.

Along the way, naturally, the Ripper has crept into all kinds of dramatic variations. *Dr. Jekyll and Sister Hyde* (1972) claimed Jekyll was also the Ripper. *Hands of the Ripper* (1971) gave the Ripper slayings a Freudian slant. His evil spirit has paid many visits to television shows, such as "Star Trek" ("Wolf in the Fold," December 22, 1967) and "Kolchak: The Night Stalker" (September 13, 1974).

The Lodger remains the king of Ripper movies, however. For all its frills, production values, and grand performances, perhaps the greatest power of *The Lodger* is its ability to lure the viewer into the Ripper's mind. Lyndon's script, Brahm's Germanic flourishes, and Cregar's virtuoso, weirdly sympathetic performance almost sucks the viewer into the psyche of the Ripper. When Doris Lloyd's Whitechapel hag stares at "us," as "we" twitch and jerk and insanely advance upon her, Hollywood magic has performed a wicked little miracle; it has given us the eyes, vision, and horror of Jack the Ripper himself.

The Lodger's director and screenwriter paid later visits to this familiar territory. Lyndon adapted Bloch's "Yours Truly, Jack the Ripper" for "Thriller" (April 11, 1961)—hosted by Karloff and directed by Ray Milland. Brahm directed and Lyndon scripted the 1962 "Alfred Hitchcock Presents" episode "Don't Look Behind You," which Mark D. Neel (in a fine Brahm retrospective for *Filmfax #31*), calls "a variation on the Jack the Ripper theme." And Brahm directed, for "The Twilight Zone," "The New Exhibit" (April 4, 1963), a Ripper variation based in a wax museum.

Finally, as for Laird Cregar, his top femme target of *The Lodger* would have her revenge on him in real life, although Merle Oberon, who died wealthy and well loved in 1979, would have been horrified to know it. Oberon's encouragement to Cregar on the set of *The Lodger* to diet into a handsome leading man helped fuel the actor's "beautiful man" campaign—a transformation Cregar personally believed would solve all his personal sexual problems while advancing his stardom. Oberon's flattery would combine with this actor's many complexities to bring on his tragic demise, which climaxed during the shooting of Fox's *Hangover Square,* a follow-up-to/variation-on *The Lodger* that was produced by

Robert Bassler, directed by John Brahm, scripted by Barre Lyndon, co-starred George Sanders, and was shot on the overhauled Whitechapel lot.

Less than one year after *The Lodger*'s premiere, and a month before *Hangover Square*'s preview, Laird Cregar was dead.

But that's a later chapter.

Bluebeard

Studio: PRC; Producer: Leon Fromkess; Associate Producer: Martin Mooney; Director: Edgar G. Ulmer; Original Story: Arnold Phillips and Werner H. Furst; Screenplay: Pierre Gendron; Musical Score Composer and Conductor: Erdody; Production Designer: Eugen Schufftan*; Production Manager: C. A. Beute; Assistant Director: Raoul E. Pagel; Art Director: Paul Palmentola; Assistant Art Director: Angelo Scibetta; Set Decorator: Glenn P. Thompson; Sound Engineer: John Carter; Master of Properties: Charles Stevens; Director of Photography: Jockey A. Feindel, A.S.C.†; Wardrobe: James H. Wade; Coiffures: Loretta Francel; Makeup: Milburn Moranti; Supervising Film Editor: Carl Pierson. Running Time: 71 minutes.

Filmed at the PRC Studios, Hollywood, May–June, 1944; opened at the Strand Theatre, Brooklyn, New York, week of January 25, 1945.

The Players: Gaston Morrell (John Carradine); Lucille (Jean Parker); Inspector Lefevre (Nils Asther); Lamarte (Ludwig Stossel); Inspector Renard (George Pembroke); Francine (Teala Loring); Renee (Sonia Sorel); Mimi (Iris Adrian); Deschamps (Henry Kolker); Le Soldat (Emmett Lynn); Bebette (Patti McCarty); Constance (Carrie Devan); Jeanette (Anne Sterling); and The Barlow and Baker Marionettes.

●

> 'Tis now the very witching time of night,
> When churchyards yawn, and hell itself breathes out
> Contagion to this world. Now could I drink hot blood
> And do such bitter business as the day
> Would quake to look on.
> —*Hamlet,* Act III, sc. ii

Sunday, October 24, 1943, was, perhaps, the most glorious night in the life of John Carradine: his *Hamlet,* hailed by *Time* as "the biggest Shakespearean premiere of modern times," opened at the Geary Theatre in San Francisco.

*Actually the cinematographer.
†Actually the camera operator.

"John Carradine and his Shakespeare Players," proclaimed the posters; the Hollywood character actor of such classics as *The Prisoner of Shark Island, Captains Courageous, Jesse James, Stagecoach, Drums Along the Mohawk,* and *The Grapes of Wrath* was producer, director, star, and sole owner of his stage repertory company. There was one empty seat in the theatre—reserved by Carradine for the spirit of his inspiration (and late drinking crony), John Barrymore. Carradine's Hamlet fascinated the audience. On the second night, a three-minute earthquake tingled the chandelier of the Geary, but nothing rattled Carradine as Hamlet—he merely spoke louder. Finally, a few sailors, awed by the star's bravery in the face of this act-of-God, took charge of the frightened crowd.

"Shut up everybody!" commanded the sailors, as Carradine acted away.

The gaunt cinema villain followed his role of Hamlet at the Geary with performances as Shylock in *The Merchant of Venice* and as Othello. He was truly an overpowering stage actor, and he proudly announced plans to tour the country with his Shakespearean Players and storm Broadway just in time for Shakespeare's April 23 birthday.

It was a dream come true—at a cutthroat price.

First of all, the stage adventure cost Carradine his family: he had fallen in love with blonde actress Sonia Sorel, who played Ophelia, Desdemona, and Portia. Leaving his wife and two sons, he announced plans to wed his co-star. His stage productions were also financially draining; to support the company, Carradine had mortgaged his home, sold his yacht, and, by his later estimation, poured $33,000 into the enterprise from his own pocket. And, professionally, John Carradine paid for the salaries, costumes, and transportation for his classical players by playing in horror movies that permanently tarnished his movie career.

The melodramatics had begun at Universal City, where Carradine transformed a gorilla into Acquanetta in *Captive Wild Woman* (1943); they followed up at Monogram, where Carradine's Nazi mad doctor unleashed *Revenge of the Zombies* (1943). In the late summer of 1943, the actor was back at Universal as Yousef Bey, High Priest of Karnak, brewing tana leaves for Chaney, Jr.'s, Kharis in *The Mummy's Ghost.*

In the fall of 1943, Carradine hit bottom. While he barnstormed as Hamlet, Shylock, and alternately Othello and Iago at an SRO-Pasadena Playhouse, prior to the San Francisco premiere, Carradine gallantly paid the troupe's bills by giving two performances for the notorious producer Sam Katzman at Monogram that truly must be seen to be believed.

Return of the Ape Man, starring Lugosi, featured Carradine as his doomed, ingenuous assistant, whose brain is transplanted into a defrosted cave man; Carradine seems to be doing a lousy burlesque of David Manners.

Carradine, on stage as Hamlet, 1943.

Hot on its heels (and even more notorious) was *Voodoo Man*, which featured Lugosi as a mad doctor, George Zucco chanting incantations in feathers and war paint, and Carradine as poor, retarded Toby, a moron in Lugosi's employ. Stroking the tresses of the female zombies, sighing "you're pretty," playing a bongo as Lugosi tries to revive his long-dead wife, Carradine's Toby would have frightened and embarrassed Chaney's Lennie of *Of Mice and Men* (1939). As he pops his eyes, rolls his mouth, runs like a toddler, and pounds that bongo, Carradine provides one of the most truly disturbing depictions of retardation ever seen on the screen.

"If this goes over," Carradine had announced of his Shakespeare

Players project, "I'm through with Hollywood forever!" *Voodoo Man* had started shooting at Monogram, October 16, 1943—eight days before Carradine's *Hamlet* opened in San Francisco—and his terrible Toby seemed to be this brilliant actor's mischievous, final nose-thumbing at Hollywood.

John Carradine's stage dream did not fulfill itself. His film career would have to go on for over 40 years and nearly 200 more movies; in 1944 alone, the financially desperate actor would play in 11 feature releases, with the melancholy air of a fallen Lucifer. On Shakespeare's birthday, Carradine was not playing the Bard on Broadway but preparing to join Karloff, Chaney, Naish, Atwill, and Zucco in Universal's monster rally *House of Frankenstein,* in which he played Count Dracula.

Strangely, in the midst of all this mad movie activity, as he "drank hot blood," as he committed movie atrocities audiences " would quake to look on," Carradine enjoyed one of his greatest cinema performances—a role some believe surpasses his performance in *The Grapes of Wrath.* The role was *Bluebeard* for PRC Studios, and the director was another fascinating "fallen angel," Edgar G. Ulmer.

●

The spirit that I have seen
May be the devil; and the devil hath power
T' assume a pleasing shape.
—*Hamlet,* Act II, sc. ii

Flashback: on February 28, 1934, Universal began shooting *The Black Cat,* the first glorious teaming of Karloff and Bela Lugosi. Directing the film, providing the adaptation, conceiving the visual style, planning the classical musical score, and even designing Karloff's satanic high priest gowns (all on a salary of $150 per week) was a 33-year-old Austrian, Edgar G. Ulmer. Shot in only 19 days at a cost just below $100,000, *The Black Cat* proved Universal's hit of the season—and one of the darkest, most perverse horror movies in Hollywood history.

By the time *The Black Cat* premiered at the Hollywood Pantages on May 3, 1934, however, Edgar Ulmer was off the Universal lot. On April 12, 1934, *The Hollywood Reporter* announced that Ulmer would direct Karloff in his new shocker, *Bluebeard;* nine days later, the trade paper reported that Universal had released the young director, due to a salary disagreement.

One ponders why Ulmer, wunderkind who had assisted Lang, De-Mille, and Murnau, who had labored at Universal so long, doing everything from working on building the set of *The Phantom of the Opera* (1925) to accompanying "Uncle Carl" Laemmle on his Tijuana gambling jaunts

**John Carradine and his second wife, Sonia (who played his victim in
Bluebeard), at their leisure.**

would select this time, the eve of a hit picture, to wage a losing war over
salary. Did free spirit Ulmer fear the temptation to "go commercial"? Did
he truly resent Universal's exploitation of his talents? Or did Uncle Carl
discover that Ulmer was in love with the assistant script girl of *The Black
Cat,* who was married to a Laemmle relative and would divorce him to wed
Ulmer in 1935?

Whatever the cause, Edgar G. Ulmer's career would never be the
same. Just as Carradine never recovered from his Shakespeare company,
so did Ulmer never regain sure footing after his Universal release. Just as
Carradine often seemed to revel in low-budget rot, so did Ulmer seem to
take a masochistic joy in fighting the outrageously low budgets and absurdly tight shooting schedules of his later films. Ulmer's years after *The
Black Cat* found him in the East, directing Yiddish pictures, but his most
famous work would come back in Hollywood, during the war years, at the
long-lamented PRC Studios. As Ulmer told Peter Bogdanovich in perhaps
his last interview, given shortly before his death in 1972 and published in
the anthology *Kings of the B's:*

> At that time I was called "the Capra of PRC." It was a nice family feel-
> ing, not too much interference; if there was interference, it was only that

we had no money, that was all. [Leon] Fromkess became head of the studio; he would listen, and when I would say I want to make a *Bluebeard,* that's what we would make.

The now defunct Producers Releasing Corporation is the most legendary of Poverty Row lots, remembered as a never-never-land of cinema schlockmeisters who recorded with secondhand equipment, shot with allegedly recanned film tossed away by the majors, and cranked out a 54-minute Western (so the legend goes) in two days on a budget of $8000. In 1944, PRC was going full force, releasing 39 films—more than MGM's 30, Paramount's 32, 20th Century–Fox's 26, or Warner Bros.' 19. "The Five Year Old in Seven-League Boots," proudly proclaimed PRC's full-page advertisement in the 1945 *Film Daily Yearbook;* the '44 output ran the gamut from the Frances Langford musical *Dixie Jamboree* to the gorilla saga *Nabonga* to Westerns with Tex Ritter and Buster Crabbe to horror movies such as *The Monster Maker,* with J. Carrol Naish as a mad doctor and Ralph Morgan in acromegaly makeup (even though real-life acromeglic Rondo Hatton was in town and about to find a home at Universal).

Founded by Ben Judell in 1939, PRC was in the hands of Leon Fromkess (Monogram's ex-treasurer). Sam Newfield was PRC's most prolific director (directing so many films for the studio that he used at least two psuedonyms). Hollywood recognized, however, that the true dynamo of the lot was Edgar G. Ulmer, who would make stylish little noir classics like *Detour* (1945) and *Club Havana* (1946) on six-day shooting schedules.

Ulmer remembered how PRC brainstormed its annual program of features:

> At the beginning of the season, Fromkess would sit down with me and Sig Neufeld, and we would invent 48 titles. We didn't have stories yet; they had to be written to fit the cockeyed titles. I am convinced when I look back all this was a challenge.

Sharing the challenge on all Ulmer's works as script supervisor, from *The Black Cat* onward, was his wife, Shirley Ulmer. Today Mrs. Ulmer lives in Beverly Hills, teaches students the art of moviecraft, and travels the world, representing her late husband at international film festivals and collecting his many posthumous honors. She remembers, affectionately:

> Edgar could persuade anybody to get in on the action. Irresistible! When I look back, I wonder how I survived some of the crazy things that I went through. It was just Edgar's enthusiasm that carried us all. We all had to have that "demonic energy"; anybody who didn't have that couldn't work on an Ulmer picture. He had almost the style of Eisen-

stein; his own little crew, and they knew what to expect. If anybody tried to fourflush, or goldbrick—God help him!

Columbia and Republic both dabbled in low-budget horror fare, but as Ulmer joined PRC, the true championship of Poverty Row* horror was waging: Monogram vs. PRC.

●

> O God, God,
> How weary, stale, flat, and unprofitable
> Seem to me all the uses of this world!
> Fie on't, ah, fie, 'tis an unweeded garden
> That grows to seed. Things rank and gross in nature
> Possess it merely.
> —*Hamlet,* Act I, sc. ii

Universal City, of course, was the three-ring circus of horror in Hollywood, but MGM, Paramount, 20th Century–Fox, and (especially) RKO could put on pretty colorful terror carnivals of their own. Monogram and PRC, Hollywood's "unweeded gardens," with their films "rank and gross in nature," were the sideshows, the peep shows, the freak shows of Hollywood horror.

Step right up at the Monogram booth, 4376 Sunset Plaza, Hollywood, and see Bela Lugosi (no longer a center-ring attraction at Universal) make faces, hiss "Ex-cellent!" and act his head off as he kidnaps brides in *The Corpse Vanishes,* or gets whipped by blonde Louise Currie as *The Ape Man,* or emits a comic sneeze in the East Side Kids' *Ghosts on the Loose* that sounds suspiciously like "Oh shit!"

Drop a few coins at the PRC Santa Monica Boulevard booth and behold George Zucco light up his eyes and purr his voice, as he turns Glenn Strange into a werewolf in *The Mad Monster* or plays the dual roles of doctor and vampire in *Dead Men Walk* or (at age 60) boisterously sprints away from Quetzalcoatl, his vengeful pet of *The Flying Serpent.*

Sometimes there were trade-offs: Lugosi visited PRC for *The Devil Bat* (1940); Zucco reported to Monogram for (apparently) a few miserable minutes of *Return of the Ape Man* before the spectacle of himself in cave man makeup made the sensitive actor so ill he had to surrender the part to Frank Moran. Of course, there was that special night at the Monogram sideshow when Lugosi and Zucco (as well as Carradine) all teamed up for

---

*Technically, "Poverty Row" was the little colony of the independent producers in "Gower Gulch," near the Columbia and RKO Studios in central Hollywood. Like the term "Hollywood" itself, "Poverty Row" has taken on larger geographic suggestions over the decades.

Voodoo Man. Although Lugosi gave one of his most striking performances as the goateed doctor trying to bring his beloved wife back from the dead, war-painted Zucco and bongo-playing Carradine would have fared better taking turns at the dunking booth.

Sometimes the sideshows were gyps, such as PRC's *The Devil Bat:* see the title horror, a spastic kite. Sometimes they were sadly exploitative, such as PRC's *Dead Men Walk:* see Dwight Frye, once the classic hunchback Fritz of *Frankenstein,* back now as Zolarr, the hunchback, terribly drawn (and weirdly effeminate), sad and desperate with one year left to live. Always, however, there was a slim but wonderful chance something special would happen in this sideshow alley, away from the ringmaster's control of the big tent, and away from the mainstream audience's sense of "taste."

Which sideshow was superior? Today, Monogram easily is the most popular; this was Lugosi's realm, and his devoted cult assures those potboilers a loyal (and growing) audience today. Karloff fans also jump on Monogram's bandwagon; "the king" played the *Mr. Wong* series and *The Ape* (1940) for Monogram (just before Broadway's *Arsenic and Old Lace* refreshed his prestige), but he never "descended" to PRC. In fact, PRC was (arguably) the more creative lot, while Zucco was (very arguably) a finer actor than Lugosi, and certainly commanded more work. He dropped by PRC between character jobs at MGM, Fox, and Paramount, and enjoyed top "heavy" status at Universal. But Zucco's following today hardly compares to the intensely loyal cult that celebrates Lugosi, a pack of worshippers comparable to Elvis Presley's and Marilyn Monroe's in fanatic passion.

There was quick money, big billing, and melodramatic vehicles for Hollywood villains at the Monogram and PRC sideshows. Early 1944 releases from PRC starred Lionel Atwill *(Lady in the Death House),* J. Carrol Naish *(The Monster Maker),* and John Carradine *(Waterfront,* in which he co-starred with Naish).

It was Edgar Ulmer who would dare to present Carradine's Hamlet — billed here as *Bluebeard* — at the PRC sideshow.

●

Angels and ministers of grace defend us!
— *Hamlet,* Act I, sc. iv

There had been a strange evolution of the working relationship of Edgar Ulmer and John Carradine.

In the early 1930s, John Carradine had been a great sideshow of Hollywood Boulevard — marching up and down in a cape and slouch hat, roaring Shakespeare to tourists, the hills, and the pepper trees, winning

John Carradine as *Bluebeard*.

notoriety as "The Bard of the Boulevard." Carradine was delighted to earn $20 per day as one of the Satan worshippers of Ulmer's *The Black Cat;* he is glimpsed playing the organ at Karloff's high mass to Lucifer. In 1936 Carradine was a hit as the snarling Sgt. Rankin of John Ford's *The Prisoner of Shark Island.* While Ulmer worked on his Yiddish oeuvres in the East, Carradine became a top character player at 20th Century–Fox and an illustrious member of the famous "stock company" of John Ford (whom Ulmer idolized). In 1942 Carradine was freelancing again—delighted to be able to accept stage roles such as the hunchbacked King Louis XI in *The Vagabond King*—just as Ulmer returned for his PRC adventures.

In 1942 producer Seymour Nebenzal prepared *Hitler's Hangman* for his "Angelus Productions," based on the infamous Nazi Heydrich, whose assassination in June 1942 brought on Hitler's monstrous razing of the village of Lidice. Ulmer worked (uncredited) on the script and set and was supposed to direct. Leading lady Frances Farmer had a severe breakdown, however, and Nebenzal (to Ulmer's disapproval) immediately replaced her with Patricia Morison. There was presumably much controversy, and Nebenzal replaced Ulmer with Douglas Sirk. Shirley Ulmer (at Edgar's insistence) remained on the picture; Ulmer's influence can be sensed in the pastoral, baroque style of this passionate melodrama. It was, in fact, so impressive that MGM bought the movie from PRC and released it in the summer of 1943 as *Hitler's Madman;* it remains one of Carradine's greatest performances.

"Carradine was a Shakespearean actor, with a reputation of going overboard," said Douglas Sirk. "A lot of Nazis behaved like Shakespearean actors."

Then, in 1943, Ulmer directed PRC's *Isle of Forgotten Sins,* (so he could use the 200 palm trees left over from John Ford's *The Hurricane,* which had featured Carradine in 1937). Fondly remembered by Shirley Ulmer as "a B stinker," it starred the priceless team of Carradine and Gale Sondergaard. The gaunt actor played (of all things) a lusty sailor seeking under-the-sea treasure and singing "Whiskey Johnny." Mrs. Ulmer remembers:

> John was *very* professional. He was suffering, on *Isle of Forgotten Sins,* from hemorrhoids. He was playing the part of a sailor, in tight, white pants, and every hour or so we had to have new pants ready, because he would bleed. He was suffering like crazy, but would never admit it ... *truly* a professional.

After a string of title-tested, six-day miracles for PRC—*Tomorrow We Live* (1942), *My Son, the Hero, Girls in Chains, Jive Junction* (all 1943)— Ulmer got the green light from Fromkess to do *Bluebeard*, a full decade after Universal had announced it for him. His old studio had kept the title on the schedule for several years, but no production ever began, despite several script writers.

The Pierre Gendron screenplay for *Bluebeard* appears definitely influenced by 20th Century–Fox's *The Lodger*. Like Laird Cregar's Jack the Ripper at Fox, PRC's Bluebeard was a sensitive soul driven to madness and murder by a whore. The psychological, sexual nature of this approach was a bit daring for a PRC production, and its sophisticated execution would establish *Bluebeard* as something of a milestone in the psychotic cinema. History's "real Bluebeard" was Henri Landru who was convicted of killing nine women and went to the guillotine in 1922.

Ulmer knew whom he wanted to star as the legendary strangler of women. But would John Carradine, who had been a top character player on the 20th Century–Fox lot, a member of John Ford's famous stock company, and a brilliant Hamlet, be willing to star as Bluebeard?

●

> The fair Ophelia! Nymph, in thy orisons
> Be all my sins remember'd.
>   *—Hamlet*, Act III, sc. i

John Carradine, in sad truth, would play virtually anybody in anything in 1944. In a glow after his *Hamlet,* Carradine's personal life was a carnival. The star and his Ophelia, Sonia Sorel, were living ("in sin," as the expression went in those days) at Villa 15 of Nazimova's legendary Garden of Allah, 8152 Sunset Boulevard. There, with Sonia, Carradine seemed to revel in his real-life role of Hollywood's hard-drinking Shakespearean screwball. In her 1970 book *The Garden of Allah,* Sheilah Graham wrote:

> John was among the most picturesque people at the Garden. He moved in with Sonia.... They were constantly fighting and chasing each other around the pool. Or rather, Sonia did the chasing. John believed in allowing the wife to be the boss. His charming boss sometimes came after him with a high-heeled shoe in her hand. Just being playful.
>
> Carradine recited Shakespeare in a loud, flat voice to impress Sonia. The recitals from the bard took place in their bungalow, but could be heard everywhere, even in the farthest corner of the Garden.... Sonia was a voluptuous blonde with her long hair flowing free. She made terracotta sketches when not fighting with her gaunt mate....
>
> There was the night that Carradine decided he was Jesus and tried to walk across the swimming pool. Marc Connelly, always a gambler, was betting on John to make it. He lost his bet.

Naturally, none of this sat well with the ex–Mrs. Carradine, from whom John separated New Year's Eve, 1943. She quickly filed for divorce, winning custody of Carradine's stepson Bruce and their son, John, Jr. (later known as David), and a settlement that, Carradine lamented, forced him to pay her about $40,000 per year "before I can buy a cup of coffee." With Ardanelle demanding her money, the Shakespearean company needing constant funds, the rent due at the Garden of Allah, Carradine could hardly give up Hollywood. At $3500 per week, the actor worked everywhere, from Warner Bros. (as Bret Harte in *The Adventures of Mark Twain*) to PRC (as a Nazi in *Waterfront*).

On May 8, 1944, Carradine completed his role of Dracula in Universal's *House of Frankenstein*. Ulmer overtured him with the title role of *Bluebeard*. The "irresistible" director even tossed in a bonus: he offered Sonia the role of Renee, Bluebeard's lover, whom he strangles and tosses into the river.

On May 31, 1944, *Bluebeard*, starring John Carradine, began shooting at PRC Studios.

●

> O'erstep not the modesty of nature. For anything so o'erdone
> is from the purpose of playing, whose end, both at the first and
> now, was and is, to hold, as 'twere, the mirror up to nature.
> —*Hamlet*, Act III, sc. ii

Bluebeard opens with a crashing, dramatic overture against the title credits as the Leon Erdody score thunders away like the overture to an opera. Indeed, Ulmer's *Bluebeard* plays in the lush style of an opera; as Shirley Ulmer says,

> My husband was a frustrated musician. . . . He wanted to be a conductor (and played a pretty decent piano). That's why he worked so well with that Hungarian, Erdody. In every Ulmer little "stinker," there's a good score.

The scene is set in Paris, 1855; a bell tolls at Notre Dame. The movie opens with a little shocker: gendarmes fishing an anonymous starlet out of the Seine. All Paris is in terror because of the Bluebeard murders, and nervously flitting through the streets at night are our brave heroine, Lucille (Jean Parker), and her frightened friends Bebette (Patti McCarty) and Constance (Carrie Devan).

"Edgar conducted his actors," says Shirley Ulmer of the music-minded director. "He used a baton all the time."

Jean Parker, our attractive, auburn-haired leading lady, was having quite a year with horror stars in 1944: Paramount's *One Body Too Many* (with Lugosi), PRC's *Lady in the Death House* (with Atwill), Universal's *Dead Man's Eyes* (with Chaney). Having begun her Hollywood career as a Metro starlet of the early '30s, Parker was a highly underrated actress who later proved her great talent in the national company of *Born Yesterday* (1946); today she is one of Hollywood's great recluses. (She was a far finer choice for the role of Lucille than Marie "The Body" McDonald, whom PRC first wanted for the role.)

Edgar Ulmer's eye for atmosphere shines in this scene from *Bluebeard*.

As the three ladies move nervously through the dark Parisienne streets, a tall Faustian figure in black cape and top hat moves through the mist, nearly walking into them. It is, of course, our Bluebeard, Gaston Morrell, the puppeteer, played by John Carradine.

Carradine, 38 years old, still tingling from *Hamlet,* is dynamic, Byronic, classically dashing. There's a touch of tragedy in his eyes (is it the role or the actor?). Certainly, Carradine relished the role of *Bluebeard* and later recalled on the PBS special *The Horror of It All:*

> *Bluebeard* hangs in my memory, not only because I was the star of it, but because it had a depth of characterization, which in that period in Hollywood, was not often seen on the screen. In the early days of Hollywood, pictures were in black and white ... not only in the film material, but in the plot lines.... There were no grays. The villains were stepped in villainy, and the heroes were just too good to be true.

A special attraction of Carradine's portrayal is his style. The Shakespearean actor, with his reputation for "going overboard," here plays very naturally. Indeed, Ulmer had demanded Carradine follow

Hamlet's advice to the players and "hold the mirror up to nature" in his own performance here. As the director later said:

> When directing John, one must be mindful of the fact that one is handling dynamite. John, without half-trying, can overpower a scene. . . . One must remind him to put the brakes on, lest he chew up the sprocket holes on the film. He is a worker, and a professional from the word "go" . . . the tenderness is there, the compassion is there . . . it must be seen.

Carradine, Parker, and Ulmer all capture a little sense of destiny and doom in the first meeting. She expresses her interest in the puppet operas he performs in the square; he flirtatiously agrees to present a puppet show the next evening if Lucille promises to attend, despite the Bluebeard scare.

"Afraid of Bluebeard?" laughs Lucille.

"Aren't you?" asks Gaston.

"What would Bluebeard want with me?"

"I should think he might find you irresistible, Mademoiselle."

In the first few minutes of *Bluebeard,* the style, the craftsmanship, the performances are all so assured that it's almost impossible to believe that Ulmer shot it all in six days. Shirley Ulmer confirms:

> *Bluebeard* was a six-day picture, but when you say six days, it was really twelve, because it was day and night. There was rehearsal in advance, so that when we came on the set, the cameramen knew what every shot was. As script supervisor, I knew every angle—Edgar made sketches long before Hitchcock ever thought of them. We'd sketch every angle and paste them in our book. We had been rehearsed to death before we ever hit a set, so there was never any correction—we were ready to go, like a stage play. The unions kaiboshed this completely in later years, you know.

At the puppet show, the opera, delightfully, is *Faust.* Performing it are the Barlow and Baker puppets; Ulmer had brought Barlow and Baker out from Philadelphia, and they had crafted the puppets in the Ulmer garage. We see our puppeteers above the stage, pulling the strings: Le Soldat (scruffy, mustachioed little Emmett Lynn) operates Faust, Carradine's Gaston pulls the strings of Mephistopheles, naturally, and Sonia Sorel, as Renee, operates Marguerite—all singing to dubbed voices (much to the displeasure of Carradine, who hoped to showcase his own basso singing voice). Sorel is a stunner. A viewer takes immediate note not only of her blonde beauty and statuesque figure, but of her resemblance to her son, actor Keith Carradine (born in 1950).

The *Faust* scene is typical of the little set pieces Ulmer loved creating: rich in atmosphere (such as the mounted gendarme who weeps at the opera's climax), emotion (closeups of Jean Parker fighting back tears as the

Lobby card for *Bluebeard* (1944).

opera concludes), and a little perversity (as Carradine, giving voice to the devil, takes time to peek out above the stage and wolfishly regard Parker). This last scene is also indicative of the awkwardness often obvious in Ulmer's films: when Carradine peers through the peep hole, he turns his favored left profile toward the camera—looking in the opposite direction of where the leading lady is watching.

Abetting Ulmer, naturally, was his loyal PRC force: art director Paul Palmentola, assistant art director Angelo Scibetta (a special help to Ulmer on the backdrops), and, most of all, his uncredited cinematographer, Eugene Schufftan (1893–1977). The German camera ace, who had introduced in *Metropolis* the famous "Schufftan process" (mirror images blended with real backgrounds), was treated shamefully by Hollywood, as Shirley Ulmer remembers:

> On *Bluebeard*, Jockey Feindel, the camera operator, was actually given the cameraman credit, because he was in the union. But it was Eugene Schufftan, one of the greatest cameramen who ever lived, who really was the cinematographer. Schufftan was a victim of Hitler. He had been in Dachau, and when he finally arrived here, by way of Portugal, and Mexico, and God-knows all kinds of horrors, he was in terrible shape. Our

union wouldn't let him in, even though he was a top cameraman from Austria. So Edgar used him a lot, anonymously, on our PRC pictures, and we had to have a union cameraman on the set. On *The Wife of Monte Cristo* [1946], for example, it was Schufftan's wonderful mirror images which helped Edgar enormously. He was an amazing man. He was a very wealthy man, because of the Schufftan process, a montage process he had invented; he had royalties coming in on that all the time, so he had plenty of money. But it was driving him crazy—because he couldn't take credit for his work.

Finally, Schufftan, thank God, did *The Hustler* in New York, got the screen credit—and won the Oscar. Which was a *big* embarrassment to our Academy.

Flames erupt climactically on the stage, and the opera ends. Gaston takes up the collection, offering his top hat for tips. He meets Lucille and her girlfriends and lures the leading lady away, up above the puppet stage. He explains that all the puppets are based on people he has known.

"And Marguerite—is she a friend of yours?"

"She was."

"Was?"

"Yes. Unfortunately, she met a tragic ending."

Gaston and Lucille move to a balcony, before a striking backdrop of Notre Dame.

"There's something in your voice that made me feel you'd suffered," says Lucille.

"You're very discerning," replies Gaston.

"It's your Marguerite.... You're keeping the tragedy alive deliberately, aren't you? ... If you wanted to forget it, you could create a new puppet. One that would remind you of someone else. Someone who might make you happy."

Gaston's face focuses more intently on Lucille. The flirtation disappears; a slightly diabolic, obsessed expression replaces it. Gaston, who has offered to paint Lucille's portrait, withdraws his offer; she, however, plans to keep her promise to make some costumes for his puppets.

Gaston returns home that night. The house number is #15 (perhaps an inside joke—Carradine's villa at the Garden of Allah was #15). Awaiting him is his lover, a fierce-eyed, jealous Renee. They quarrel, Ulmer giving both lovers terrific closeups. The flying sparks are indicative of the off-screen relationship, says Shirley Ulmer:

> On *Bluebeard,* there was lots of jealousy on the part of Sonia. John flirted! Sonia was very jealous, but he was enamored of her, and he toed the mark, for a little while. At that time, it was still early in their relationship, so they were very "together." They had a lot of separations, between and betwixt, but Sonia was good for John, because she played along with

him—she was a great straight woman; she played along with all the same kinds of nonsense and acts that he did.

"Gaston—these girls—I've known they didn't mean anything to you really," says Renee, her face marvelously lit with doom-promising shadows. "But Gaston—what's happened to them?"

Gaston removes his cravat. Renee screams. Bluebeard sadly carries the cadaver via a secret passageway down into the sewers, and shortly afterwards, we see gendarmes pulling Sonia's soaked corpse out of the Seine.

Bluebeard introduces its other leading players. There's Inspector Lefevre, played by Swedish Nils Asther, once a matinee idol of MGM silents. Sound had damaged his career; he later denied the popular story that Garbo (with whom he starred in Metro's 1928 *The Single Standard*) later recognized him working as an elevator boy and fainted. In truth, he had acted regularly in European films and was quite active in the early '40s, playing such roles as the mystic of Universal's *Night Monster* (1942) and the rapidly aging hero in Paramount's *The Man in Half-Moon Street* (1944).

There's Lamarte, Morrell's evil art patron, who knows Gaston is Bluebeard (Gaston notes earlier that Lamarte was one of his inspirations in creating the puppet of Mephistopheles); the role is perfectly played by bald, round Ludwig Stossel (1883–1973), who in this performance strangely resembles Werner Krauss's Dr. Caligari. "He was a fine German actor," says Mrs. Ulmer of Stossel. "Edgar knew him from his Reinhardt days." Stossel was featured in such Universal horrors as *The Climax* (1944) and *House of Dracula* (1945); his greatest fame came as "The Little Old Wine Maker" of television commercials during the 1960s.

And there's Francine, Lucille's sister, played by Teala Loring; Francine is actually an undercover police agent on the trail of Bluebeard. Loring had previously appeared with Carradine in *Return of the Ape Man*, in which she is carried off in the arms of cave man Frank Moran; she played that film under the name of Judith Gibson. In real life, Loring was the sister of '50s starlets Debra Paget and Lisa Gaye.

Ulmer directs *Bluebeard* rather in the voyeuristic style he displayed in *The Black Cat*. There's some "ooh-lah-lah" '40s style: Le Soldat breaks into Lucille's salon with a message from Gaston, scaring a model, who screams in her corset; when Gaston calls on Lucille and first meets Francine, she's dressing behind a screen.

> GASTON: How do you do?
> FRANCINE: Usually better than this!

Ulmer even injects a comic courtroom scene where the police interrogate models who might have known the artist who is Bluebeard; Iris

Adrian, as Mimi, a model-turned-prostitute, does a hip-swaying, out-in-left-field burlesque of Mae West.

Lefevre traces clues to a painting of Bluebeard's fourth victim, sold by Lamarte to a duke. The inspector plans to present Francine (his girlfriend, by the way) as a wealthy young lady from South America, with agent Deschamps (Henry Kolker, from *The Black Room* and *Mad Love*) posing as her father, who wants her portrait painted. The undercover pair visit Lamarte, hoping he will find the painter of the portrait and the police will find Bluebeard. Lamarte agrees to do so for 150,000 francs; he offers Morrell 30,000. Gaston, needing the money desperately, reluctantly agrees to paint Francine from behind a screen (and in strict anonymity).

Francine arrives at Lamarte's studio. Gaston begins painting her but, unhappy with her pose, he steps out from behind the screen. Although he doesn't recognize Francine (he saw only the top of her head when she was changing at Lucille's), she recognizes him.

"Lucille's puppeteer!" she gasps. "So *you're* Bluebeard!"

The panic on her face maddens Gaston and his eyes grow wide.

Lamarte tries to escape with the 150,000 francs, leaving Gaston with Francine's cadaver and the unconscious Deschamps, whom Lamarte has recognized as a policeman and knocked out. Gaston stops him and accuses him of betraying him. As Lamarte breaks down in fear, Carradine's Bluebeard walks across the set, turns, reaches out his arms, and—in a move that can only be called balletic—sweeps across the studio to strangle him.

●

I am but mad north-northwest: when the wind is
southerly I know a hawk from a handsaw.
                              —*Hamlet,* Act II, sc. ii

"John Carradine was a person I could hang onto," said Edgar Ulmer late in life, remembering *Bluebeard*. "He knew what we were trying to do. Yeah, it was a very lovely picture."

In fact, the relationship of director and star was very close indeed, for it was at the time of *Bluebeard* that an unusual event took place, bringing together both men, as Shirley Ulmer recalls:

> John was in trouble. He was in the process of getting a divorce from his first wife. John came to dinner—we called him "The Man Who Came to Dinner"—and ended up staying for a while with his son Jackie (today "David"). He had his rooms at the Garden of Allah, where he was living with Sonia, but he couldn't make his alimony payments—and he was hiding from his wife.

Shirley Ulmer describes the Ulmer house, high in the Hollywood Hills, where Carradine found his sanctuary:

> We lived at 1969 N. Kings Road, way up the winding road above Sunset, almost to the top, with the most magnificent view. We were next to Hopalong Cassidy, and across the street from poor darling Zachary Scott; it was quite an artists colony, right up the hill there. It was there that John came, and he and Edgar just hit it off. It was great to listen to their dialogues. And "Jackie" was a chip off the old block. We called him "Captain Midnight," his favorite radio hero at that time. Jackie would pretend he was Captain Midnight—climbing over the balcony of our daughter Arianne's room, and up onto our Mediterranean, red-tiled roof. He'd flap his arms, and make like wings—and break all the tiles!

Shirley Ulmer loved listening to her husband and Carradine, debating everything as they sat up late into the night:

> They discussed Shakespeare, they discussed Europe, they discussed philosophy; John was very erudite. He was not what I would call *very* educated—but, if he hadn't learned it in school, he was self-taught. They argued a lot, which was good. With my man, you got along well if you weren't afraid to stand up to him—and John wasn't the least bit afraid to stand up to anyone in this world. Edgar would scold him, and thought he was ruining himself by acting so crazy offscreen, and John didn't agree. He said, "That's what people want, and that's what they can have, and f--- them"—and that was it!

As John Carradine hid out in the Ulmer aerie, Shirley came to understand the actor, his show-off behavior in Hollywood, and his anxieties:

> John Carradine was a kid—a grown-up kid. When you got him in a serious mood, like Edgar did, you were surprised that, mentally, he was very much more than you expected. But he was acting, playacting, to the public, all the time. These pranks were just to gain attention—he must have been very unloved as a youngster. He missed his father, who died when John was very young, and I think he felt very unloved, and he wanted to be admired, and he wanted attention.

It must have been a haven for Carradine to be living with such stimulating and sympathetic friends. It was a feeling that carried down Kings Road, across Sunset, and south to the PRC studios as *Bluebeard* completed its dizzy six days of shooting.

●

> What would he do,
> Had he the motive and the cue for passion
> That I have?
> —*Hamlet*, Act II, sc. ii

The latter scenes of *Bluebeard* are little pieces of bravura acting, directing, and cinematography that are ample illustration of why Shirley Ulmer is so often away from Beverly Hills accepting international awards for her late spouse.

A mournful Lucille stands near the casket in the funeral parlor with a deeply shaken Lefevre. He shows Lucille his only clue: the murder weapon, a stitched cravat—the very one she had stitched for Gaston.

Suddenly, as an organ hits a chilling note: the dark, shadowed form of Carradine's Gaston falls across the doorway. The effect is spine-tingling; here Ulmer transforms Bluebeard into the spectre of Death itself, with the gall to pay respects to its victim. Gaston offers flowers, but all Lucille can focus on is his new cravat.

Of course, Lucille realizes that Gaston is Bluebeard. Being a horror heroine, she naturally doesn't tell Lefevre, but visits Gaston to accuse him. Just as an opera would afford its lead singer a climactic aria, just as Shakespeare would have provided his lead actor with a magnificent soliloquy, here "Bluebeard" affords Carradine a long, rich, dramatic speech as he confesses his mania and his murders.

He had been a young, starving painter; then one night he found on the street a starving girl named Jeanette. Ulmer presents Jeanette (Anne Sterling) in a weird, twisted flashback, complete with a cockeyed lampost. Jeanette was blonde, and indeed, she resembled Morrell's puppet of Marguerite. Gaston nursed her back to health, and as he fell in love with her, he painted her portrait. It was an inspired portrait, and Lamarte came one day with the news that Gaston's "Jeanette" would hang in the Louvre. Gaston felt compelled to share the glorious news with Jeanette and went to find her.

The flashback shows Ulmer at his best. Jeanette is, of course, a whore—"a low, coarse, loathsome creature." Ulmer and Schufftan tilt the camera to a dizzy, downward angle as Jeanette drags the stiff-armed Gaston down through the film frame, toward her bed. She laughs at the horrified artist and throws money at him. The sight of his inspiration-turned-doxy unhinges him, and he strangles her—all under Erdody's mounting music.

Carradine beautifully delivers his tragic monologue:

> I thought that would stop her defiling the image I created of her, stop her degrading my work, I thought that would be the end of what she could do to me—but it wasn't. Every time I painted again, I painted Jeanette.

Jean Parker and John Carradine in a scene from *Bluebeard*.

> I turned to making puppets, because I could make them of wood. Because when they became Jeanette, I could take out my fury on them.

Carradine grabs a puppet and madly, viciously, breaks its neck.

> There was no money in puppets—at least not enough for Lamarte. I owed Lamarte a lot of money. Only he knew that I had killed Jeanette, so I had to paint for Lamarte. He wanted pictures of girls he could sell. But again, every girl I painted turned out to be Jeanette, and I couldn't permit it, I couldn't stop myself. Every time I painted her—I had to kill her again. Finally, life came to mean nothing to me, not even my own. Then I saw you.

Gaston believes Lucille can cure his mania. He almost bows beside her, before a fireplace, the Faustian flames raging below them in the frame. But she will have none of it; he has killed her sister.

"Anyone seeking to destroy our happiness is a menace," rants Gaston. "A menace that would have to be done away with!" The tenderness is still there, the compassion is still there, but now Carradine is truly letting it rip—wonderfully mixing the madness of Bluebeard with the acting power of John Carradine.

Lucille is going to the police. "You wouldn't do that!" says Gaston. "Wouldn't I!" hisses Lucille.

"Lucille! You *couldn't* do that to me! Not you, Lucille. . . . I wouldn't let you turn against me too, oh no, not you Lucille, not you!" Carradine's Gaston grabs her, embraces her, tenderly and mournfully holds her — and then suddenly notices his hands are near her neck.

And there's a closeup of the mad eyes.

"It wasn't a bad picture until toward the end when they got those two former Mack Sennett cops in," lamented Carradine years later. Indeed, before Bluebeard can strangle Lucille, Lefevre and his police break into the studio in pure melodrama style. As Lefevre comforts Lucille (with whom he's clearly in love), a chase scene ensues, the "Mack Sennett" gendarmes pursuing the villain over the rooftops of PRC Paris. Our Bluebeard climbs atop a roof, Carradine receiving one more wonderful closeup before the roof breaks away and he falls, far below, into the Seine.

The Notre Dame bell rings. The Erdody score booms beautifully, deliriously, almost maniacally. And, with this wild, baroque finale, *Bluebeard* comes to its tragic, madly operatic end.

In the summer of 1944, Carradine and Sonia had a horrific fight at the Garden of Allah. He downed 12 double Scotch and sodas and tried to drown himself in the pool. Three male nurses saved him. The lovers reconciled and, on August 13, 1944, Carradine and Sonia wed in Nevada.

On October 9, 1944, the *Hollywood Reporter* offered a review of *Bluebeard.* Ulmer had fooled the astute *Reporter:* the critic had no conception that this was a typical PRC six-day quickie. Expecting a sideshow, he had seen an opera:

> It has been the avowed and advertised purpose of PRC for some time to lift itself above the status of an organization devoted to the making of lower-budgeted films and strike out for a better trade by pouring into the market films with a "flexible budget." . . . PRC has done this with *Bluebeard.* It is the kind of picture any company, or any producer, would like to release. It is a class product from start to finish, with every opportunity to entertain, regardless of expense, utilized to the fullest. In comparison with other movies with the same premise, it is head and shoulders a superior. . . . Carradine has never been seen to better advantage. Gone are the familiar, hammish chin-stroking and the leering eye. He gives a sensitive, yet virile portrayal of the mad painter that will be marked as one of the finest pieces of acting in a long time. . . . Edgar Ulmer's direction is studied and exact. There is a gentleness and an understanding permeating the entire film that can be attributed to him.

Bluebeard opened at the Strand Theatre in Brooklyn, New York, the week of January 25, 1945. *Variety* was impressed:

One of the best pictures to come out of the PRC mill, *Bluebeard* is a horror film that should be able to bring good returns as the top film on neighborhood duals.... John Carradine gives an excellent portrayal.... Production has some expensive settings and pretty costumes.

Before *Bluebeard* could have its Hollywood premiere, Carradine ran into new trouble: ex-wife Ardanelle claimed he had rewed before their divorce was final. So, Carradine and Sonia wed again March 25, 1945. "Jackie" (aka David) was ringbearer, the Ulmer's daughter Arianne was flower girl, and it was a Shakespearean wedding, with bride and groom in full classical attire. "I don't know how that minister ever approved of it," laughs Shirley Ulmer, "but John insisted on a Shakespearean wedding. It was kooky as hell!"

In the last week of June 1945 *Bluebeard* finally opened at the Hawaii Theatre in Hollywood, supported by PRC's Lionel Atwill/George Zucco *Fog Island*. The film received a sad publicity bonus later that week when Carradine, preparing to visit Coney Island to play in *My Dear Children* with Sonia, was arrested on charges of alimony contempt and tossed into jail, where he suavely posed through the bars of his cell for photographers.

Edgar G. Ulmer remembered that *Bluebeard* earned "tremendous money in France," but this wonderfully stylish, dramatic horror film — perhaps the finest Poverty Row horror film ever made — did nothing to boost the career of its director or star. Ulmer stayed on at PRC, creating marvelous curiosities like *Detour*. Carradine, shortly after reprising Dracula in Universal's *House of Dracula* (1945), paid one more visit to the PRC Studios for *Down Missouri Way* (1946), playing a hammy director seeking a "hep" mule to star in a musical. Shortly afterwards, he fled a new alimony arrest and went east with Sonia (who had played in Ulmer's 1945 *Strange Illusion*); there he worked on Broadway, in stock, and in the cheaply-made, New York City–filmed movie, *C-Man* (1949). Edgar Ulmer and Carradine would never work together again.

And as for PRC, the studio went its crazy, ruthless, irreverent way. Maris Wrixon, heroine of PRC's *White Pongo* (1945), saga of an albino gorilla, remembered (in a *Filmfax* interview with Don Leifert) that PRC was the only Hollywood studio not to close down for the day when President Roosevelt died. For a time, PRC could at least pride itself that it had never stooped so low as "Big Top" Universal by promoting real-life acromeglic Rondo Hatton as its "monster without makeup." However, when Rondo Hatton died February 2, 1946, just after completing Universal's *The Brute Man*, his home studio, possibly plagued by distaste and guilt, certainly believing it had a disaster on its hands, desperately offered to sell the film off to an independent studio.

It was PRC, shamelessly, who released *The Brute Man*.

There's a divinity that shapes our ends,
Rough-hew them how we will.
—*Hamlet,* Act V, sc. ii

By 1972, three strokes had left Edgar Ulmer paralyzed and unable to speak, yet his mind was keenly alert. He could move only the forefinger of his right hand, but he would signal Shirley to bring him a pen, and he would scribble his inspirations.

He was, of course, rich in memories. The irrepressible Ulmer had worked his crazy magic for two decades after *Bluebeard;* for a time, he carried on for PRC: *Strange Illusion* and *Detour* (1945), *Club Havana, The Wife of Monte Cristo, His Sister's Secret* (all 1946). In 1947, Eagle-Lion bought the studio, releasing Ulmer's 1948 *Ruthless* (Shirley Ulmer's personal favorite of her husband's films). In the early '50s, the Eagle-Lion lot was mad with activity, housing not only the "EL" forces, but over 20 independent producers; it soon was acquired by United Artists. Edgar Ulmer, not surprisingly, had survived his old studio.

The Ulmer oeuvre had grown to include costumers like the 1949 *The Pirates of Capri* (shot in Italy), low-budget "Sci-Fi" like *The Man from Planet X* (UA, 1951), and nonsense like *Babes in Bagdad* (UA, 1952, starring Paulette Goddard and Gypsy Rose Lee). Inevitably, Ulmer's shooting schedules were farcical, his budgets ridiculous; but the films were always personal, and whenever possible, they were family affairs. For example, on *Beyond the Time Barrier* (AIP, 1960), Ulmer directed, Shirley script-supervised, and daughter Arianne played the femme fatale, Markova.

Ulmer was erratic. Take *Daughter of Dr. Jekyll,* released by Allied Artists in 1957. Early in the movie, heroine Gloria Talbott arrives at the Jekyll home and undresses, revealing a nineteenth century Victorian corset. A while later, our monster (Arthur Shields) goes madly rampaging across the moors and leers inside a cottage where blonde '50s starlet Marjorie Stapp is cavorting about in a black, Frederick's of Hollywood–style body girdle, playfully hooking and unhooking her stockings to her 1957 garters. *Daughter of Dr. Jekyll* suddenly turns into *Lingerie Through the Ages.*

The final Edgar Ulmer movie was *The Cavern* (20th Century–Fox, 1965), which he hoped to film in caves high in the snowy mountains of Yugoslavia. In his book on George Sanders, *A Dreadful Man,* the late Brian Aherne recalled Ulmer as "a florid, temperamental character" who was left in the mountains with not even half the money necessary to shoot the movie. The Ulmers were unconquerable, however, and, as Aherne wrote, "Ulmer and his loyal, overworked wife, who acted as assistant producer, script girl, wardrobe mistress, secretary, cashier, and everything else necessary, plunged into their tasks and scarcely slept for many weeks." The caves had to be closed, the crew had to move to Rome, crews went on strike, and Aherne finally finished the picture—"thankful to be alive." For Edgar and Shirley Ulmer, it was all part of the mad challenge of movies they had shared for thirty years.

"He had humor and passion and a kind of demonic charm," wrote Peter Bogdanovich after interviewing the legendary director early in the 1970s. Always, despite his terrible illness, Ulmer dreamed of new projects, using the pen in his forefinger to try to write them down. Shirley Ulmer still has them.

Edgar George Ulmer died September 30, 1972, at the Motion Picture Hospital and is buried in the Abbey of the Psalms in Hollywood Memorial Park.

●

As for John Carradine, late in his life, he appeared (at Shirley Ulmer's invitation) at a UCLA showing of *Bluebeard.* He was very ill, almost crippled by arthritis, which had destroyed the shape of his hands and feet. A nurse had to be with him, and Shirley almost felt guilty for asking him to appear. But he was keen and bright and spoke warmly about *Bluebeard* and Edgar Ulmer.

The decades since *Bluebeard* had been tempestuous for Carradine. His marriage to Sonia (which produced Christopher, Keith, and Robert Carradine) had ended in ugly, sordid headlines in 1957; a third estranged wife (actress Doris Rich) had died in a fire; a fourth wife had left him. He had played in such films as *The Ten Commandments, Around the World in Eighty Days, The Man Who Shot Liberty Valance, The Shootist;* he had acted in many stage successes, on Broadway and in stock and classical repertory; and, indeed, he had fathered an acting dynasty. By the late 1980s, however, Carradine sadly survived primarily by playing cameos in low-budget, porno horror films like *Vampire Hookers* (1978) and *Evils of the Night* (1984). Watch him in the latter film—gnarled, crippled, looking up at aging Julie Newmar, looming over him in her hot pants—and it's hard to believe this man was our tall, suave Gaston of *Bluebeard.*

Adding to the sadness was the fact that even such rot never made Carradine financially comfortable. Late in his life, he lost his house in Santa Barbara to a finance company; at the end, he was reportedly living in a Quonset hut near San Diego, looked after by an agent who farmed him out for whatever work came along. Over 40 years after his Shakespearean company and his first divorce, John Carradine was still paying the price, having never regained solvency.

The last movie came in 1988: *Buried Alive,* shot in South Africa. Robert Vaughn and Donald Pleasence starred in this bloodbath about horrors in a private school for bitchy young ladies; Carradine has an embarrassing cameo as a mad, cackling geek in a wheelchair. It's as if his retarded Toby, from the 1944 *Voodoo Man,* has survived the decades and is now making a comeback.

One would have hoped at least that Carradine had made peace with his "crazy" ways by the end of his life, perhaps to take a joy in his defiance of convention during his many years. Even this never came true. Researching his life turns up wonderfully offbeat tales (Phyllis Coates, in a *Starlog* interview with Tom Weaver, recalled Carradine visiting her one night with a lady friend, staying so late that Phyllis went to bed—only to awaken at three in the morning to find Carradine reciting Shakespeare to the girlfriend in the living room—stark naked.) Yet he was compelled in interviews to deny he ever was eccentric. A special hot spot with Carradine was the story that, in the late 1920s/early 1930s, he stalked Hollywood Boulevard reciting Shakespeare. Carradine time and again denied it (even though veteran actor Fritz Feld gave me a wonderfully detailed eyewitness account of the spectacle). But nobody was fooled; *The Hollywood Reporter* included the legend in Carradine's obituary, eulogizing him as "The Bard of the Boulevard."

Certainly, the end was in character, sadly and colorfully, for John Carradine. While many details of his death are shrouded in mystery, the popular account insists that Carradine and his agent, en route home from *Buried Alive,* were in Milan on Thanksgiving Day, 1988. Carradine wanted to visit the Duomo, the 328-step Gothic cathedral where priests of olden days climbed the steps on their knees, flagellating themselves all the while. Arriving at the tower, Carradine learned the elevator to the top was out of order.

"I'll *walk* up," Carradine announced.

The 82-year-old actor, twisted by arthritis, managed to climb to the top, but later collapsed. David and Keith Carradine took a plane to Italy and found their famous father, unknown in Milan, in a paupers ward of the hospital. John Carradine died, reportedly in his son David's arms, on November 27, 1988. While newspapers listed "heart and kidney failure" as the cause of death, David Carradine reportedly told friends his father had died of malnutrition—a remarkable cause of death for a working actor who played in hundreds of films, TV shows, and plays.

The funeral was at St. Thomas the Apostle Church, Hollywood, to which Carradine had contributed in his palmy days. One onlooker noted that the corpse, in the casket, seemed to be without arms or legs; it had perhaps been dismembered by the autopsy doctor in Italy. His sons gave eloquent eulogies; David cried during his speech. The final hymn was *Onward Christian Soldiers,* and the Hollywood community filed out of the church.

Then came one, final eccentricity for John Carradine.

All his life, Carradine had adored John Barrymore. One of Hollywood's great stories (probably apocryphal) is that Errol Flynn's cronies stole Barrymore's corpse from the funeral home and took it to Flynn's house for one last drink (to Errol's horror). After the Carradine funeral, David — apparently familiar with the Barrymore legend, certainly familiar with his father's love for Barrymore — returned to the empty church, and to the casket. There, David cradled his father's corpse and tried to give John Carradine one last drink, spilling it all over the corpse. Photographers reportedly rushed to shoot the macabre scene, but fortunately — possibly out of deference to one of the movies' greatest character actors — the shots have never been published. David Carradine married a few days later in the same church.

The body of John Carradine was cremated, and the ashes scattered over the Pacific. On December 6, 1988, *The Hollywood Reporter* printed a full-page tribute that would have pleased Carradine very much. There was a picture of his very gloomy Hamlet, on stage in 1943. Beneath it were the words Horatio spoke over Hamlet's corpse, and the words Lionel Barrymore had carved into the crypt of his brother John:

> Good Night, Sweet Prince,
> And Flights of Angels
> Sing Thee to Thy Rest

Edgar Ulmer once described one of his favorite movie moments — from King Vidor's war epic *The Big Parade* (MGM, 1925) — "when Renee Adoree hugs John Gilbert's boots and hangs onto him as the truck pulls out to the front." Most of Ulmer's best works have some single, haunting vignette that refuse to leave the subconscious: in *The Black Cat*, it is when Karloff suddenly, startlingly, yelps like a wolf as Lugosi skins him alive; in *Detour*, it is when Ann Savage, as the horrid she-bitch, defiantly, frighteningly turns to glare at Tom Neal as he tries to steal a peek at her in his car.

In *Bluebeard* the haunting moment (for me) comes just before Lucille visits Gaston to confront him with the death of her sister. With all the melancholy of Hamlet, Carradine's Bluebeard stands alone in his studio, his arms dropped over the staircase, the shadow of the puppets shrouding him like some horrible, mocking curse. The scene is silent; only the music plays gently, mournfully. The shot seems a cameo of a truly lost soul, a man, as Shakespeare put it, tragically "sick at heart"; a little moment of time in the movies, created by a very gifted director and actor.

"These are the moments," said Edgar Ulmer, "that make pictures worthwhile."

●

Finally, as for the sites of Hollywood's old horror sideshows: KCET-TV of Los Angeles now owns the Monogram property, or what's left of it. There are only two, old red-brick buildings today at 4376 Sunset Plaza, where Monogram Studios used to churn out its product. As for PRC, visit 7324 Santa Monica Boulevard today, and you'll find a 24-hour towing service. Walk down to the back of the property, and there are some old buildings that appear to be forsaken soundstages, presumably the remains of all that's left of what once was Hollywood's most notorious Poverty Row studio.

The rest is silence.
                              —*Hamlet,* Act V, sc. ii

The Picture of Dorian Gray

Studio: Metro-Goldwyn-Mayer; Producer: Pandro S. Berman; Director: Albert Lewin; Screenplay: Albert Lewin (based on the novel by Oscar Wilde); Musical Score: Herbert Stothart; Director of Photography: Harry Stradling; Second Cameraman: Sam Leavitt; Assistant Cameramen: Frank Phillips, Eddie Davis; Painting of the degenerate Dorian: Ivan le Lorraine Albright; Painting of Dorian as a young man: Henrique Medina; Special Assistant to Mr. Lewin: Gordon Wiles; Recording Director: Douglas Shearer; Art Directors: Cedric Gibbons and Hans Peters; Set Decorator: Edwin B. Willis (Hugh Hunt and John Bonar, Associates); Men's Costumes: Valles; Women's Costumes: Irene (Marion Herwood Keyes, Associate); Makeup: Jack Dawn; Editor: Ferris Webster; Assistant Editor: Don Hall; Assistant Director: Earl McEvoy; Second Assistant Director: Frank Myers; Unit Manager: Keith Weeks; Casting: Mel Ballerino; Researcher: Viola Pettit; Gaffer: C. A. Philbrick. Running Time: 110 minutes.

Filmed at the MGM Studios, March 8–August 5, 1944. Premiere, Capitol Theatre, New York, March 1, 1945.

The Players: Lord Henry Wotton (George Sanders); Dorian Gray (Hurd Hatfield); Gladys Hallward (Donna Reed); Sibyl Vane (Angela Lansbury); David Stone (Peter Lawford); Sir Basil Hallward (Lowell Gilmore); James Vane (Richard Fraser); Lord George Farmoor (Reginald Owen)*; Allen Campbell (Douglas Walton); Adrian Singleton (Morton Lowry); Sir Robert Bentley (Miles Mander); Mrs. Vane (Lydia Bilbrook); Lady Agatha (Mary Forbes); Sir Thomas (Robert Greig); Duchess (Moyna Macgill); Chairman Malvolio Jones (Billy Bevan); Young French Woman (Renie Carson); Kate (Lilian Bond); Lord Henry's Wife (Lisa Carpenter); Narrator (Sir Cedric Hardwicke); Mr. Erskine (William Stack); Mrs. Vandeleur (Natalie Draper); Lady Harborough (Anita Bolster); Street Preacher (Arthur Shields); Cabby (Alan Edmiston); Butler (Charles Coleman); Gladys (Carol Diane Keppler); Parker (Emily Massey); Davenant (Sir Sidney Lawford); Waiter (Frank Dawson); Sandwich Man (Leo Mostovoy); Violinist (Joe Bernard); Woman (Dorothy Ford); Waiter (Mitchell

---

**Reginald Owen's footage was deleted.*

293

Lewis); Piano Player (Jimmy Conlin); 1st Stage Hand (Bernard Gorcey); Xylophone Act (Taylor and Sinclair); Shopkeeper (Colin Campbell); Butler (Harry Adams); Cabby (James Aubrey); Stage Manager (Joe Yule); Victor (Guy Bates Post); Lackey (Guy Bellis); Duke of Berwick (Arthur Mulliner); Another Gentleman (Leonard Mellin); Friend (Crauford Kent); 1st Club Member (Evan Thomas); 2nd Club Member (Herbert Evans); Mayfair Hostess (Lillian Talbot); Beautiful Young Woman (Ann Lundeen); Other Woman (Barbara Woodell); Young Woman (Lorraine Miller); 1st Jewel Merchant (James Logan); 2nd Jewel Merchant (John Good); Butler (Norman Pogson); Old Pianist (Pedro De Cordoba); Barkeeper (Pedro Regas); Hunchback (John George); Asst. Barkeeper (Skelton Knaggs); Ant Man (Tom Pilkington); Girl Character (Kay Medford); Butler (John Valentine); Queen (Helena Benda); King (Tom Tamarez); Prince (Jerome St. John); Policeman (Larry Williams); Francis (Frederic Worlock); Lady Gwendolyn Rugby (Ann Curzon); Lady Ruxton (Renie Riano); Lady Alice Goodbody (Audrey Manners); Lord Gerald Goodbody (Rex Evans); Ernest Harrowden (Edward Cooper); Cabby (Charles McNaughton); Sir Geoffrey Clouston (Kenneth Hunter); Loader (George Jenner); Thornton (Lumsden Hare); Driver (Gibson Gowland); Cabby (Robert Cory); Station Master (Lee Powell); Housekeeper (Betty Fairfax); Footman (Charles Knight); Farmer (Harry Allen); Club Members (Toby Doolan, Charles K. French, Eric Mayne, Major Sam Harris, William Holmes, Hugh Greenwood, Scott Seaton, Richard Earle, J. C. Fowler); Footmen (William O'Brien, Wilson Benge); 1st Maid (Lotus Thompson); 2nd Maid (Glenna Kendall); 3rd Maid (Alice Keating); 4th Maid (Margaret Roberts); Patrons (T. Arthur Hughes, Al Ferguson, Bruce Carruthers, George Broughton, William Eddritt, Ila Lee, Doris Stone, Herberta Williams); Beautiful Girl (Helen O'Hara); Doorman (Reginald Simpson); Flirting Girl (Ruby Newport); Man (Lloyd Ford); Footmen (Walter Rode, Tom Costello, Art Berry, Sr., Joseph Marievsky, Alex Pollard, Ray Flynn, Frank McClure, Leslie Sketchley); Beaters (Eddie Acquilina, Buck Bucko, Pascal Perry); Hunters (Fred Aldrich, Allen Schute, Whitey Sacks, Stuart Holmes, Donald Kerr, Wally Dean); Loaders (Larry Stanton, Bud Harrison, Mike Jeffries, Lee Powell, Will Patton, Frank Pharr); Footman (Sam Simone); Dorian's Friend (Paul de Corday); Members of London Club (Oliver Cross, Ward Carson, Bob MacLean, Jack Lee, Allen Schute); Footman (Carl Leviness); Guests at Mayfair Tea (Mary Benoit, Volta Boyer, Elyse Brown, Monica Bannister, Olive Jones, Richard Collin, Kerry Vaughn); Sailor (George Peters); and Devi Dja and her Balinese Dancers.

●

I sent my Soul through the Invisible,
Some letter of that After-life to spell:
And by and by my Soul return'd to me,
And answer'd: "I myself am Heaven
and Hell."

— *The Rubaiyat of Omar Khayyam*,
prologue and epilogue to *The Picture
of Dorian Gray*

During the last act of its late-lamented Golden Age, Metro-Goldwyn-Mayer produced one of the most controversial horror films ever made—

Poster for *The Picture of Dorian Gray.*

one (arguably) years before its time, a film that has won an increasingly loyal audience over the decades: *The Picture of Dorian Gray* (1945).

Elegant, sophisticated, haunting, this film version of Oscar Wilde's classic (and, in 1890, notorious) novel has so much to admire: the arrogance of George Sanders as Lord Henry, Dorian's Faustian influence; the mystical direction of Albert Lewin; the tragedy of Angela Lansbury as Sibyl Vane, driven to suicide by Dorian; the horror of the shocking, Technicolor painting of the old, spiritually ravaged Dorian by the Albright brothers; the Oscar-winning black and white cinematography by Harry Stradling; the moody, powerful score by Herbert Stothart; the dry, literate narration by Sir Cedric Hardwicke.

The most indelible memory of *The Picture of Dorian Gray*, however, is the enigmatic, stylish performance of Oscar Wilde's tragic hero by Hurd Hatfield. For generations of moviegoers, Hatfield *is* Dorian Gray, the decadent British aristocrat whose face and form revealed no sign of his horrific spiritual decay, even as his painting became a masterpiece of grotesque horror.

In August 1988 Hurd Hatfield, called "America's least known great actor" by Arthur Penn, was in Baltimore, filming *Her Alibi* for director Bruce Beresford (for whom he had previously acted in *King David* and

Crimes of the Heart). I called the publicist to arrange an interview and headed the next morning to Baltimore, with some trepidation. I hadn't seen Mr. Hatfield's recent films; the last time I saw him on the screen was in the 1968 *The Boston Strangler*. The cruel things that the years can do to an actor, both physically and temperamentally, are always a bit worrisome for a journalist, and in the case of Hurd Hatfield were a fascination.

How had Hurd Hatfield, Hollywood's Dorian Gray, aged? The melodrama of the question was irresistible, and I let my imagination go merrily macabre en route to the actor's hotel, reminding myself that, except for Angela Lansbury, he is the only star from that film shot over 44 years before who is still alive today. I think of the very minimal personal publicity he has allowed over the years. I think of the reports that he lives all alone, in an old country house in Ireland.

When I report to the hotel and the publicist's office, a new twist presents itself. The telephone rings; it is Mr. Hatfield, who has spent a "very bad night." The publicist apologizes a few minutes later and asks to postpone the interview. Suddenly, in my mind, the "very bad night" takes on the aura of all kinds of Wilde debauchery, florid decadence flourishing in his hotel suite high above Baltimore. I resist the crazy conjurings and ask the publicist if (or when) I might reschedule the interview.

"Oh, we only have to postpone it for a few minutes!" he genially smiles. "Hurd just needs a few extra minutes to get himself together. He just didn't want you to think he was being rude while you were waiting."

We board the elevator; the door of Hatfield's hotel suite opens. And greeting me, warmly, is a smiling Hurd Hatfield. He is tall, handsome, almost startlingly youthful; not the slightest hint of physical or spiritual ravishings. The new temptation is to wonder if the septuagenarian Hatfield, (like Dorian), has a magical portrait stashed away in some attic room.

Soon the Dorian connection stops altogether. Hatfield seems more like an animated, happy, sophisticated graduate student than he does Wilde's waxy antihero. It's hard to imagine Dorian Gray doing impromptu impressions of such acquaintances as Katharine Hepburn, George Sanders, and Walter Huston. It's almost impossible to picture the icy Dorian being homesick for his 400-year-old house in Ireland, proudly showing snapshots of the house's restoration, warmly describing the Dalmatian that he misses so much, and discussing his very active work for People for the Ethical Treatment of Animals.

Indeed, Hurd Hatfield talks so much, about so many things, that it's difficult to focus him on *The Picture of Dorian Gray*. Not that he resents the movie. With a long, rich career in movies, television, and on the stage and a new career impetus in the Beresford films, Hurd Hatfield has long made peace with the infamous role with which he is most identified.

"No actor ever got so much mileage out of one role," laughs Hatfield. "It still gets me good tables in restaurants. But it was also the kiss-of-death, really. After all—what could follow? *Son of Dorian Gray?*"

> The first duty in life is to assume a pose; what the second duty
> is no one yet has found out.
>   —Oscar Wilde

Louis B. Mayer hated horror movies. The moralistic champion of the studio's *Andy Hardy* and *Lassie* movies, Metro's almighty patriarch had acquiesced here and there during his reign, only to be personally ashamed by some of the wildest and most notorious shockers of the era, including *Freaks, The Mask of Fu Manchu,* and *Mad Love.* There had been no MGM horror films since *Dr. Jekyll and Mr. Hyde* in 1941; even with its classic literary title, superstars Spencer Tracy, Ingrid Bergman, and Lana Turner, and esteemed producer/director Victor Fleming, the movie had embarrassed Mayer with its kinky Freudian montage and aura of sexual sadism.

Enter Albert S. Lewin. "I'm the only college-bred man in the studio," lamented Lewin, a Harvard graduate with a masters degree in literature and a former English professor at University of Wisconsin, after he had joined Irving Thalberg's staff at Metro in the 1920s. "They resent me!" Five feet tall, mousey, and bespectacled, Lewin became Thalberg's "pet" and Metro's resident intellectual during the MGM glory years of the early 1930s, personally supervising such prestigious films as *The Guardsman* (1931), starring the Lunts. Lewin took over the completion of *The Good Earth* (1937) following Thalberg's September 14, 1936, death; shortly thereafter, he was exiled from the studio in a purge that Mayer (whose battles with Thalberg are the stuff of Hollywood legend) vindictively mandated.

Lewin based himself at Paramount, producing such fare as Claudette Colbert's *Zaza* (1939). Then in 1942 he directed *The Moon and Sixpence,* released by United Artists. This Somerset Maugham saga of a Gauguin-like painter (George Sanders) who forsakes British convention, runs away to Tahiti to paint native girls, and ultimately dies a leper was considered the last word in Hollywood exotica and sophistication. Lewin now set his sights on Oscar Wilde and passionately planned to shoot *The Picture of Dorian Gray.*

On May 13, 1943, *The Hollywood Reporter* wrote that Lewin was preparing the screenplay for *The Picture of Dorian Gray,* with expectations of directing it. The trade journal cited the "abnormal sex theme" of the "exotic literary classic" and reported that Lewin believed he could fashion a screenplay to get by the censors (just as he had with *The Moon and*

Sixpence).* On May 21, the *Reporter* claimed production depended on securing the rights from Wilde's estate.

That MGM acquired the rights to *The Picture of Dorian Gray* for the sum of only about $800 was yet another testimony to the fallen glory of Oscar Fingal O'Flahertie Wills Wilde (1854–1900). The great aesthete and playwright was himself stuff of Faustian legend—a Victorian genius, whose plays *Lady Windermere's Fan* (1892) and *The Importance of Being Earnest* (1895) were enormous popular successes. *The Picture of Dorian Gray*, originally published in the June 20, 1890, issue of *Lippincott's Monthly Magazine*, was his most famous work.

"After this date," wrote the late Richard Ellmann in his best-selling 1988 *Oscar Wilde*, "Victorian literature had a different look." As Ellmann dissected the relationship between Dorian and Oscar:

> It was also premonitory of his own tragedy, for Dorian has, like Wilde, experimented with two forms of sexuality, love of women and of men. Through his hero Wilde was able to open a window into his own recent experience. . . . By unintentional suicide, Dorian becomes aestheticism's first martyr. The text: Drift beautifully on the surface, and you will die unbeautifully in the depths.

Wilde's downfall was epic: in 1895, the Marquess of Queensberry, hellbent on ending the relationship between his son, Lord Alfred Douglas, and Wilde, publicly denounced Wilde as a homosexual. Wilde sued for libel, lost, was convicted of sodomy, and served two years of hard labor at Reading and Pentonville prisons. His wife and friends deserted him, and he ended his life an exile, completing *The Ballad of Reading Gaol* in France and traveling to Italy with Lord Alfred Douglas. Oscar Wilde died in Paris in November 1900.

Curiously, MGM already had a Wilde work on the boards—*The Canterville Ghost*, which would star Charles Laughton, Robert Young, and Margaret O'Brien, be directed by Jules Dassin, and be released in 1944.

Why did Mayer sanction such a "decadent" property as *The Picture of Dorian Gray?* The reason was probably personal; the "Hollywood Rajah" apparently had moments of remorse over the Thalberg wars of the '30s and now welcomed Lewin back to the Metro fold with open arms, even allowing him his "exotic literary classic."

Lewin completed the screenplay, while Pandro S. Berman became producer of the project. This was a comfort to Mayer. Berman had pro-

---

*The Picture of Dorian Gray *already had undergone several film transitions: a 1910 Danish version; a 1913 U.S. adaptation; a Russian film in 1915, as well as another American version; a British 1916 film, starring Henry Victor, with an appearance by "the devil"; and, in 1917, versions from both Germany and Hungary (the latter possibly featuring Bela Lugosi).*

duced such legendary RKO films as the Astaire/Rogers *The Gay Divorcee* (1934), Katharine Hepburn's *Mary of Scotland* (1936), and Laughton's *The Hunchback of Notre Dame* (1939). Joining MGM, Berman had specialized in such slickly packaged mass entertainment as *Ziegfeld Girl* (1941), the Clark Gable/Lana Turner *Honky Tonk* (1941), and Abbott and Costello's *Rio Rita* (1942). Mayer indulged himself in indulging Lewin, all the while realizing that if *The Picture of Dorian Gray* possessed any "showmanship," Berman was the producer to exploit it.

So in 1943 Berman began MGM's well-publicized search for the ideal actor, "the beautiful man," to star in *The Picture of Dorian Gray*. It was Scarlett O'Hara all over again, and many stars were tested and rejected. Gregory Peck was throught to be too American. Robert Taylor, at this point, was thought to be too old. For about a year, the studio tested scores of actors, famous and unknown, for one of the most coveted roles in Hollywood.

Ironically, the actor who eventually won the role of Dorian Gray had no desire to play it or to have a Hollywood career. As Hurd Hatfield recalls:

> I never wanted to be an actor. When I was going to the movies, Gable and Garbo seemed like gods and goddesses — another world — and I never dreamed I'd be a part of this world. And I never wished to be, actually — I wanted to be a painter, or a writer. But, through dramatics at Bard College, I won a scholarship to study in England with Michael Chekhov, nephew of the playwright. Chekhov was a brilliant man, a genius. I toured the U.S. in Shakespearean repertory . . . eccentric old men with putty noses — Gloucester in *King Lear*, Aguecheek in *Twelfth Night*, a bizarre comic character . . . I was really a comedic character actor.

Hatfield had made his Broadway debut as Kirilov in *The Possessed* (Lyceum Theatre, October 24, 1939), followed by the Religious Man in *The Strings, My Lord, Are False* (Royale, May 19, 1942), directed by Elia Kazan. He originally came to Hollywood not to crash the studio gates, but to visit some repertory friends. While there, the chance to test for *The Picture of Dorian Gray* opened up for him through Iris Tree, daughter of Edwardian actor/director Sir Herbert Beerbohm Tree. It was an adventure he almost avoided:

> The original Dorian of Wilde's is blonde and blue-eyed, and here I was, this gloomy-looking creature! I almost didn't go, and when I did, all these blonde Adonises were to the right and left of me — I looked like one of the agents! But, on Iris Tree's advice, I improvised from the book, bits and pieces. Then Albert Lewin and associates started arguing about what they were going to do with my hair, and so on. I tested for three months — and finally was given the role. I wired my parents with the news,

and my father sent me a wire that I've never forgotten: "Confident that you have accomplished miracles!"

Albert Lewin cast me because he thought I looked the part. But, in reality, I had never worn evening clothes, I had never had to be icy, to underplay—and I realized this would be a terrible stretch for me.

On November 5, 1943, *The Hollywood Reporter* noted that Hatfield had "hit the jackpot" by winning the role of Dorian Gray. "Aside from being a talented actor," promised a Metro press release, "Hatfield is as handsome as the description of the character in Wilde's novel."

As things evolved, Hatfield received his cinema baptism of fire not in *The Picture of Dorian Gray*, which was still meticulously preparing, but in *Dragon Seed*. Pandro Berman was seeking an actor to play Katharine Hepburn's brother, Lao San, who becomes a bloodthirsty warrior against the Japanese in this Pearl Buck saga, and the role became Hatfield's screen debut.

Dragon Seed was some experience. They sent me to the back lot, where I met a retired actress from *The Good Earth*—a Chinese water buffalo. One of the most difficult actresses I've ever worked with. I had to learn to ride her, and her back wasn't made for the human crotch—I couldn't stay on. A nightmare! I was very skinny, and I thought they'd make me look better; instead, they gave me this terrible Chinese pajama suit. And the cast—Walter Huston was my father, Katharine Hepburn was my sister, Aline MacMahon from New York was my mother, Turkish Turhan Bey was my brother, Russian Akim Tamiroff was my uncle—it was a *very* odd Chinese family!

I had these Chinese eyepieces—mine always came loose just before each shot. On location, in the San Fernando Valley, the loudspeaker would order, "Hatfield to the cameras!" The first day, Hepburn, who terrified me, came out to watch this new young actor; I got on my Chinese water buffalo—and the buffalo, quite logically, being a *water* buffalo, went straight into the water, soaking my costume. I hit him with my antique Chinese flute—and broke it.

And, of course, I knew nothing about continuity. In the scene on the old Chinese farm, I was to play my flute. In the master shot, I played the flute one way; in the medium shot, to be creative, I played it another way; in the closeup, a new way. Suddenly, there was this terrible pause. Jack Conway, the director, came up to me and said, "Have you been playing that flute the same way all morning?" "Oh no!" I said, very proudly. "I played it here, and this way, and this way." Well, he threw his hat down, stamped on it, shouted implications and oaths . . . I had ruined most of the morning's shooting! I thought, "Why did I ever leave the theatre?"

Dragon Seed would open at Radio City Music Hall July 20, 1944, and the *New York World-Telegram* praised Hatfield's performance as "outstanding."

Meanwhile, while Hatfield had labored on *Dragon Seed, The Picture of Dorian Gray* was still preparing its elaborate production. The true "plum" role of the movie was Lord Henry Wotton, the aristocrat whose wicked wit and cynical sophistication lure Dorian to his downfall. MGM seriously considered three masterful actors for this coveted part.

There was Basil Rathbone, who had enjoyed the status as Hollywood's top "legitimate" actor (at $5000 per week) and was the cinema's greatest costume villain in such films as *Captain Blood* and *The Adventures of Robin Hood.* A popular visitor to MGM in such films as *David Copperfield* (1935), *Anna Karenina* (1935, with Garbo), and *Romeo and Juliet* (1936, as Tybalt), Rathbone was actually on contract to Metro in the mid–'40s, the studio marketing him out for the Sherlock Holmes Universal series and radio show. As such, he seemed the perfect candidate for Lord Henry, and the November 29, 1943, *Hollywood Reporter* wrote he was "huddling" with his home studio for the flamboyant role.

There was Laird Cregar, 20th Century–Fox's star villain, who had just completed his tour de force as Jack the Ripper in Fox's *The Lodger* that fall. Cregar had triumphed on the Hollywood stage in 1940 in the title role of *Oscar Wilde,* which had led to his Fox contract. On December 9, 1943 (exactly one year before the actor's tragic death), the *Hollywood Reporter* employed the same word it had used in regards to Rathbone (huddling) to describe Cregar's wrangling with MGM for the Lord Henry role; "If the deal is consummated," noted the *Reporter,* "he will be borrowed from Fox."

There was George Sanders, who also had just completed *The Lodger* at his home studio Fox, in the role of the Scotland Yard hero. Sanders had starred in Lewin's *The Moon and Sixpence,* and his notices had him campaigning for leading man roles after celebrated villainy in such movies as Warners' *Confessions of a Nazi Spy* (1939), UA's *Rebecca* (1940), and Fox's *Man Hunt* (1941). It seemed that Sanders was the dark horse for the role — not because of talent, but because his notorious arrogance at Fox was known to Mayer. In fact, Sanders, who professed to hate all studio moguls on basic principle, boasted he had once stood up Mayer for lunch when the producer hoped to entice him to the MGM fold.

On Christmas Eve, 1943, the *Hollywood Reporter* announced the winner of the Lord Henry role: George Sanders. He was Lewin's top choice, and Hurd Hatfield says:

> Lewin was a little man, quite deaf, and he used Sanders several times
> in films because I think Sanders was his idol, what he wished he could be.

Most of the other key roles of *The Picture of Dorian Gray* were cast from MGM's contract roster. Donna Reed, who had spent several years at MGM in adventures with the Thin Man, Andy Hardy, and Dr. Kildare, won the female lead of Gladys Hallward. Angela Lansbury, future Broadway powerhouse and "Murder She Wrote" TV star, who had just given an Academy-nominated Best Supporting Actress performance in *Gaslight*, was cast as the tragic Sibyl Vane. (Sam Katz, Metro producer, tried very hard to dissuade Lewin from casting Lansbury and offered him MGM starlet soprano Kathryn Grayson. But Lewin held firm—Lansbury got the role, and her real-life mother, Moyna Macgill, won a part in the film as a duchess.) Peter Lawford, who had just scored in MGM's *The White Cliffs of Dover* (1944), was cast as David Stone, Dorian's rather callow nemesis.

It was a huge, imposing cast, and a major feature, mysteriously uncredited, was Sir Cedric Hardwicke, who spoke the narration.

One of the most fascinating talent forces signed for the film was the pair of Albright brothers. "They Paint Gruesome Masterpieces in an Abandoned Methodist Church," headlined *Life* magazine (March 27, 1944) of Ivan and Malvin Albright, 47-year-old, 5'2" bachelor identical twins, whose abandoned church near Chicago contained (according to *Life*) "rows and rows of paintings of men and women who look as if they had been dug up from the grave." Late in the fall of 1943, MGM paid the Albrights a reported $75,000 to produce four pictures for *The Picture of Dorian Gray*. The *Life* profile featured photographs of their paintings, as well as a picture of the horrid, cadaverous model of the decayed Dorian they produced prior to the painting. *Life* noted of these "masters at portraying decaying flesh":

> For research for these paintings the twins made the rounds of the local insane asylums, alcoholic wards and hospitals for the incurably diseased. Their father, Adam Albright, who followed them to Hollywood to see what they were up to, left hurriedly after a few days for Lower California where he could quietly paint little barefoot Mexican children.

Finally, production for *The Picture of Dorian Gray* was set to go before the camera of Harry Stradling (1902–1970). Mayer continued to favor Lewin with all the resources he might have given a back-from-the-dead Thalberg. The schedule was 52 days, and the original budget for the movie was a walloping $1,129,969—almost the final negative cost of the Tracy/Bergman/Turner *Dr. Jekyll and Mr. Hyde*.

On March 8, 1944, shooting began on *The Picture of Dorian Gray*. The scene is London, 1886.

Herbert Stothart's beautiful score plays a street ballad startlingly similar to the prelude to the "Who Will Buy" song in Lionel Bart's 1961 musical *Oliver!* (based on *Oliver Twist*). A coach rides down the street with a most elegant passenger.

"Lord Henry Wotton had set himself early in life to the serious study

**The Albright brothers, Malvin (left) and Ivan (right), at work with their
mannequins and portraits of the "young" and the "evil" Dorian Gray;
Henrique Medina painted the youthful portrait ultimately used in the
film.**

of the great aristocratic art of doing absolutely nothing," purrs the uncredited narration of Sir Cedric Hardwicke. "He lived only for pleasure.
But his greatest pleasure was to observe the emotions of his friends while
experiencing none of his own. He diverted himself by exercising a subtle
influence on the lives of others." George Sanders, in beige suit and top hat,
black mustache and goatee, looks dashing and properly Faustian. As the
music plays a mysterious, Oriental theme, ominous yet sadly beautiful,
Sanders' Lord Henry invades Basil's study, where he discovers the artist's
new painting and deliciously delivers a bevy of Wilde epigrams.

"Intellect destroys the beauty of any face." . . . "The one charm of
marriage is that it makes a life of deception absolutely necessary for both
parties." . . . "I'd believe anything, providing it's quite incredible." . . . "I
like persons better than principles, and persons with no principles better
than anything else in the world."

Sir Basil, well played by Lowell Gilmore (1907–1960), who (according to MGM PR) was himself a landscape painter, is mysterious about his

latest subject. Lord Henry proclaims the portrait the best work Basil has ever done, but the artist will not exhibit it. "We suffer for what the gods give us," says Basil, "and I'm afraid Dorian Gray will pay for his good looks." He says there is something "mystic" about the painting— "whenever Dorian poses for me, it seems as if a power outside myself were guiding my hand. As if the painting had a life of its own independent of me."

Naturally intrigued, Lord Henry wants to meet Dorian Gray. Stradling's camera first captures Hurd Hatfield at the piano—looking very young, aristocratic, and, indeed, quite beautiful. As James Beuselink incisively analyzed in his feature "Albert Lewin's *Dorian Gray*" in *Films in Review* (February 1986):

> Dorian is seated at Basil's piano. Dorian plays an aubade from a music book. This is an extremely subtle touch from Albert Lewin. An "aubade" is defined as a song greeting the dawn or the morning. It is from the Latin word "albus," meaning "white" or "pure." One may take this as a description of Dorian's soul as it is when we first encounter him.

With almost baroque symbolism, Sanders' Lord Henry traps a butterfly with his top hat to kill it for his collection, as he proclaims his philosophy to Dorian:

> There's only one way to get rid of a temptation and that's to yield to it. Resist it, and the soul goes sick with longing for the things it has forbidden to itself. . . . The gods have been good to you Mr. Gray. . . . You have the most marvelous youth—and youth is the one thing worth having. . . . What the gods give, they quickly take away. . . .
> Live! Let nothing be lost upon you. Be afraid of nothing. There's such a little time that your youth will last—and you can never get it back. As we grow older, our memories are haunted by the exquisite temptations we hadn't the courage to yield to. The world is yours for a season. It would be tragic if you realized too late, as so many others do, that there is only one thing in the world worth having—and that is youth.

"Dorian Gray had never heard the praise of folly so eloquently expressed. . . . Dorian stood as if he were under a spell," says narrator Hardwicke. Lord Henry, meanwhile, has caught his butterfly, poisoned it in paint thinner, and pinned it to a card.

Basil's little niece Gladys appears as the portrait is finished. She has never missed a sitting (she has a child's crush on Dorian), and Basil has her add her signature "G" to his now-finished work. Lord Henry asks if she prefers Dorian or the painting. "I like Dorian better," she insists.

"You prefer him today, my dear," laughs Lord Henry, "but when you're a young lady and are turning all the handsome heads in London, you may prefer the portrait. For it will look just as it does today, but we shall all be changed—and not for the better."

At these words, the face of Hatfield's Dorian looks like that of a woman who has been slapped. He promises little Gladys he will never change. And Lewin now finally shows us the portrait.

It *is* exquisite (the actual painting is the work of Henrique Medina) and in a grandly theatrical touch, it is displayed in Technicolor, a lush surprise in this black and white film; a symphonic whiff of the "aubade" theme accompanies the unveiling. When the film was revived in 1988 at Baltimore's Museum of Art (with Hatfield as guest of honor), the audience sighed at its beauty. So does Dorian.

"As I grow old, this picture will remain always young. If it were only the other way. If it were I who was always to be young—and the picture was to grow old."

Lord Henry warns Dorian that he shouldn't express the wish in the presence of the cat statue, which Basil has included in the portrait. It's one of the 73 great gods of Egypt. He even suggests Basil send the cat along with the statue to Dorian's home—"I don't think the god or the picture should be separated."

"If only the picture could change," said Dorian, "and I could be always what I am now. For that I would give anything. Yes, there is nothing in the whole world I would not give. I would give my soul for that."

The music swells as the camera focuses on the Technicolor painting; a blast of Chopin's Prelude 22 in G Minor, Opus 22, joins his Faustian promise. Everything about this opening is elegantly, quite brilliantly realized, from Sanders's casual delivery of the epigrams to Hatfield's vain, vulnerable Dorian Gray.

Hatfield posed for the Henrique Medina painting of the young Dorian (sold to a private collector at the MGM auction for $25,000); he also confronted the horrid, grotesque Albright portrait of the demonic Dorian (now in the Chicago Institute of Art). The shooting would take five months (as long as *Dragon Seed,* which had much exterior shooting) and would prove another adventure for the young actor:

> We shot in sequence, which was wonderful (and very rare in films), and I was catching the style as I worked—not so much due to Al Lewin, who was enormously helpful, but to my training with Michael Chekhov, which kept us flexible. They had to stop me from going to the rushes, because I would be so neurotic the next day; whenever I see myself in a film, I always think myself the person I'd least like to meet with the voice I'd least like to hear.

"Dorian began to venture alone on warm summer evenings," narrates Hardwicke; curiously, he ventures into the twisting streets of lower-class

London. One of the famous Lewin "metaphysical" touches appears here: as Dorian walks the street in his black cape and top hat, a man wearing huge advertising boards strolls behind him, hawking an optician with a huge eye painted on the boards. It's clearly Lewin's symbol of the "Eye of God," and it follows Dorian right to the little music hall theatre, the Two Turtles, where he meets the first great tragedy of his life. It's just one of the frequent touches that delight many aficionados of the film (just as they alienate others).

"Eat, Drink, and Be Merry" is the motto on the door of the Two Turtles. There Dorian sees Sibyl Vane, who sings the famous song, "Little Yellow Bird." (In Wilde's original, Sibyl is a Shakespearean actress, not a cabaret singer.) There is an instant sadness, innocence, and haunting pathos about Sibyl, unforgettably played by a blonde, 18-year-old Angela Lansbury.

The atmosphere of the Two Turtles is wonderful: from Sir Malvolio Jones, the host of the show (played by mustachioed Billy Bevan of *Dracula's Daughter*—the first of many horror movie veterans to appear in *The Picture of Dorian Gray*), to the stagehand in the rafters dropping snow on Sibyl as she sings, to the crowd warmly joining in for the final chorus. Naturally, the lyrics of the song forecast the doom to come: how "a common sparrow should refuse a bird with blood so blue."

"I'll gladly introduce you, sir," says Sir Malvolio to Dorian, "but she's proud." Dorian's intense gaze attracts her, however. Dorian does not go backstage that night, but he returns every night for a fortnight to see her. Finally he goes backstage, plays "Little Yellow Bird" for her, and she sings for him alone. Then Dorian plays Chopin's moody prelude. Sibyl is fascinated by the music and her admirer.

"What's the music called?" she asks.

"It's called 'Prelude,'" says Dorian, and they kiss passionately.

Sibyl's mother (Lydia Bilbrook) and brother James (Richard Fraser, later the Quaker hero of Lewton's 1946 *Bedlam*) see the kiss, and James disapproves. After all, Sibyl doesn't even know the man's name. As James prepares to leave that night to sail away, Sibyl tells her brother about her admirer:

> For me, he's like one of King Arthur's knights, that we used to read about when we were children. Who took the vow of chivalry . . . to defend the right to protect all women.

And on her wall is a drawing of her "Sir Tristan."

Dorian announces his engagement. Basil and Lord Henry join Dorian at the the Two Turtles to meet Sibyl Vane, where she now sings "Little Yellow Bird" rapturously and right to Dorian.

"I believe she loves you so much," says Lord Henry, "you have no need to marry her."

Hurd Hatfield in *The Picture of Dorian Gray*, followed by the "Eye of God"—one of the movie's many metaphysical flourishes.

Lord Henry cynically proposes a test: invite her to the house to see Basil's portrait and as it grows late, ask her to stay. Then if she leaves, "I'd believe her to be as good as she is beautiful and beg her forgiveness and marry her."

Dorian tests the breathlessly-in-love Sibyl. At his domicile, he again plays the Chopin prelude for her. The Egyptian cat sits omnisciently in the center of the scene, as if eyeing the action; "It's that cat," says Sibyl, "I thought I saw its eyes move." And Dorian reads to her from Wilde's 1894 poem, "The Sphinx":

> Hideous animal, get hence!
> You wake in me each bestial sense.
> You make me what I would not be.
> You make my creed a barren sham.
> You wake foul dreams of sensual life.

Dorian asks Sibyl to stay. Heartbroken by her "Sir Tristan," she turns and slowly walks away, a tear in her eye, Stothart's music sympathizing with her sadness. "I suppose I should have expected a conventional reaction," says Dorian, playing out the test as Henry had proposed it. Then he begins playing the Chopin prelude, and Sibyl, dazed, miserable, and fatally in love, returns, as the MGM orchestra plays evil, triumphant chords.

The next day, Dorian writes to the compromised Sibyl, with a token of money:

> You have killed my love.... You used to stir my imagination—now you are nothing to me. I will never see you again. I will never mention your name. I will never think of you. Henceforth I shall live only for pleasure ... and if this leads me to the destruction of my soul, then it is only you who are responsible.... My real life begins—my own life—in which you cannot possibly have any part.

We see Sibyl reading the merciless letter at the theatre. In a simple but superbly chilling gresture, Lansbury responds by aimlessly raising her arm, dazed and shattered. It is, of course, the last we will see of Sibyl Vane. The Oscar-nominated work of Lansbury is so touching, so haunting that it's almost a comfort to the audience to realize that this lady went on to four Broadway Tony awards and acts away today, almost 50 years after *The Picture of Dorian Gray*, as the perennially popular Jessica Fletcher of TV's "Murder She Wrote," one of the industry's most powerful stars.

Meanwhile, Dorian has an ominous feeling. At his Mayfair house, he looks at his portrait. "The lines of cruelty about the mouth were unmistakable," says Hardwicke's narration. Dorian remembers his oath at Sir Basil's in the presence of the cat and is frightened. He decides to implore Sibyl's forgiveness and beg her to be his wife. He pens a new letter.

And then Lord Henry arrives with news: "Sibyl Vane is dead."

It is, perhaps, the most genuinely disturbing scene in the film: Sanders's Lord Henry casually describes how Sibyl had left the theatre with her mother, gone back for something, and then poisoned herself. "It's tragic, of course" says Lord Henry, playing with a stereoptical slide and hand viewer, "but you mustn't let yourself brood over it. You must learn to see it in its proper perspective.... You should look upon this tragedy as an episode in the wonderful spectacle of life." Lord Henry then invites Dorian to dine with him that night and go with him to see *Don Giovanni,* and he exits singing opera. Sanders is awesomely wicked in this episode; he's all the more impressive after one hears Hurd Hatfield recall that the actor himself was kind and helpful, with "a heart of gold."

"So I have murdered Sibyl Vane," says Dorian when he hears the news, "as surely as if I'd had cut her throat." But he falls under Lord Henry's influence. When Basil arrives later that rainy night to see Dorian, the butler informs him that Dorian has gone to the opera.

"You went to the opera while Sibyl Vane was lying dead in some sordid lodging?" demands Sir Basil the next morning. "What's past is past," says Dorian, enjoying a huge breakfast and refusing to repeat his emotion of early the previous evening. Basil gives him *The Light of Asia,* the story of Buddha, to read, hoping it will cancel some of Lord Henry's ideas. And he asks to see the portrait.

"I don't offer any explanation, and you are not to ask for any. But if you try to look at that picture, Basil, on my word of honor, I will never speak to you again!"

Dorian moves the painting upstairs, to his old schoolroom. Here Lewin allowed his love of symbolism to run rampid. As James Beuselink wrote in his *Films in Review* study:

> As Dorian stands next to a table, looking at the painting, his foot knocks over a toy knight that is on the floor. The knight is on horseback and holding a lance, as if to charge. It falls over next to some wooden blocks.... The letters on the two blocks nearest the knight form the initials of the name "Sir Tristan." In a sense, Dorian is a "fallen knight."

Also, there are toy blocks lying about—one with the initial "D" for Dorian, another with the number "8" (there are eight letters in the word "portrait"). And nearby, there are two little blocks bearing the initials S. V.

●

As *The Picture of Dorian Gray* was being filmed at MGM, the production soon ran awesomely over schedule and over budget. The original 52 days passed by, with the conclusion nowhere in sight, but the front office seemed oblivious to its excesses. Mayer granted Lewin's every whim, and all the members of the company were treated as if they were royalty.

For Hurd Hatfield, the experience was, naturally, unforgettable.

I noticed that sets would become social gatherings, which I found very unnerving. One day, Signe Hasso, a lovely Swedish actress, had come on the set with the whole Swedish delegation from Washington. I couldn't work, and Lewin put them off—from then on, it was a closed set. Of course, Hedda Hopper came on the set; everything stopped, the crew put down their hammers, "Hello, Hedda," and so forth, and I'm in the middle of a scene. But she was very nice and wrote "I met the young man with the pearl gray voice in the pearl gray vest." The next person who came on the set was Hepburn, of whom I was so frightened on *Dragon Seed*. She came right over to me in that forthright manner, so terrifying to a young actor, and said, "I hear you're perfectly wonderful. *Are* you?"

Hatfield found the whole company very congenial—even George Sanders, who killed himself in 1972 because he was "bored." Sanders's arrogance was Hollywood legend, as Hatfield recalls:

We had our first costume test in the evening, and Sanders, whose work I admired, said, "Lewin thinks this is amusing, all these costume fittings after six o'clock. I want my dinner!" I was afraid Sanders would be difficult. But about the second week, one Saturday night, he said, "Would you like to have dinner with me?" No one had asked me anywhere, and I said, "Yes, I'd love to." Well, he took me to his pseudo-English country house, behind the Beverly Hills Hotel (Hollywood is full of architecture which belongs someplace else). Driving there, George said, "You know, you should really marry, as I have done, a reputable waitress, and make her into a lady." So we arrived—I don't think his wife knew we were coming—and she was playing cards with another lady. And George said, in that offhand way, "This is my wife, and this is my mistress"—I don't think she was, or meant to be—"and this is Dorian Gray."

He was wonderful to work with, very skilled, very polished. He recognized that I was a greenhorn, and he was very affectionate and kind.... Years later I met George, after his divorce from his second wife, Zsa Zsa Gabor. I asked what it had been like to have been married to her, and he said, "I don't know. I never really saw her. She was always under the hair dryer."

Hatfield developed a lifelong friendship (and, according to the *Hollywood Reporter* of that era, a romance) with Angela Lansbury:

This was Angela Lansbury's third film.... She, of course, was wonderful—and, unlike me, she had that incredible quality of having both feet planted firmly on the ground. She was charming, and we became lasting friends; later, she was my neighbor, in Ireland, and I was the first guest star she requested for "Murder She Wrote."

As the star of such an extravagant production, Hatfield enjoyed the pampering that only a Metro attraction could know. And despite Lewin's painstaking methods and arrogance and his subject matter, *The Picture of Dorian Gray* seemed magically to escape censure—even from the front office of MGM:

> Lewin was intellectual, bright, kind; he wouldn't photograph me after four o'clock, and as soon as I began to look tired, he would take only long shots. I must mention Lewin's assistant, Gordon Wiles; he was continually at Lewin's side, with matters of taste—moving objects, and things. You'll notice in the film that the blocks have the initials of the people Dorian killed; the figure of the Egyptian cat, which I have in my house in Ireland, is a symbol of evil. The film is full of things they had fun with, giving it a subtext, and making it very rich.
>
> And I must mention Louis B. Mayer. One would have thought Mayer, with his great sense of "morality," who loved those folksy things with June Allyson, would have hated *The Picture of Dorian Gray;* his secretary, Ida Koverman, despised it! But he came on the set one day, shook my hand, and said, "I'm delighted to be making a prestige film again, Mr. Hatfield."

Those who visited *The Picture of Dorian Gray* set were delighted to find the title character to be in life such a charming young man with such a sense of humor. In turn, Hatfield enjoyed making the rounds of the other productions then shooting on the MGM lot:

> Of course, I would escape the grim set whenever I could and explore MGM. Next door, Fred Astaire was dancing with Lucille Bremer. And Judy Garland was at Metro then. So charming. I asked her once, "Do you like singing?" and she said—rather tragically, in retrospect—"Yes, it makes me feel healthy."

●

"As the years passed, the miracle of Dorian's changeless youth caused wonder, but rarely suspicion," narrates Hardwicke as the film begins its second half. A nice touch shows Dorian and the maturing Lord Henry chatting at a garden party as they stand beside a sundial. But Dorian's behavior is suspect. He is perhaps guilty of all variety of scandal.

And Gladys, Basil's little niece, has grown up, in the form of a lushly beautiful Donna Reed. She is so in love with Dorian that she plans to propose marriage to him at his party that night, even as her beau, David Stone (Peter Lawford) objects, believing Dorian to be a "devil."

Hatfield recalls both co-workers:

> Donna Reed was lovely; we were friends, and I was at her funeral, a few years back. Peter Lawford was always on the telephone, arranging

a date, and sometimes I'd have to say, "Come on, let's get back to the work."

It's a bizarre party: Dorian and his Egyptian cat watch Devi Dja and her Balinese dancers (in the release print, it's only one dancer—presumably Devi herself) as the host steals glances at Gladys. There's a tinge of decency left in Dorian, however; he refuses Gladys's coy proposal, claiming that to wed her would be "an incredible wickedness."

Then late one foggy night, on the eve of his 38th birthday, Dorian passes Sir Basil Hallward on the street; Sir Basil is en route to the train to leave for Paris. In one of the highlights of the film, Basil visits Dorian's house and asks him to deny the "hideous" rumors he has heard about him and that "wretched boy in the guards who committed suicide, and Adrian Singleton, and Lord Wayne's son." Dorian blames the demises of the "wretched boy" and Lord Wayne's son on women, but the hint of bisexuality is undeniable. And Lord Wallace, one of Basil's best friends at Oxford, has shown Basil a letter his wife had written while she was dying alone at her villa. "Your name was implicated in the most terrible confession I've ever read."

"Do I know you?" asks Basil. "Before I could answer that I should have to see your soul. ... Only God can do that."

"You shall see it yourself—tonight," says Dorian.

Dorian escorts Basil upstairs to the old schoolroom to see the portrait. As they walk up the stairs, the camera retreats, and we see the Egyptian cat watching.

"You think it's only God who sees the soul," says Dorian as he uncovers the portrait. Lewin directs the moment beautifully; at first we don't see the portrait because the focus is on Basil's shocked expression at his own work and Hardwicke's narration ("It was from within apparently that the foulness and the horror came"). Then, with a blast of Stothart's music, there is the portrait, leering at us in horrific Technicolor.

"If this is what you've done with your life, it is far worse than anything that has been said of you," laments Basil as Dorian plays with a knife, nervously sticking it in the old furniture. "Do you know how to pray, Dorian?" As Basil sits at the table, praying for Dorian, the light reflects a cross on the door; he recalls Gladys mentioning the portrait just the other day, and how she paced her "G" on it. "If she could see it now...."

"Gladys must never know," narrates Hardwicke. "An uncontrollable feeling of hatred for Basil came over him.... Panic seized him, he felt like a hunted animal."

And as Basil prays for Dorian's soul, Dorian attacks him with the knife and stabs him in the back. It's a virtuoso scene: as Basil's body knocks the hanging lamp above the table awry, the light blinks Dorian's face from

***The Picture of Dorian Gray:* Peter Lawford, Donna Reed, and Lowell Gilmore.**

darkness to light and Basil's arm falls near the blocks, two of which display his initials. Then we see the portrait.

"It was as if the painting," intones Hardwicke, "had sweated a dew of blood."

Dorian must get rid of the body. He sends for Allen Campbell (played by Douglas Walton, Percy Shelley of *Bride of Frankenstein*), a rising scientist and by all hints a former lover of Dorian. "You must destroy that thing that is upstairs," says Dorian. The sexual tension between the two men is powerful, and when Allen refuses, Dorian shows him a blackmail letter he's written.

"It would kill her," says Allen. He leaves to get chemicals from his laboratory. Later, we learn through a Scotland Yard inspector, Sir Robert Bentley (Miles Mander), that Allen Campbell has killed himself.

Dorian attends a dinner party. Lord Henry is there, with Sanders dropping more epigrams ("When her third husband died, her hair turned quite gold from grief" ... "It's monstrous the way people go about nowadays saying things behind one's back that are absolutely and entirely true"). Also there (for sharp-eyed horror fans), as "Lord Goodbody," is Rex Evans, the raving Vazec of *Frankenstein Meets the Wolf Man.* And so are David and Gladys—to whom Dorian proposes marriage, to the delight of the guests and Gladys herself.

After his engagement to the niece of the man he has killed, Dorian seeks "other roads to forgetfulness than the one Allen Campbell took." He has his coachman take him to an opium den in Bluegate Field. Once again, the film offers some familiar faces to horror aficionados: the bartender is Skelton Knaggs, the pockmarked English grotesque who played Steim-muhl in *House of Dracula* and also acted in several Lewton films; Kate, a prostitute, is played by Lilian Bond (once a leading lady of *The Old Dark House* [1932]); and the wonderfully depraved Adrian Singleton, Dorian's old artist friend, is acted by Morton Lowry (the villain of *The Hound of the Baskervilles* [1939]). Adrian sketches Dorian's caricature with a gallows around the head; as Dorian leaves in disgust, Adrian calls out, "Goodbye, Sir Tristan!"

And James Vane—Sibyl's bereaved brother, who has been scouting London in hopes of finding the man who drove his sister to suicide 18 years before—happens to be there to hear it.

"How old do you think I am?" Dorian smugly asks Vane when he accosts him. But as Dorian walks off into the night, Adrian laughs, "Dorian Gray has looked twenty-two for the last twenty years." He chalks Gray's name and address on the wall.

Vane stalks Dorian. The haunted aristocrat takes a train to his country house in Selby (with Lord Henry, who insists, "To get back my youth, I'd do anything in the world except get up early, take exercise or be respectable"). Gray hosts a shooting party at his country home in Selby; there a guest accidentally shoots James Vane while Vane hides in the bushes. As wind howls, Dorian goes out to the barn where the body rests and looks at the face.

Conscience catches up with Dorian. On a snowy night at Selby, he breaks off his engagement with Gladys and returns to London. Meanwhile, David appears and reports he's been investigating Dorian. He has been in the schoolroom.

The finale of the movie is unforgettable. In his schoolroom, Dorian stares at his portrait—desperate to find some sign of salvation following his sacrifice of giving up Gladys. "Surely it was there!" narrates Hardwicke, "in the eyes, struggling through the horror and the loathsomeness." Hatfield and Lewin pull off the eleventh hour repentance with delicacy and power. The "Sir Tristan" theme plays as Dorian symbolically lifts a fallen toy knight from the floor. "The knife that had killed Basil Hallward would kill his portrait also," announces the narrator.

Dorian stabs the portrait through the heart.

"But when the knife pierced the heart of the portrait, an extraordinary thing happened."

Hatfield's Dorian lunges in the shadows. "Pray, Father, forgive me, for I have sinned . . . through my most grievous fault." And the portrait slowly returns to its original state of beauty and innocence.

Once more we see the blocks on the floor. The initials of Allen Campbell have joined the group and so have those of James Vane. Henry Wotton's initials are also now in the blocks, and off to the left is a block with an "O"—a nod to Mr. Wilde. A "G" for Gladys now dominates the blocks, as the symbol of the decency that proved Dorian's salvation. And above all, there is one single block, with the letter "L." Just as Basil Hallward signed the portrait, Albert Lewin has signed his own film.

Lord Henry, Gladys, and David break into the schoolroom to see the pierced portrait and the horrible, decayed cadaver on the floor (apparently a dummy was used for the shot).

"Heaven forgive me," sighs Sanders's Lord Henry.

David and Gladys depart the house. For the final shot, we see the Egyptian cat, looking out into the audience, perhaps seeking a new master, and a book opened to the *Rubaiyat:*

> I Sent my Soul through the Invisible,
> Some letter of that After-life to spell.
> And by and by my Soul returned to me and
> answered: "I myself am Heaven and Hell."

Finally, the finale and final credit music appear. As in MGM's *Dr. Jekyll and Mr. Hyde,* the ending is inspiring and beautiful, as if it were appropriately celebrating the saving of a lost soul.

●

> You will be repelled, mystified, or fascinated—but you will not remain indifferent to this incredible story by Oscar Wilde. . . . Not for the kiddies.
> —*Photoplay* review, May, 1945

The Picture of Dorian Gray finally wrapped at MGM on August 5, 1944. The shooting schedule, originally set for 52 days, had stretched to an incredible 127 days—nearly five months of shooting. On August 8, the fastidious Lewin began retakes but soon he acquiesced to preview the film. It was a night that Hatfield remembers with a shudder:

> They told me *not* to go. The front office said it wasn't really finished, the music would be "canned," and so on—but I couldn't resist. So I went to the preview—in disguise as an old man, in case the studio executives saw me. I wore bifocals, and a mustache, and sat in the balcony—as it

Director Albert Lewin's symbolism works through blocks as Peter Lawford, Donna Reed, and George Sanders behold the dead Dorian and the reverted painting.

turned out, *right* behind Mayer and his associates—and I was terrified they'd find me. When it was all over, my girlfriend and I fled the theatre, down the fire escape.

After all was over and the magnificent Stothart score was added, *The Picture of Dorian Gray* tallied a walloping negative cost of $1,918,168.38. This was more than the production costs of the 1930 *The Unholy Three*, *Freaks*, *The Mask of Fu Manchu*, *Mark of the Vampire*, *Mad Love*, and *The Devil-Doll* combined. Mayer had allowed Lewin's every desire for this "prestige" picture; now came the test of Producer Berman's showmanship and the film's box office appeal.

In February 1945 MGM hosted a trade show of *The Picture of Dorian Gray*. The February 26, 1945, *Hollywood Reporter* was very impressed:

In the entire history of the production of fine pictures by Metro-Goldwyn-Mayer, from a production standpoint, few if any can compare with the achievement accomplished with its screen transition of the Oscar Wilde story, *The Picture of Dorian Gray*. Its magnificence of production can hardly be approached by any picture that has ever been made. The sets, their decorations, the photography, the direction, the acting are truly inspired creations. Just how much the public will realize and appreciate this excellence can only be judged after the picture is played, the tickets counted and the verbal reactions of the customers analyzed.... But whether it's a hit or a flop, MGM can take great pride in the production, even though it may later condemn itself for its hope in the attempt to bring so risky a subject to the screen.

The MGM publicity department despaired for an angle with which to sell *The Picture of Dorian Gray.* Thoroughly stumped, they finally slapped a tag on the posters that to anyone familiar with Oscar Wilde or the movie, seems hilariously ingenuous: "Youth's Adventure in Living."

Finally, on the night of March 1, 1945, *The Picture of Dorian Gray* had its premiere at New York's Capitol, MGM's showcase Broadway theatre, complete with a big stage show. "B'way Has Never Seen So Many Top-Ranking M-G-M Stars *in Person!*" promised the *New York Times* opening day advertisement: featured on the Capitol stage were Lena Horne, Xavier Cugat and his orchestra, the Dancing Garcias, impressionist Paul Regan, and—in a strange stab at wholesomeness—MGM star Robert Walker (fresh from *See Here, Private Hargrove*). Hurd Hatfield was there too, in the audience, and the opening night fully awakened him to the literal dangers of movie stardom:

> I went with my parents; I remember we sat in the balcony—with Sinclair Lewis, of all people. The usher came up, and said "Mr. Hatfield, follow me." Well, the crowd suddenly realized I was there, and went mad. We got into the limo out front, and then all the people in the street surrounded the car and pushed the chauffeur against it, and he couldn't get around to get inside. I started to laugh. My father said, "I'm getting claustrophobic, open the window." And my mother said, "Don't! They'll all be in here." Finally, they got the police, and they escorted us to 21 for the party.

Reviews the next day were predictably controversial. Eileen Creelman of the *New York Sun* praised the film's sophistication and vision:

> *The Picture of Dorian Gray* bids fair to be the season's most-discussed movie. . . . Mr. Lewin, by making the picture as he felt it should be made, has contributed greatly to the art of motion pictures. . . . Mr. Hatfield, in his first important role, and one of the toughest assignments an actor could wish, plays the cold, soulless Dorian Gray with a deliberate dead-pan quality, making the man as deadly and as fascinating as a beautiful snake.

Meanwhile, in the *New York Times,* Bosley Crowther blasted the movie:

Aside from the fact completely that Oscar Wilde would probably have split his portly sides laughing at the mawkish pomposity of the film which has been made from his elegant little novel, *The Picture of Dorian Gray*, there is good and sufficient reason for a modern to do the same thing. As a matter of fact, one might venture to slip it a ribald razz. For the elaborately mystical treatment which Metro has given the tale is matched in egregious absurdity by the visual affectations of the film.

The public made its own decision, and it was a shocker. *The Picture of Dorian Gray* broke all first-week records at the Capitol, with a top first-week gross of $80,049. The gross was all the more remarkable (as the *Hollywood Reporter* noted) due to Manhattan's bad weather and a curfew. The movie set a new record at the Capitol for its first two weeks; by its fifth week, *The Picture of Dorian Gray* had won the #2 spot for highest figure of any MGM film for that length of run, topped only by MGM's 1943 Spencer Tracy/Irene Dunne/Van Johnson *A Guy Named Joe*.

Meanwhile, on March 27, 1945, *The Picture of Dorian Gray* had its Hollywood opening at the Egyptian, Fox Ritz, and Los Angeles theatres. "The picture is strictly for adults," warned the *Los Angeles Herald-Express;* "one of the most unusual ever brought before the public," praised the *Los Angeles Times*. Once again, the box office performance was astounding: the film capped the third largest Los Angeles opening day gross of any MGM film; it was surpassed only by the Greer Garson/Walter Pidgeon *Mrs. Parkington* and the Marlene Dietrich/Ronald Colman *Kismet* (both in 1944).

As audiences lined up at theatres, *The Picture of Dorian Gray* inspired wildly conflicting reviews. The *New York Journal-American* hailed Sanders as "outstanding," while the *Sun's* Miss Creelman (who had so loved the film) criticized his "careless mumble that passes in some British circles as speech." The *New York Daily News* praised Angela Lansbury as "the cinema find of the year," while the *New York Times* (in a follow-up broadside against the film) panned her as "plump and unethereal." *PM's* John T. McManus wondered about the film's timeliness, opining that the movie's "excruciating Briticisms and effete epigrams from a buried era" were hardly appropriate for wartime audiences. Even the grotesque Albright portrait rated controversy: the *Los Angeles Herald Express* hailed it as "nightmarish in its horror," while the *New York Sun* turned thumbs down on "this horrible Albright fantasy" that "harms the illusion of a picture which is one of the year's most interesting productions." Naturally, poor old *Variety* got into the act, calling the movie "an interesting and daring experiment," then missing the point entirely by opining that Hatfield "should have been aged a little toward the end."

Albert Lewin, meanwhile, reveled in the debates and controversy and must have beamed when he read the *Los Angeles Times* understatement assessment: "not exactly pap for morons."

On March 7, 1946, at Grauman's Chinese Theatre, *The Picture of Dorian Gray* competed in the Academy Award race for Best Supporting Actress (Angela Lansbury), Black and White Cinematography (Harry Stradling), and Best Black and White Interior Decoration (Cedric Gibbons and Hans Peters; Edwin B. Willis, John Bonar, and Hugh Hunt). Lansbury, winning her second Best Supporting Actress nomination in two years, was up against Eve Arden and Ann Blyth for Warners' *Mildred Pierce*, Joan Lorring for Warners' *The Corn Is Green*, and Ann Revere, who had played Angela's mother in MGM's *National Velvet*. The winner was Revere. Cagney/UA's *Blood on the Sun* took the Interior Decoration Award, but *Dorian Gray*'s Harry Stradling won the Academy Award for Cinematography (he later won a Best Color Cinematography Oscar for Warners' 1964 *My Fair Lady*).

By the time the picture went into general release, "horrific" copy was accompanying the film:

- *"Lover* by day . . . a romantic *beast* by night!"
- *"Women were his prey . . . romantic thrills his bait!"*
- *"Warning to women:* Bring your smelling salts!"

And as for the commercial fate of *The Picture of Dorian Gray*, the film maintained its weird box office allure, becoming a surprise hit. It reaped a domestic gross of $1,399,000 ($120,000 more than the 1941 *Dr. Jekyll and Mr. Hyde*), while the foreign gross was even bigger: $1,576,000, making a world-wide gross of $2,975,000. Hence *The Picture of Dorian Gray* has the distinction of having won the largest initial release audience of any MGM horror film of the 1930s and 1940s. Of course, no one had expected the top-heavy production to make a profit, and *The Picture of Dorian Gray* lost $26,000 — a tiny loss, considering the prestige and publicity it afforded MGM (which enjoyed a 1945 fiscal profit of $12.9 million).

Finally, one more controversy about *The Picture of Dorian Gray:* one might have expected Albert Lewin, with his highly sophisticated style, to have been an idol of Val Lewton, RKO's literate, poetic, legendary producer of such beloved "B" films as *Cat People* and *The Body Snatcher*. Such was hardly the case. In his milestone 1973 book on Lewton, *The Reality of Terror,* Joel Siegel originally included a personal letter Lewton had written after he and his wife (and Mark Robson and his spouse) had passed a "badly misspent" evening seeing *The Picture of Dorian Gray*. The publisher cut the letter from his manuscript, but Siegel published it in *Velvet Light Trap* magazine (#11, Winter, 1974). In this letter, Lewton lambasted the work of MGM's Lewin as "a disgustingly pretentious piece of poopishness" and elucidated:

> We make horror films because we have to make them, and we make them for little money and fight every minute to make them right. Here's

George Sanders, Donna Reed, and Hurd Hatfield in *The Picture of Dorian Gray.*

a man who makes a bawdy horror story out of a classic, with no compulsion upon him to do so and with every facility that money and time can provide for the making of a good film. Mr. Lewin just hasn't got it—he must be a poop.

As for Albert Lewin, he was director and screenwriter for UA's 1947 *The Private Affairs of Bel Ami* (featuring *Dorian Gray* alumnae George

Sanders and Angela Lansbury), another very sophisticated tragedy based on Guy de Maupassant's works. He was also screenwriter for such films as *Call Me Mister* (Fox, 1951) and *Alice in Wonderland* (1951), and was producer/director/original author/screenplay writer of *Pandora and the Flying Dutchman* (1951), a lushly metaphysical controversy starring Ava Gardner and James Mason. Lewin's final producer/director/screenwriter credit was *The Living Idol* (1957), another dose of dramatic metaphysics. He died in 1968.

And in the case of Hurd Hatfield, *The Picture of Dorian Gray* won the new MGM star as much infamy as it did stardom:

> The film didn't make me popular in Hollywood. It was too odd, too avant-garde, too ahead of its time (after all, Lewin always said he had made it for six friends). The decadence, the hints of bisexuality, and so on, made me a leper. Nobody knew I had a sense of humor, and people wouldn't even have lunch with me!

Of course, Hurd Hatfield went on to work with Jean Renoir (*The Diary of a Chambermaid* [1946]), Victor Fleming (*Joan of Arc* [1948]), Arthur Penn (*The Left-Handed Gun* [1957] and *Mickey One* [1965]), Nicholas Ray (*King of Kings* [1961], as Pontius Pilate) and most recently, Bruce Beresford. Hatfield also acted on the stage, where he was directed by such legends as Elia Kazan, Eva Le Gallienne, Sir Laurence Olivier, and Sir John Gielgud. He played in over a hundred television programs, winning an Emmy nomination for his performance as Baron Rothschild in "The Invincible Mr. Disraeli" (on "Hallmark Hall of Fame," 1963). He revealed his wonderful versatility in many roles, while *The Picture of Dorian Gray* has remained his trademark film. (He even did a TV take-off on the role on the "Wild Wild West" episode "The Night of the Man-Eating House," December 2, 1966.) Over the years, *The Picture of Dorian Gray* has presented Hatfield with many surprises. He's met many people who claim to have tested for the Dorian Gray role; indeed, years ago, at a New Year's Eve party, Hatfield met Greta Garbo and learned she had wanted to play Dorian Gray herself at MGM, dressed as a man.

Today, *The Picture of Dorian Gray* survives as one of the most popular MGM classics of its celebrated era. While in the East in 1988, Hurd Hatfield appeared in conjunction with showings of the movie for the Baltimore Film Forum and the American Film Institute at the Kennedy Center; all proceeds were donated to People for the Ethical Treatment of Animals.

"I'm glad *The Picture of Dorian Gray* found its audience," says Hurd Hatfield (now at work on writing his memoir), "but, for the longest time, I worried that people wouldn't realize that, for me, Dorian Gray was a character part. That wasn't me."

It's a distinction that anyone who meets Hurd Hatfield would have no trouble in recognizing.

●

Sir Cedric Hardwicke, the voice of Oscar Wilde in *The Picture of Dorian Gray,* had a Wildean cynicism about Hollywood. He once remarked that the movie capital lured the most talented directors, producers, actors, writers in the world, spent millions to make a movie, took it out to preview, and if one miserable teenager scrawled "lousy" across the preview card, the studio was in hysteria the next morning, second-guessing its talent force and planning to revise the film for the masses.

To the contrary, there is an admiringly arrogant quality about *The Picture of Dorian Gray.* It plays with a rapier-sharp style and with absolutely no apology for its intellectualism or mystical frills. It still survives today as one of the most controversial of horror films; some fans despise it for its pretensions (just as Bosley Crowther and Val Lewton did), while others admire its daring intellectual arrogance (in a genre where intellect often had no place at all).

If Sam Katzman's Lugosi Monogram "B" movies are the cheeseburgers of the horror movies (often delicious in spite of themselves), *The Picture of Dorian Gray* is its Lobster Newburg, with caviar—too rich for many tastes, but a masterful creation all the same. If the horror genre is presently overrun by writers who are English professors (as a few colleagues have lamented), *Dorian Gray* might be one of their pet movies. It remains a daring art film, an "elitist" indulgence, a vision captured by an eccentric director who got away with making a major Hollywood movie aimed to please only six friends. And if one can enjoy many of the Poverty Row horror movies, finding them endearing for their incredible lack of intelligence, isn't it possible to admire *The Picture of Dorian Gray* for its airs and arrogance?

It would be too easy, however, to dismiss *The Picture of Dorian Gray* as a pet indulgence of movie fans with masters degrees. Just as Sir Basil Hallward managed to invest some supernatural evil in Dorian Gray's painting, so did the company of MGM's *The Picture of Dorian Gray*—director Lewin, stars Hatfield, Sanders, and Lansbury, cameraman Stradling, et al.—provide a hypnotic, civil, yet curiously depraved magic, fascinating to "the masses" in 1945, just as it fascinates so many today. The film's commercial achievements—its record-breaking early engagements, its surprising release grosses, the huge international success, the early (and popular) release of the film on video by MGM, its perennial status as one of the most-requested pictures in MGM's film library—all attest to this power. Champions of this Jekyll/Hyde variation, this study of a man's diseased soul, swear by this mystical lure—even if this magic is as hard to describe (and, to many, probably as preposterous) as Wilde's original novella.

The fascinating themes of *The Picture of Dorian Gray* naturally spawned other versions. On January 23, 1953, John Newland starred as Dorian Gray on an episode of TV's "Tales of Tomorrow." In 1970 *The Secret of Dorian Gray,* an Italian/German/Lichtensteinian production, starred Helmut Berger, Richard Todd, and Herbert Lom and updated the film to the present. *"The Picture of Dorian Gray,* released 25 years earlier, is vastly superior," claims Leonard Maltin in his *TV Movies* book, however. Dan "Dark Shadows" Curtis produced a 1973 two-part TV movie, featuring a well-publicized Dick Smith makeup. And there was the 1983 made-for-TV movie *The Sins of Dorian Gray,* in which Dorian was a *woman.*

For all the versions filmed of Wilde's classic, MGM's 1945 *The Picture of Dorian Gray* reigns supreme, with Hurd Hatfield indelibly linked with the depraved Dorian. Even with Dorian Gray's Egyptian cat in his Irish country house, Hatfield remembers his infamous performance with little mysticism and much humor:

> Hollywood, today, is just an open-air opium den. On one of my recent trips there, I went to a party, and the host offered me "a little Coke"—meaning cocaine, of course. "Thank you," I said, not comprehending at all, "but can you make it a diet Coke?"
> I must have disappointed him terribly!

Hangover Square

Studio: 20th Century–Fox; Producer: Robert Bassler; Director: John Brahm; Screenplay: Barre Lyndon (based on the novel *Hangover Square,* by Patrick Hamilton); Musical Score: Bernard Herrmann; Cinematographer: Joseph LaShelle; Art Directors: Lyle Wheeler and Maurice Ransford; Set Decorator: Thomas Little (Frank Hughes, Associate); Film Editor: Harry Reynolds; Costumes: Rene Hubert and Kay Nelson; Special Photographic Effects: Fred Sersen; Make-up Artist: Ben Nye; Sound: Bernard Freericks and Harry M. Leonard; Running Time: 77 minutes.

Filmed at 20th Century–Fox Studios, August 21–October 25, 1944; retakes, November, 1944. New York Premiere: Roxy Theatre, February 7, 1945.

The Players: George Harvey Bone (Laird Cregar); Netta Longdon (Linda Darnell); Dr. Allan Middleton (George Sanders); Carstairs (Glenn Langan); Barbara Chapman (Faye Marlowe); Sir Henry Chapman (Alan Napier); Supt. Clay (Frederic Worlock); Detective Inspector King (J. W. Austin); Detective Sgt. Lewis (Leyland Hodgson); Watchman (Clifford Brooke); Butler (John Goldsworthy); Mickey (Michael Dyne); Yvette (Ann Codee); Ogilby (Francis Ford); Manager (Charles Irwin); Newsman (Frank Benson); Maid (Connie Leon); Costermonger (Robert Hale); English Policeman (Leslie Denison); Drunk (Jimmy Aubrey); Voice of Child (Roddy McDowall).

●

Laird Cregar . . . Twentieth–Fox star, passed away Saturday afternoon at 4:52 P.M. of myocardial failure following an operation at Good Samaritan Hospital. Private funeral services. . . .
— *The Hollywood Reporter,* December 11, 1944

Today, almost 50 years after its nightmarish production, *Hangover Square,* 20th Century–Fox's 1945 Victorian sex melodrama, is finally winning a belated reputation as a minor terror masterpiece. Long shrouded in the shadow of *The Lodger* (sharing that 1944 film's producer, director, writer, and two leading men), this release has strikingly come into its own, offering unforgettably chilling vignettes.

The closeups of Laird Cregar suffering a Jekyll/Hyde fit, his eyes heartbreakingly shining fear, bewilderment, and horror on a dark, White-chapel street are memorable. Then there is the Guy Fawkes bonfire, where singing and dancing revelers place their dummies on a huge pyre, and Cregar carries the masked corpse of strangled Linda Darnell to the top, cremating his dead lover to the eerie piccolos of Bernard Herrmann's de-monic music. In the fiery, Wagnerian climax, George Sanders, the crimi-nal psychologist who finally trapped Cregar, rescues the madman's loyal love from the flames as Cregar pounds the final notes of the concerto he had composed while violently losing his sanity.

The superb direction by John Brahm, the taut screenplay by Barre Lyndon, the exquisite cinematography by Joseph LaShelle all contributed to a movie that *Time* praised in 1945 as an "excitingly horrid story ... a top drawer horror picture."

Time's testimonial, however, was an exception to the critical rule; *Hangover Square* is a movie whose popular reputation was decades long in coming. It was a film that none of its three stars wanted to make, a property that its screenwriter didn't want to write, a movie whose most celebrated scenes were not in the novel and were in fact bitterly disowned by the novelist. It was a film in which one of the stars physically assaulted the pro-ducer, another star verbally assaulted the director, the musical director alienated virtually everybody, and the on-set tension became so severe that the crew dispatched a signed petition to *The Hollywood Reporter*.

And all three stars of this horror show were in real life sadly destined for horrific deaths.

Finally, the brilliant star of *Hangover Square*, suffering torments brought on by the part and his own private demons, would never live to see the film.

> *Click!* ... Here it was again! He was walking along the cliff at Hunstanton and it had come again ... click! ... "Dead" moods—yes, all his life he had had "dead" moods.... A silent film without music—he could have found no better way of de-scribing the weird world in which he now moved....
>
> Then he remembered, without any difficulty, what it was he had to do: he had to kill Netta Longdon.
>
> —from the novel *Hangover Square*, by
> Patrick Hamilton (1942)

On January 19, 1944, *The Lodger* had premiered at New York's Roxy Theatre, complete with a big musical stage show and Laird Cregar, Fox's 6'3", 250-pound super villain, who enjoyed the triumph of his life as the lodger—aka Jack the Ripper. Reprising a scene from *The Lodger* on the Roxy stage, Cregar won a five-minute ovation from the

***Hangover Square* poster.**

audience and joyously extended his engagement, thrilled by the cheers and the glory.

On December 16, 1943, before *The Lodger*'s premiere, *The Hollywood Reporter* noted that a very important conference had taken place at 20th Century–Fox: producer Robert Bassler and screenplay writer Barre Lyndon, both late of *The Lodger,* would be preparing a new vehicle for Laird Cregar at Fox. The *Reporter* described the unnamed property as "a modern story" dealing with a schizophrenic whose moods tragically swing from love to murder.

The mysteriously anonymous property was, in fact, *Hangover Square,* by Patrick Hamilton, author of the phenomenal hit play, *Gaslight* (which became the MGM 1944 hit movie and won an Oscar for Ingrid Bergman).

Cregar himself had persuaded Fox to buy the rights to the 1942 novel; he was intrigued by the book's doomed protagonist, George Harvey Bone, a lost, lonely soul who takes care of the hotel cat, cries at movies, and humiliates himself time and again in his sick love for an unspeakably bitchy actress named Netta. Bone suffers from "dead moods" and climactically, during one such spell, drowns the wicked Netta in her bathtub, then gasses himself, leaving a note asking that someone look after the cat.

Lyndon had known Hamilton in London, where Lyndon's play *The Man in Half Moon Street** and Hamilton's *Gaslight* were both playing simultaneously. Later, Hamilton and Lyndon met again and cordially traded each other copies of their respective scripts for *Gaslight* and *The Amazing Dr. Clitterhouse.* As it turned out, Lyndon didn't share Cregar's admiration for Hamilton's new novel. An erudite man who collected H. G. Wells memorabilia, Lyndon told Joel Greenberg in *Focus on Film:*

> So when I saw that he'd written *Hangover Square* I bought a copy, or got one sent over here. I read about half of it and thought, "This is a weird one, I can't understand it at all," and gave it to the guy at the garage to read.

When Bassler conferred with Lyndon about a new project, the author rejected the first two offerings; the third, to his chagrin, was *Hangover Square.* Reluctant to read it again, Lyndon visited the story department and asked for the three-page synopsis. He began imagining how he could alter the novel's story so that it would best suit Laird Cregar:

> As I began reading it I suddenly saw the way to do it. You see, this fellow is supposed to suddenly go off his head, and it just "happened." What triggered me off was the thought, "Now if there were a noise, or something we could see—either hear or see—something big, something noisy, like a truck spilling a load of piping—if you've ever heard that you won't forget it! And then—oh boy!—I went straight back and sold this to Bassler. "Oh yes," he said, "of course!"

Lyndon did not reveal how many stabs he took at adapting *Hangover Square* to Zanuck's demands. The 20th Century–Fox collection at the University of Southern California contains no less than five separate drafts of shooting scripts for *Hangover Square,* produced over a six-month period. Lyndon's original, 183-page script of February 12, 1944, bore little relation to either Hamilton's novel or the final film. In 1937 London, George Harvey Bone is a gentle, brilliant musician who finds his inspira-

---

Lyndon's play inspired the Paramount 1944 film and still later, Hammer's 1959 The Man Who Could Cheat Death.

tion by visiting St. Saviour's Church at night and dreaming his beautiful compositions. Tragically, Bone falls madly in love with a sexy chanteuse named Netta and provides music for her songs (which featured these Lyndon lyrics): "I've a jungle urge ... I'm a bad little girlie and I don't give a damn ... Love me-e-e!"

George has his admirers: Humphrey Leigh, a doctor concerned with George's dead moods; Barbara, Humphrey's wife and George's devoted friend; Sir Henry Chapman, a maestro who offers George the chance to perform his concerto; and 12-year-old Christopher Wyndham, who idolizes George and his musical genius. The discordant sounds that propel George into his schizophrenia turn him into a suave man-about-town who visits a criminology club to discuss murder. Tormented and cheated by Netta, Bone strangles her during a "dead mood," throws the body into the excavation ditch of a theatre, and pours a ton of wet concrete over the cadaver. An old, retired Scotland Yard man named Middleton, who regrets having never trapped a murderer, now traps one as Bone finally realizes the severity of his mania while triumphantly performing his concerto. He escapes the authorities, and exhausted and fatally ill, goes with little Christopher to his haven—St. Saviour's Church.

"If a man could ... stand upon a cloud ... and listen," says the dreamy, dying composer. As he dies, Bone says to the child, "Play my music, Christopher.... Play my music."

Actor Cregar was thrilled that Lyndon had changed George Harvey Bone from the jobless loser of the novel to a genius composer. The character star had been taking singing and piano lessons and hoped to showcase his talent; Fox even promised him he could perform some of his own compositions. He was delighted at the chance to portray the schizophrenic character switches from gentle genius to suave criminology aficionado. And, naturally, he loved the dramatic, moving death scene offered in this contemporary vehicle.

Hangover Square was further delayed, however. Lyndon did two rewrites, one dated April 7, 1944, another June 23, 1944. Each followed the basic pattern of the original scenario. As the film firmed up on the production slate, Cregar took off for Stamford, Connecticut, to star in a summer stock production of *The Man Who Came to Dinner,* which opened July 10, 1944.

Cregar was presumably unaware of this directive on *Hangover Square,* which Zanuck dictated after studying the June 23 script:

> The story should be laid in London in 1910. It is essential that we put it back to 1910 in order to get the flavor of mystery that goes with that period....
> The story is entirely overwritten from the standpoint of sets, and it will

have to be radically confined to a budget of $850,000. . . . I see no reason why we cannot use all of the streets and sets as they are from *The Lodger.*

While Laird Cregar took bows in Connecticut, Lyndon finalized *Hangover Square* in Hollywood. The new July 12, 1944, script set back the time to the turn-of-the-century (1903, as it evolved), opened the melodrama with the muder of an antique dealer, and found a new way to dispose of Netta's corpse. As Lyndon remembered:

> Well, I'd got a body and I didn't know what to do with it, you see, because it was 1903, and at first I had the idea of sinking it in the foundations of a building beneath falling cement and limestone. But I have a feeling that Zanuck didn't like the idea, so I had to think of something else, and suddenly I thought of Guy Fawkes Day, November 5. I don't know if kids do it now in England, but they used to go around collecting pennies with "Guys" in a perambulator. Also organizations like breweries used to have a yard and they often did have a big bonfire in it for their employees, who'd go and drink beer in the yard.

On July 17, 1944, Zanuck's office issued his response:

> Mr. Zanuck thinks this is a tremendous improvement over the previous script. We now have a story which is not only psychologically interesting, but physically interesting as well. . . . The Guy Fawkes thing is great; so is the first killing.

Zanuck had also transformed old Scotland Yard man Middleton into a romantic role designed for George Sanders. Barbara Leigh had shed her husband in the rewrites, becoming Sir Henry Chapman's daughter and George's girlfriend, while little Christopher Wyndham had disappeared entirely during the script revisions. Excited about the revised *Hangover Square,* Zanuck sought a leading lady.

"We must get a very sexy woman, possibly a foreigner, for the role of Netta," Zanuck had dictated. "She should have the same lure that Marlene Dietrich had in *The Blue Angel.*" Sure enough, the July 25, 1944, *Hollywood Reporter* announced that Fox would probably close a contract "within 48 hours" to star Marlene Dietrich as femme fatale Netta in *Hangover Square.* Then everything fell to pieces.

Laird Cregar, returning from his stock engagement, read the shooting script of *Hangover Square* and absolutely refused to play it. "First thing you know," said Cregar, "I'll be known as the Bette Davis of 20th Century-Fox."

Hollywood was shocked. Zanuck had bought *Hangover Square* just for Laird Cregar—who now refused to star in the picture. Dietrich, sensing a doomed production, bailed out of the role of Netta and Zanuck slapped Cregar with an eight-week suspension.

On August 1, 1944, *The Hollywood Reporter* announced that Fox contractee Glenn Langan would inherit the Laird Cregar role in *Hangover Square.*

●

> I soon became adjusted to the idea that I would always be cast as the villain. . . . I made a much better adjustment in this sort of thing than did our poor late-lamented Laird Cregar, an actor of great talent, who was virtually assassinated by Hollywood.
> —George Sanders, *Memoirs of a Professional Cad,* 1960

What happened? Why did Cregar refuse *Hangover Square?*

Since *The Lodger,* Laird Cregar had lost three roles he dearly wanted. MGM had cast George Sanders as Lord Henry in *The Picture of Dorian Gray.* Zanuck had awarded Cregar the role of Waldo Lydecker in *Laura,* but Otto Preminger (who took over the film from Rouben Mamoulian) felt Cregar was too obvious a villain and replaced him with Clifton Webb (while replacing Jennifer Jones with Gene Tierney in the title role). Cregar had campaigned for the role of Private Francis Marion, Southern aristocrat soldier of Fox's *The Eve of St. Mark,* but was told he was too big and heavy; Vincent Price got the part. For a man who so passionately loved acting, Cregar was horrified at the threat of typecasting. It became an obsession.

Even more obsessive, however, was a private anxiety: his homosexuality. The super actor, who had virtually come out of the closet in his mincy moments in *The Lodger,* was now involved in a romance with a young lady. It was, by all reports, traumatic, and Cregar, desperate to consummate the affair, believed he could do so only by shedding his villainous bulk and becoming a glamorous leading man. The *Hangover Square* revamping agonized him; it had been set back to a period show. George Harvey Bone no longer visited the criminology club, but stalked the streets like a Golemesque monster, and the same producer, director, writer, male co-star, and even the sets threatened to turn *Hangover Square* into a carbon copy of *The Lodger.*

For Laird Cregar, terrified of typecasting, desperate to be a lover on and off the screen, the concept of life as Jack the Ripper was horrifying. As George Sanders wrote in his memoir:

> The change wrought in the story by the studio was too much for him and he refused to do the part. The studio, in accordance with

its policy at the time, brought pressure to bear upon him and he finally succumbed.

Richard Widmark once told *Films in Review*'s Michael Buckley about trying to refuse *O. Henry's Full House* at Fox. The next morning when he called his agent, "He had Zanuck on the other line and held the phone up to my receiver. Zanuck is saying, 'I'll ruin the s.o.b.—professionally, socially, morally!' He was screaming like an insane man. So I did it." The young, sensitive Cregar must have received the same sort of threats, bullying, and abuse. He hadn't completed a film in a year, his option was due at the studio, so he surrendered. Something snapped, however, when Laird Cregar accepted the role of Bone in *Hangover Square*.

"A tragic resolve was born in Laird's mind," wrote George Sanders, "to make himself over into a beautiful man who would never again be cast as a fiend."

August 11, 1944: Louella Parsons reported that Laird Cregar "went on eight weeks suspension but apparently thought better of his revolt and is back on the lot." Parsons also announced that Jack Warner would loan Geraldine Fitzgerald to Fox for the "femme lead" in *Hangover Square*.

August 15, 1944: The *Hollywood Reporter* announced that Bernard Herrmann, who had won the Oscar for his score of *The Devil and Daniel Webster* (and had composed the milestone score for *Citizen Kane*), "has composed a concerto which will be the theme in *Hangover Square*."

August 17, 1944: The *Hollywood Reporter* notes, "John Brahm takes the script and shooting blueprints of *Hangover Square* to his beach home today for five days of pre-shooting work before going into work with the picture." There has been no more mention of Fitzgerald and no leading lady has been named.

August 21, 1944: *Variety* reports, "*Hangover Square* starts today at 20th–Fox. . . . Picture was held back several days for Linda Darnell, who has just finished in Bing Crosby's *The Great John L.*"

August 24, 1944: The *Hollywood Citizen-News* reports, "John Brahm, directing *Hangover Square* for 20th, has a 'hangover headache'—must work out with special effects expert Lou Witte: three fires, three fog sequences, a windstorm, a rainstorm, and a snow scene."

Fox also had to cope with the censorship eye of the Breen Office, which attacked the *Hangover Square* shooting script in this letter of August 11, 1944:

> In accordance with the Association's agreement, the word "fire" should not be shouted out, but used in a completed sentence, this to avoid any possibility of panic in the theatre . . . the costume of Netta,

described here and elsewhere, must not be objectionably revealing. . . .
The attitude of George in wanting to come to Netta's apartment to play
his new composition should not contain any suggestive inference. This
is essential . . . there should be no closeup details of the thuggee cord . . .
[the] dissolve on Netta and Carstairs seem suggestive of illicit sex. It must
be revised to get away from any such flavor. . . . George's line, "I'll neither
be held nor be hung," should be revised to get away from any indication
he intends to commit suicide to avoid being taken by the officers. This
is important.

Special effects, censorship problems, and a bitterly disturbed star all
posed threats for *Hangover Square*. It would, in fact, prove a far more
unhappy and tragic production than anyone ever imagined.

●

Laird Cregar was my uncle. . . . "They tell me at the studio
I will be a great leading man," he wrote me once. "My size is
the only disadvantage. I've got a picture coming up called
Hangover Square, which is one of those thrillers you like. . . . I
will play a tormented and deranged killer, who is a concert
pianist." . . . As I read, I could imagine myself sitting in the
local theatre with a few friends, watching them cringe and hide
their eyes at the scary parts. But I knew better than that. I had
lived in his house, shared his glory and fun, and loved him very
much.
　　　　　　　　　　　　　—Elizabeth Hayman, Laird Cregar's
　　　　　　　　　　　　　niece, in a tribute in *American Classic
　　　　　　　　　　　　　Screen* (1982)

The motif of *Hangover Square* is fire. The very first shot is a flame
burning at night on the old Whitechapel back lot; a hurdy-gurdy plays and
Brahm provides an immediate homage to *The Lodger*. The camera of
Joseph LaShelle (who would win a 1944 Academy Award for his work on
Laura) sweeps up to the second story of Ogilby's Antique Shop, where the
old dealer (Francis Ford, ex–serial hero and fixture in so many of his
brother John's films) is fighting off an attacker. The attacker is the camera;
just as it "killed" the old doxy in *The Lodger,* the camera quakes and jerks
and advances on Ogilby. A knife is raised and stabs the old man; a hand
pulls down a lamp and fire erupts.

The camera shifts in a burst of Bernard Herrmann music, and we see
the killer, George Harvey Bone—Laird Cregar.

Out in the street, Bone stumbles along, bumping into passersby. He
turns at the corner and stares back toward the fire—Cregar's first close-up.
It is a shock—not only because of the evidence of the diet that killed him,
but because of a frighteningly tormented look in his eyes. This is no

showboat performance, like *The Lodger;* it is Cregar's most natural screen work, played with a sadness and anxiety that are both pitiful and haunting.

While acting the role, Cregar was planning his "beautiful man" strategy. The actor, mercilessly dieting, laid grotesque plans to subject his face to plastic surgery and to undergo a major operation that would both correct a hernia and limit his intake of food. The bitter man perhaps never realized that future audiences, seeing him with a new face and form, would possibly reject him as some sort of freak; if he did, he was beyond caring. The transformation was underway, and as George Sanders wrote:

> He confessed this to me on the first day of shooting. He told me he was going to have an operation on his eyes and make various other changes. And that above all he was going to reduce until he became as slender as a sapling.

Fox, meanwhile, only aggravated the actor's mania. Zanuck had announced Cregar for the role of Inspector Javert in *Les Misérables*. It had also been announced, however, that if the actor lost sufficient weight, the studio would consider switching him to the role of hero Jean Valjean.

Bone arrives home, where his girlfriend, Barbara (Faye Marlowe), is playing his unfinished concerto for her father, impresario Sir Henry Chapman (Alan Napier). Chapman offers the young composer the chance to present his concerto at a soiree at Sir Henry's home in early December; Chapman himself would conduct. "I am enormously complimented," Bone was to reply.

A Hollywood scribe reported to the Baltimore *Evening Sun* the on-the-set tension that surrounded this simple line:

> Over at 20th Century–Fox, the thermometer on Stage 14 registered 104, and Laird Cregar, who, in spite of his dieting, is still a mighty fat boy, was blaming the heat for his repeated blow-ups. Usually Mr. Cregar is letter-perfect in his lines.... The star has only four words to say ... "I am enormously complimented." But still he can't get them out.

Finally come take #11, Cregar tried again and out came, "I am enormously *complicated.*" Brahm and company—familiar with the gossip about Laird Cregar—all burst into laughter. Producer Robert Bassler was more concerned; he called lunch half-an-hour early to let his disturbed star cool off.

"I wish I could tell you Laird Cregar's nickname," gossip columnist Sidney Skolsky cryptically wrote in his September 1 column. "Oh, the things you learn on a movie set."

Bone confesses his fear of having committed a crime to Barbara just as a newsboy hawks the edition about a murder in Fulham. Bone decides to

"Retouch" was the order on this original still from *Hangover Square*. Cregar had lost 100 pounds by the time this scene was filmed.

see a criminal psychologist at Scotland Yard, Dr. Allan Middleton, played by George Sanders.

Just back to Fox after playing the hedonistic Lord Henry in MGM's *The Picture of Dorian Gray*, Sanders was at the peak of his outrageous "noncooperation" (as his friend Alan Napier put it) as he reported for *Hangover Square*, a project he approached with total contempt. He refused to learn his lines. A dialogue director would try to hear them as Sanders flopped half-undressed in his dressing room, but the star declared his dialogue "unspeakable." Then Sanders would summon his friend Alan Napier to his dressing room and ask Napier to write him new dialogue.

"Nape, write me something," Napier remembered Sanders saying. "I can't possibly say this crap!"

It was an awkward spot for Napier, who was also a good friend of script writer Barre Lyndon. As Napier recalled, only "minimal changes" were made in Sanders's "unspeakable" dialogue.

Bone, accompanied by the loyal Barbara, explains his blackouts to Middleton: "When I'm tense or worked up, then any discordant sound seems to do it."

Dr. Middleton performs blood tests, investigates. He calls on Bone and Barbara. "If Mr. Bone had done it," says Middleton, "we wouldn't be able to prove it." Middleton suggests Bone escape his world of music and get out among ordinary people: "learn how they work and—above all—learn how they play."

"But Dr. Middleton," says Bone, "Music is the most important thing in the world to me."

"No, Mr. Bone. The most important thing is your *life.*"

Middleton walks Barbara home across the square; Sanders and Marlowe stroll through the night across the magnificent exterior "Hangover Square" Fox built on the back lot. Meanwhile, George Harvey Bone decides to attend a smoking concert.

Linda Darnell was one of the most beautiful actresses in Hollywood history. She had joined Fox in 1939, at the age of only 15, proving gorgeously decorative in such costumers as *The Mark of Zorro* (1940) and *Blood and Sand* (1941).

"She was like Spring, young, sweet and innocent," said the late Rouben Mamoulian, director of both these films, in Ronald L. Davis's 1991 Darnell biography, *Hollywood Beauty.* "The whole crew behaved differently when she was on the set. There was a kind of innocence about her that was enchanting."

Arriving in Hollywood from her Texas hometown complete with a pet rooster (Weedy), Linda had become very popular at Fox; Zanuck engaged her to appear (anonymously) as the Blessed Mary in Fox's *The Song of Bernadette* (1943). A marriage to cameraman Peverell Marley (not approved by Zanuck) had caused her virtual banishment, however. She went on loan-out as the vixen of UA's *Summer Storm* (co-starring with George Sanders); advance word of her sexy performance was so great that Zanuck, screening *Summer Storm* before its release, took a fresh interest. John Brahm (whose new term contract with Fox was announced in *Variety* on September 11, while *Hangover Square* was shooting) had a tough time persuading Linda to play evil, vampy Netta Longdon:

> Miss Darnell wanted to do the part, felt instinctively that here was a new role for her of greater depth. But she was frightened to death and at first refused. I argued with her, pleaded, showed her the marvelous drawings of Toulouse-Lautrec, who so admirably caught the demimondes of music halls. I told her, "Remember, you are low class, but you are a girl with a purpose, however dishonest or sinister." And I taught her how to kiss with her mouth open.

We first see Darnell, in "Toulouse-Latrec" costume, singing "Have You Seen Joe?" in a smoky pub, kicking and dancing in her fishnet stockings and high heels. She is a treat. *Time,* reviewing *Hangover Square,* hailed Linda's "memorably expressive pair of thighs," hailing her as "Hollywood's most rousing portrayer of unhousebroken sex." And this the girl who, the previous year, was playing the Virgin Mary.

Bone is captivated. He follows her, meeting his colleague Mickey (Michael Dyne, who landed his *Hangover Square* role after playing in a stage production *There's Always Juliet* directed by Brahm); Mickey is Netta's "agent," accompanist, and—so it's implied—lover. As Netta gripes about the lousy crowd and her lousy song, smoking a cigarette, playing with a high heel, Bone plays one of his tunes for her.

"Is he important?" she asks Mickey.

The three get drunk together and walk home through Hangover Square, George having written a song for Netta, "All for You." He agrees to take home her cat, whom the landlady has put out. The cat nicely symbolizes Netta's invasion of Bone's life and provided some tension of its own; when *Hangover Square* opened in Hollywood, the *Los Angeles Times* critic noted the girl behind him—"The only thing that worried her was that Bone would skin his cat alive."

George neglects his concerto and Barbara. Madly infatuated with Netta, he squires her about town. One night, in a fancy restaurant, she meets musical comedy impresario Eddie Carstairs (Glenn Langan, who had been set to replace Cregar as Bone in *Hangover Square* before the star changed his mind). While poor George telephones for seats to the symphony, Netta flirts outrageously with Carstairs, persuading him to let her sing for him that night at his club. She tells George she has a headache and must go home. In the carriage, she seductively sings to him and implores him to finish the new song he's writing for her that night.

"Then you could bring it over after a while," purrs Netta. "It wouldn't matter how late, George."

Poor George finishes the song. As he sits at the piano, Netta's cat is curled up in his lap—a suggestive touch that crept right by the censors. He rushes to Netta's, where she takes the song and begs off seeing him, due to a headache. Of course, behind the door, she's all dolled up, ready to go to Rafini's to sing the song her slavish beau just gave her. In a handsomely hateful touch, Netta watches through her window as George walks away, down the cobblestone streets; Brahm then gives the little vixen a closeup, as she smiles merrily at her own treachery.

George doesn't go all the way home. He stops for a hot drink at a stand where an old timer awaits a late night delivery of pipe. He sees a coach pull up at Netta's, and he watches her run out to board it.

Netta snaps at George, "Sometimes you can be an awful bore ... Come later if you like, when you're in a better temper, darling." The carriage rides off. To add to George's shame, Sir Henry and Barbara have just returned from the symphony and witness the scene.

"Aren't you rather letting yourself down?" asks Barbara.

"Hollywood's most rousing portrayer of unhousebroken sex," was how
Time **described Linda Darnell in** *Hangover Square.*

"If I am, isn't that my own affair?" replies George.

The angry, humiliated man is left alone in the dark streets. Along comes the wagon carrying the pipe. A wheel falls off the carriage, and the pipe crashes to the street.

"Click!"

The crash, of course, propels George Harvey Bone into one of his horrid dead moods. The transformation of Cregar's Jekyll to Hyde is masterful: the actor stares, wide-eyed, helplessly, horribly, into the camera, as Herrmann's shrill piccolos chillingly accompany his mania. The madman goes to his house, takes a cord off a curtain, ties it into a "thuggee cord," stalks the streets, and a scream is heard from Barbara's house.

As Middleton and Scotland Yard investigate the attack, Bone, still wandering the darkness in a daze, falls into a ditch and comes out of his trance. Seeing the excitement at the Chapman's, he runs over. He apologizes to the girl he has just attacked for having quarreled with her that evening and promises to get back to work on his concerto.

Of course, the various motifs played throughout the film — the hurdy-gurdy playing during the antique dealer's murder, the tune for Netta, etc. — are all part of the concerto that Bernard Herrmann wrote before the film was shot. Barre Lyndon confessed to *Focus on Film:*

I'll tell you: I wrote in the idea of the concerto. I don't think I ever conceived what it did to him musically, because that was beyond me. They commissioned somebody from New York to do it. He came out, a typical New Yorker who didn't think anything of pictures—two minutes spent with him was enough, if you know what I mean. After that he wrote the concerto and it was recorded. "You must hear this," John [Brahm] said, so we went up to his office where he played it; and I hated it, I absolutely hated it. But he laughed at me when I said it was lousy. "No," he said, "this is good, this is exactly what it should be."

Years later, Lyndon saw the *Hangover Square* climax on television and thought the music was "wonderful." "I take my hat off to him now, whatever his name was," Lyndon said of Herrmann, whose arrogance and temper became legendary as he went on to score (brilliantly) many Hitchcock films (including *North by Northwest* and *Psycho*) and such fare as *The Day the Earth Stood Still*, *The Seventh Voyage of Sinbad*, and *Jason and the Argonauts*.

●

> The time is too short for all I want to do.
> —remark made by Laird Cregar
> during the shooting of *Hangover Square*

Twentieth Century–Fox was a busy lot in the fall of 1944. There were three Technicolor musicals shooting: *Billy Rose's Diamond Horseshoe*, starring Betty Grable, Dick Haymes, and Phil Silvers; *Nob Hill*, with George Raft and Joan Bennett; and the Ira Gershwin and Kurt Weill fantasy *Where Do We Go from Here?* with Fred MacMurray and June Haver (they later wed). Also, the legendary Tallulah Bankhead was on the lot, playing Catherine the Great in the Lubitsch-produced farce *A Royal Scandal*, with William Eythe and Vincent Price.

Amidst all this activity, *Hangover Square* inspired plenty of gossip. There was talk about how sexy Linda Darnell was as Netta and about the misconduct of the incredibly arrogant and lazy George Sanders. The most disturbing news, however, was about Laird Cregar, his temperament, and his obsessed dieting.

This was a different "Sammy" Cregar from the delightful ham who used to cartwheel across the Fox lot. When John Brahm visited New York City for the opening of *Hangover Square* early in 1945, after Cregar's death, the director told Irene Thirer in a *New York Post* interview:

> Laird wanted so badly to do *Hangover Square* that the story was bought especially for him. Yet, all through the film he behaved so badly, like a

naughty little boy, whereas he'd been charming when I directed him in *The Lodger*.

From start to finish of the picture [sic] he lost 100 lbs. and in some of the closeups he is wonderfully handsome in a true poetic manner which is perfect for his interpretation of a musical genius with a split personality. Actually, his confused and confusing off-screen personality coincided a good deal with his last screen characterization.

Cregar had to rehearse diligently at the piano to place his hands in accord with the notes being played by Ignace Hilsberg on the soundtrack; the actor bitterly complained about the arduous rehearsals. The star also gave interviews, such as this one to journalist Inez Wallace:

> The other day a woman wrote about what she called my "spectacular rise" to fame. I came out here in 1937. That's seven years ago. Do you think seven years is a quick rise? I don't. All fans ever see is the time *since* one arrived—not the years of heartbreak that lead up the ladder to success.

Poor Cregar didn't realize that many people work their whole lives for success, never experiencing any.

●

> In *Hangover Square* . . . an 11-minute concerto (composed by Bernard Herrmann) is played, ostensibly by Cregar—and I defy anyone to tell me that the photographed music, expressing the musician's thoughts, is not equally as engrossing as any of the romantic sequences; as truly exciting as a chase!
> —John Brahm, is a *New York Post*
> interview with Irene Thirer, 1945

George Harvey Bone works on his concerto. One night, Netta, corseted into a black, skin-tight, low-cut gown, visits his study. He defies her, but her allure is too powerful; she wants a piece of his concerto for her new song and he surrenders it to her. As they kiss, in a wonderfully wicked touch, Darnell's Netta opens one eye to the audience to celebrate her triumph.

Of course, Netta is a cheat; she has toyed with Bone to get songs for her new musical show (with the retrospectively ambiguous title of *Gay Love*). On the day of her premiere, George visits her apartment to propose marriage.

"I'm afraid you're a little late, old boy," says Eddie Carstairs. He has already proposed to Netta, and she has accepted.

"But at the piano . . . She whispered to me . . . 'You could have me,' she said," rants Bone. Cregar builds like a volcano, attacking the producer, his face in a horrible grimace as he tries to strangle him. Netta and her maid pull him off. He goes home, angrily tosses the ring box across the room, and knocks down the violins.

"*Click!*"

The Hyde nature of George Harvey Bone once again stalks the streets. He enters Netta's boudoir. The she-bitch is primping in her mirror, and Bone swoops down on her just as the cat is killed in the street. Strangely, Cregar begged Brahm and company not to have him kill Linda Darnell on screen (even though the audience would be pining to see her get it).

There follows *Hangover Square*'s most famous vignette: The Guy Fawkes bonfire.

"John Brahm had the entire studio fire department standing by," wrote the *Hollywood Citizen-News*, "and outside companies on call, for the huge bonfire scene." Fox built a special square for *Hangover Square*'s bonfire and engaged 200 extras to caper about the 40 foot pyre. It's a masterpiece: Cregar's Bone, marching through the singing chanting crowd, carrying the corpse of Netta, disguised by a grotesque mask. Arriving at the bonfire in the carnival atmosphere, Herrmann's music shrilly accompanying the scene, Cregar climbs a ladder to the top of the bonfire as the camera notes the mask slightly sliding away to reveal Darnell's mouth. Bone deposits Netta's cadaver atop the bonfire and climbs down. The revelers attack the pyre, madly hurling their torches into it. As the flames rise, Bone is caught in the singing crowd that is dancing in circles; his face is horrible as he stares at his lover being cremated. There's a demonic quality about the scene, as it suddenly erupts into hell on Halloween night.

Ironically, Cregar almost *was* burned in the scene. The shaken actor amused the 200 extras by quipping to Brahm, "Boy you sure like your ham well-smoked!" His animosity toward the director, however, was brewing.

Sanders's Dr. Middleton soon traces the disappearance of Netta Longdon to the bonfire and to Bone. On the night Bone's concerto is to be performed, Middleton visits his quarters and accuses him of Netta's murder. Because the psychologist is aware of Bone's mental illness and the influence his concerto has had on his crimes (and vice-versa), he forbids him to play that evening. But Bone escapes him, and that night, before the guests at Sir Henry Chapman's, George Harvey Bone performs his "Concerto Macabre."

It took Brahm a week to film this wonderfully dramatic scene. As Bone plays, his crimes all come back to him in shadowy flashbacks; finally he breaks down. Sanders's Middleton, who has escaped the room where Bone had trapped him, leads him off to a sideroom while Barbara tearfully plays the rest of his beloved concerto. Bone begs to hear the rest, but two

Scotland Yard inspectors (Frederic Worlock and Leyland Hodgson) arrive, demanding to take Bone away. Bone throws a lamp at them. The room catches on fire.

In a superbly dramatic touch, Bone reaches a balcony overlooking the musicians just as his Concerto Macabre nears its climax. In a heartbreaking closeup, the tragic man tenderly wipes a tear from his eye. Then the fire erupts. The crowd screams and tries to escape.

"Go back!" rants Bone, using a piece of bric-a-brac as a weapon, "Go back! You must hear the concerto to the end!"

George Harvey Bone runs to his piano and resumes playing, slowly, mournfully; as the fire rages, his concerto becomes a haunting dirge. Barbara tries to rescue her deranged love, and Middleton heroically manages to save her. Sanders and Marlowe were to run to the outside, in prop snow.

"Listen," says Napier. "Why didn't he try to get out?"

Sanders's reply, literally, almost stopped the show—and *Hangover Square*'s production.

Producer Bassler, Director Brahm and Scenarist Lyndon had all seriously discussed the final dialogue of *Hangover Square;* they needed dialogue that would be sympathetic to Bone, but avoid glorifying a murderer.

For all their pains, George Sanders felt the final dialogue (which, unfortunately, appears lost to the ages) was stupid and decided to reveal his displeasure.

The *Hangover Square* company assembled one night on the Fox back lot for the huge fiery destruction of the Chapman house. "At the first rehearsal run-through," remembered Alan Napier, "George told John Brahm that it was a bloody, awful line and that he did not intend to say it."

Brahm, concerned with the logistics and mechanics of a giant fire sequence, ignored George. Finally, the fire was lit. The house went up in flames. Sanders and Marlowe ran to Napier and hit their marks outside the conflagration, in the prop snow.

Silence.

Time and again, the crew put out the fire, lit the house ablaze again— only to have Sanders say absolutely nothing. Brahm, stunned, seeing thousands of dollars burning away in every take, finally sent for Bassler. Everything stopped. Sanders calmly strolled to his studio chair on the back lot and stretched out to take a nap.

"Then I heard the rustle of a stiff, Mackintosh raincoat," said Napier. "It was little Bobbie Bassler, hurrying to enforce authority. I'm sure he'd had two or three quick Scotches to nerve him for the battle."

Bassler accosted Sanders. The actor refused to answer him. Finally, Bassler exploded.

"How dare you, you arrogant son-of-a-bitch!"

Laird Cregar and extras on *Hangover Square* watching the Guy Fawkes bonfire (note the dummy behind Cregar's hat).

Sanders didn't even rise from his chair. He simply extended his arm and knocked Robert Bassler out cold.

"Fox arranged for all the parties to have lunch together the next day," remembered Napier, "and, after Bassler had apologized to George for throwing aspersions on his mother, a happy compromise was reached over the offending line." On October 11, 1944, the *Los Angeles Examiner* heralded Sanders, saying, "Hollywood had a new contender for the duration one-punch championship of the film colony" and printed Bassler's "post battle communique": "I'm sorry the news leaked out because we shook hands and straightened the whole thing out.... I'm not carrying any scars."

Also on the 11th, Bassler, desperately trying to be upbeat about the whole thing, fired off this memo to Brahm:

> Here is a revision on the last scene in *Hangover Square.* I really feel good about it. Middleton's line has more significance, is less dry in its implications, and can be read, I believe, with considerable feeling, because it signifies that no matter whether or not Bone escapes the fire, his fate is nevertheless sealed—either he will be hanged for murder or committed for life to the asylum for the criminally insane at Broadmoor ... it is important that the lines be read with sadness and resignation and weltschmerz.

Once more the back lot house went up in flames. The final lines were simplicity itself:

NAPIER: Listen ... Why didn't he try to get out?
SANDERS: It's better this way, sir.

The final shot inside the inferno is a spectacular and haunting one: LaShelle's camera retreats past the burning chandelier, and we look down on Cregar's Bone, pounding away at the piano, with the house in flames around him and above him and the smoke rising as he sounds the final flourish of his genius. Herrmann's music dramatically hits crescendo, as *Hangover Square* ends.

On Friday, October 20, 1944, as *Hangover Square* was in its final days of shooting, *The Hollywood Reporter* announced that John Brahm would direct *Jean Valjean*, Fox's remake of the 1935 *Les Miserables*. Cregar, as originally announced, would play Javert; although he had been dieting brutally during *Hangover Square*, reducing to about 225 pounds, Fox still decreed him too heavy to play the title role with which they had baited him a while before.

Hangover Square wrapped October 25, 1944. "Laird Cregar has dropped a total of a hundred-and-two pounds," wrote Edith Gwynn in her "Rambling Reporter" column of the *Hollywood Reporter* on October 26, 1944, "but the end isn't in sight." The following day, October 27, Gwynn filed this *Reporter* tidbit:

> If a canvas were made among the principals and extras of the *Hangover Square* company, we don't think John Brahm would win any personal popularity poll. Not from the remarks that have poured into our shell-pink ears! When they finished the last scene, Laird Cregar in saying good-bye to the director, said: "Well, I think we've worked together long enough to know that we never want to work together again." Cregar is off to Del Monte for three weeks' rest before having that long-delayed operation.

This report appalled the *Hangover Square* crew; they believed Cregar to be the villain behind the production mayhem (as well as Sanders, of course). Certainly it didn't bode well for the proposed third Cregar-Brahm collaboration, *Jean Valjean*.

Then, as Brahm and his crew sighed relief to be done with the neurotic Cregar and outrageous Sanders, there was big trouble: Zanuck did *not* like the rough cut of *Hangover Square*. As Lyndon told Joel Greenberg:

> I remember that he called everybody in to see the rough cut. He saw that in his private projection room near his office, and he had everybody

in there, the writer, the producer, the wardrobe people—everybody who'd had anything to do with making the picture was there. He ran it reel by reel and at the end of each reel he'd stop it and make his remarks and ask his questions—and you'd better have some answers too! . . . He'd consider shooting new scenes or cutting others out. He went right through it, and we were there till past three-thirty in the morning and back again at nine next day.

The result was that *Hangover Square* went back into production. Brahm's loyal crew, expecting possible trouble from the stars, rallied totally behind the director.

"Whatever John Brahm's troubles with the cast in *Hangover Square* may have been," noted Edith Gwynn in the November 2, 1944, issue of the *Hollywood Reporter*, "the crew is for him 100% and just sent us a signed petition saying so."

Also on November 2, Brahm began his first big new scene: the dance hall episode, with Linda Darnell singing "Have You Seen Joe?" The *Reporter* noted several times that Brahm had completed *Hangover Square*, only to report a few days later he had wrapped again. As late as November 24, the *Reporter* was still noting that Brahm had "completed added scenes." The troubled picture went on and on—Laird Cregar fanatically dieting all the while.

Based on the shooting script, there were no newly created scenes penned for *Hangover Square;* however, there were apparently many retakes and some cuts. Zanuck, who had ordered the role of Middleton beefed up for Sanders, tailoring romantic situations for him with Barbara, now cut his part drastically, eliminating situations the producer had personally mandated. This seems to be more the result of spite for Sanders's horrid conduct than pace: *Hangover Square* runs a very tight 77 minutes, making it one of the shortest Fox "A" films of that period. These cuts inevitably reduced the roles of Faye Marlowe and Alan Napier, and Cregar lost a few moments of his largest screen role as Zanuck vindictively pruned the Sanders footage.

All agreed that Linda Darnell was a sensation in her fishnets; on November 22, the *Reporter* announced Fox had lifted her option and signed the actress for another year.

Throughout all the revisions and postproduction on *Hangover Square*, Laird Cregar, about to enter the hospital for his operation, was unusually professional. John Brahm thought he detected the sad reason why:

> For all his obstinacy and childishness, he attended to every necessary detail—such as retakes, dubbing, stills—before going to the hospital, even though I suggested that many matters could be left for his return, since the release date was far off. He insisted on finishing up, and then—

he made a will, carefully disposing of all his personal belongings. No doubt, he had a premonition that he would not return.

Completing *Hangover Square,* Laird Cregar accepted *Photoplay*'s invitation to join such stars as Greer Garson, Van Johnson, and Shirley Temple in a "What I Want for Christmas" feature for the Christmas issue. Even in this whimsy, Cregar revealed his obsession:

> Dear Santa:
> ... I know. You're typed, too. But nobody hates a jolly fat man, especially when he's so free and easy with the presents. But my kind! Little kids whimper when they pass me in the streets. ... Nothing can save me but a miracle, or a word from you, dear Santa, to the headman at my studio.

Thursday, November 30, 1944: Laird Cregar left his cottage, 9510 Cherokee Lane in the mountains above Beverly Hills, and checked into Good Samaritan Hospital for his abdominal operation.

Saturday, December 2, 1944: Cregar signed his last will and testament. He left his estate (later estimated "in excess of $10,000") to his mother and aunt, who shared quarters in Beverly Hills.

Monday, December 4, 1944: The abdominal operation was performed. "Laird Cregar called before going into Good Samaritan for that big operation," wrote Edith Gwynn in the *Hollywood Reporter,* "and said he'll have only a local anesthetic and will watch the entire proceedings. Well, that's one way of being entertained!"

Wednesday, December 6, 1944: *Variety* announced that Brahm and producer William Perlberg were "huddling on possible early start for *Jean Valjean* at 20th–Fox."

Friday, December 8, 1944: *Variety* mysteriously reported, "With the possibility that *Jean Valjean,* his announced next assignment, will be pushed back on the 20th–Fox schedule, director John Brahm is reading several other scripts, one of which he may do as his next picture." The *Reporter* settled for gossip: "John Brahm and Maria Palmer are having a fling around town."

Saturday, December 9, 1944: About 4:00 A.M., Laird Cregar suffered a heart attack at Good Samaritan. By noon he had suffered a second one. His mother and a brother kept a vigil by his bedside; at 4:52 P.M. Laird Cregar died. He was 31 years old.

Wednesday, December 13, 1944, the *Hollywood Reporter:* "Funeral services for Laird Cregar, 20th–Fox star who died last Saturday of a heart attack following an abdominal operation, have been arranged for 2:30 P.M. today at the Church of the Recessional in Forest Lawn. The funeral will be private."

Vincent Price, who had acted with Cregar in *Hudson's Bay* (1941), delivered the eulogy at the request of Laird's heartbroken mother. In an interview with David Del Valle in *Video Watchdog* (May/June 1992), Price said:

> Laird was an extraordinary man. He was an *enormous* man. He was a giant, you know, and all of his family were giants. I happened to know his mother and his brothers.... I read the eulogy at his funeral, strangely enough, though I didn't know him that well. His mother wanted me to do it because I'd been with him in his first picture. He was a wonderful actor, Laird, and he died much too young.

●

You'll not dare to even *scream*...!
So terrifying is the horror of *Hangover Square*
          —20th Century–Fox publicity, 1945

Even after Laird Cregar's tragic death, it seemed *Hangover Square* would never be finished. On Saturday night, December 23, 1944—two weeks after Cregar's demise—Brahm finally completed supervising the dubbing on the film. The studio set a New York premiere date and planned what promised to be a sad publicity campaign.

On January 15, 1945, 20th Century–Fox hosted a trade show of *Hangover Square*. The *Hollywood Reporter*, which had so avidly followed the film's production melodramatics, praised the picture as a "dynamic, powerful drama," full of "superb screen artistry":

> Naturally, one of its most notable features is the fact that it marks the last screen appearance of the late Laird Cregar. It is gratifying to be able to state that his valedictory is one of the finest performances of his career, one fully worthy of his great talent.... Linda Darnell gives one of her finest performances to date as the sexy, heartless charmer, again proving herself a most alluring siren. George Sanders scores as usual.... John Brahm's direction is an example of virtually flawless artistry.... There is especial praise for the music by Bernard Herrmann.

Hangover Square premiered at Broadway's Roxy on February 7, 1945, complete with a lavish stage show hosted by Milton Berle, who, ironically, had been one of Laird Cregar's friends in Hollywood (they had even collaborated on writing a song, "Would It Make Any Difference to You").

"Let Yourself Go! *Broadway's Biggest Show!*" promised the opening day advertisement in the *New York Times*. Connie Russell, Ben Yost's Vikings, the Slayman Ali Troupe, the Three Rockets, the Gae Foster Roxyettes, and Paul Ash and the Roxy Theatre Orchestra were all on hand. No doubt some remembered that only a year before, Cregar had been a part of the Roxy's stage show for *The Lodger,* triumphant in his success and mercifully unaware of the cataclysmic fate awaiting him.

Reviews for *Hangover Square* were mixed; "There is not a first-class shiver in the whole picture," carped the *New York Times,* while the *New York Mirror* opined, "The suspenseful direction of John Brahm makes this a 'must' for those who crave their thrills vicariously." Brahm visited New York to promote the picture, finding himself there just in time for the release of both *Hangover Square* and UA's *Guest in the House* (on which he had replaced Lewis Milestone).

Twentieth Century–Fox tried to be upbeat about *Hangover Square,* and the March 1, 1945, *Hollywood Reporter* claimed the film was "outgrossing *The Lodger* by 23% in the first seven situations." The film still seemed doomed for trouble. When it opened in London, Patrick Hamilton was aghast at the changes wrought in his novel, and the British press gave the film a vicious reception. Nevertheless, Fox insisted that the movie "is now breaking all records in London and topping Brahm's *The Lodger.*"

Hangover Square finally had its Los Angeles premiere on March 30, 1945, opening simultaneously at Grauman's Chinese Theatre, the Carthay Circle, the Fox Uptown, and Loew's State (oddly supported at each of the four movie houses by a Columbia Western, *Swing in the Saddle,* with Jane Frazee and Guinn "Big Boy" Williams). It was a great time for horror fans in Hollywood; *Hangover Square* was opening at Grauman's Chinese Theatre and MGM's *The Picture of Dorian Gray* had opened just days before at the Egyptian Theatre, across Hollywood Boulevard.

"Cregar did a swan song that will long be remembered by his followers," wrote the *Los Angeles Examiner.*

Over a year later, April 7, 1946, CBS's "Hollywood Star Time" radio show presented a version of "Hangover Square." Playing George Harvey Bone was the actor who had read Laird Cregar's eulogy: Vincent Price, who was now Fox's top star villain. Linda Darnell reprised her bewitching Netta. Price also had won the role of the evil "patroon" of *Dragonwyck* (1946), which Fox originally had considered for Cregar, and played two other Cregar roles on radio's "Hollywood Star Time": the title role of "The Lodger" (May 19, 1946, with Cathy Lewis) and the insane detective of "Hot Spot" (aka "I Wake Up Screaming," July 27, 1946, with Brian Donlevy).

Hangover Square, while helping Fox enjoy a 1945 fiscal profit of $12.7 million, strangely bore a stigma of tragedy. In later years, it became critically fashionable to dismiss the film as an inferior follow-up to *The Lodger* (just as Laird Cregar had feared).

But while *The Lodger* is a wildly theatrical movie, *Hangover Square* is demonic—a more frightening and haunting film than its predecessor.

Linda Darnell's evil Netta truly and chillingly conjures up the word "vampire" in the old Theda Bara sense, yet in a sexy, streamlined 1944 package. Her sensuality is almost frightening, her painted mouth almost ferocious. Rarely has sex been so predatory in a horror film, and her cremation atop the Guy Fawkes bonfire seems an appropriately satanic demise.

Herrmann's magnificent "Concerto Macabre" sounds like something Lucifer would play on a moody night, while Joseph LaShelle's photography made gaslight London seem a shadow land of vanity and trickery where a "painted sepulchre" like Darnell's Netta might indeed feed and thrive.

Hangover Square is probably John Brahm's finest work, and his staging of the Guy Fawkes bonfire one of the great episodes of Hollywood horror.

Of course, *Hangover Square* truly belongs to Laird Cregar. He made George Harvey Bone no flamboyant Jack the Ripper, but a sad, tragic, doomed young man, terrified by what he really is, destroying himself as he tries to be someone different. It was *Variety,* after a New York preview, that really pinpointed the strange, almost eerie power of *Hangover Square:*

"This is a picture more notable for the omniscience of a single player than any other factor."

●

> [The] picture is odd in that we don't care if Cregar murders Darnell, because she's really a louse. . . . The enjoyment comes from watching the heavy-set Cregar in his final film (before suffering a fatal heart attack) give one of his best psycho performances (in a role that Vincent Price, Victor Buono, or Raymond Burr might have had fun with in later years); the wonderful period detail, and Brahm's exciting, bizarre direction, [is] especially impressive during the blackout sequences.
> —Danny Peary, *Guide for the Film Fanatic*

Linda Darnell, whose Netta was cremated on *Hangover Square*'s Guy Fawkes bonfire, had a fear of fire that went all the way back to her childhood; indeed, she had a strange premonition she would die by fire. On Fox's *Anna and the King of Siam* (1946), Linda was terrified when the fire of her death scene singed her.

"Next time, I prefer being shot or stabbed," the composed star later told the press. "At least that kind of dying is painless."

Fire almost killed Linda on *Forever Amber* (1947), Fox's ambitious costumer that won Linda notoriety as Kathleen Winsor's racy heroine; in the great fire scene, a roof caved in, nearly falling on the star. En route to the shooting of *No Way Out* (1950), Linda almost burned again when her car exploded.

Laird Cregar attacks Faye Marlowe in a scene not to be found in the release print of *Hangover Square*.

After Fox dropped Linda in the early 1950s, her career gradually toppled into summer stock and night clubs. Her personal life was fraught with bad marriages and debts, and she seemed cursed with everything from a weight problem to hair loss. There were also suicide attempts. In April 1965 after watching herself in *Star Dust* (1940) on the "Late Show" while staying with friends in Chicago, Linda was caught in a burning house and suffered third degree burns over 90 percent of her body, including her face. In his book on Linda Darnell, *Hollywood Beauty*, Ronald L. Davis provides a heartbreaking account of the visit to Linda's hospital room by her adopted daughter Lola. She found her mother with skin and hair burned away, clad in a hospital diaper, whispering in a "horrible voice" (due to a tracheotomy) to her daughter, "I love you baby, I love you."

Linda Darnell died April 10, 1965, thirty-three hours after the fire; she was only 41 years old.

As for George Sanders, the star prospered in Hollywood, winning the Best Supporting Actor Academy Award for Fox's 1950 *All About Eve*. Divorced from his "waitress wife" in the late 1940s, he wed Zsa Zsa Gabor in a doomed union that ended in the mid–'50s. His marriage to actress Benita Hume, Ronald Colman's widow, supplied the happiest years of his life, and he never recovered from her death in the late 1960s. (A fourth marriage, to Zsa Zsa's sister Magda, ended quickly when Sanders, feeling trapped, had the marriage annulled on the grounds he was impotent.) A heavy investment in a sausage company left him bankrupt. Sanders's final miserable years ended April 25, 1972. Hotel staff at Castelldefells, Spain, entered his room and found his naked body, five empty tubes of Nembutal, and this suicide note:

> Dear World:
> I am leaving because I am bored. I feel I have lived long enough. I am leaving you with your worries in this sweet cesspool—Good luck.

Finally, a word about John Brahm. After Laird Cregar's death, Fox dropped *Jean Valjean* from the production roster (when the studio remade *Les Misérables* for 1952 release, starring Michael Rennie and Robert Newton as Valjean and Javert, Lewis Milestone directed). Brahm had a success on loan-out to RKO for the multiflashback *The Locket* (1946) and ended his Fox stay with *The Brasher Doubloon* (1947), a Philip Marlowe mystery (starring George Montgomery). He reportedly was unhappy with Fox and departed the studio.

Brahm directed only about a dozen more films, including Columbia's *The Mad Magician* (1954), starring Vincent Price (and containing features from both *The Lodger* and *Hangover Square*); his final film was MGM's *Hot Rods to Hell* (1967). Brahm worked extensively in television, directing the pilots for "Naked City" and "M-Squad," as well as such shows as "Playhouse 90," "General Electric Theater," and "Dr. Kildare." It was, however, his work on such shows as "Alfred Hitchcock Presents," "The Twilight Zone," "The Man from U.N.C.L.E.," "The Girl from U.N.C.L.E.," and "Thriller" that best displayed his gifts.

John Brahm died in his sleep at his Malibu home October 11, 1982; he was 89 years old. He had survived the horrors of *Hangover Square* by 38 years; twice divorced, he was survived by two daughters and two grandchildren. In a career of mainly memorable moments, Brahm's *The Lodger* and *Hangover Square* blaze as his masterpieces; indeed, when Laird Cregar died, the impetus of Brahm's career sadly expired too.

In June of 1973, Brahm, following a stroke, had taped a rambling (and, sadly, sometimes incoherent) oral history for the University of Southern California. "They're all dead," he sadly marveled as he remembered his 20th Century–Fox days of *The Lodger* and *Hangover Square*.

And he remembered, of course, Laird Cregar. "A great loss," said John Brahm of his late star, "because we did *Hangover Square* . . . and there was a great understanding that couldn't be continued."

Bedlam

Studio: RKO–Radio; Producer: Val Lewton; Executive Producer: Jack J. Gross; Director: Mark Robson; Screenplay: Carlos Keith (aka Val Lewton) and Mark Robson (Suggested by the William Hogarth painting *Bedlam,* Plate #8, *The Rake's Progress*); Cinematographer: Nicholas Musuraca; Art Directors: Albert S. D'Agostino and Walter E. Keller; Set Decorator: Darrell Silvera; Special Effects: Vernon L. Walker; Music: Roy Webb; Musical Director: C. Bakaleinikoff; Costumes: Edward Stevenson; Editor: Lyle Boyer; Sound: Jean L. Speak and Terry Kellum; Assistant Director: Doran Cox; Running Time: 79 minutes.

Filmed at RKO Studios, Hollywood, July 18–August 17, 1945. Premiere, Rialto Theatre, New York City, April 19, 1946.

The Players: Master Sims (Boris Karloff); Nell Bowen (Anna Lee); Lord Mortimer (Billy House); Hannay (Richard Fraser); The Gilded Boy (Glen Vernon); Sidney Long (Ian Wolfe); Oliver Todd (Jason Robards, Sr.); John Wilkes (Leyland Hodgson); Dorothea the Dove (Joan Newton); Mistress Sims (Elizabeth Russell); Tom, the Tiger (Victor Holbrook); Dan, the Dog (Robert Clarke); Podge (Larry Wheat); The Warder (Bruce Edwards); First Maniac (John Meredith); Solomon (John Beck); Queen of the Artichokes (Ellen Corby); Judge (John Ince); Varney (Skelton Knaggs); Chief Commissioner (John Goldsworthy); Scrub Woman (Polly Bailey); Lord Sandwich (Foster Phinney); Cockney Girls (Donna Lee, Nan Leslie); First Stone Mason (Tom Noonan); Second Stone Mason (George Holmes); Third Stone Mason (Jimmy Jordan); John, the Footman (Robert Manning); Pompey (Frankie Dee); Second Commissioner (Frank Pharr); John Lard (Harry Harvey); Sam's Friend (Victor Travers); Bailiff (James Logan); Bit Girl (Betty Gillette).

●

Val Lewton was a dreamer, who made a lot of his dreams come true. He would die very young, only in his late 40s, and I never wondered why—the man never got any rest. He'd be up late, writing, wondering how things would go—and it eventually just caught up with him.

He was anything but what you would visualize in your mind's

eye as a Hollywood producer—he was just a real person. And
when you actually sat down and talked to him, you knew he belonged in another century, really—he was not of that era, he was
way beyond it, way ahead of his time.

> —Glen Vernon, portrayer of "the
> gilded boy" in Val Lewton's *Bedlam*
> (RKO, 1946)

If you accept the traditional credo that Hollywood's Golden Age of
Horror ran from 1931 through 1946, *Bedlam* drops a glorious final curtain
upon a magical era.

It features Karloff's last great horror role of the '40s as Master Sims,
evil apothecary general of St. Mary's, Bethlehem (although the star would
have insisted it was a "historical" role). It boasts Anna Lee as Nell Bowen,
horror's first true "feminist" heroine. It was the last of Producer Val
Lewton's legendary RKO horror films. And it tackled one of the true horrors of history.

Even in its crusader spirit, with its moving finale pointing to a true
"age of enlightenment," *Bedlam* seems a grand valedictory to horror's
Golden Days.

Researching the art and production of *Bedlam* adds more layers. It
was in production at RKO Studios during the fall of both atomic bombs
on Japan; World War II ended during its shooting, and the world itself
seemed on the dawn of a new age. Val Lewton was soon to depart RKO
to become a "big" producer for Paramount. Karloff, a major Hollywood
character star, thanks to Lewton's *The Body Snatcher* (and his stage
triumph in Broadway's *Arsenic and Old Lace*), appeared destined for
"legitimate" work in all media. Hollywood seemed on the eve of a new
sophistication, a true enlightened time free of Hitler and the Axis, a new
direction for the movies and the world.

Of course, all this failed to happen. Hollywood's "enlightened era,"
in the decade after *Bedlam,* took horror movies through atomic bomb-
inspired spiders, ants, and Edward D. Wood, Jr. (director of *Plan 9 from
Outer Space*). Val Lewton's dream of being a major producer became a
nightmare that tormented this sensitive man into an early death. Karloff
indeed triumphed as a character star, playing everything from an Indian
chief in DeMille's *Unconquered* (1947) to Captain Hook in Broadway's
Peter Pan (1950). But Karloff never escaped (nor really ever wanted to
escape entirely) the genre that made him a movie immortal; he ended his
career in the notorious 1968 Hollywood/Mexican horrors that he graced
simply because they provided him the joy of working.

Well praised in 1946, *Bedlam*, in retrospect, remains a fascinating production: a bravura star performance by a horror great, a properly Gothic
subject, a fastidious production by Lewton, who not only manages to

blend horror picture with costume picture, but also makes it a "message" picture as well. The rosy "new age" that *Bedlam* forecasts in its finale might never have happened, but it was a lovely dream, charmingly, touchingly imagined in a beautifully classic melodrama.

●

> I was about 12 when my father passed away. He was interested in teaching me, so I had a little workshop, and tools, because he was interested in woodworking. He taught me how to sail, on his yacht.
>
> —Val Lewton, Jr.

Success had not changed Val Lewton. He was still the poet with the Boy Scout knife, the artist with the Hemingway complex. He sailed his yacht, the *Nina,* and inspired tales in Hollywood that he killed coyotes with a bow and arrow. Val Lewton, Jr., recently set the record straight on the coyotes—simultaneously providing insight into his sensitive and complex father:

> Our house was a very long, rambling, low ranch house that had belonged to Jack Holt, the actor. It was on Corsica Drive, in the "Riviera" colony, just before you got to Pacific Palisades, below Sunset Boulevard. You could see the ocean from the house and, on a clear day, see all the way to Catalina Island.
>
> The area was partly rural; my sister had a donkey, and we had bantam chickens and turkeys. Sigrid Gurie, the actress, lived next door, and her husband, a doctor, had a menagerie—four hundred rabbits, two Great Danes, peacocks, and even ocelots. Well, the coyotes used to come down from the hills; you could stand in front of our house and see coyotes run across the field, past the haystacks harvested for the horses at the Riviera Country Club. The coyotes also would come and try to get our turkeys, and the turkeys were ferocious, defending their eggs. So, my father got the idea that he could shoot one of these coyotes with a hunting bow.
>
> He planned to build a crossbow—he devoured magazines like *Popular Mechanics*—he was very excited about that, because apparently the muzzle velocity of such a crossbow exceeded anything, including high explosives. He never built that, but he did buy some hunting bows—and we worked together, learning to shoot these metal-tipped arrows, firing them up like an arc, and setting up targets. Well, I think this really appealed to him because he knew he could never do it. He might have kept watch at night with the bow and arrows to defend the turkeys, but with his sensitivity, he would have felt terrible if he ever actually hit a coyote.

Coyotes, for Val Lewton, must have been a welcome diversion from the varmints at RKO.

In 1944, Jack Gross, who had been a Universal producer (*The Wolf Man* and the 1943 *Phantom of the Opera*), joined RKO to supervise Lewton's work. Lewton proclaimed Gross a barbarian and originally was appalled when the new executive producer signed Karloff (who ironically became one of Lewton's best friends) to a two-picture contract. It seemed to Lewton a violation of all he had strived to create.

On May 10, 1945, Val Lewton's *The Body Snatcher*, which starred Karloff and was based on the Robert Louis Stevenson tale, opened at Hollywood's Hawaii Theatre. It was Lewton's greatest hit since *Cat People*. Karloff was magnificent as Gray, "the body snatcher," unforgettable in his top hat, jolly smile, and climactic apparition. In his new book, *Alternate Oscars*, Danny Peary opines that Karloff truly deserved the 1945 Best Actor Oscar for this performance. Henry Daniell was superb as the tragic Dr. MacFarlane; there was a humdinger cameo by Bela Lugosi as a dimwit blackmailer; and the climax is one of the most wildly, richly terrifying finales of all horror movies. Robert Wise directed, perfectly daubing the movie with strokes of Lewton mood, atmosphere, and poetry, evoking a wonderfully spectral Edinburgh, complete with the castle, eerie graveyards, and a doomed streetsinger.

In *The Body Snatcher* (this author's favorite Lewton film), the producer fully blossomed — mixing rich, dramatic fireworks with his beautiful cinematic poetry.

"I can't begin to tell you," rejoiced Karloff to *Silver Screen* about the Lewton unit, "how happy such a setup makes me!"

Audiences were happy, too: *The Body Snatcher* broke records at Hollywood's Hawaii Theatre. It reaped excellent reviews and also scored a triumph for Lewton that was very significant: it won the producer (who had rewritten the screenplay by Philip MacDonald so extensively that he used the old nom de plume of Carlos Keith) the respect long overdue him at RKO.

With Karloff vehicle #2, the moody *Isle of the Dead*, set for late summer release, RKO gave Lewton a splash of money, publicity, and resources to produce what would be his final RKO picture: *Bedlam*. Mark Robson, in an interview with Charles Higham and Joel Greenberg in *The Celluloid Muse*, claimed credit for the concept of what evolved as Val Lewton's final horror movie:

> *Bedlam* ... originated rather strangely. A Hearst paper, *The American Weekly*, used to run a Sunday supplement featuring offbeat articles like for example, "Secrets of the French Police." One day I noticed in this supplement the name Tom O'Bedlam. I'd never heard of this name. Out of curiosity I looked it up in some research books and found that there was a word, "bedlam," and that the word had something to do with the St. Mary of Bethlehem Hospital for the Insane.

Poor Tom, that eats the swimming frog, the toad, the tad-
pole, the wall-newt and the water; that in the fury of his heart,
when the foul fiend rages, eats cow dung . . . swallows the old
rat and the ditch-dog; drinks the green mantle of the standing
pool; who is whipped from tithing to tithing.
—from Shakespeare's *King Lear*, re
Edgar, who escapes death by masquerading as "Mad Tom O' Bedlam"

"It seems strange that anyone should recover here," reported a journalist after visiting St. Mary's of Bethlehem in the late seventeenth century. "The cryings, screechings, roarings, brawlings, shaking of chains,
swearings, chaffings are so many, so hideous, so great." A small social
epidemic of "love" and "responsibility" had caused the founding of the
first specialized institution of its kind in 1247 in a clammy stone building
near Charing Cross (and several neighboring leper houses). The purpose
was to house the "distraught and lunatik"—who in the thirteenth century,
ranged from the violently deranged, all the way to aged paupers and pro-
miscuous females.

Notoriety grew rapidly. By the late 1300s, the King decreed that
"Bedlam" be moved farther away from the royal palace, insisting he could
hear the howls of the inmates. In the late sixteenth century, the city of London took over the hospital; over the next 200 years, horrible rumors and
tales circulated, amidst scandalous mismanagement. Managers of the
asylum often embezzled the hospital's funds as the patients starved to
death.

Three fates generally awaited the hapless patients of Bedlam. Many
committed suicide, and their bodies were not discovered until whatever
time the "keepers" (hired for their fearsome looks, hot tempers, and
bellowing voices, and equipped with bullwhips) decided to patrol the cells
(where unsegregated patients were herded like cattle). Others perished
through "accidents," often brought on by neglect or violent frustration.
Such "accidents" inspired the creation of the strait jacket ("[which]
soothed the mind, induced reflection, prevented over-excitement, encouraged relaxation, and also had the desirable effect of increasing
perspiration"). Some patients finally were released—not as "cured," but
as "Bedlam social beggars," sent off with metal armbands identifying them
as Bedlam veterans who were legally free to beg in the streets via special
royal decree. (This spawned "pseudo–Bedlam social beggars," who forged
bands to beg with the protection of the law; the fraud became so obnoxious
that the king revoked his magnanimous decree in 1675.)

For all its horrors, Bedlam prospered; it was (until the mid–1700s) the

Bedlam poster.

only hospital of its kind. Neglected patients lost toes and even feet to frostbite, but keepers made extra money by escorting the curious through the cells of Bedlam, where the onlookers (for a penny per trip) shrieked at the sight of the insane. The most famous sufferer of Bedlam was one William Norris; nothing is known of his prior life, other than these facts presented in an 1815 report to the House of Commons:

> In one of the cells, the Committee saw William Norris. He stated himself to be 55 years of age and that he had been confined about 14 years in consequence of attempting to defend himself from what he conceived to be the improper treatment of his keeper. He was confined in the manner in which the Committee saw him, namely—a stout iron ring was riveted round his neck, from which a short chain passed to a ring, made to slide upward or downward on an upright massive iron bar inserted into the wall; round his body a strong iron bar, about 2" wide, was riveted; on each side of the bar was a circular projection enclosing each of his arms, pinioning them close to his sides; the waist bar was secured by two smaller bars, which passing over his shoulders, were riveted to the waist bar, both before and behind; the iron ring round his neck was connected to the bars on his shoulders by a double link; from each of these bars another short chain passed to the ring on the upright bar.

This committee was the result of several factors. There was the impact of Dr. Philippe Pinel (1745–1826), who claimed a mental hospital should be a *curing* agent, not just a custodial one. More concrete was Samuel Tuke's *Description of the Retreat*, which focused on York Asylum (the most notorious of Bedlam's sibling asylums), and Edward Wakefield's article on Bedlam in the April 1814 *Medical and Physical Journal.*

Dr. Best, chief physician of York Asylum was so terrified of a parliamentary investigation and an examination of his records that he quite obviously burned down a section of the hospital housing the records, killing four patients in the process. He was forced out of his position after a lengthy battle.

Dr. Thomas Munro—the socially prominent apothecary of Bedlam—suavely escorted the committee through Bedlam with perfect aplomb, convincing them that Bedlam was as fine an institution as any in England. He even rationalized the perverse chaining of William Norris (actually described in the committee's report as "rather a merciful and humane act rather than a rigorous and severe imposition"). The confidence trick succeeded only temporarily; Munro finally cracked under parliamentary cross-examination and surrendered his resignation.

By 1844 the Pinel theories and Quaker-inspired reforms were taking root. Reforms came, albeit gradually, and St. Mary's of Bethlehem survives today, very much "a modern institution."

With his love for historical research, Lewton himself tackled the screenplay (which, at various times, was titled *Chamber of Horrors* and *A Tale of Bedlam*), employing his nom de plume of "Carlos Keith" (as he had on *The Body Snatcher*). He was assisted by Mark Robson, the editor of *Cat People, I Walked with a Zombie*, and *The Leopard Man*, who had progressed in the Lewton unit to direct *The Seventh Victim, The Ghost Ship, Youth Runs Wild*, and *Isle of the Dead*. Lewton researched Bedlam passionately and checked references to it in the letters and memoirs of historical figures ranging from Casanova to Ben Franklin.

Lewton was especially fascinated by the William Hogarth paintings of the era; indeed, Hogarth's "The Rake's Progress" became the inspiration for the film (just as Boecklin's *Isle of the Dead* painting inspired Lewton's previous film). As Robson recalled:

> From there it was only a short step to reproducing much of Hogarth's "The Rake's Progress" in our film; in fact, we virtually used Hogarth as our art director. The dialogue was an amalgam of all kinds of eighteenth century characters, including Lord Sandwich and various others.

RKO awarded Lewton a *Bedlam* budget of $350,000—double what he had spent on *The Body Snatcher* and over $200,000 more than he had spent on *Cat People*. It was a notable figure in terms of the Lewton competition: Universal had spent the exact sum on *House of Frankenstein* (1944), boasting Karloff's mad doctor, Chaney's wolf man, Carradine's Count Dracula, Glenn Strange's Frankenstein monster, J. Carrol Naish's hunchback, Elena Verdugo's Gypsy girl, and cameos from Lionel Atwill and George Zucco—all in a monster rally attempt to blow the RKO challenge right out of the water. (*The Body Snatcher*, opening at Hollywood's Hawaii Theatre five months after *House of Frankenstein*'s 1944 Yuletide engagement, did bigger business.)

Following his initial two-picture contract, which was made for *The Body Snatcher* and *Isle of the Dead*, Karloff had wanted to stay with Lewton and his RKO friends. He and Val Lewton had become great pals, and Ruth Lewton says:

> Boris Karloff was a dear—a darling. At one point, he wanted to have some pictures taken, and he felt he wasn't living in a proper home to have them taken in—so Boris borrowed our house. He left me a "Thank You" note—"Thanks for the hire of the hall." Oh, I really liked him tremendously. Very, very delightful.

Karloff signed a new RKO contract in January of 1945, for three films and a grand total salary of $100,000. Karloff won *Bedlam*'s starring role of Master Sims, the evil apothecary general of St. Mary's. Karloff loved the role and waxed enthusiastic to *Silver Screen:*

The character I play in it is that of the Apothecary General, whose job is a political sinecure. I'm a poet, a wit, toady and a scoundrel who got his job by sucking up to the great and is always "making a leg" to his patron. On his home grounds in the asylum, he is hard and cruel. Not sadistic, merely a product of his age.

Lewton personally selected Anna Lee for the plum leading lady role of Nell Bowen. The superb British actress, who had survived many British film adventures, such as brain-swapping experiments with a mad Karloff in *The Man Who Changed His Mind* (1936), discovering *King Solomon's Mines* (1937), and being shot out of a cannon ("I really did that—no double!" she smiles) in *Young Man's Fancy* (1939). Arriving in Hollywood, she had worked with such directors as John Ford (*How Green Was My Valley* [1941]), Fritz Lang (*Hangmen Also Die* [1943]), and Douglas Sirk (*Summer Storm* [1944]).

Lewton naturally chose many of his regulars to create *Bedlam:* the cinematography was by Nicholas Musuraca (from *Cat People, The Seventh Victim, The Ghost Ship,* and *Curse of the Cat People*); the art direction was by Albert S. D'Agostino and Walter E. Keller (who had worked on all of Lewton's RKO films); and the music by Roy Webb (who had scored all of Lewton's horror films except *Isle of the Dead*).

While $350,000 was a fortune for a Lewton production, it still required the use of leftover sets: hence Lewton inherited Leo McCarey's old church from *The Bells of St. Mary's* (1945) for his St. Mary's of Bethlehem. The company would work at the RKO Hollywood lot, the RKO–Pathé lot in Culver City, and the RKO ranch in Encino, scavenging old props and sets wherever possible.

By the summer of 1945, *Bedlam* was ready to begin shooting, just as the war in Germany had ended and the war with Japan was drawing to an atomic finale. One wonders if our alliance with Great Britain influenced Lewton to be diplomatic and set the period of the film (and its Quaker-inspired reforms) half-a-century before they ever truly began.

In his research, Lewton probably also came across an historical tidbit that must have been difficult to resist. King George, III, ruler of England from 1760 to 1820, had himself suffered from fits of "mania." The king was a victim of porphyria, a disease that causes a myriad of physical ailments, as well as hallucinations and delusions. George's personal fits caused him to believe that an oak tree in Windsor Park was his ally Frederic the Great of Prussia, to attack violently the Prince of Wales, and to expose his genitals to the aghast ladies of the court. To control the king, his physicians, assistants, and sons had him bled, purged, straitjacketed, gagged, and strapped to his bed, where a servant sat on him to guarantee his bondage.

The most hallowed figure in England was thus subjected to the same tortures that befell the patients of Bedlam. (King George III lived to be 81; he became deaf, lame, almost blind, and demented beyond recall.)

What a follow-up to *The Body Snatcher* it might have been — Karloff as Master Sims of Bedlam and Henry Daniell as mad King George, III — or vice versa. However, with World War II finally drawing to a close, this was no time for an exposé of a British king.

On July 18, 1945, Val Lewton began shooting *Bedlam*.

●

London, 1761. The people of the eighteenth century called
their period "The Age of Reason."
— Prelude to *Bedlam*.

Roy Webb's eighteenth century period music plays right over the RKO–Radio tower logo; Hogarth's paintings serve as a dramatic backdrop for *Bedlam*'s title credits.

Bedlam begins with a bang. Musuraca's camera frames a looming edifice — Gothic and gloomy, under a sky of stars. And on the roof, hanging from the spouting, is a man who is trying to escape the building. A warden arrives on the roof and approaches the escapee. There is a close-up of foot on hands, a scream, and the victim falls to his death. A crowd gathers below, and we see the sign on the gate: St. Mary's of Bethlehem Asylum.

A coach worthy of Cinderella comes rolling over the cobblestones. Inside, however, is no Cinderella; it's Nell Bowen, classical actress-turned-protégée of the grossly fat and jolly Lord Mortimer. A brunette Anna Lee, complete with beauty marks and a breathtaking gown, totally suggests the amoral lady of the stage, enjoying her pet cockatoo, which recites:

Lord Mortimer is like a pig,
His brain is small, his belly big.

Nell laughs, but then so does Lord Mortimer. Billy House (1890–1961, who also scored at RKO in Orson Welles's 1946 *The Stranger*) is superb as the obese Mortimer. As Ed Bansak wrote in his "Fearing the Dark: The Val Lewton Legacy" in *Midnight Marquee* magazine, House's Mortimer is not so evil as ignorant: "in his white wig he resembles Old King Cole more than anyone else." Pauline Moore, a bridesmaid in *Frankenstein* (1931) and a 20th Century–Fox starlet of the late '30s, acted with House in Broadway's *Murder at the Vanities* (1933), an Earl Carroll spectacular featuring Olga *(Freaks)* Baclanova and Bela Lugosi. She remembers Billy House's "show-must-go-on" temperament:

He had a heart attack one night, and every minute he wasn't on the stage he was sitting there, the sweat just running off of him. But the minute his time came for an entrance—on he went!

Mortimer's coach stops at the accident. The fat man jumps out; Robson focuses on the coach's foot pedestal, which suffers under Mortimer's weight as the coach rocks in response. Lord Mortimer sputters away the incident—until he learns that the escapee was *not* an inmate, but his friend Lord Colby, who was in Bedlam to examine the asylum. He vows punishment, saying that someone will pay for this.

We meet that "someone" the next day—Master Sims—Karloff.

As Mortimer lounges in his bed in nightcap, tending to his own beauty marks and Nell (in her riding togs, hat, and crop) toys with the cockatoo, Sims waits hours for his audience. Karloff looks like a dapper devil in his black wig, period finery (even if the breeches almost comically accentuate his bowed legs), and silver-topped cane; still, he's instantly the butt of *Arsenic and Old Lace*-style jokes about his famous face. A little black houseboy in a turban named Pompey (Frankie Dee) grimaces horribly at himself in a mirror and then explains to Lord Mortimer that he wants to look like "the visitor in the hallway."

"Sims!" roars Mortimer with delight, as if such a face could only be his.

Finally admitted, Karloff's Sims is a spectacle as he bows, makes faces, flatters—and denies he murdered Colby out of jealousy. "Murder? There was no murder! Colby was my guest. He chose to leave by a window before I could open the door for him. And then—that—that *monstrous* accident." The real show is the sparks that fly between Karloff and Lee—a wonderful, dramatic animosity that will provide the top fireworks of the film.

"You have a tender heart," sneers Sims to Nell. "Most people laugh at my ugliness."

"It offends me, sir," sniffs Lee's Nell.

"To move a lady so beautiful in any way," volleys Karloff's Sims.

Lord Mortimer had wanted Colby to write a play for his upcoming fete; Sims, ever the toady, eager to display his wit, volunteers to write one of his own. "What if the masque were performed by my company of wits—the Bedlamites?"

Mortimer is delighted; Sims claims he was inspired by "milord, and the beloved of milord." Nell replies, in a speech that must have pleased the Legion of Decency: "I think you misunderstand, Master Sims. I am the milord's protégée. I entertain him, and he has no more freedom with me than any other man."

"In any case," smooth-talks Sims, "if milord will but give me the day and the hour of the fete, I will prepare a masque of madness that will set you howling."

Sims exits, with flair, of course, and Lee announces her opinion of the scoundrel:

"If you ask me, my Lord, he's a stench in the nostrils, a sewer of ugliness, and a gutter brimming with slop."

"But *witty*!" exclaims Mortimer, who suggests Nell visit the "loonies" at Bedlam to see just how "funny" they are.

Karloff, in three-cornered hat and bowed legs, walks to Bedlam, past two Cockney girls singing in the streets (one of whom is Donna Lee, who played the tragic street singer murdered by Boris in *The Body Snatcher*). A man awaits him: Hannay (Richard Fraser, Sibyl Vane's doomed brother in *The Picture of Dorian Gray*). A Quaker carpenter, he hopes to build an addition to the hospital. Here, we see the other side of Sims: he decides to make Hannay wait as he consults his rhyming dictionary. When he finally speaks to Hannay, he offers him a bribe (which the Quaker refuses) and mocks the man's "Thee and Thou" cant. Relaxing, Sims also pulls off his black wig, exposing his head of stubbly, gray hair.

Enter Nell. Sims dives for his wig—a delightful comic touch, played to the hilt by Karloff, as well as Lee, who looks away and rolls her eyes at the man's vanity before she focuses on the handsome Hannay.

"I had not looked forward to the pleasure of seeing you again so soon, Mistress Bowen," says Sims, wig in place.

"I have a curiosity to see the loonies in their cages," announces Nell.

Sims, all pomp and jolly, becomes her tour guide for a tuppence.

The first entrance into Bedlam is a tour de force of direction, cinematography, and performance. We hear the cacophony of screams, moans, and wails—all as the camera focuses on Nell's beautiful and slightly alarmed face, while Karloff grins like a gargoyle behind her. Then Musuraca's camera retreats, and we see the giant room and the herds of inmates like cattle, just as the history books describe the tragic Bedlam of the 1700s. A man plays a violin, with a book on his head as a hat; an inmate makes a cat's cradle with string ("to catch peacocks for the royal dinner," smiles Karloff); another sits alone in a dunce cap. Dominating all, however, is Nell's arrogant face and the flicker of compassion that begins to light there.

"They're all so lonely," she marvels. "They're all in themselves and by themselves ... like separate dreams."

Karloff, too, is in his dramatic glory, offering this soliloquy on his patients:

They're animals. Some are dogs; these I beat. Some are pigs; those I let wallow in their own filth. Some are tigers; these I cage. Some, like this one, are doves.

The casting of these "types" is fortunate. One of the actors portraying a patient was Robert Clarke, an RKO stock player who had played one of the medical students in *The Body Snatcher* and later starred in such cult films as *The Man from Planet X* and *The Hideous Sun Demon* (also producing, co-directing, and co-writing the latter). Clarke plays "Dan the Dog," acting the role with a cringing fear and an odd likability. Strongman Victor Holbrook makes a fearsome, brooding "Tom the Tiger." Joan Newton—as "Dorothea the Dove"—looks like a Catholic Madonna statue leftover from Karloff's *The Black Room.* And while Sims does not specify what he does to "the Dove," the lascivious pat on the cheek the actor gives suggests volumes.

The effect of this scene is haunting and powerful. As "Dr. Cyclops" wrote in a video review of *Bedlam* for *Fangoria:*

> There are ample opportunities for shock moments in the asylum scenes but the script (written by Lewton and director Mark Robson) opts instead to humanize the inmates, touchingly presenting them as piteous figures. . . . *Bedlam* literally towers over the better-known *Freaks,* another vintage melodrama which purports to sympathetically portray its tragic protagonists but is actually nasty and sensationalistic.

Nell can take no more and makes her exit. "That mad girl with her staring eyes!" she exlaims, and strikes Sims across the face with her crop. Hannay sees the strike and compliments the woman on her humanity as they meet outside the asylum. But worldly Nell feels compelled to deny her sympathy for the inmates; she claims she slapped Sims "because he is an ugly thing in a pretty world." Atop her horse, Lee's Nell makes a grand little speech:

> My heart is a flint, sir. It may strike sparks, but they're not warm enough to burn. I have no time to make a show of loving kindness before my fellow men. Not in this life. I have too much laughing to do.

She rides away. Hannay (and the audience), however, knows that her liberal spirit is stirring.

Incidentally, awaiting Nell in the street is her devoted personal servant from her theatre days, Varney—played by the ubiquitous Skelton Knaggs (1922–1955). The pockmarked, British ex–Shakespearean mime had already played in Lewton's *The Ghost Ship* and *Isle of the Dead,* Fox's *The Lodger,* Universal's *The Invisible Man's Revenge,* and MGM's *The*

Picture of Dorian Gray, as well as the 1944 Broadway play *Hand in Glove,* directed by James Whale. Knaggs's Varney is a surprisingly effeminate performance for the era, possibly acceptable so nobody would guess that loyal Varney had tended to Nell in private ways as well. (After *Bedlam,* Knaggs reported to Universal for what is probably his most famous performance — Steinmuhl, the village grotesque of *House of Dracula.*)

The night of the Vauxhall garden party is perhaps *Bedlam*'s most famous episode.

Karloff's Sims, full of poetry, flair, and himself, presents his amusement. The true star of Sims's masque is "Reason," played by "the gilded boy" — a "loonie" painted head to toe in gold gilt. It was only a three-minute role, but very significant, and RKO awarded the part to Glen Vernon, a rising juvenile actor at the studio, who would make those three minutes unforgettable.

In the spring of 1993, Glen Vernon was playing on the Hollywood stage in the drama *Edith Stein* and acting in a new Don Rickles comedy pilot. He had joined RKO in the early '40s after playing Broadway in such plays as *Best Foot Forward* and *Sons and Soldiers;* he was excellent as the lead in *Youth Runs Wild,* Lewton's 1944 juvenile delinquency film.

"Val Lewton was a Selznick of RKO," says Vernon, "just as dynamic, but he never had the financing to do bigger things." He remembers his audition for the role of "the gilded boy":

> I did the audition in Mark Robson's office. I just stood up, and he said, "Give it a little 'Shakespeare' touch, and play it as though you're not really here — you're in another world." He wanted it to look like the lines were rehearsed into me by Karloff, with that stick of his. So I auditioned in the office, and Robson said, "Now, with all the illusion and the effect and the gold, I think it will work" — and it did!

The aristocrats laugh decadently as "Reason" recites his ode to Lord Mortimer, even as the boy grabs his throat and gasps for air.

"To this pretty world — there came — heaven-sent, divinely inspired ... the blessing ... of our age..."

"Come on, come on, I spent all morning beating it into your head!" says Karloff, jabbing at the gilded boy with his stick.

"Somewhere I heard that the human body must breathe through its pores," observes Whig John Wilkes, rival to Tory Lord Mortimer (Wilkes is played by Leyland Hodgson, the smoky-voiced actor of such Universal fare as *The Wolf Man, The Ghost of Frankenstein,* and *The Invisible Man's Revenge*). "If you shut those pores...."

"This prince of men — this paragon — Lord — Lord Mortimer," concludes "Reason," and he collapses.

Karloff's Sims introduces Anna Lee's Nell to Joan Newton's "Dorothea the Dove."

Laughter bursts out. Sims suggests he be tossed in the river, and the gilt rubbed off with canvas and coarse sand, but Nell protests.

"If I understand you properly," says Sims, "this boy is dying." He pauses, looks at "Reason," and then says, "This boy is dead because his pores are clogged by the gilt. Well then, sweet Mistress Bowen, since you are such a stickler for the correct definition, you will grant me the legal fact that this boy died by his own exhalations. You might say he poisoned himself."

There is again laughter, and Nell walks out. As she leaves, Sims presents his new attraction, the "queen of the artichokes." An inmate in a grotesque mask sings quaveringly—a memorable bit played by Ellen Corby, later a noted character actress.

Glen Vernon recalls he did his role of "the gilded boy" "in two takes." He remembers it as "no problem," except for one detail:

> I almost died!
> For *Bedlam*, they painted me in gold gilt; it took about three hours in makeup. And they put too much gold on me! It really hardens, like cement! Incredible! They had painted my entire body, and didn't leave

Karloff's Sims presents the "gilded boy" in *Bedlam.*

anyplace to breath—like on my back. I was getting weak and wondered why—it was because the oxygen wasn't going into the blood!

It was Boris Karloff—very friendly, very nice, very gentle, very quiet, nothing like he played—he was the one who got the nurse. Evidently, he knew quite a bit about medical problems, and he said, "This could be fatal, if you let it go too long, because the gilt will get into the bloodstream." Fortunately, the nurse made a spot on my back, about as big as a quarter or half-dollar, so my body could breath; she put some alcohol on it, and then I was fine.

Well, meanwhile, the whole RKO lot got all shook up! I said to Karloff, "You really do frighten people!" It took about six hours to get the gold off with a shower. Then all I did was drink a lot of orange juice and get a lot of oxygen.

I *really* lived that role!

"The gilded boy" is prophetic of Shirley Eaton's "golden girl" of *Goldfinger* (1964), and the party scene is a cinema ancestor of *Marat/Sade* (1966); the powerful episode still strikes a chord in audiences. And it appalls and inspires Nell Bowen, as Anna Lee throws herself into a performance that makes her the women's liberation heroine of horror films.

Nell demands that Lord Mortimer begin reformation at Bedlam.

Sims persuades him otherwise, pointing out the taxes Mortimer will suffer funding such reforms. Outraged, Nell insults her corpulent "lover," who replies she'd still be a strolling player if she hadn't caught his eye.

> Do you call that weak and watery vessel your eye? I would not want to look at the world through it. I would not want to be a dull man forever in need of amusement. I would not want to bribe and be bribed or fawn upon the king and kick the commoner. In short, my lord, I would not want to be Lord Mortimer. . . . Maybe being rich and great and powerful is infectious. It's a disease I don't want to catch. Goodbye, my Lord!

"Such angry words!" says Karloff, rolling his eyes.

Mortimer spitefully reclaims Nell's property. Nell, in reply, takes her cockatoo into the town square to sell it, where the bird regales the crowds with its "Lord Mortimer is like a pig" limerick. Sims, meanwhile, brings his beer-and-gin-loving niece Kitty to meet Mortimer, in hopes of making her his lord's new protégée. It's a delightful performance by Elizabeth Russell, Lewton's "cat woman" of *Cat People* and familiar of *The Seventh Victim, The Curse of the Cat People,* and *Youth Runs Wild.* Joel E. Siegel, in his book on Lewton, *The Reality of Terror,* describes Russell's Kitty performance as being "perched somewhere between Marie Wilson and Judy Holliday."

"My father liked Elizabeth Russell a lot," says Val Lewton, Jr., "and she used to come over to our house quite a bit." Ruth Lewton still remembers her as "the woman who looked like a cat." While Russell played delightfully with Karloff in *Bedlam,* she has no warm memory of him:

"The English were very 'superior' to us," Elizabeth Russell said in an interview with the author at the 1990 FANEX convention in Baltimore. "And Karloff, an Englishman, perhaps had a right to be that way—he was a very well-to-do actor. He was never affable with me."

Kitty claims she tried to buy the cockatoo, and Mortimer sends Pompey to buy it for 100 gold guineas. Nell refuses to sell, however, preferring to humiliate Lord Mortimer by letting the bird caw its limerick in the streets. What to do about Nell?

"We can always make her my guest," suggests Sims, sinuously.

Good-natured Mortimer is shocked, but agrees to arrest Nell, Varney, and the parrot. Hannay is with Nell, Varney, and the bird when the police drag them into Mortimer's quarters, where the fat lord draws a sword on the Quaker. Hannay merely pushes the sword away, and Mortimer trips, falling on his bed, much to the amusement of Nell, Kitty, and the parrot. The humiliated Mortimer reconsiders Sims's suggestion.

Nell gains the politically dangerous Wilkes as an ally. Lord Mortimer tries desperately to make peace with her, and at tea, Sims offers her money to take a vacation at Bath.

Nell contemptuously makes a sandwich of the money and takes a bite out of it. Then she slaps Sims—who persuades Mortimer to sign a paper committing Nell to Bedlam.

Nell appears for her sanity hearing clad in a flowing black cloak. Sims sits in on the hearing.

"Mistress Bowen," asks the Judge, "is it true that some days past you refused the sum of 100 gold guineas for a parrot not worth five shillings? ... Can you explain why you ate a bank note?"

The decision is a quick one: Nell Bowen is committed to Bedlam. The judges and Sims walk out of the room as Nell cries and collapses. That night, she is in Bedlam, and Sims pays a call, with a coin.

"Here in Bedlam, my dear, we can't feed you bank notes," mocks Sims. "Try chewing on this."

And the apothecary general shoves a coin in her mouth.

●

> I was very fortunate, because I was working in Hollywood during what I still say are the Golden Years, the '40s and the early '50s. They don't make films like that anymore!
> —Anna Lee, 1991

In January of 1993, Anna Lee received a traditional cinema honor: her own star on Hollywood's "Walk of Fame." Indeed, Anna Lee would survive more than the horrors of *Bedlam;* she has survived five decades in Hollywood and is still working today, in her 80s, as Lila Quartermaine on ABC's top-rated soap opera, *General Hospital*. The widow of author Robert Nathan *(Portrait of Jennie)*, she lives in a cottage in West Hollywood and is so fresh, beautiful, and blonde in her 80th year that one is surprised to hear her speak nostalgically of the old Hollywood.

"John Ford's *How Green Was My Valley* and Val Lewton's *Bedlam* are my favorites," she says. "I love them. And my role in *Bedlam* was such a good part!"

Anna Lee recalls her first meeting with Val Lewton:

> Val was a friend of my first husband, director Robert Stevenson. I think I met Val at a party, down in Santa Monica, at the home of the big German director, Berthold Viertel—for whom I had made *The Passing of the Third Floor Back,* with Conrad Veidt, in England—and his wife Salka. They had a sort of "soiree" every Saturday night, and they'd invite certain people, mostly writers. However, Garbo used to come there. That was the only time I ever met Garbo; she sat herself down—and didn't say a word all the time. It was wonderful just to be in the same room with her. But that was when I met Val.

Starring enemies: Anna Lee's Nell Bowen and Boris Karloff's Master Sims.

Then I became friendly with Ruth, his wife, and his children, and of course, I'd heard about his aunt—Nazimova. When I first came out to Hollywood, the first place I ever stayed was the Garden of Allah, which was full of memories of her. But I liked Val enormously.

Lewton had *Bedlam* in mind for some time and told his friend Anna that he envisioned her for the leading lady. RKO had other ideas:

Val had always told me he wanted me to do *Bedlam,* but I think whoever was in charge at RKO wanted an American to play it—though it was a very English part. I think it was Jane Greer they wanted. But anyway, Val fought for me, and finally I did it. As far as I'm concerned, it was the best part I ever had—really a wonderful part.

Bedlam was all Val—Val supervised every bit of it. The picture really led Mark Robson to becoming one of the top directors, but it was Val's picture. He was always there on the set, very meticulous in everything. Val had done a lot of research on the Hogarth drawings; he had them all screened and used as background for shots. He was such a stickler for every detail.

Bedlam provided a very jolly reunion with Boris Karloff. Anna had co-starred in the British 1936 thriller, *The Man Who Changed His Mind,* with Boris as the chainsmoking mad Dr. Laurience, with wild eyes and a shock of gray hair—one of his most delightfully "over-the-top" portrayals:

> Boris Karloff—oh yes, a *dear* man. We both loved poetry, and apparently, we both loved the same poems. On *The Man Who Changed His Mind,* we'd have a sort of "poetry jam"; we'd say a poem—for example, *The Children's Hour* ... I'd say the first two lines—
>
> "Between the dark and the daylight,
> when the night is beginning to lower,"
>
> and then Boris would *boom* out,
>
> "Comes a pause in the day's occupation,
> which is called the Children's Hour!"
>
> So always, on *Bedlam,* we'd recite poetry to each other, for hours—poems I hoped he *hadn't* remembered, but he always *did!*
> The reunion with Boris was wonderful, as was the atmosphere on the set of *Bedlam*—because Boris had a great sense of humor, and he used to laugh about everything. When I had the bank note in the sandwich, and ate it, Boris said, "Anna, you're not really going to eat that?" And I said, "Don't you think I could?" "*No, no,* you *wouldn't* do that!" said Boris. "Yes I will!" I said—and I did! I swallowed a piece of it! And I remember the scene where he pushed a coin into my mouth—Boris was giggling all the time!

Anna Lee recalls a very famous costume she inherited as *Bedlam*'s Nell Bowen:

> Oh yes, my riding habit. You see, we had the costume designer, that wonderful man who had designed all the clothes for *Gone with the Wind*—Walter Plunkett. As the movie was done on a budget, he did

everything he could to cut the costs. And he said, "Well, you must have a lovely riding habit. How would you like green velvet?" I said, "That sounds wonderful," and he said, "I have just the thing! I have one of the dresses Vivien Leigh wore in *Gone with the Wind*, where she took down the curtains. We had to make three or four of them, and I have the one she wore in the second scene, and we'll just adapt that." So my riding habit was Vivien Leigh's dress! And that other dress, the lovely dress I wore when they showed the painted man — that had been Hedy Lamarr's dress. And it was gorgeous.

Always, there was the dynamo of Val Lewton behind every aspect of *Bedlam*'s production.

Val was a great workaholic. I don't think he ever stopped working on any project he was doing. Val was very unrecognized; nobody really thought about his creativity then, and thinking about it now, all these years later, has made people realize how good he was. He had a great imagination, and was very erudite in everything he did. But it had never dawned on me, in those days, that Val was driving himself that way to death.

At the time of this interview, Anna Lee had just signed a new two-year contract with *General Hospital*. Spinal surgery five years earlier had deprived her of the use of her left leg, and she had been working on the show in a wheelchair. "However, my right leg is fine, she smiles, "so I can still drive my car and still go to work. That's the main thing. I call myself 'The Great Survivor'!"

●

The name "Nell Bowen" echoes throughout Bedlam as the lunatics parrot the cry of Quaker Hannay in the streets. Hannay joins some masons bringing mortar into Bedlam and goes looking for Nell. The search provides for two memorable Lewton "busses," when an arm lunges out of the bars to clutch the Quaker and when — a moment later — a hag suddenly appears against the bars, cackling madly at our hero. He manages to find Nell; they are falling in love, and the smitten Quaker, despite his pacifist ways, surrenders to Nell's plea to give her a trowel, in case she needs to defend herself.

Nell forms a friendship with the "people of the pillar" — mad lawyer Sidney Long (Ian Wolfe), alcoholic Oliver Todd (Jason Robards, Sr.), who refuses to speak, and gentle Dan the Dog (Robert Clarke). They all play paroli, and Dan bets dogs — "Five whippets, ten bassetts, one greyhound." All provide a true warmth to the film. Robert Clarke remembers shooting the scene:

Robson was a fine director, and so painstaking in his efforts to achieve—for example in the scene where we were playing paroli, with the names of dogs.... We went over it and over it. I remember my mother was on the set that day, out at Pathé Studios, where David O. Selznick had shot *Gone with the Wind,* and my mother stood there for a couple of hours while we did the scene. She said later, "Oh! The hardest work I ever saw. I certainly hope that you make a lot of money, because I wouldn't do it for anything in the world!"

The "people of the pillar" also provide Lewton's most famous in-joke: Wolfe, as the mad lawyer, shows a book of sketches that, thrown up against the wall behind a lantern, will flicker like action—Lewton's insinuation that a madman first devised the concept of the movies.

At length, Nell personally begins reforms, making the inmates more comfortable. She even comforts a chained man imprisoned in his own cage—perhaps Lewton's nod to the William Norris of the real-life Bedlam who was mentioned in the report to the House of Commons. Nell becomes, in Sidney Long's words, "an angel in this darkness." Of course, her triumph in the asylum incenses Sims. The passion between Karloff, unwigged, leering, hissing his lines, and Lee, strong, unbending, defiantly mocking, is superbly dramatic, as is Sims's sentence for her: caging the lady up with the man called Tom the Tiger.

"Enter the cage," commands Sims. "Gently, and with a word. Conquer him with kindness. Or admit that your Quaker lies!"

"I always loved the scene where Karloff says I wouldn't go into the cage with Tom the Tiger," says Anna Lee. "He *dared* me to go in, and I tamed the tiger!"

Karloff's Sims appears again—all dressed up; the wig is back and he looks very rakish. He informs Nell that she is to have a new hearing the next day, but before this can happen he will give her "the remedy." The expression is enough to send chills into the inmates (just as Karloff's delivery of the line chills the viewer).

However—perhaps predictably—the inmates come to Nell's rescue. They overwhelm Sims as Nell escapes with Tom the Tiger, turning back for a final mocking smile at the trapped Sims. The Tiger gets her through a window and to the roof to safety. The scene is Lewton poetry: the Tiger, so long imprisoned, is filled with wonder as he sees the moon and the stars, and he lets our heroine dangle precariously until he refocuses his attention.

"In the closeups," says Anna Lee, "we were six or seven feet off the ground—it wasn't all that high. But the Tiger was very strong."

Meanwhile, the inmates have attacked Sims, stripping him of his wig and his dignity. A kangaroo court prosecutes; Wolfe's Todd is the star lawyer, while a "judge" officiates and an inmate named Solomon intones, "Split him in two!" Our villain offers an eloquent defense:

> I was frightened . . . of the great world. . . . I've had to fawn and toady
> and make a mock of myself until all I could hear was the world laughing
> at me. But once I had what I wanted—this—my place here . . . I had to
> please those to whose favor I owed everything. I was afraid.

The inmates allow Sims to go free; the terribly abused populace is merciful.

"The Dove," however, is not.

As Sims retreats, the Madonna-like beauty silently raises her hand, and there is the missing trowel, which she stabs into Sims's back.

The result is the final shock moment of Lewton terror—and a winner. Fearful of punishment, the inmates try to hide the body. À la Poe's *The Black Cat*, they wall up the body behind a fresh wall of mortar and brick.

And then, just before the final brick can be put in place, Sims's eyes open.

It's too late; the brick goes into the wall, and the wounded man is buried alive in his asylum.

A brief epilogue ensues. Persuaded by the Quaker, Nell agrees to return to Bedlam and tend to Sims. Of course, he cannot be found; but Hannay, seeing the freshly mortared wall, suspects what has happened. So does Nell, who convinces him not to divulge his suspicions out of concern for the patients and out of love for her.

A glowing, triumphant Nell Bowen seems to suggest promised reforms for Bedlam and a promised Age of Reason.

While *Bedlam* was in its final days of shooting, the B-29 *Enola Gay* dropped the atomic bomb on Hiroshima. By the time *Bedlam* wrapped on August 17, 1945, a second atomic bomb had fallen on Nagasaki. World War II was over, and the atomic age had dawned.

In this new age, the days of Hollywood horror seemed numbered, but Universal pursued the rivalry. Aware of RKO's new Karloff shocker, Universal put *House of Dracula* before the camera in September—a new "monster rally," with Chaney's wolf man, Carradine's Dracula, Strange's Frankenstein monster, a mad doctor (Onslow Stevens), and even a hunchbacked nurse (Jane Adams). It would be the Christmas attraction at the Rialto Theatre in New York City for 1945—four months before RKO's *Bedlam* would play there.

●

Beauty—at the mercy of madmen!
—RKO publicity for *Bedlam*, 1946

The inmates strike: Karloff's Sims, unwigged, caught by the inmates, including "Dan the Dog" (Robert Clarke, on right).

On February 25, 1946, *Bedlam* won a bonanza of publicity: *Life* magazine featured the film as its "Movie of the Week." The story hailed Lewton as "The virtuoso of B-film producers," noted the leftover *The Bells of St. Mary's* set and *Gone with the Wind* costume, and proclaimed, "*Bedlam* is an interesting and imaginative terror film, marred only by uneven pace and occasional verbosity."

RKO hosted a trade show for *Bedlam* at the studio April 16, 1946. The preview was timely; Hollywood was gossiping about Karloff's divorce the week before from his wife Dorothy (the movie colony was amused by the horror king's charge of "cruelty" against her), as well as his new marriage to wife Evelyn, which took place just after the divorce. It was indeed a new age, even for *Variety,* which actually provided a discerning review:

> *Bedlam* is a suspenseful exploitation picture from which RKO may expect heavy grosses. Produced by Val Lewton, whose past offerings in this field have netted high revenue for the company, the film has been directed forcefully by Mark Robson, with many a sock dramatic moment.... Narrative permits spicy melodramatic action.... Karloff makes a picturesque and sinister character of madhouse keeper, and Miss

Lee scores definitely. . . . Nicholas Musuraca's photography, always in low key, is an exceptional piece of camera work. . . .

The trade reviews were excellent, such as this notice in *Motion Picture Herald:*

A powerful, manifestly painstaking account . . . the film is not to be confused with the routine horror picture, but possesses more impact than any of them. Boris Karloff, the top name, has this time an assignment which gives him scope for the fine acting talent he seldom gets a chance to display . . . it will make itself remembered as a powerful use of the camera to tell a story of importance.

There was one unhappy member of the *Bedlam* company. The genial Robert Clarke, so good as "Dan the Dog," recalls:

Val Lewton was a very, very sweet man—he was kindly and all, but on *Bedlam*, at the studio preview, I was shocked by the fact that my name was not on the credits. After all, I'd had a good part in it. . . .
I said, "Mr. Lewton, my name's not on the credits!"
He said, "Oh, of course it is. You just didn't see it."
I said, "I looked several times—I didn't see it!"
So Lewton said, "Look—come to my office tomorrow . . . I know you're wrong, I know it's there, because I approved the cast list!" So the next day, I went to his office. . . . He said, "I'm going to look at the picture and make sure, because I *know* your name was on the list." Well—I got a beautiful letter of apology from him . . . "Regretfully, Bob. . . ." It was too late to change it; my name's not on the list.

Glen Vernon, on the other hand, would enjoy the notoriety his role of "the gilded boy" brought him:

After the preview of *Bedlam*, I used to call myself an "Oscar." I always tell people, "I invented the gold Oscar—they saw me in *Bedlam* and said, 'Hey, that's an idea! Let's make the Academy Award an Oscar—call it the Golden Boy!'" I'd say, "Next year, they're giving *me* away! Put me up on a mantle!"

On Good Friday, April 19, 1946, *Bedlam* opened at New York City's Rialto Theatre, showplace of the Universal and RKO horrors of the war years. There was big competition in town for melodrama fans: 20th Century–Fox's *Dragonwyck,* starring Gene Tierney and Vincent Price, had just opened at the Roxy. Yet *Bedlam* drew crowds and impressed the Manhattan critics.

"Val Lewton is the custodian of one of the most restlessly roaming imaginations in Hollywood," reported the *New York World-Telegram,* while the *New York Daily News* praised Karloff's performance as "the personification of evil genius." *Cue* provided a review that was virtually an ode to the great horror star:

> A mild-mannered, lisping ex–Shakespearean actor—who used to be a farmer, truck driver, stevedore and real estate salesman before he turned to the movies—is the person mainly responsible for giving Rialto audiences heebie-jeebies, and the theatre its harrowing reputation as Broadway's Mansion of Menace and House of Haunts. . . . Boris Karloff, or the monster of *Frankenstein, Bride of Frankenstein* and *Son of Frankenstein,* is filmdom's most famous gargoyle. . . . Karloff in *Bedlam* is a perfect example of a Karloffian nightmare on the march. . . . It sounds pretty frightening, and it is. But *Bedlam* is actually far less horrible than most of the Rialto's film offerings, and is considerably more intelligent in writing, production, direction and performance.

Bedlam was also a triumph for the leading lady. "Anna Lee plays the principal role with spirit and zest," noted the *New York World-Telegram,* "apparently not bothered by the flowery writing." The film had all the earmarks of being Lewton's biggest hit to date.

Studio politics can be lethal, however, and they plagued *Bedlam.* Charles Koerner, Lewton's champion at the studio, had died early in 1946, and the new front office never fully got behind *Bedlam.* The first West Coast reviews in Academy files note it as a New Year's Eve, 1946 attraction at Hollywood's Marcal Theatre, supported by RKO's *A Game of Death* (Robert Wise's remake of the studio's 1932 *The Most Dangerous Game*). One wonders if the new RKO management was acting in spite because of Lewton's desire to leave RKO (he eventually defected to Paramount). One also wonders why RKO dropped Lewton's project, *Blackbeard,* which was to star Karloff as a has-been pirate seeking security in his mellow years.

Whatever the studio intrigues, the *Los Angeles Daily News* praised *Bedlam* and its stars:

> Done realistically and with a sense of responsibility to its subject, *Bedlam* reaffirms the conviction that a problem drama can combine thoughtfulness with traditional entertainment elements.

Finally, there was one problem in the foreign market. England outright banned *Bedlam* in 1946, and, as far as anyone knows, the movie is still banned there today—47 years after the film's release and over 175 years after reformation first worked its way toward the tragic walls of Bedlam.

●

As Nell's Quaker friend (Richard Fraser) states, Providence was responsible for having Nell confined to Bedlam so she could initiate reforms which will continue long after her departure. It's fitting that it's Providence rather than sinister Fate that is triumphant in Lewton's one postwar horror film, for it allowed him to leave RKO on his first positive note. For the only time in Lewton films, man can understand his own life's course and change things for the better. Terrific performances by Lee and Karloff are enhanced by intelligent, witty script, offbeat supporting characters, and classy direction by Mark Robson.
— Danny Peary, *Guide for the Film Fanatic*

The five years Val Lewton lived after departing RKO were traumatic. He was bogged down in studio machinations at Paramount (where he produced *My Own True Love* [1948]) and at MGM (where he produced *Please Believe Me* [1950]). While independent production seemed ideal for Lewton, Val Lewton, Jr., doesn't believe it would have suited his father:

My father was getting older, and Hollywood was changing. Although he would have railed against the idea, I can see, looking back, that he fit into a studio system where he was an employee, and somewhat protected. Working for a studio gave him a base; maybe projects would fall through, but he had a salary. He had a basic insecurity which needed that protection. An independent producer had to be somebody who could stand a lot of stress.

Lewton did make an ill-fated attempt to produce independently with old RKO protégés Robert Wise and Mark Robson, but "Aspen Productions" ended traumatically when they felt compelled to drop Lewton, who had been slow in providing story material. Ruth Lewton says:

The really bad thing that happened to Val was that Mark Robson and Robert Wise decided to hit out on their own as producers, with Val. But Val, by that time, was so stressed that he couldn't work as fast as those guys wanted. I think it was a great disappointment to Val.

Lewton's daughter Nina (who became the mother of five children and, sadly, was also fated to die at an early age) called the Aspen disaster "the most horrible thing that ever happened" to Lewton. He plunged into depression; indeed, his secretary would hear him crying alone in his office. (Ruth Lewton is quick to note, however, that Robert Wise managed to stay friends with Val.)

"My father was a somewhat volatile person," says Val Lewton, Jr. "He could have a real temper. And late in his life, he was sick, he was ill, and he was anxious all the time."

Shadows seemed to be closing. DeWitt Bodeen, for all his affection for Lewton, remembered the producer becoming "a psychological case" in his last days, who had "lost all faith in himself" and become "impossible to work with." Lewton managed to produce a good Technicolor Western "B" for Universal-International, *Apache Drums* (1951) — but the old insecurity and hypersensitivity were destroying him inside. He had joined Stanley Kramer Productions and was working on the projects *My Six Convicts* and *The Member of the Wedding* when he suffered a heart attack.

Val Lewton died at Cedars of Lebanon Hospital on March 14, 1951. He was only 46. Alan Napier delivered a beautiful eulogy. The mourners were in tears, but Napier believed his friend would have laughed: "He had always been trying to find me a good part in one of his pictures, and here I was, having a triumph at his funeral."

Ruth Lewton lamented after her husband's demise that his early death came, fundamentally, because he lacked faith in himself. Ironically, it was a neurosis that had destroyed some of his most memorable film characters. Simone Simon destroys herself in *Cat People*, fatally tormented by the fear she will transform into a leopard. Jean Brooks in *The Seventh Victim* allows her morbid fascinations to run so rampant that she finally hangs herself. Henry Daniell is so tormented by Karloff's *The Body Snatcher* that he summons up the scoundrel's cadaver and spirit from the beyond, scaring himself to death.

Light vs. Darkness — Val Lewton's obsessive theme.

These characters, and others in Lewton films, all lacked faith in themselves — or, perhaps, preferred to believe the *worst* about themselves. So, ultimately, did Val Lewton.

Soon after her husband's death, Ruth Lewton, who believed childhood insecurity was a root of her husband's unhappiness, paid tribute to his memory in a moving and dynamic way:

> About three or four years after Val died, I got a job working with emotionally disturbed children in a hospital setting in Los Angeles, under the direction of the Child Guidance Clinic. I tried to figure out what in life would be the most important thing I could do, in a helping way; something to help people who were disturbed. Especially children — because I felt my husband's childhood background had influenced his life to such a degree that it was difficult for him not to be governed by the peculiarities in his thinking. He was talented, that's for sure — but his childhood had left him so stressed.
>
> I felt that stress was a wicked thing.
>
> So I wanted to help children who were disturbed, and did so for 16 years. It was the only thing I could think of that would help *me*. And it was very rewarding.

●

Only a few horror movies followed *Bedlam,* in the late-lamented 1931–1946 "Golden Age of Horror," such as Warner Bros. *The Beast with Five Fingers,* which premiered in December of 1946, its amok hand making for a weird Christmas attraction. By the summer of 1948, it was officially over, via the release of Universal-International's *Abbott and Costello Meet Frankenstein.*

So *Bedlam* could serve, proudly, as the curtain-dropper on a fascinating era of screen magic.

It was richly rewarding to behold a heroine who not only survived her fiend, but defeated him as well, providing a dynamic social significance — and did it all without a single scream.

It made horror addicts proud to see a terror movie also serve — and very well — as a historical picture, and a message picture.

And, it was poetically proper that Boris Karloff, most famous as Frankenstein's man-made monster, beautifully saluted Val Lewton by calling him: "The man who rescued me from the living dead and restored my soul."

For many, even in the post Oscar-winning wake of *The Silence of the Lambs,* the 1930s and 1940s still are the Golden Age of Horror.

And the fascination — like folklore, the power of drama, and the beauty of imagination — never dies.

INDEX